This book is dedicated to my family, trail family, loved ones, friends, and friendly strangers that supported and believed in me during this adventure and the writing of this book. Thank you all from the bottom of my heart. I wish I could have mentioned every single one of the wonderful people that I met while out on the trail, but I'm afraid I simply wouldn't have had enough pages to say all of the good things that you all deserve. If one person is helped or inspired to change their life or pursue their outlandish dreams by the reading of this book, then I have succeeded.

INTRODUCTION

LOST ON THE APPALACHIAN TRAIL

A tale of grand adventure about losing yourself in the wilderness, only to find the things that truly matter...

I stood there terrified...my entire journey riding on the proceedings of the next several minutes. I could feel the Ranger's eyes on me; looking me over, searching for any inconsistency that might reveal my true intentions. I silently wondered if I looked as guilty as I felt. I was all nerves, yet at the same time, deep down, calm and resolved in what I was doing and about to do. I had not walked 2,170 miles up to this point and traversed more than four hundred mountain peaks, only to be stopped now. I remembered all of the rain, sleet, hail, snow and ice. I remembered the mud, the rocks, the bogs, and the bug hoards; the rivers, the injuries, the blood and blistering heat. Not to mention the hurricane force winds, rattlesnakes, copperheads, poison ivy, poisonous spiders, and porcupines. Then there were the skunks, bull moose, and enough bears to build a small army, as well as countless other setbacks and obstacles. Had it all been for naught? Not a chance! I was not about to be stopped a mere fifteen miles from my final destination after trekking through all of that over the course of the last 194 days. The reality of the situation was however.... that the contents of my backpack were putting me in serious jeopardy of not completing this hike.... should they be discovered. Not to mention, get me in a heap load of trouble. I knew what I was gambling and had weighed the risks. I found the reward to greatly outweigh the consequences, no matter what happened in the end. Nevertheless, I had faith in my best friend. After everything we'd been through, I had every confidence that she could pull this off. The ranger began to slowly walk around me. My heart began to sink while simultaneously beating into the top of my skull. "SO..." the Ranger began. "Congratulations on making it this far. It's quite an accomplishment, BUT, before you go any further..."

Over 2,170 miles, one and a half years, and a lot of blood, sweat, and pain earlier... a plan is hatched.

CHAPTER 1: FLORIDA

"Jumping Off the Hamster Wheel."

Like so many people I met these days, I felt like I was missing something. Perhaps not missing something, so much as missing OUT on something. I felt like I was trapped in an endless cycle of wake up, drive to work, work all day, drive home, go to bed and repeat again and again until the weekend; where I would then do any number of things that I always did, with the people I always did them with. Suffice it to say, it was beginning to feel a bit repetitive; driving over the same roads to go to the same places, day after day, week after week, year after year. What did I think was going to happen? Doing the same thing over and over again whilst expecting different results is the tell-tale sign of insanity, and insanity is exactly what it was. It was insane to think I was going to spontaneously wake up one morning and be overjoyed with my standard, mundane routine. I needed to do something different, something exciting... I needed an adventure, but what?

I owned a small personal training studio that provided me a modest living, but I knew if I could simplify my life and do without a few indulgences for a while, I could save up the funds to do something truly fantastic. I began to spend my free time, as well as my not-so-free-time, day dreaming about places where I could travel or adventures I could pursue. I read dozens of online blogs and tirelessly researched ways to travel and adventure on a shoe string budget or even for free. This went on for months, but I couldn't decide or settle upon something that I deemed worthy enough of turning my life and small business upside down in its pursuit.

One day while sitting at my laptop searching for some work related folder, a different folder labeled "gear list" caught my eye. I'd created it years ago and out of curiosity and boredom, I opened it only half remembering what I originally made it for. "Appalachian Trail Gear List" was the heading at the top. "Aha! I remember now!" Six years ago, when we were teenagers, three other friends and I had made plans to hike the Appalachian Trail together. We all made our own fantasy gear lists of what we'd take with us. Money wasn't an issue at the time, because in our minds, we were going to hunt and fish all the way through. Through to where? We had no clue. In fact, I don't think we did any research whatsoever. It was simply a fantasy designed to get away from it all, live in the woods like manly men, all the while hunting and fishing for our food. I smiled to myself as all our crazy notions flooded back to me. Then out of an even deeper curiosity, I decided to look into that "Appalachian Trail" just a little bit more. Needless to say, the rest is history...

Upon discovering the trail was a continuous footpath that stretched across the eastern wilderness nearly 2,200 miles from Springer Mountain in Georgia to Mount Katahdin in Maine, and took on average anywhere from five to seven months to complete, absolutely blew my mind. I was instantly obsessed! How do I find food and water? Where do I sleep? What do I sleep in? How dangerous is it? Can I hunt? Can I fish? How many people do it or have done it? When do you start? How much does it cost? How cold does it get? What gear do I need? How many people die? An endless stream of questions poured through my mind and every time I thought I'd researched every question that could possibly be asked, I found myself coming up with more. This all began in the mid spring of 2013...

After weeks of continuous reading and research, I finally felt like I had enough information and motivation to start amassing the couple thousand dollars in gear that I had painstakingly researched and written down. I also decided to announce my decision to my friends and family, but I can only describe their reactions to the description I gave them of my future endeavor as "humoring." I could tell none of them took me serious and chalked it up to something that I would get over and move on from after a few weeks. This only motivated me more. "They think I can't or won't do it! I'll show them!"

I only had less than a year to buy all the gear I needed, as well as save the funds to complete the hike. I had a timeline and a window of opportunity I wanted to meet for embarking the trail. If I got on the trail too early, then it might be too cold. If I got on the trail too late, then I might find myself hiking into the winter months in order to finish. I was trying to save what my research had described as the "low end" of the budget scale for completing the entire trail. My plan was to save at least three to five thousand dollars for the hike and I considered anything over that amount a bonus. While I'd found that some people had finished the trail for as little as six hundred dollars and as much as fifteen thousand dollars, I figured that somewhere in between those two numbers, on the lower end, would be sufficient for me.

As 2013 progressed, I slowly checked things off my gear list as I bought them. Amazon and eBay became my best friends, as well as the Bass Pro Shop and the Army Navy Surplus store down the road. All I could think about was finishing the whole trail. I had to complete the entire thing no matter what. If I was going out there, then there was no way I was coming back unless it was in a body bag or I'd hiked every inch of that damn trail.

I began coming up with fallback plans as I went over every scenario I could think of that might possibly keep me from reaching Maine. "Quitting" was never one of them, and in the end I could only settle on two things that could possibly stop me: an injury or running out of money. I knew I had very little control over the first one, other than being extra cautious and not doing anything overly stupid. The second one I associated directly with food. If I didn't have money, then I couldn't buy food when I went into towns. The way I figured it... once I had all my gear, then all I needed to get to Maine was food in my belly. No money = No food = No Maine. That's what it came down to in my mind.

During my research I'd found that you could have packages mailed to you in different towns that resided along the trail. You could send them to the post office or any other local businesses that held packages for hikers. I came to the conclusion that while I was still working with a decent income, I needed to buy food and package it in advance. This way the packages could be mailed to me in the event that I ran low on money before reaching Maine. As a result of learning this information, I went to Sam's Club and got slightly carried away. I ended up with thirty large USPS flat rate shipping boxes, each weighing between eight to ten pounds full of food. I had dozens of honey buns, summer sausage, oatmeal packets, grits packets, Ramen Noodle packets, cereal bars, thirty- six military MRE's, banana chips, pumpkin seeds, almonds, coconut chips, tuna packets, pasta sides, and instant mash potatoes. I ended up with more than two months' worth of food stacked up in boxes at my parent's house, ready to be sent to me in the unlikely event that I went broke out there.

After covering what I considered to be a critical component to the success of my venture, my mind was at ease and confident that nothing was going to stop me. The next order of business was to begin making arrangements for my business to be taken over while I was gone. This also ensured that I would have a small income trickling into my account while away on my adventure. Only once I'd made these arrangements and had everything lined up accordingly, did everyone begin to take me serious...

By December 2013, I had everything I needed, or so I thought. I made the executive decision to do the hike using a hammock instead of a tent as my shelter. I'd done my research and based on that research I found myself to be a "hammock guy." Forget needing flat, smooth ground to pitch a tent; give me two trees and the world is my camp spot. If there were no trees, then who wanted to camp there anyway?

The pack I chose was a 41-liter military style radio backpack. Looking back, I have no idea why in the hell I went with this as my backpack choice and I can only chalk it up to being a "rookie mistake." With my major pieces of gear finally squared away, the adventure began to feel very real. I had my hammock and my backpack. I was saving money to buy food on the trail, but also had food stored away in case I ran out of money. I had a filter for water and containers to carry it in. Food, Water, Shelter! Check! Check! Check! The big three items that I needed to be a happy and thriving human being.

Of course I had more than just those items. I had my summer sleeping bag. A sleeping bag liner in case I got cold inside my first sleeping bag; warm and cold weather clothes. Rain gear for when it rained; A pot and an alcohol stove for cooking; a lighter for fires; fuel to sustain those fires; a knife for cutting; a headlamp for nighttime; a rain cover for my backpack; a dry bag for my clothes, sleeping bag, and food; a pair of waterproof hiking shoes; two pairs of socks; a phone charger to charge my phone which also doubled as a camera to capture my memories; a spice wheel to flavor my food, a spoon to scoop it and a fork to impale it; also, one hundred feet of

550 Para cord because rope is important; a shemagh (desert scarf) to protect me from high winds; gloves to warm and protect my hands; a hat to cover my head; sunglasses to protect my eyes; batteries for my headlamp; pain killers for pain, Neosporin for infections, medical tape for blisters, band aids for boo boos and my handy dandy watch for telling time! That was how I went over my gear list in my head and also assured myself of the function and importance of each item. When all was said and done, my pack topped out at just over fifty pounds. It was only rated for forty-five, but I didn't care. As far as I was concerned, I was ready to be dropped off anywhere in the world and survive.

My planned departure date was March 10, 2014 and at first it felt as if it would never arrive. Then, as the tenth slowly approached I began to feel not the least bit anxious and nervous. I kept going over all of my gear. "Do I have everything I need? Do I need everything I have? Am I missing something? What am I missing? IM SURE I'M MISSING SOMETHING THAT I CAN'T POSSIBLY LIVE WITHOUT!" This feeling lasted for a while, but I never quite figured out what my paranoia was trying to tell me I was leaving behind. One thing that occupied my time quite a bit, was figuring out how to pack all my gear. I must have unpacked, packed, rearranged and reevaluated all of my gear five times a week for three months. To be honest, I enjoyed it. It kept me focused, it kept me motivated, and it kept me familiar with everything I had.

There were other ducks to line up as my departure date approached; I focused on the expenses that I would have back home and began trying to eliminate them. I moved out of the house I was renting with my girlfriend and moved all my stuff back to my parent's house. That was over $700 a month back in my pocket right there. Luckily, my car was paid off, so I dodged a bullet in that arena. Car insurance... canceled it. Cell phone bill... I told my mother I would cancel it because the whole point of me going out there was to get away from it all, therefore, I didn't want to contact or be contacted by anyone. This had the planned effect that I hoped it would.

"Well what about an emergency?" my mother asked. "What if I need to contact you?" she added. I simply looked at her with a "sorry face" and shrugged my shoulders. "Well, I'll just pay your cell phone while you're out there, because I want to be able to reach you!" Hook, line and sinker! ... "If you insist mom," I replied. It was mission accomplished. Yes, I was cheating by using my mother's unconditional love to help me pay one of my bills, but I had expenses to cut.

Being 24, I still had over a year and a half of coverage on my parent's health insurance, so I was golden in that department. The personal training studio expenses were covered by the people that I'd leased it to, and I had every confidence that they could handle it. In the end my only expenses back home were some very small credit card bills that I was paying the minimum amount while I was gone.

Physically, I have always kept myself in good shape. Being a personal trainer and wanting to look the part, I usually kept myself in what could be described as a little bit better than your average "good shape." Unfortunately, like all mortal beings, I went through highs and lows of just how well I took care of myself. Preceding my decision to hike the trail, I had been in a low place of unhappiness, boredom, and dissatisfaction with the life I was leading. I hadn't been working out consistently and my body had de-conditioned from the level of fitness I normally maintained. Upon my decision to hike the trail and throughout my accumulation of gear and information, I'd still continued to neglect my fitness.

In November of 2013, I had elbow surgery to remove a bone spur from my ulna. That spur was a partial reason for why I hadn't been working out previously, as it had been causing me a great deal of pain and discomfort. Surgery was a success and the recovery time was relatively short, but still, the sensitivity of my elbow further prevented me from working out and provided excuses not to stay active. I gained thirty-five pounds before my departure and topped out at a personal high weight of 255 pounds. At 6'2, I've always had a relatively solid built frame that carried any extra weight well. To the random passer-by I probably looked like a big, husky, muscular guy. To family and friends, I looked like a blimp compared to the lean athletic shape I usually kept. How ironic that I'd spent virtually my entire life in good physical condition, but right before the biggest physical undertaking/challenge of my life, I would neglect my health more than I ever had before. I didn't let any of this bother me however, as I knew that I'd lose weight on the trail and through muscle memory, I would adapt and be back in shape in no time. I mean it was just walking, how hard could it possibly be?

Originally, I had no plans to take my dog with me. She is a Shiba Inu and her name is Katana. She's an ancient, purebred Japanese hunting dog, and at about fifteen pounds, with a curly tail, as well as the features and colors of a fox, she could very well be the cutest dog you've ever seen. Fiercely independent, cunning, and always looking for trouble, she is my little princess. Unfortunately, I've let that little princess walk all over me since the day I brought her home.

In all my research of the trail, everything I read about hiking with dogs had basically said the same thing. "Do not bring one unless you have no other choice! A dog will dominate and inhibit your hike, as well as increase your budget and your chances of not completing the trail due to possible injury to the dog and other factors." I was determined to follow that advice, as my little princess was disobedient and couldn't go anywhere without a leash or attempting to run away. I was forced to make arrangements for her care in my absence.

My girlfriend had also moved back into her parent's house, and although she was not overly thrilled with my decision to hike the trail, she was still supportive. Her and her mother agreed to watch Katana for me while I traipsed across the eastern seaboard. They had two little Weiner dogs and one Chihuahua that I was praying Katana would get along with in my absence. My parents couldn't watch her because they had two Corgis that she always fought with, so my girlfriend's parents were my only option. With my fur baby being watched, I finally had all the bases covered. All that was left to do was await my departure date and drive up to Georgia.

March 10th was days away when I checked the weather conditions in northern Georgia where I'd be starting. They showed snow, ice, and ice storms. Being from Florida, I don't do ice very well, so all my macho-ness and preparedness went out the window. There was no way I was starting in the freezing cold, so I postponed my departure by a couple weeks. During that time of anxiousness and extreme boredom, I cut down a small magnolia tree that was growing in the woods near my house. I removed a thin, straight section of the small tree and shaved off the bark before carving some grips as well as some other designs into it. "Voila!" I'd created my own personal walking staff! Most people would have fancy $100 + trekking poles, but I would have my homemade walking stick.

The days dragged by and a couple of painfully slow weeks later, I was in the car with my girlfriend headed up to Georgia. I was more nervous and scared than I would've ever projected or admitted to anyone at the time; I was second guessing everything. Every piece of information I'd learned about the trail suddenly felt unreliable. I told myself I was crazy for thinking that way and everything would be fine. I'd done everything I could possibly do (other than workout) to prepare up to this point, and all that was left was to get out there and start walking.

We arrived in the small town of Dahlonega, Georgia on March 30th. It was windy, sleeting rain, and freezing. The whole situation seemed to be filled with bad omens. We checked in at a hotel where I spent a relatively sleepless night thinking about anything and everything related to the journey ahead. I even unpacked and packed my bag again… twice.

The next morning was beautiful and clear, albeit very, very cold as we set out towards Amicalola Falls State Park. I had butterflies in my stomach the entire way, but during the ride over, every reservation, ounce of anxiety and nervousness that I'd been plagued with before, had dried up and transformed into pure adrenaline-pumping excitement. I felt as if I was riding a rollercoaster slowly up that first big climb.

We reached the park a little before 9:30 am and stopped in at the welcome center. Everything from there on seemed to happen so fast, that I can hardly believe it happened at all. I don't know what I was expecting; perhaps something a little more drawn out to precede such an epically long adventure, but no.

I walked into the welcome center and informed the employees that I was a "thru-hiker." They almost rolled their eyes at me as if to say, "Not yet-you're not!" Every person that walks into that building and says they're a thru-hiker must look like the biggest "wannabe" ever in their eyes. They asked me to sign the "thru-hiker roster" and I did. It was March 31, 2014 and I was the 779th person to begin an attempted thru-hike of the Appalachian Trail that year. I asked the employee where the trail started and she replied, "The 8.5-mile approach trail starts right behind this building; you can start here or you can drive to the top of Springer Mountain and begin there."

I'd read about this "approach trail" during my research. Most pieces of information said that if you skipped the approach trail, you weren't a thru hiker. This was because it used to be a part of the original trail built back in the 1930's. That was all I needed to know. What was an extra 8.5 miles out of 2,185.3 anyway? I was definitely doing the approach trail.

I walked back outside to my anxiously awaiting girlfriend. "It starts right back there," I told her as I pointed around the building. We walked behind the welcome center to an archway that announced the start of the approach trail. We had someone snap a picture of us together underneath the arch before we said our goodbyes and goodbye kisses (that just didn't seem to last long enough). I turned and looked through the archway; I could feel my rollercoaster rounding up over the top of the first climb. I stepped through the stone arch and started walking. My rollercoaster began to plummet down that first big drop and wasn't about to stop for the next 195 days....

CHAPTER 2: GEORGIA

"A Major Gut Check!"

A Journey of 2,185.3 miles begins with a single step. Or perhaps 600 consecutive steps straight up the face of an enormous waterfall in the case of the 8.5 mile Appalachian Approach Trail. As I stepped through the archway and began my adventure, I could hardly contain the butterflies fluttering around my stomach. It wasn't long before they almost made their escape in the form of me puking all over the stair case leading up Amicalola Falls, the tallest cascading waterfall east of the Mississippi. With day hikers, tourists, and possibly other thru-hikers around me, I tried to make it look as if I was stopping to enjoy the scenery, and not because I felt like I was going to hurl on death's door.

Reaching the top of the falls was the first great climb and accomplishment of the journey. For many of the first few weeks, it would be a common question amongst thru hikers to ask each other if they'd hiked the approach trail. If you answered "Yes," the response would almost always be, "How bout them stairs!"

The approach trail meandered through the Georgian wilderness marked by rectangular "Blue Blazes" that were painted on trees. Blue blazes always marked official trails that branched off the AT (Appalachian Trail) but weren't the AT. They normally marked side trails that led to water sources, shelters, towns, bypasses, and bad weather trails.

Along the approach, there were a myriad of different climbs and descents of varying difficulty and steepness. One thing was certain - if the trail wasn't mud or mud puddles, it was jagged rock or exposed tree roots. It wasn't even noon before my feet were feeling sore and bruised. I couldn't help but wonder what everyone wonders when beginning their first thru-hike - "What have I got myself into?"

By 11:45 my pack was lighter by two liters of water, one pack of Skittles, one Tootsie Roll and half a Subway sandwich. After my little lunch break, everything but my feet were feeling better. I would later come to realize that many of my emotions out on the trail would be tightly connected to my hunger. Out on the trail, your level of hunger would dictate if it was a good day or a bad day.

I finally reached the base of what I assumed was Springer Mountain sometime in the early afternoon. Up, up, up... the trail went as it endlessly ascended over rocky steps. It was a rocky stairway to heaven that burned like hell. Being from the Sunshine State, I wasn't used to anything more than a gentle slope. My legs burned like they'd never burned before.

At one point, both of my legs completely cramped and seized up on me. I collapsed onto a large rock and began massaging my thighs. After a few minutes I attempted to stand up, but they immediately cramped and seized again, sending me back onto my rock. For the second time on the first day... I questioned the predicament I'd gotten myself into. I knew that it was going to be rough starting out, but I never dreamed the pain would be this bad on the first day. After nearly fifteen minutes of massaging and resting my legs, I was back up and walking.

In the grand scheme of the Appalachian Trail, Springer Mountain isn't really that big or difficult. On this day however, Springer Mountain was my Everest. I finally rounded up over some rocks to find there was no more mountain above me. I walked forward to a smooth precipice of rock to find the plaque marking the southern terminus of the Appalachian Trail set into the stone of Springer Mountain itself. It read, "Georgia to Maine, a footpath for those who seek fellowship with the wilderness." This was a famous plaque that I'd seen many times in pictures during my research of the trail. Elation swelled inside me as I thought to myself... "THIS IS IT!"

I admired the plaque and the amazing view of the landscape below for several minutes. Ultimately, I would have liked to have stayed longer, but was driven away by powerful gusts of freezing wind whipping across the summit. I turned back to the trail and walked several more yards before my eyes fell upon a beautiful sight. It was like a beacon of hope shining through the forest, as well as my guide for the next 2,185 miles; I saw my first white blaze. If it hadn't been for the horrible chaffing on my thighs and other areas I probably would've broken into a skip.

The entire Appalachian Trail is marked by "white blazes." A blaze is nothing more than a small rectangle painted on a tree, a rock, a road, a sign, a building, an archway, a bridge, a boat, anything! The purpose of blazes is to serve as a marker that lets you know that you're on the right path. Blazes marking the Appalachian Trail are white, and can be anywhere from several yards apart, to several hundred yards apart, to sometimes over a mile apart. You always have to keep a wary eye open lest you stray off the path or onto a different trail.

I made my way down the north side of Springer while taking note of every white blaze as I walked. In less than a mile I reached a road; the road where I assumed most people were dropped off when they skipped the approach trail. There was a parking lot next to the road, and in this parking lot I met a man named "Mountain Squid." This wasn't his real name of course - it was his trail name.

Nobody calls you by your real name out on the trail because you get a trail name given to you. Some people name themselves, but this is secretly frowned upon. The only way to get a true blue trail name is to earn it. As you might guess, there are many ways in which to earn a trail name. You can earn it through the things you commonly say or do, or by things that happen to you. Sometimes you may even be named according to the way you look or the things you wear (red headed people beware). How someone gets the name "Mountain Squid," I'll never know, mainly because I never asked.

Mountain Squid wasn't hiking the trail this year. He was just hanging out and giving advice as well as snacks to any thru-hikers that passed by. Old Squid gave me a juice box as I walked across the parking lot. This was my first experience with what is called "trail magic." Trail magic may come in many forms, but mostly it comes in the form of food and drink provided by benevolent and thoughtful strangers. It can also come in the form of rides to and from town and pretty much any random good deed or act of kindness. After a few golden nuggets of advice from Mountain Squid I pressed on. I was chaffing so badly that I likely had tears in my eyes. I made it almost another three miles from the road and wound up at Stover Creek Shelter.

There are quite literally hundreds of shelters set up along the AT and every single one of them is unique. They can be anywhere from several to ten miles apart, or even fifteen to twenty miles apart in some sections of the trail. The shelters are usually nothing more than a three sided wooden lean-to that is completely open to the elements on one side.

Your typical shelter can accommodate anywhere from five to thirty people and forty to one thousand mice. The average is usually five to ten people and one hundred mice, but all along the trail fantastically elaborate and beautiful shelters of varying sizes can be found. It's always smart to plan your daily miles around the shelters that lie ahead of you, because they are normally placed in ideal locations that are almost always next to a reliable water source.

The majority of shelters will also have a "privy" (outhouse) somewhere within the vicinity. The reason for the privies is to consolidate human waste. If everyone went to the bathroom in any convenient spot within the vicinity of a shelter, then things would get pretty poopy and unhealthy out there. The privies certainly help to keep the waste centralized, but they are not always the better alternative to simply digging a hole. This is due to the critters that tend to call these small wooden outhouses "home." The standard privy will be filled with spiders, spider webs, flies, and other insects as well as mice, rats, chipmunks, woodchucks, and sometimes snakes that come to feed on them. Yes, the Appalachian Trail privy is a miniature ecosystem in itself and it takes a special person to get used to one. Just imagine a brown recluse spider sitting just under the lip of the makeshift seat you're sitting on as you do your business. I promise this thought will be stuck with you for the next several dozen times you sit on a toilet, especially an Appalachian Trail privy...

It wasn't even 4 o'clock yet, but upon seeing the shelter through the trees, I felt like I was saved. I half walked, half ran up to the shelter with my awkward chafing gait, dropped my pack, plopped down on the edge of the wooden floor and laid back. I must have passed out quickly because I don't remember anything else after that and when I awoke it was after 5 pm. There were now two other people at the shelter, milling around and trying to get a fire started. They didn't succeed due to the damp conditions from the previous day's rain. It would be a while before I mastered the art of making fires in wet and soggy conditions (shave the superficial wet bark off with your knife until you reach the dry stuff).

I opened my pack and pulled out a container of chicken wings that I'd bought at Wal-Mart the previous day and devoured them. I was still hungry, but didn't eat anything else.

More hikers showed up and set about eating and making camp. A couple of them set up their air mats and sleeping bags on the floor of the shelter. This prompted me to begin setting up my camp.

I had set up my hammock probably a hundred times while practicing back home without a single problem. Today I felt like the pressure was on. I was so nervous and didn't want to look like some rookie in front of these strangers by fumbling around trying to get my hammock hung just right. I had no idea if these other hikers were amateurs like me, or expert mountaineers with a lifetime's worth of experience in roughing it and surviving in the wilderness. Nevertheless, I wanted to look as if I knew what I was doing in front of my peers.

I found two suitable trees not far from the shelter and slung my atlas straps around their trunks about six feet off the ground. "So far so good," I thought. Then I proceeded to unpack my hammock and get it all unfurled. "No problems yet!" I clipped my carabineers to a loop on each of the atlas straps and found the hammock to be slightly lopsided at first. After two or three moves to higher and lower loops on either strap, I got it just right. I looked around to see if anyone was watching me, but of course they weren't. Everyone was busy keeping to themselves while dealing with their own gear. They were probably thinking about the same things as me.

I climbed into my hammock for a little "test" run. "Ahhh, just right," I thought as I put my hands behind my head and stared up into the tree canopy. Almost at once, my eyes fell upon an enormous tree branch that had snapped and was hanging precariously among the other branches directly above me. "Shhhit!" I hissed under my breath. I'd hung my hammock right under a widow maker (a lumberjack term for a branch that falls and kills you while you're cutting down a tree). I looked around again to see if anyone had noticed my blunder. As before, no one was paying any attention to me. I looked back up at the huge branch that was dauntingly dangling twenty feet above my head. "There's no way I can get up and move my hammock now," I thought. "Everyone will think I'm an idiot!" Then I imagined the news headline back home. "Local Man Goes to Hike Appalachian Trail; Killed by Falling Tree Branch First Day."

At this moment I felt like I was trapped in a lose-lose situation. I could move my hammock for seemingly no reason and look like a moron in front of these total strangers, or stay where I was and maybe get killed in my sleep. To me at the time, this was big. It was my first executive life or death decision on the trail. I had no idea that I'd be making them so soon!

I scrutinized the branch a little more before deciding that it had been hanging up there for quite some time. The chances of it falling on this night were probably very slim. Since the wind had also calmed down, I figured it was no longer a factor. I made the decision to stay put.

My eyes slowly closed, the branch fading from my vision and thoughts as I began to relax and reflect upon my first day on the trail. Mostly I thought about how much pain I was in and how much worse it was going to get before it got better. This was especially true for my chafed and burning thighs. That's when it hit me! I suddenly remembered what I'd forgotten in my meticulously thought out accumulation of gear... body-glide and baby powder! My thighs and other areas had reminded me with their molten lava-like burning.

Nobody stayed up to converse much on that first night. I'm sure this was due to a combination of being worn out as well as the lack of a campfire. I made up my mind that if my chafing thighs and sore feet hurt as much in the morning as they did that evening, I would hang around the shelter a while longer. I fell asleep to the sounds of people fending off mice inside the shelter. I heard the pounding of fists and feet and the shaking of sleeping bags as the mice hoards descended upon the now sleepless, shelter-dwelling hikers. I couldn't help but chuckle as my decision to sleep in a hammock was reaffirmed.

I was awoken early around 6 am to the sound of rain lightly falling on my canopy. I hadn't set up my rain fly the night before, so my protection from the rain was minimal. I was more overjoyed to realize that I hadn't been killed by the widow maker overnight than I was upset about getting wet by a little drizzle. The rain was light enough that it wasn't soaking through my canopy, so I didn't immediately jump out and set up my rain fly. I waited for several minutes and it passed, never to be seen for the rest of the day.

After perhaps another hour of lying in my cocoon, I decided it was time to get the day started. I cooked some grits for breakfast, did my hygiene routine, filtered some water, and packed up camp. The whole process took me nearly an hour. "I'll get faster," I told myself.

My chafed regions had miraculously healed over night, but my feet were another story. They were swollen and sore as I squeezed them into my shoes. "At least I don't have any blisters yet," I thought. All in all, it was a beautiful day and I was feeling great. I was ready for some hardcore walking as my spirits were sky high.

In the early days when just starting out, I'd wanted to put Georgia behind me as fast as possible. I thought it would make me feel better psychologically if I chalked up some big miles in the first days and weeks. Despite everything in my body telling me "NO," I still wanted to push what I considered bigger miles. In the beginning I didn't care as much about the journey as I did about just finishing. I later found that to be the wrong train of thought, as hiking the Appalachian Trail is 100% about the journey and experience, and not just saying that you did it.

A word to the wise, NEVER try and push bigger miles when you begin a long distance hike without any prior experience or conditioning. Listen to your body, and unless you absolutely have to go further due to water or an emergency, stop when it tells you to stop. It will save you a tremendous amount of pain and heartache. I can't tell you how many people I saw quit the trail due to overdoing it in the beginning and hurting themselves or causing themselves more pain than they could tolerate. There is no harm in going slow and building yourself up gradually. You have plenty of time and distance to grow stronger, and believe me, you will!

I can only describe the first miles out of Stover Creek as peaceful and enjoyable. The trail ran along a beautiful stream with banks covered in rhododendrons. The scenery had been bleak in most parts of the forest, but all along the stream the plant life was bountiful. Blood Root, Chickweed, Toothwort and Trout Lily all shaded under a canopy of Sweet Gum, Cedar, Hickory and Beech trees. The level ground and beautiful scenery was not to last long. Soon, I was climbing mountains again.

The mountains kept coming one after the other with no breaks. When you came down one mountain, the next one was right there going straight back up again. While climbing Hawk Mountain I heard what sounded like no less than thirty coyotes screaming in a nearby gully. "The first signs of wilderness predators!" I thought excitedly.

After Hawk Mountain and a few other little bumps, I reached Sassafras Mountain. This mountain was a plague unto my soul that day. Up until this point in my life, Sassafras was the steepest thing I'd ever climbed. This mountain was a big jokester too. It was only on my second day that I became very familiar with what a "false summit" was. A false summit is pretty much exactly what it sounds like. You round up over a ridge or incline thinking that you've reached the top of the mountain when in fact that is "FALSE," the jokes on you and there's still an indeterminable distance to traverse in order to reach the real summit. I encountered no less than three false summits on Sassafras Mountain. I felt as if I was dying and must have stopped every forty steps to catch my breath and allow my legs to stop burning.

Halfway up, as I was trudging along, staring at my feet, I noticed a red gummy bear lying in the middle of the trail. For about four seconds I contemplated picking it up and eating it. That little red bear made of yummy gummy looked so delicious at the time, lying there all alone in the dirt. It was painfully obvious that the food cravings were already setting in. In the not so distant future, I would do crazier things than picking up random food out of the dirt and eating it in the name of extreme hunger.

I daydreamed of skittles for most of that day, which was strange because I've never really been a big fan of skittles. The previous day had been the first time I'd had them in years, but now I was craving them. Looking back, I now know that it wasn't actually the skittles I was craving back then, but sugar in general. Skittles just happened to be the last sugary thing I'd eaten; therefore, they were sticking out in my mind because I wanted more sugar.

The descent down Sassafras was as steep and unforgiving as the climb up. Once again this was the steepest descent I'd ever encountered. I couldn't decide which I despised more, the burning of hiking uphill or the hurting of going down. Going uphill was slow and painful in the beginning, requiring frequent breaks, while every step downhill jarred my joints and smashed my toes to the front of my shoes. Before the end of the journey, I would learn to love the climbs and hate the descents. The descents did so much more damage to my body.

After Sassafras I stopped for a rest in Cooper Gap. A gap is the space between two mountains or hills. Usually a small level area right where one mountain comes down and another goes up (depending on which way you're going of course). While leaning against a tree in the middle of this gap, I happened to look down and see an enormous wolf spider sitting on top of my foot. I was too tired to do anything about it, so I just stared at the octagonal arthropod, daring it to head north up my leg. Lucky for him, he didn't. As I began walking again, the leggy demon hopped off and continued on its own adventure. This was a milestone in itself, because this was the first spider to ever touch me and not get turned into spider dust. I was already finding my harmony and fellowship with nature and the wilderness; just like the plaque said!

No short amount of huffing and puffing later, I finished my last big climb of the day as well as another five miles to Gooch Mountain Shelter. Along the way, I ran into a guy who told me a story of a bat that'd repeatedly flown between his legs earlier that day while he was filtering water from a stream. The only thing I could say was that the bat was lucky it wasn't me, or it would've wound up a "bat pancake" between my now chafed and trail blazing thighs. Ozzy Osbourne would seem like a walk in the park compared to the misery that being trapped between my sweaty, chafing thighs would bring.

When I arrived at the shelter, there were more than a dozen other hikers already there. "Where were these people yesterday?" I thought. None of the people from Stover Creek were anywhere to be found. Everywhere I looked there were new faces. I surmised that I must have gone further than the people I camped with the night before and that these were people that had been ahead of me yesterday. I'd gone far enough that day to catch up to the people in front of me. This made me feel good because it was right in line with my plan to put Georgia off my mind and behind me as quickly as possible. I was moving right along and had finished a thirteen-mile day on top of the twelve miles I'd done the day before. I was surprised that I wasn't as chafed as I was the day before, but my feet felt destroyed. I could feel hot spots and blisters finally starting to form. Each foot felt like one big bruise.

I was too tired to cook anything and only ate a few spoonfuls of peanut butter as well as some peach slices before calling it a day. I wasn't even worried about people watching me as I set up my hammock. I'm sure they weren't worried either. I decided not to hang my food away from bears and instead shoved it all into different pockets on the underside of my hammock.

The hammock I bought was designed as a "four season" hammock. It had six huge pockets sewn into the bottom where I could store all my gear. These pockets also double as insulators. When you put things inside them, it creates an open pocket of dead air that warms up as you lay in the hammock. This open space of air between the outside of the pocket and the main fabric of the hammock itself also acts as a shield from direct wind chill. It's quite functionally fancy if I do say so myself.

After setting up, I made my way over to the shelter in an attempt to be social. I met six other hikers by the names of Schweppes, Coma, Picachu, War Story, Chester, and Jim. I know what you're thinking. "What a line up!" Some of these were their real names, while some were trail names. I stayed up and talked with them for a while and learned that each of them had gone out there by themselves just as I had. I didn't know it at the time, but some of these people were going to become lifelong friends whom I later thought of as family.

It wasn't too long before dark that I retired back to the hammock that I now affectionately referred to as my "nest." I wasn't worried about a bear ravaging my hammock for the tasty contents within (the food; not me) because there were plenty of other food bags hung up around the shelter to keep it busy. I was a firm believer, as well as an avid practitioner in the game of odds, and I felt like I had a good chance of being overlooked. In the end, the worst that happened that night was a squirrel getting into one of the hanging bags and scattering the contents all over the forest floor.

Day three proved to be a pivotal day in the grand scheme of the entire adventure and even my life after the trail. If the events that happened on this day had not happened, my hike would've undoubtedly been quite a different experience. Things would have happened along a much different timeline and I wouldn't have met or reconnected with certain people. What happened to me on this day later reaffirmed my belief in synchronicities and the notion that all things happen for a reason.

The day was filled with its usual ups and downs that I had more or less come to terms with. Dreading and complaining wasn't going to make the mountains disappear. I took it slow while stopping for many breaks throughout the day. Fantastic views were plentiful, as I was determined to enjoy every single one of them.

Then unexpectedly, on a pile of rocks and dirt they called Big Cedar Mountain, I had a little accident. It was supposed to be my last big mountain of the day and should have gone off without a hitch. I was tired and looking forward to making camp for the night when an incident happened that would change my hike for the rest of the journey.

The trail was still covered with leaves from the previous fall as I made my way down the steep slopes of Big Cedar Mountain. Everything was going smoothly until I stepped on a small rock hidden beneath the leaves and rolled my ankle completely over. It rolled so hard and so far that the ball of my ankle hit the dirt and even scraped some skin off. I stumbled but miraculously didn't fall; the only thing keeping me on my feet was my wooden staff. Intense pain washed over my body as I stood there leaning on my staff and gritting my teeth. My worst fear had been realized and only on the third day...INJURY!

After a minute or so, I did some range of motion exercises with my ankle and determined that it wasn't broken; however, it was throbbing and had swollen to the size of a softball. There was nothing I could do other than keep walking. I checked my guidebook and saw there was a spot called "Lance Creek" just over a mile from where I estimated myself to be. I hobbled the rest of the way there and set up my hammock at the top of a ravine that had the narrow, as well as shallow, Lance Creek flowing steadily down below.

I took off my shoes and set about popping blisters, as well as further examining my ankle. The swelling had gotten worse. I decided the best thing to do was go down to the creek and soak it in the cool water. I slowly ambled down the steep ravine using small saplings and shrubs to steady myself before finally making it down in one piece. Lance Creek itself was very narrow and shallow, except for one spot that opened into a pool about a foot deep. I sat on a rock and soaked my ankle. I decided that it felt so good (and also because I hadn't showered in three days) that I was going to go ahead and take a bath while I was at it.

I sat down in the pool and began to rub water all over my legs, arms, armpits, shoulders, and everywhere else. The chafed spots burned as the water reawakened the dried sweat that had been crusted to my skin. I switched to a sitting position on my knees and leaned over to splash water onto my face. On about the third splash I felt something stick to my forehead just above the bridge of my nose and next to my right eyebrow. I subconsciously assumed it was a leaf, but seconds later I felt the leaf start climbing towards my prematurely receding hairline. Instantly startled, I swatted at my face and knocked whatever it was back into the water. I looked down to see a baby salamander paddling away. Actually I have no idea if it was a baby or not; it was just so small that the word "baby" seemed like the best description for it.

I scooped the salamander back up while chuckling at my overreaction and examined him for several seconds. It was dark brown with black spotty markings all over its body, maybe two inches long. The little guy was apparently an amazing swimmer too. I sent little Salamander Phelps back on his travels down Lance Creek. I could once again feel my level of harmony with nature rising.

After bathing, I climbed onto a rock wearing only my compression underwear. I sat there while air drying and contemplating my new predicament. I stared down Lance Creek for more than half an hour in blissful solitude. In those thirty minutes I had some of the most peaceful moments of clarity and calm that I'd ever had in my life up until that point. I felt very lucky to be where I was and doing what I was doing. There was no way that I could let this injury stop me from accomplishing what I'd come out there to do. "It may slow me down, but it's not going to stop me." I told myself.

I made my way back up the ravine to find Schweppes and two other hikers with their tents pitched near my hammock. We built a fire and had dinner together as we talked about the day's adventures that were unique for each of us. It was during these conversations that I discovered how Schweppes had received his trail name.

Schweppes was 22 years old; a ginger with red hair, pale white complexion, and blue eyes - a ginger in every sense of the word. "Schweppes" just so happens to also be a brand of "GINGER ale." The similarities don't stop there. "Schweppes Ginger ale" comes in a green aluminum can. Coincidentally, all of Schweppes's clothes were green, as well as his tent and much of his other gear. He seemed to have a slight obsession with the color green. Naturally it was said that he was a "Ginger in a green can" every time he crawled into his tent. It was quite ingenious and the name "Schweppes" stuck. That is a first rate trail name story, as well as a text book scenario of how a trail name is coined and earned.

It was also on this night that I discovered a new way to eat summer sausage. Let me rephrase that, I discovered the ONLY way to eat summer sausage. Roast it in chunks over an open fire until the outsides are charred and dripping with grease. It tastes like a cross between bacon and steak, and a wilderness dinner isn't complete without it. Throughout the journey I would end up experimenting with a lot of different foods in a lot of different ways.

Sitting around the campfire that night, I felt like I'd found new friends in these other hikers and I didn't want to lose them. Unfortunately, my new injury had other plans for me. Even though I'd made new friends, I decided that if my ankle didn't feel better the next morning, I would take the day to rest. I had plenty of food and my first resupply was only a day's hike away, so I wasn't sweating it too much.

The next morning my ankle was even more swollen and painful. It was stiff and I could hardly stand on my right foot. Every time I put my full weight on it, a sharp piercing pain would shoot through my ankle and up my leg. The decision to stay was practically made for me. It was sad to watch my new friends leave, but there was nothing I could do. I was left alone at my secluded camp spot on the edge of the ravine. I lay in my hammock for most of the day and did nothing. This is what's called a "zero day," or a day that you hike zero miles. You simply relax or take care of things that might need taking care of and don't hike.

I had an entire day of uninterrupted thought whilst listening to the creek below and the gentle rustling of the leaves in the cool breeze. It gave one a lot of time for personal reflection and introspection. My only wish was that it could have been under different circumstances. Out of boredom I ended up eating most of what food I had left, leaving myself with only one option... I had to hike out the next day no matter what.

That evening, no less than a dozen new hikers arrived near my encampment. In anticipation of my mystery guests, I had already built a large fire as the evening drew nearer and the prime hiking hours came to an end. As I predicted, everyone gravitated towards the circle of flames. Fires have always had the uncanny ability to bring people together. I got to know some of the other hikers while recounting my accident and explaining how I'd come to be at Lance Creek since late afternoon the previous day.

One of the hikers joked that I was "The Mayor" of Lance Creek, since I'd been there for so long and created the fire that brought everyone together. Everybody pondered on making that my trail name, but it was left undecided between two other names. Some wanted to call me "Captain America" because of my American flag short-shorts that I wore. Others wanted to call me Gandalf because I only carried a wooden staff while everyone else wielded dual trekking poles made of expensive, space age composite materials. In the end, I was temporarily crowned "Captain Gandalf the Mayor" as a joke.

I spoke to one hiker in particular that had some advice for me regarding my predicament. He said to me, "I have a Japanese poem for you to remember when you feel like your injury is holding you back." The poem went like this... "The snail goes up Mount Fuji, slowly... slowly." It was short and sweet and said more with those eight words than you could have written on a full page. In later days I only wish that I could've told that guy how much his poem helped me out. I only saw him one more time shortly after Lance Creek and then never again. I have no idea if he ever made it all the way.

I retired back to my hammock as "hiker midnight" approached (9 pm). I had come to realize that this whole place and experience is what you make of it. Your attitude and frame of mind determined everything. It wasn't hard to see how this undertaking could be the worst or best experience of a person's life. In the case of it being the worst, they probably wouldn't make it very far. I have yet to meet anyone that hiked the entire trail and said they had a terrible experience overall. Every single obstacle can be seen as either a blessing or a curse. It is completely up to you to decide. The trick is not to let it grind you down; roll with the punches and don't fight against anything that happens to you - adapt to it. The great irony of the trail is that even though it's so unforgiving and easy to injure yourself, it is without a doubt a place of healing. You just have to slow down and let it work its magic.

The next day my ankle was no less swollen or tender, although it didn't hurt quite as bad as the day before. After a few stretches and carefully hobbling around, the muscles and tendons warmed up and I decided to make a go of it. I only had one major obstacle standing in the way of me and my precious resupply. The name of that obstacle was "Blood Mountain" and at close to 4,500 feet tall, it's the tallest mountain on the Georgia section of the trail. The climb wasn't too terribly bad, but I kept reciting the Japanese poem to myself, reaffirming that no matter how slowly I went, as long as I kept moving, I would get there.

Descending Blood Mountain was a different story. To say that it was steep would be an understatement. To me at the time, this behemoth was a treacherous deathtrap, made even more dangerous by my crippled and fragile state. Huge areas of the climb down the north side were massive, smooth sections of rock sometimes as steep as seventy degrees with nothing for my staff to grip or catch onto. "So this is why they call it Blood Mountain," I remember thinking.

After completing the descent, I made it another couple miles to a road that crossed through an area known as "Neels Gap." On the side of the road was a famous outfitting store called Mountain Crossings. What made it so famous was that it had been there for decades and resided approximately thirty miles into the Appalachian Trail (not including the 8.5-mile approach trail). This building was usually the first sign of civilization that people saw when they first began this journey. The trail itself actually goes through a small archway and tunnel that bisects the big building.

When your eyes first fall upon Mountain Crossings, the first thing you'll notice is that the building is old. It's built almost completely out of a stone that gives it a very old timey look. The next thing your eyes will fall upon is the giant "boot tree" that dwells on the front left side of the building. It's called the boot tree because it's ordained with hundreds of old hiking boots that have been tied together by their laces and thrown up into the boughs. It's so completely covered in boots and shoes that it almost looks natural; as if the tree had one day began sprouting footwear from its branches. The boots belonged to past thru-hikers that had finished the trail, as well as hikers that had decided the trail wasn't for them and subsequently didn't need their hiking boots anymore. In essence, the tree is full of realized and unrealized dreams.

After five days in the woods, full of sweating, hurting, eating bland food, and tripping all over the steep learning curve of long distance hiking, this building looked better than a winning lottery ticket. Mountain Crossings had every piece of hiking gear you could possibly need and also carried a limited but still decent variety of foods to resupply with. Not to mention they also had ice cream and pizza. The employees were friendly and would do "shakedowns" of your gear to help you get rid of things you didn't need and maybe add some things that you were missing.

During my five days on the trail I had only come to realize that I was missing body glide and baby powder. I quickly fixed that situation and passed on getting a pizza, instead settling on a Snickers Bar. I was really trying to budget my money until I had a good feel for what things were going to cost out there. A good rule to follow is to keep the price of your current resupply at or under the number of miles you've hiked since your last resupply. I'd hiked more than thirty miles of the trail up until this point and my resupply cost me $28. That was a damn good ratio by thru hiking standards, although it's nearly impossible to maintain throughout the entire journey. Still, it's a good strategy to utilize if you're worried about money. You will almost surely end up spending extra bucks at restaurants or replacing worn out gear when you go into towns.

Throughout my time on the trail, I learned of many different people completing it with various amounts of money. As I mentioned earlier, people spent as much as fifteen thousand dollars and as little as six hundred dollars on an entire thru-hike. How much money you spend is usually tied into your comfort level and self-discipline. Many people end up running out of money due to lack of discipline, when they had more than enough to complete a thru-hike at the beginning. Besides food, the main things some people spend their money on (that don't tie directly into completion of the trail) are: restaurants, hotels, alcohol, transportation, hostels, postage, and new gear.

While it's almost impossible to avoid all or most of those things at some level or point in the journey, doing so would help reserve a pretty good chunk of extra change. I will say that the experience would lose something if you spent all of your time out in the woods and not in towns having some fun, as well as a reprieve from the elements. The small towns that reside along the trail are as much a part of the experience as the mountains and forests.

After packing away my food, I decided to hang around and relax a while. I noticed a congregation of other thru-hikers on the side of the building and went over to investigate. They were all crowded around a middle aged gentleman that I later learned went by the name of "Baltimore Jack." He had traversed the entire trail a total of nine times and was one of the most polarizing characters I've ever met. He dazzled us with hysterical and crazy stories from his past exploits of the trail, all the while sipping on a small bottle of bourbon. Story after story he told, as his audience stood entranced and consumed with interest and laughter. Any question or piece of advice you needed about the trail, he had an answer that was spot on. Probably the greatest advice he gave was that it wasn't a "one size fits all" answer. He encouraged and gave you the confidence to trust in yourself to figure things out on your own and find out what works for you, while simultaneously dropping little hints to help you along.

After a short time, Baltimore began asking everyone what their trail names were. People who had them readily shared them. When he got to me, I gave him the three names that I'd been given so far.

"Definitely not Gandalf," he began. "Every other schmuck who comes out here with a wooden staff is named Gandalf, so you don't want that one." That made good sense to me. As much as I loved and respected the great Gandalf from my favorite book trilogy of all time, I had to admit that it was very cliché.

He went on to say, "Captain America is good, but it's too obvious. People are going to refer to it as a joke; it's the first thing that comes to mind when you see someone wearing anything related to the American Flag." This also made perfect sense to me. "This guy's good!" I thought.

Baltimore then looked at me and put his fingertips together in front of his chin while he made the successive drumming motion with his fingers that you might see someone do on a desk when they were feeling impatient. As he did this he said, "Ooooooh... The Mayooor... That's a good one." He continued thinking out loud, "If anybody ever asks you what you're the mayor of, you can look at them and say... right here.'" That settled it for me. In my mind his logic was undeniable and how cool it would be to say that your trail name was decided by a living trail legend. So on my fifth day of hiking the Appalachian Trail, I officially became "The Mayor." The Mayor of wherever I was standing at the present moment, according to Baltimore Jack.

I wrapped up the day with a shower and some laundry before setting up my hammock in the woods behind the building. I was completely tickled by my new trail name and somehow felt that I was going to have extra responsibilities with a name like "The Mayor." It was the kind of name that people would defer decisions and responsibilities to, even if only in a joking manner.

I had gotten in touch with my girlfriend and she was "overnighting" an ankle brace and some other goodies that were supposed to arrive at Mountain Crossings by noon the next day. So this meant I would be hanging around for at least another half day.

My package made it on time and I was thrilled to put my ankle brace on. As a bonus the package was also filled with bacon jerky, summer sausage, and a pile of Pay Day candy bars. With half the day already gone I was faced with the decision to stay another day or see how far I could get with the daylight I had left. I was feeling pretty good and my ankle had loosened up quite a bit over the last couple days. I decided to go for it and despite the late start I still managed to make it more than eleven miles before 6 pm. Once I got moving, I felt like I needed to prove to myself that my ankle wasn't going to inhibit me. Although it throbbed and caused me a great deal of pain, I stayed relentless and tackled five good climbs over the course of those eleven miles. I managed all of that during a slight drizzle and without taking more than two breaks... I was feeling unstoppable!

About halfway through the afternoon I descended into a gap that was next to a road that briefly curved by. In this gap I met a fellow by the name of "H.G." He was probably close to four hundred pounds and standing on the side of the road looking very defeated. I immediately felt bad for him. As someone that had been active for almost their entire life, the terrain had still been incredibly challenging for me. I couldn't even imagine how challenging and painful, mentally and physically, this must be to someone that is obese or even just overweight.

I went over to him and asked how he was doing. He said he'd been trying to hitchhike out for more than an hour with no luck. Try to imagine the helplessness you might feel if it were you that was stuck in that spot, completely exhausted and in pain with steep 1,000 foot climbs on either side of you. Imagine how defeated you might feel if you knew that you had to climb one of them in order to reach any kind of decent cover for camping.

I sat down with him and talked for a while. Everyone has their reasons for going out there and attempting this journey. The important thing is not to forget or lose sight of those reasons. Pain and suffering do funny things to the human brain that can cause us to make rationalizations in the heat of the moment that we may regret later on. The ability to look beyond your present pain and discomfort to see the payoff is an important attribute to practice and possess.

H.G.'s reason for coming out there was to turn his life around, get more active, lose weight, and see how far he could get. I gave him a little pep talk and passed on my new Japanese poem. I told him not to give up, that he was right to be out here and he just needed to keep chipping away at his own pace and eventually he would beat the terrain. Our talk seemed to pick up his spirits a bit. I continued on and left him there to excogitate our conversation.

After ascending several hundred feet, I glanced back down at him one last time. He was still sitting right where I left him. I hoped he would continue, but I would never know. With such a difference between our two paces, I knew our paths would never cross again.

That night I hung my hammock across a small creek. Not the smartest decision I've ever made, since the coolest temperatures are always going to be near sources of water and high elevations. Nevertheless, the cold temperatures were outweighed by the tranquil sound of the water gurgling beneath me. I had only been out there for barely a week, yet it felt like an eternity.

My one-week anniversary on the trail was a low-key one, as the terrain I traversed that day was relatively easy. Without having to focus on the usual pain of walking over rocks or up steep climbs, my mind was free to wander. As the trail meandered through the rolling hills and along the sides of mountains, my mind began to do the same. When you have an entire day to yourself, you tend to think about things that you normally wouldn't think about. I began to contemplate how good I had gotten with my walking staff. Believe it or not, there is a lot of technique involved when going over different types of terrain. It's considerably different than using two trekking poles. The staff is obviously much wider at the end and cannot grip rocky or hard surfaces as well as a trekking pole can. Therefore, I had to aim precisely where I put my staff with each step so that it was as effective as possible and didn't slip. In the rocky terrain that abounded there, it could get a little technical on some of the downward slopes.

That day I realized that I could thrust my staff anywhere ahead of me and hit exactly where I was aiming every single time. Whether it was tiny rocks, twigs, or individual leaves, I could bulls-eye them with the end of my staff. Out of boredom, I began to wonder where this skill might be applicable in the normal functioning world. "It must be applicable somewhere… but where?" I thought. I walked, and I thrust my staff, and I thunk, and I walked some more before I finally figured it out. There could only be one answer! I could use this new found skill to gig the snot out of some frogs! I was excited to stumble upon this realization for several seconds before another thing occurred to me (to my temporary dismay). Most frog products probably came from some mass producing frog facility or farm. There really wouldn't be a market for a professional frog gigger, as most wild frogs were probably only taken by hobbyist frog giggers. This was a problem because the hobbyist angle wouldn't make me any money. So then I thought, "What if there was someone who was so incredibly good at gigging frogs, that they could meet the supply and demand of the possibly nonexistent "wild caught frogs" side of the market?" By putting up numbers never before seen by "lesser" frog giggers, my skills could possibly usher in the era of a whole new industry.

People go ape-shit over the wild caught, free range, and cage free concepts these days. That was the angle I would have to play. Problem solved. Of course I wasn't really going to become a professional frog gigger after the hike, but those kinds of thoughts kept me entertained. That is a glimpse inside the mind of someone presented with too much time to think. It's not the most productive train of thought, but it's enough to keep the brain occupied.

Besides my wandering mind, I was also kept busy by the multitude of blisters that were appearing all over my feet. They were mostly developing on the outside edges, as well as on my toes. Luckily my heels had been invulnerable to blistering so far, unlike many other hikers. It seemed like most other people developed blisters on their heels, while I developed them everywhere BUT my heels. I sat down periodically throughout the day to tend to them. When I say the word "tend," I mean slice them open with a knife and wrap medical tape around them. I didn't have any moleskin with me, so I was resigned to using medical tape.

One blister in particular was giving me a run for my money. It had popped up on my pinky toe the day before and I'd slayed it with my knife without too much trouble. I thought I'd seen the last of it, but alas it'd come back even bigger than before. This blister took up almost my entire right pinky toe. My fifth little piggy looked like a blood filled grape, and I'll be honest, it kind of freaked me out. The damn thing had seriously taken over nearly my entire toe. I was almost under the impression that if I popped it, then my pinky toe might actually disappear in a spray of blood and puss.

Maybe I should have just cut the entire toe off so that I didn't have to look at it anymore. Or was it looking at me? That blister was big enough to have its own brain and nervous system by now and could have developed consciousness at this point in the blister game. "What could it be plotting against me?" I wondered. I wasn't taking any more chances and wrapped piggy number five up so tight with medical tape that no amount of shoe friction was ever going to reach it. As I always say, out of sight out of mind.

My days spent in Northern Georgia were hard days, as it felt as if I was there longer than I actually was. Although only seventy miles of the trail lay across this state, it might as well have been a thousand. I thought about all the pain and suffering I'd already been through and tried not to imagine how much more I'd have to endure before the end. If I was completely honest with myself, Maine felt like a fantasy land that existed only in my dreams and nowhere else; a place, that try as I might, I would never get to. The entire goal of walking to Maine seemed nearly unattainable during those days. This was mostly due to the illusion that it would take a lifetime of walking and an insufferable amount of pain to get there.

I hardly made any contact with the outside world during my first week in Georgia. I couldn't make up my mind if this was a good or bad thing. I ended up deciding that it was a good thing because I needed to figure things out for myself and learn to be comfortable with constantly being uncomfortable. The reality was that I couldn't have made contact with the outside world even if I'd wanted to. I literally had zero reception on my cell phone, except for rare occasions on the tops of certain mountains.

On my eighth day I was running low on food once again and decided to make my first trip into town. I descended Blue Mountain into Unicoi Gap in order to reach a road that would take me into Hiawassee, Georgia. Whilst standing on the far side of the road, Chester, Coma, Picachu, Jim, and War Story appeared off the trail on the other side. I was pleasantly surprised to see them all. I had been fairly certain that they were way ahead of me due to my zero day, and half day, but apparently they'd all been going slower than I was. As it so happened, they were also trying to get into town.

Here is some back story on each of them as I understood it up until this point in my adventure. Chester was a 22-year-old guy from Pennsylvania that had just gotten out of the marines. His real name wasn't Chester; that was just a name he'd given himself because he hadn't accepted anything else. He was very loud as well as talkative and would say pretty much anything that popped into his head to pretty much anyone who would listen.

Coma was a 30-year-old guy from Savannah, Georgia. He had attempted a southbound hike of the trail the previous year, but stopped just short of 300 miles and went home for unknown reasons to me. He got his trail name because he put people in a coma. I'll let you decide the meaning of that for yourself.

Picachu was a 34-year-old guy from Annapolis, Maryland; however, he looked much younger than he actually was. He had previously been a financial investigator that worked closely with the FBI. He was very witty and incredibly intelligent. He also had an equally incredible dry sense of humor. You could never tell if he was serious or not because he never laughed at his own jokes and half the time they were so dark and morbid that you didn't want to laugh until you were sure he was joking. Supposedly he'd gotten his name from the bright red rain jacket he always wore. I'll be honest, I don't know what the significance or correlation between the name and his jacket was, and I don't think he did either. I felt kind of bad because he was a very muscular dude and "Picachu" didn't seem befitting.

War Story was a big guy in his mid-thirties from Ohio. He was quite hefty and you could tell that he used to be in great shape, but had let himself go. He was a veteran of the Army Scouts and had received his name because he'd been shot six times in the line of duty while serving in Iraq. The story of how it all went down is a crazy one. So crazy and incredible that he was dubbed "War Story" and it stuck. I know the story quite well, but I feel it would be disrespectful to recount it on these pages, so I'll just leave it at what I've already recounted.

Last but not least, we had Jim. Jim was a 21-year-old guy from Columbus, Ohio and had earned himself a trail name since the last time I saw him at Gooch Mountain. His new trail name was "Laser Pussy." Don't get offended just yet! Allow me to explain. Jim had a hat, and illustrated on this hat were more than a dozen different cute and cuddly cats. All of these cats were outlined in neon lasers of different colors. Hence the name "laser" for the neon lasers and "pussy" as in pussy cat. So you see it's really not that bad after all. For the sake of brevity and also to avoid misunderstandings and offending people, we always called him "Laser." Laser would go on to say that his father had warned him that the other hikers would call him a "pussy" if he wore that hat out there. His dad was only half right.

So there we were, a motley crew of stinky homeless looking hikers standing on the side of the road attempting to hitchhike into town. When you decide to go into town, you have three options. Your first option is that the trail may go straight through the town all on its own. When this happens, then you obviously have no choice but to go into town whether you needed to or not. This is a semi frequent occurrence in the grand scheme of the overall trail, as most of the time you'll have to hitchhike in order to get into towns.

The second option entails walking alongside the road in order to get into town. This is referred to as "road walking." Depending on how far away the town is, road walking could take anywhere from less than an hour to the better part of a day or even an entire day. Even longer when you factor in the round trip distances and times. This isn't any fun because those are considered "sideways miles." Sideways miles are miles that don't contribute to your completion of the trail. Even though we're walking all day, every day, we really don't want to walk any further than we have to, and especially not anywhere that isn't bringing us closer to Maine.

Your third option, that may or may not have preceded the second option, based on your success or willingness to even attempt it, is hitchhiking. Hitchhiking can be a touchy subject for some people. Good people who end up having to hitchhike are plagued by visions of being abducted and/or murdered by the people who pick them up. While the good people who normally don't pick up hitchhikers are plagued by visions of hitchhikers robbing and/or murdering them. Everything you learn growing up tells you not to hitchhike and not to pick up hitchhikers.

Subsequently, the number of people out there hitchhiking is fairly small, while the number of people who pick them up is even smaller. HOWEVER, there is an exception on the roads that bisect the Appalachian Trail. The people that live in the small towns along the trail are very familiar with the yearly migration of hikers and many of them are usually quite inclined to pick them up... usually.

Despite the likelihood of people picking you up, there is still a fine art to hitch hiking that I like to think I have mastered over the course of my great journey. It is a subtle art that requires more psychology than you might think. Prepare to be amazed at the amount of thought that goes into hitchhiking and the different situations that require different tactics. If you are an attractive female, then you can pretty much disregard everything you're about to read because your good looks alone will land you a ride in almost any situation.

The first rule is to pick out a suitable spot in which to hitchhike. The most important thing is visibility. Your potential ride needs to be able to see you from a good distance away. This is so they have time to slow down, and more importantly, give them time to judge your appearance and make up their mind over whether they want to stop or not.

The next important rule of hitchhiking is accessibility. You have to make sure that now that people can see you, you are also in a suitable spot for your potential ride to pull over. This means that if you're trying to hitch east, then you can't be standing on the westward traveling side of traffic. That only works if you're on a remote road in the back woods or a road with very little traffic that your potential ride would have no problem pulling across to get to you. There is only one other time that you would stand on the opposite side of the road from the direction you are trying to go. You would only do that if there is literally nowhere for a vehicle to pull over safely, or nowhere for you to safely stand. In these cases, you have to hope for a break in traffic at the moment your potential ride sees you, or pray they are charitable enough, and not so much in a hurry, that after they pass you, they turn around, pick you up, turn around again and continue in your desired direction as well as their original direction. It's not rocket science.

The third rule and major factor that you have to worry about is appearance. This is where most people mess up. If you're a hiker, then you already look homeless and unapproachable. The main goal is to make it very clear that you ARE a hiker. Make sure that your backpack is visible on your back or at your feet. Homeless people have backpacks too, so make sure that you have your trekking poles out as well, because homeless people don't carry trekking poles. If you have a wooden staff like me, then you're already half way screwed.

You must look approachable. Make sure you smile at the passing cars while you stick your thumb out. Don't be lazy and only half stick it out or rest your arm on your side. Achieve a 90-degree angle between your arm and torso. Get that baby out there loud and proud! Make sure you wave at the cars that don't slow down or stop. This makes you look friendly as well as understanding and sometimes people will turn around to come back and get you. Sometimes the people behind them will see your friendliness and stop instead. On some occasions you may have people competing to give you a ride. Make sure you comb your hair and your beard; that is if you have hair, a beard, or a comb.

Let us delve further into appearances and focus a little bit on strategy. Sometimes when you're a big intimidating guy with a beard and filthy clothes, standing on the side of the road by yourself trying to look friendly, you won't be able to get a ride to save your life. A tactic that will increase your chances exponentially is to always hitchhike with a female when one is readily available. You can even borrow one to hitchhike for you while you hide somewhere out of sight, then let them go on their way after your ride has stopped. This kind of decoy cheating will sometimes backfire when your ride sees you step out of the woods and the girl step back into the woods, but sometimes you have to take risks.

When people see a female on the side of the road hitchhiking, they usually associate it with "damsel in distress" as opposed to "she looks like she might cut my head off and put it in her backpack." As a result of this thinking, the lone female hitchhiker almost always gets a ride right away. This also goes for the male hitchhiker that teams up with the female hitchhiker. Your potential ride will think to themselves, "Oh, what a lovely couple, they seem harmless, I'll pick them up!" or... they will think, "If that girl is hitchhiking with that guy, then he must not be a murderer because she is obviously still alive and therefore safe to pick up." I'm telling you, this is what lurks in people's minds.

Another strategy is to use the weather to your advantage. If it's raining, windy, freezing cold or any combination of the three of those things, then you're in luck. As the cars go by, try to look as miserable as possible, but also manage a hopeful look/smile as they approach. This will tug on the heart strings of your potential ride. No one wants to feel like they're responsible for another person's suffering... usually.

The next strategy is hitchhiking with a dog. People instinctively associate someone who owns a pet with being stable. Why is this? It's because unstable people don't usually own pets. They don't own them because their pet has died or they don't want a pet in the first place because they're, well... unstable. Your potential ride will see you and your lovely animal and think to themselves, "that guy is definitely stable enough NOT to be an axe wielding murderer... I think I'll pick him up."

Last but not least is what I call "active hitchhiking." There is a saying that goes like this, "No matter what you do, never do nothing." This can be true for hitchhiking. Sometimes the distance you're trying to hitchhike isn't far at all. Maybe it's less than two miles. This is a very walkable distance. In fact, it's so walkable that you might be able to walk it faster than you can signal down a ride. When you find yourself in this situation, you should start walking and hitching at the same time. Hold that thumb out loud and proud as you saunter down the road towards town. If you're lucky or helpless enough looking, then someone will pull over and get you into town that much quicker.

The strategy of active hitchhiking can also backfire. In some situations, you may have a longer walkable distance. We will say between three to five miles or more in some cases. You start walking under the assumption that someone will feel bad for you and pull over. No one does and eventually the side of the road may get so narrow or winding that there's simply no way for your potential ride to safely pull over even if they wanted to. In cases such as this, you have officially screwed yourself and your chances to get a ride have just gone to zero. Your options are to grit it out and walk the rest of the way into town, or walk back to the trailhead and continue stationary hitchhiking.

Here are a few other quick nuggets. You should never hitchhike in a group of more than three or four people at the most. Any more people than that and most folks won't have room in their vehicle or even want to deal with that many individuals. Also, you can just forget about hitchhiking at night. It almost never works unless you're a very attractive girl or your potential ride is an overly trusting saint.

That is the fine art to hitch hiking along the Appalachian Trail and can probably be applied to almost anywhere else. Of course there are exceptions to every rule, but for the most part, those guidelines will hold true in almost any situation. I can proudly and not so proudly say that every situation I've described above has happened to me during my adventure at one point or another.

Eight days into my journey however, none of us had acquired any of this information or experience. We settled for calling a cab, and a Crown Vic showed up twenty minutes later. Packing six, full grown, sweaty, smelly hiker men as well as all of their gear into that vehicle was a farce to say the least, but somehow we managed it. Keep in mind; if you ever need to hide a body or six, then a Crown Vic is the car for you. Those are the most spacious trunks I've ever seen.

We got into town and proceeded to raid the "Ingles" grocery store. Another word to the wise, never resupply when you're hungry. Eat first and then enter the store with a full stomach and level head. I ended up buying more food than I could fit in my pack and was forced to eat some of it while still in the parking lot.

After putting away our groceries, the next order of business was finding somewhere to eat. We heard tale of a pizza buffet somewhere in town and upon further inquiry we learned it was called "Big Al's Pizza Buffet," and that it was only about a mile from our current location at the grocery store. After receiving directions, we set off on our pizza quest. "How ironic," I thought... "A quest within a quest." I would later come to realize that hiking the Appalachian Trail is nothing but a series of small adventures within bigger adventures that were all wrapped up into one enormous adventure!

We made contact with the pizza buffet and promptly got to work. In that moment I felt like it was my job to eat pizza. It had been eight days since I'd had a real meal and I felt like I owed it to myself. I felt like in order to be successful at my new job that I needed to eat as much pizza as I could possibly cram inside my body. Everyone else seemed to be tracking along the same thought process.

Less than twenty minutes into the gorge fest, and for seemingly no reason, Laser abruptly got up from the table and bolted towards the front door. He wasn't even all the way through the door when he puked all over the front step. One entire pizza worth of vomit hit the sidewalk in front of the restaurant. We erupted with laughter thinking that he'd eaten too much like the rest of us and consequently made himself sick. This was not so! After he cleaned up the mess, he returned to the table and informed us that he was actually lactose intolerant. "WHAT!? Why would you come with us to a pizza buffet if you were lactose intolerant?" we inquired. He simply replied, "I don't let my problems control me." That's a good philosophy I suppose, but I can only hope the taste going down was worth the taste coming up.

While sitting around the table, I let everyone know that I'd been thinking about some things I wanted to run by them. The first was Pikachu's name. I told him I didn't feel right calling him Pikachu and that I'd come up with a different title for him. I ran the name "DSOH" (pronounced Dee-So) by everyone. I explained it was an acronym for "Dry Sense Of Humor." Everyone approved, especially DSOH.

"Furthermore, I would like to run a new name by Chester," I said. I told him that it was a molester's name and that he really couldn't get away with naming himself. I told everyone "Muzzle" would be a better choice, since he had no filter and didn't know when to shut up. "You just want to put a Muzzle on him," I said. Surprisingly, Chester jumped on this one faster than anybody else and took it with pride. "Muzzle it is!" I was now the father of two trail names and feeling quite accomplished in knowing that my Mayoral duties were well received.

Not long after eating, the weather quickly deteriorated into heavy rain and lightning storms. The six of us ended up splitting a room at a local hotel. It was a cramped fit, but the experience provided a fine opportunity for all of us to bond. I was afforded the opportunity to learn a lot more about my new friends.

The next day was no different. Freezing rain, heavy winds, and constant lightning was the name of the game. We really didn't want to pay for another night, so we ended up calling a local shuttle to take us back to the trailhead. Once we'd been dropped off, it was every man for himself. There were no plans of going any great distance that day, as we only wanted to get to the first Shelter and out of the terrible weather. Georgia wasn't going to make it easy though. It was only a little over five miles to the shelter, but all of it was steep climbs and descents. The first climb was one thousand feet straight up over Rocky Mountain. Three guesses why they named it that.

The rain was coming down so furiously that the trail had become a series of miniature raging rapids. Water was surging around my legs on its wild descent towards level ground as I waded through the madness the whole way up. Descending Rocky Mountain was no different, except now the water was hastening my descent instead of slowing my climb.

Up until this day, Sassafras Mountain had been my least favorite of the mountains I'd climbed so far. Now Trey Mountain loomed above me with a 1,500-foot climb that seemed to go straight up. Trey had more false summits than I care to talk about. It was infuriating! When I wasn't about to be blown off the mountain by raging winds, I was screaming up at the heavens "WHERE IS THE TOP OF THIS THING!?" The entire experience was incredibly miserable, as this was my first bout of extreme bad weather on the trail. Little did I know that this was just a taste of things to come...

Everything I was wearing was soaked and freezing. My rain cover hadn't fit properly over my backpack because of everything I had strapped to the outside of it. As a consequence, quite a bit of water had gotten inside and everything that wasn't stuffed into a dry bag got wet. I was even wearing my rain gear and still got soaked to the bone.

A heavy fog rolled in over the mountain as the visibility closed to less than fifty feet. I kept going, desperate for salvation. Suddenly out of the gloomy blanket of rain and fog, the shrouded shadow of a shelter appeared through the loose thicket of trees. "I'm not going to die!" I thought excitedly. I quickly scrambled inside to find Muzzle and Laser already there along with three other hikers named Viking, Baguette, and Trail Lobster. A tarp had been hung across the entire front of the shelter to help trap warmth inside as well as provide some protection from the wind. Within an hour, DSOH, Coma, and War Story arrived too.

There was no more room in the shelter, as it was packed to the brim with all of us and our gear. Everyone and most of their belongings was soaked. We were stripping our freezing wet clothes off and putting dry ones on to warm up. The challenge was trying to find enough places to hang everything so that it could have a chance to dry during the night. What resulted was the inside of the shelter looking like some kind of foreign Bazaar with all of the different items draped and hung all over the place. We took it to a whole new level when Muzzle and I both managed to get our hammocks hung up inside the shelter, subsequently freeing up two more spots on the floor. Those spots were soon filled by other hikers arriving out of the storm and packing everyone like sardines again.

Once dry and off the nasty floor, I was feeling quite cozy. As soon as everyone else was settled in and tucked away in their sleeping bags, you could almost call the place home. Of course when you get that many guys sleeping in a confined area, united by the misery brought on by the storm as well as the commonality of being on the same epic adventure, camaraderie and brotherhood is forged. However, other side effects of having that many guys in a confined space are to be expected as well; a symphony of farts and other bodily noises, as well as raunchy jokes and no holds barred conversations. It didn't matter because all of it helped to distract from the freezing cold and pass the time.

As evening set in, it became a race of who could fall asleep the fastest, and no one wanted to be last. The more people that fell asleep before you did, meant the more snoring and other noises you had to contend with before you finally got your turn to fall asleep. Being the insomniac that I was, with a brain that I could never seem to shut down, I lost. At one point, I was halfway asleep when Laser had some sort of nightmare and let out a blood curdling shriek that gave me a heart attack as I nearly flipped out of my hammock. Oh the hazards of sleeping in shelters...

My last two days in Georgia proved to be mostly uneventful. On my second to last day I came across a rather large dog leash hanging in some bushes on the side of the trail. Since I was a good Samaritan who was "one with nature," and also because it looked shabby and out of place, I decided to carry the leash out and dispose of it in the next town. After carrying that damn dog leash in my left hand for over four miles, I began to wish that I'd left it where I found it. For some reason it never clicked that I could have simply put it in my pack. I think part of me refused to carry any more extra weight on my shoulders. It wasn't before long that I came to the edge of a rather large cliff. Peering over, I figured it must have been close to a hundred feet down. I guiltily glanced around to see if anyone was nearby or watching. The coast was clear as I casually dropped the leash over the side, did an about-face and continued on my way.

It wasn't my problem anymore and I doubted anyone would ever see it, let alone find it down there. Mother Nature could dispose of it however she wished. Despite my rationalizations, I still felt guilty about it. Sure it wasn't in a place that interrupted the unbroken views of nature anymore, but I highly doubted that a single dog leash would have any kind of ecological impact on the forest. In the end, guilt was what I got for trying to do a good deed.

I finished that day at a gap called "Dicks Creek." In my guidebook there was no apostrophe in the name to imply possession; I was a little worried at the plural implications of the name of this creek. Upon going down to collect water, I was very pleased to find that there were in fact no dicks in it (PHEW!).

Towards the end of Georgia, I had also made the executive life or death decision to stop filtering my water if the source was over 3,000 feet in elevation and coming straight out of the rocks. I hated filtering water because of how long it took. I felt like I was losing precious minutes of my life every time I stopped to filter two liters of water. I can equate the feeling to that of sitting at a stop light. You have places to go, things to see and all you want to do is move, but you can't. That's because your life probably depends on waiting those extra couple of minutes. If I could have chosen one super power at this point in the adventure, it would have been the ability to see down to one micron. That way I could instantly decide if my water was safe or not. I think everyone back home reading this information on my blog at the time, thoroughly expected me to drop dead and lose contact any day. I continued this practice up until Virginia when farms and pastures became more common. When crossing pastures and farmlands became commonplace, the threat of Giardia did too, and I began to filter religiously once again.

Giardia was one of the biggest and most common threats out on the trail. It's an intestinal infection brought on by consuming untreated or contaminated water. It's caused by parasites in the water that usually got there because the water source came in contact with infected feces. It can be transmitted through food and person to person contact, but normally it's contracted through drinking backcountry water sources.

I had heard of many people contracting Giardia out on the trail. Coma ended up being one of them, but he was able to get over it and continue. There were plenty of others that contracted it and didn't continue or had to get off the trail for many weeks in order to recover. Whether you got off the trail or not due to a Giardia infection was completely up to you and the level of suffering and discomfort you could bear. The main symptoms of Giardia were bloating, cramps, and chronic diarrhea. Depending on how severe it was, you could hike through it or lay low while you took some antibiotics and let it run its course.

On the day of April 9th-2014, something wonderful happened...I walked clear out of the state of Georgia. It was around 2 pm and quite the hot and buggy day. I thought I was lost or had misread my guidebook, because I was certain that I should've hit the state line at least thirty minutes' sooner. Then I almost missed it! On a narrow stretch of trail that overlooked a steep ravine, nailed to the side of a tree, was a tiny 10 x 4 inch sign that simply read "NC/GA." It was pretty anticlimactic but I was still overjoyed as I did the stupid "hop from one state to the other" a few times before waving "hasta la vista" to Georgia. "WOOHOO! No more Georgia!"

I stood there at the state line gazing into North Carolina and I'll be damned if it didn't look exactly the same as Georgia. None of that mattered though, as I was too elated with this first state crossing and even happier to put Georgia behind me. My happiness was short lived, because within spitting distance of the state line, I began the first climb of North Carolina. It was a mountain called Courthouse Bald, and this son of a gun went almost vertical. The peak topped out at exactly 4,666 feet. Was this a number joke? A coincidence? I think not! This was a sure sign from the hiking Gods that North Carolina was going to be hell!

In all actuality, Georgia wasn't that bad. When I really thought about the obstacles and the terrain that I faced in that state, I realized it was all bush league compared to what I encountered further up the trail. Everyone who starts in the south associates Georgia with mountains of pain and discomfort. This is due to the steep learning curve that surrounds an attempted thru-hike for the first time, as well as the still soft texture of our bodily souls and the soles of our feet...

CHAPTER 3: NORTH CAROLINA

"One More Mouth to Feed"

The first morning I awoke in North Carolina my hammock was covered in ice. I realized on that morning I wasn't equipped to deal with many colder nights such as that one. I knew I'd have to get some extra protection/insulation from the elements if I was going to keep myself from turning into a Floridian Popsicle during the freezing nights.

Right off the bat I encountered a gradual climb and descent over Standing Indian Mountain. That mountain became my favorite mountain for a very long time. With the terrain so agreeable, I was able to focus on important things like remembering the lyrics to "Don't Stop Me Now" by "Queen," and "Holy Diver" by Dio. Of course I couldn't remember them all, so I always ended up stuck on the same catchy parts over and over again.

While walking and singing in my head as well as out loud, I periodically began to hear a sound that I couldn't place. Not only did I hear the sound, but also felt it vibrating through the ground beneath my feet, as well as the airborne shockwave vibrations in my chest. I could only describe the sound as being that of a generator starting up. It would start out slow and then get faster and faster until the sounds and vibrations all ran together before abruptly cutting off.

It sounded like Thump... thump... thump... thump... thump... thmpthumpthumpthumpthump and then silence. Every five to ten minutes I would hear it reverberating through the forest. I was completely perplexed.

I'd never heard anything like it before in my life, and if I hadn't known any better, I would've said it was the distant impact of bombs. I didn't even know how to research what it could be. How would I phrase it in the Google search box? "What is that thumping noise in the forest?" That would certainly get a specific response on Google.

This sound had me so bothered that I began to imagine ridiculous sources of the commotion. I began to imagine entire civilizations of advanced subterranean creatures/beings living beneath the ground, much like the "Morlocks" in the book "The Time Machine." I imagined great networks of tunnels winding under the endless expanses of rolling hills and mountains that covered the landscape out there. Whatever was making those sounds; this little "Eloi" didn't have the answers. The mystery of the "thump" noise went unsolved that day and for a great many days after. I didn't know it at the time, but I would be hearing this sound nearly every day for almost my entire journey.

My first full day in North Carolina also marked the completion of my first one hundred miles of the trail. I was feeling like hot shit until a half second's worth of math calculations later I realized that I still had 2,085 miles to go. That number was mind boggling to me. I'd just walked one hundred miles and still hadn't completed even a twentieth of the entire trail.

After several more very cold nights in North Carolina, it became exceedingly apparent that I needed to take some extra precaution against the elements. Despite the insulating properties of the storage pockets on my hammock, cold chills brought on by the wind and cooler air was still making its way through the fabric to my butt and lower back. This is a condition known amongst hammockers as "cold butt syndrome." My cold butt syndrome was causing some very sleepless early mornings between the hours of 2 am and 5 am, when temperatures for the night were normally at their coolest. The only cure was to get an under-quilt or a sleeping pad to provide extra protection and insulation. Since I didn't want to fuss with the extra effort and cost of a decent under-quilt, I decided that I would instead purchase a sleeping pad during my next trip into town.

That next town ended up being the busy little metropolis of Franklin, North Carolina. I made the trip in with DSOH, Coma, Laser, War Story, and Muzzle. Once again our hitchhiking skills left much to be desired as we alternately resorted to catching a small bus into town. The bus was fairly full when it arrived, carrying around ten other hikers that'd been picked up from a different road crossing. With the number of hikers nearing twenty, this was probably the smelliest god awful bus you'd ever been on.

The driver of this chariot was a real character who thought himself a comedian. Our Chauffer was an upper middle aged man by the name of Roy. He spoke loudly and confidently to everyone onboard and claimed to have been born and raised in the town of Franklin. He had a very thick southern drawl and the way he spoke about the town; you would've thought he was the commissioner. In fact, I think he even mentioned something about running for commissioner or maybe already being the commissioner. I don't recall exactly...

From near the back of the bus I watched Roy gaze into his rear view mirror. I watched him watching us, and I watched his eyes pass over every single passenger, as if accounting for attendance. I thought this strange at first, but what happened next was explanation enough for why he did his little "audience check." After his audience inspection was complete, Roy began attempting to entertain us with long, drawn out, old southern jokes (The kind that might offend some). As far as jokes go, they had clever punch lines and were even humorous; albeit in a distasteful and not so politically correct way. One could feel the uneasiness and discomfort in the air throughout the bus. The people that laughed did not do so openly and without regard. It was mostly uneasy chuckles, forced out of humoring or perhaps sympathy at his brash attempts to entertain us during the fifteen minutes into town.

Upon our arrival in town, we resupplied our food and paid a visit to the local outfitting store where I bought an inflatable sleeping pad. By the time we'd resupplied, gone to the outfitter and patronized a local burger joint, it was early evening and getting dark. We decided on splitting another hotel room. Since the room smelled like an armpit that'd been deep fried in urine, due to our gear being stored inside, we spent most of our time sitting on plastic chairs in a circle out in the parking lot.

In the early days on the trail, hotel or hostel stays were important in the grand scheme of your physical and mental health. It was sometimes very difficult to juggle groceries, laundry, restaurants, showers, injuries, Wi-Fi connections/blog updates, post office visits, gear replacements and other chores without staying overnight in a town or having a home base (hostel or hotel room) to work from. If the sun went down on you while still in town, then you could kiss your chances at hitchhiking out goodbye. You would either be looking for a place to camp within, or just outside the town (which can be dangerous or stressful), or paying exorbitant prices for a cab or shuttle (assuming the town had such services). That money was better spent splitting a room or staying in a hostel if the town even had either of those.

At around 8 pm we heard the sound of sirens. As the sound drew nearer and nearer, we caught sight of a fire truck. As it reached the hotel, the truck pulled into the parking lot with emergency lights shining and horns blasting. It came to a stop in front of our congregation. We didn't see a fire or any other emergency in the immediate vicinity, so this was quite unexpected. Perhaps our smell had been reported as some kind of toxic leak or spill?

Firemen began to pour out of the truck carrying different trays covered in foil. I could hardly believe my eyes. The local Franklin Fire Department had brought us all a spaghetti and meatball dinner! They also brought salad and pudding for desert. This was an example of trail magic at its finest. I'd only been out there for two weeks and already my faith in humanity was being restored.

The next morning Roy gave us all a ride back to the trail. Funny enough, everyone had coined his new name "Racist Roy." Despite his initial remarks from the ride into town, Roy was probably one of the friendliest, most genuine, and most helpful locals that I ever met while on the trail.

Either way, his new title had a ring to it and wound up sticking. We would always remember and affectionately refer to him as Racist Roy later on down the trail.

I'd only been into town twice on the journey so far and already I was noticing how much I'd adapted to the peacefulness of the woods. Going into town was a nice reprieve from bad weather, uncontrollable temperatures, as well as a sore body. Having a hot meal, a shower, electricity and climate control reminded you of all the things we take for granted on a daily basis. What I noticed was that it was never long after arriving in town that I found myself longing to be back in the woods. A place with no cars to run me over, no loud sounds to accost my ears, no neon signs to distract my eyes, and no rude people in a hurry to go nowhere. Town was nice for some things, but the woods were infinitely better for everything else regarding sanity, mental health, and clarity of mind.

Coming out of Franklin, we took a short day and stopped at the first shelter we came to called Siler's Bald. The inside of the shelter itself was covered in elaborate artwork and graffiti that'd been left by past hikers and campers. Most of it was actually very beautiful and the shelter log itself was also full of drawings and comments about the drawings within the shelter.

All the shelters along the Appalachian Trail have what is known as "Shelter Logs" or "Trail Registers" inside them. They are usually nothing more than a simple spiral ringed notebook and a pen that's been stuffed inside a Ziploc Bag to protect it from moisture. The purpose of these log books is to keep track of where people were on certain dates and also to pass messages or thoughts to friends and strangers that may be behind you on the trail. Whenever a person goes missing on the trail, it's the shelter logs that are checked first in order to better understand their last position on specific dates. It's completely up to you whether you sign them or not. Some people do it religiously, while others do it semi-frequently or not at all.

You don't even have to sign your name and date; you can write whatever you want in a shelter log. You can talk about your day, write a poem, draw a picture, leave an inspirational quote, tell a story or simply pass on information or advice to whoever's behind you that might read it. Advice and information like, "This shelter sucks, don't sleep here," or- "There is a large black snake living under this shelter," or- "The mice at this shelter are worse than other shelters," or- "Hiker so and so is a snore bastard, avoid him at all costs." You could find almost anything in a shelter log. I even found a Marijuana joint that was taped to the inside of a shelter log that had "Cheers" written underneath it. I left it where it was, but that's the sort of crazy random things you could find in one of these journals... not just signatures.

I've seen people obnoxiously take up entire pages to themselves writing nonsense messages or even just writing their name really big like a kindergarten child. You can be sure to find a little bit of everything in a shelter log, but most importantly you will get a better idea of who's ahead of you. Not only that, but it can also give you something to talk about with a hiker you're meeting for the first time. For instance, much further along in my journey while meeting a fellow hiker for the first time, I recognized their name from a journal entry that I'd read many weeks before. After learning their name and remembering their log entry, the conversation went something like this. Me: "Oh I read that you were attacked by a donkey while crossing that field outside of Daleville; how have you been since then?" Them: "Oh yeah, I had to fend it off with my trekking poles, but I've been good! Just climbing mountains and shit every day, you know how it is."

In the beginning I signed almost none of the Shelter Logs, but as time went on they became a bit of a game as well as an outlet to relieve boredom. I would write the lyrics of songs that were stuck in my head or write excerpts of a fictional story that I'd made up while walking along. I always left the story in a state of suspense and "to be continued" at the next shelter log. It kept things interesting and entertaining while out there in the wilderness. We had few diversions and did what we could to bring the entertainment to us.

Towards the end of the journey, I signed or read almost none of the shelter logs. The novelty had worn off and there were so few people left on the trail that there was hardly anything worth reading in them anymore. Everyone had run out of things to say besides just signing their name and dating it. "So and so was here on such and such date"- period. Unless you were curious about who was in front of you, there was almost no reason to look at them anymore.

That evening at Siler's Bald we built a grand fire and enjoyed a pleasant night of deep conversations while sitting around the crackling logs. Later on, while lying in my hammock I heard that "thumping" noise again. The mole people were expanding their empire, or the trees were talking to one another, or maybe I was going bat shit crazy. I figured it was probably one of the first two.

April 15th was a nasty, wet, and freezing day. Out of my seventeen days on the trail so far, this one was my least favorite and the most miserable. I never counted how many days it actually rained on me during the entire adventure, but I'm sure it was close to, or more than half.

The morning had begun with ease over modest terrain while a heavy fog blanketed the entire forest. The visibility was probably no more than twenty to thirty feet at certain times. In the bleak woods that had not yet bloomed, the thick fog created a very eerie setting. I felt as if I was in a horror movie and something or someone was going to materialize out of the fog at any moment and attack me. I had a strong impression of Sleepy Hollow and the Headless Horseman.

In the end, the only thing that lifted the fog was the torrential downpour that ensued. Before long, the level areas of the trail were no more than giant puddles of mud and water while the inclines and declines became miniature rapids once again. Even though the temperature was close to freezing, I intentionally tried to wear as few clothes as possible. This was so that when I made camp, all of my warm garments would be nice and dry. Trey Mountain had taught me the misery of getting multiple layers of warm clothing wet. There is a bit of a catch 22 to hiking in freezing rain, and there are only a couple of good options.

You can be wet and warm while you're hiking, then freezing when you stop to camp; or you can be wet and freezing while you hike, then warm and dry when you camp. If you choose the first option, then you've undoubtedly chosen to layer your clothes underneath your light, rain shell jacket, thinking that it will keep them dry. Yes, your rain shell does keep your layers underneath dry, but your body still sweats like crazy. So while there's a monsoon of rain on the outside, there's also a monsoon of sweat on the inside. Once you get to where you're going and take off your rain jacket, you'll be very displeased to find that your nice warm clothes underneath are also soaked. Not with water, but with stinky sweat that's designed to cool you off even faster as it dries. As soon as you're not moving anymore, this sweat becomes just as freezing, if not more freezing than the rain outside. You traded being warm while you hike for being cold in your shelter, because several of your layers just became practically useless. That's at least how it works for me, because I sweat like a pig. Always remember, it's more important to be dry than warm; that goes for your warm clothes staying dry!

Your second option is to wear as little as possible while you hike in freezing rain. You can wear just a t-shirt and your rain shell, or just your rain shell by itself. If you're really crazy, you might wear no shirt at all (I practiced this religiously later on in the hike). You may get cold, but as long as you keep moving, while keeping your breaks short or nonexistent, you'll be alright and have all your warm, dry clothes to look forward to when you finally stop. Of course there are times when it's so cold and intense that you'll have to wear as much as you can or learn when to call it a day and remain bundled up in your shelter. Further on in New Hampshire and Maine, it would get so cold and windy that I couldn't possibly move without layering some clothes.

During this particular freezing downpour, I opted for less clothing. I wore my shorts, a T-shirt and my rain shell. My extremities were a little cold but nothing serious, or so I thought. I kept up a quick pace to generate internal body heat that would keep me warm. I knew that I could only stop if it was for a few seconds at a time, or if I was calling it a day and stripping off my wet clothes to put on dry ones.

At one point I was forced to climb over a fairly large fallen tree. As my leading foot hit the ground on the other side, it began to slide forward in the mud before my other leg had made it over the branch. What ensued was me very nearly doing the splits, falling backwards onto the log and squashing the family inheritance. Luckily I caught the log with my hands and stopped myself from experiencing what would surely have been a major emergency.

The temperature continued to drop as I made my way further along the trail. My torso felt fine, but it wasn't until I stopped for a quick breather that I realized my hands and fingers were almost completely numb. I tried to unbuckle the hip belt and chest strap of my backpack but couldn't. My fingers were so numb that I'd lost the strength and dexterity to unsnap the buckles. This surprised and frightened me quite a bit at the time. I skipped the break and decided to keep moving at an even faster pace while trying to breathe warm air into my hands to thaw them out. They began to feel better after a while and my mind was put back at ease.

Sometime in the late afternoon, the rain stopped and the sun peeked through the clouds. Feeling much better about the entire situation, I decided to take my break. While sitting on a rock, gazing out at the soaking wet forest and listening to the water drip out of the trees, a bird began to whistle the most beautiful tune. I started whistling back and to my pleasant surprise, the bird mimicked my whistle. I felt my harmony with nature continue to rise. It got to the point where the bird wouldn't whistle until it heard me whistle first. If I stayed silent long enough, the bird would eventually give what sounded like an "inquiring" whistle, to which I always replied. They were going to have to change my trail name to "Papa Nature" if this kept up.

My feet were mush and swimming in my shoes when I finally reached the top of Copper Ridge Bald. I wasn't going to force myself to go any further, as I could feel the skin peeling off my feet and the rain starting up again. Against my better judgment, I decided to make camp right there, near the top of the mountain.

In the early days of the hike, I never took into consideration that the coldest temperatures were at the highest altitudes. I knew the information, but for some reason never applied it. I was so worn out and beat up at the end of those early days, that when I wanted to stop, I simply stopped wherever I was. As you might expect, I was usually the most worn out after climbing to the top of a mountain. In the early days, avoiding immediate misery usually trumped proper judgment, which almost always resulted in prolonged misery.

That night was so cold that I thought I might freeze to death. I spent the night alone, atop Copper Ridge Bald at over five thousand feet. I hardly slept as I kept myself tucked into the fetal position for most of the night while trying to hold onto as much body heat as I possibly could. All I could think about was how this hike was turning out to be so much harder than I ever dreamed it would be.

The next morning the entire forest was a blanket of ice. Sleeting rain drizzled steadily down for most of the day, while icicles of every size hung from everywhere. Whenever the wind would pick up through the trees, hundreds of icicles would fall to the ground all over the forest. I wanted no part of it. Since the sun had come up, I'd managed to find some warmth within my hammock that I was determined to hold onto. Most of the day I laid there listening to the icicles pattering off my rain fly while I read a book on my kindle.

Around 3 pm I received a message from DSOH informing me that he'd made it to the "NOC" (Nantahala Outdoor Center) about twelve miles ahead of my current position. He informed me that he and the rest of the posse had rented a cabin for the night and they hoped that I could get there by that evening.

I weighed my options. I could stay atop Copper Ridge Bald another night and miss the opportunity to shower, do laundry, and get warm inside the cabin; or I could pack up in the freezing, rainy conditions and try to haul my ass over twelve miles to the NOC. It was after 3 pm when I made the decision to haul ass, and close to 4 pm by the time I actually started walking. The sleeting rain had stopped, but the ice still clung to everything. To add to my already freezing situation, it began to snow just after 5 pm. "You have got to be kidding me!" I thought.

Maybe it's because I'm from Florida and I had virtually no experience with snow, but for some reason it scared me. The whole experience was still very new and I felt like every extreme situation involving the elements was out to kill me. Go ahead and laugh. I laugh at myself now too. When you first get out on the trail, anything feels possible. Attacks from wild animals, freezing to death, starving to death, getting lost forever, you name it. It isn't until you've been out there for a while and get comfortable with everything that you really start to relax.

At the time, I felt like if the conditions got worse or I slipped and hurt myself, I'd be screwed. I'd never been in a situation quite like that one before, and it made me nervous. I knew that I'd be hiking into the night for the first time and I had no idea if the weather was slated to get worse. All I could think about was getting to that cabin and out of the unfamiliar elements.

I wrapped my Shemagh tightly around my head to protect my ears and nose form the snow laden wind as I trudged on through the icy mud. I was trying to go as fast as I could without putting myself at risk of a bad fall. I descended Copper Ridge and climbed Wesser Bald before tackling a nearly three-thousand-foot plunge back towards sea level and the NOC.

The entire descent was a combination of jagged rocks and mud; made all the more dangerous by the thin blanket of snow that was now covering it all. The winds were intermittently gusting up to what I imagine was close to 40 mph, whipping snowflakes into my face and sweeping them out of the trees. I nearly fell off a cliff as my momentum carried me over a steep and rocky patch of trail. The path made a sharp right turn just before a ledge that was blocked by nothing more than a couple of small bushes. I later found out this spot was called "The Jump-off." I think the "The Fall-off" would've been more appropriate.

I pushed on into the dark and through the freezing air. I didn't know how much further I had when I finally saw the lights twinkling below me. Those distant signs of humanity were a huge source of comfort that spurred me on even faster. After descending one last steep embankment covered in thick evergreen foliage, I crossed a small wooden footbridge, then a road to arrive safe and sound at the NOC a little after 9 pm.

With the surrounding darkness and dimly lit streets, I couldn't get a good look around the place. I did notice however that the area seemed very large and was also a ghost town at this hour. "Where do I go from here?" I thought. I was freezing and had no cell phone reception. After sitting for a while and getting colder by the minute, I finally discovered there was free Wi-Fi at the outfitter building in front of where I sat. I managed to get a hold of DSOH and he called a shuttle to pick me up and bring me to the cabin.

What was very evident upon my arrival at the cabin, was that the word "cabin" had been very generously applied to what this actually was. I've never thought of the words "cabin" and "trailer" as being synonymous, but when you think of an enclosed space that holds heat, they might as well be the same thing. I didn't care what it was called, as I felt overjoyed to be there nonetheless. Having a heater, shower, washer and dryer, this trailer was a palace to me!

The next morning, I was finally able to have a proper look at the "NOC." The place looked like some bizarre mountainous Disney Land at first glance. It wasn't a town and there weren't any houses to be seen anywhere. It was simply an area that was completely dedicated to having fun in the mountains and on the river. Everything was built on and centered along the large, Nantahala River that flowed swiftly past. There was a restaurant, an amazing outfitting store, gazebos, picnic areas, and places to rent kayaks and rafts to partake in river adventures. It was one of the most unique and fun looking locations I encountered on the journey.

DSOH, Coma, Laser, and Muzzle all hiked out that morning. I decided to hang back and relax. This entire area looked like something out of a fantasy world. I had a strong impression of "Rivendell" from Lord of the Rings. This was a place that you didn't simply pass through. You had to soak it up for all it was worth. War Story ended up staying behind as well, due to some knee pain that he was experiencing.

I spent nearly the entire day sitting by the edge of the river with my feet propped up, drinking a six pack while watching kayakers and rafters go by. That night War Story and I slept in a bunkroom with four other men that were at the NOC for one reason or another. All I knew was that none of them were hikers. Try as I might, I never made it through the entire night in that room, because at around midnight I got up and left. I had to go anywhere but inside the confines of that bunkroom.

This leads me to a fun fact about War Story. The guy snores louder and more obnoxiously than anyone I've ever heard. At this moment you think I'm exaggerating for the sake of the story. You're thinking of someone you know right now and saying to yourself, "they're probably much worse than this War Story guy." I think not... I'm firmly convinced this guy could hold a spot in the record books if he pursued one. It's not even how loudly he snores, but how incredibly annoying the different sounds were. It sounded like a gargantuan beast slowly suffocating on a large object stuck in its windpipe, and then miraculously coming back to life as the object is pushed clear.

When you listen to most people snore, you can usually find a rhythm in the snoring and then eventually tune it out and fall sleep. Not with War Story. Each breath is as unique as the snowflakes that I'd walked through the day before. There is no rhythm or uniformity to the sounds that issue from this human snore machine. Sometimes the volume of the snore will rise so quickly and so loudly that it will literally make you jump in your sleeping bag. I've been startled out of sleep by his snores, while lying in my hammock, even when he was encamped more than a hundred feet away.

Around midnight, after hours of staring at the dark ceiling of the bunkroom and wondering how a human being could produce such noises, I decided I couldn't take it anymore. I got up, packed my things, walked out the door and hung my hammock on some trees behind the building. I could still hear him snoring through the thin walls of the bunkroom, but it was muffled enough that I could finally drift off to sleep. I never brought headphones or music with me on the journey, but this would've been the perfect time to have them.

In the morning, as I was eating a pop tart, I was approached by a middle aged man. "Was that your friend in the bunkroom last night? You know, the one snoring." He said almost angrily. I very nearly told him that I'd never met the guy in my life, but I bashfully owned up to knowing him. The man continued, "I'm 56 years old, retired from the Army, and I HAVE NEVER in my life heard anything like that!" I shrugged as I said, "I know, me too." I couldn't tell if the man was angry, amazed, or a combination of both. He couldn't seem to put into words how he felt about another human being that could make those kinds of noises in their sleep. He went on and on about War Story needing to seek professional medical help and that his relationships would be almost impossible to maintain with snoring like that. The man vented to me for close to five minutes before finally wishing me luck on dealing with the "snore bastard" (as he referred to him) for the remainder of my journey.

I hiked out of the NOC at 7 am that morning wanting very badly to catch up with my other companions. It wouldn't be easy, as they already had an entire day's lead on me. I decided the only way to fix that was to hike as hard and far as I could that day. The climb out of the NOC was an almost continuous seven-mile 3,300-foot ascent up Swim Bald and Cheoah Bald that set me down at over 5,000 feet above sea level, again.

I remember that seven-mile climb being powered by hit songs of the 80's. Mostly, Love Shack, Whip it, and Another One Bites the Dust. Since I never brought any music with me, I always had to resort to singing the songs myself. Later on in the journey, I would actually look up the lyrics to certain songs and try to memorize them so that I could sing them more completely while out on the trail. You never knew who might be listening and it was good for my mental health not to repeat the same catchy lyrics two hundred times over the course of several hours. I refused to wear headphones or play anything out loud over speakers like so many other hikers did. This was just my personal preference but I didn't mind, sometimes, hiking next to someone that was playing their music out loud.

Not long after the big climb out of The NOC, I encountered my first snake of the journey. It was a small garter snake slithering up an embankment to get away from me. It was definitely warmer than the last couple of days, but it was still too early for the frequent encounters with snakes that I would have later on. All my life I've loved everything about snakes, and in addition to bear and moose, it was one of the creatures that I was looking forward to seeing the most while on the hike.

As the day progressed, I finally settled on a final destination based on my pace and fatigue level. I was going to shoot for Cable Gap Shelter, and if I made it all the way, it would be my biggest day yet.

44

It was close to 5 pm and I was only about seven miles from Cable Gap when I ran into a couple of teenage boys headed in the opposite direction. One had long, straight blond hair that was shiny, conditioned, and worn in a feminine style; while the other had a bit of a squint in one eye, kind of like Forest Whittaker. They stopped me and immediately asked where I was headed. "What are you, the trail police?" I thought to myself. I replied that I was aiming for Cable Gap. One-eyed squint replied, "We left there at 9:30 this morning, I don't think you can make it that far today." I did some quick math calculations to myself and realized they'd only made it seven miles in the nearly eight hours since they'd left.

"Ooohhh Reeeeeeally?" I thought in my head, before saying out loud, "Wanna bet?" Squinty replied, "Well, where did you start today?" "The NOC," I answered. Squinty's eyes got big (well one of them did) as he said, "Wow, and you're here already...yeah, you'll probably make it." "Yup," I replied as we wished each other well and parted ways.

It felt good to be impressing people with the miles I was starting to put in on a daily basis. It made me feel like I was getting stronger. Despite how far I'd already come that day, I'd made another rookie mistake and neglected my hydration. I was so concerned with not stopping that I'd forgotten to collect water along the way. My initial two liters had run out some time ago and I was now parched beyond words. My lips were cracking while my tongue was sticking to my teeth, as well as the roof of my mouth. Now that I wanted water and was actually thinking about it, I couldn't find it anywhere. Most of the last seven miles were a waterless slog done at a snail's pace. As the sun was setting, I finally found a shallow creek a short distance off the trail and a couple miles before Cable Gap.

I once again hiked into the night by myself. Hiking at night was something that I never thought I would do before this journey. Before the adventure's end, "night hiking" would become somewhat of a common occurrence and even something that I enjoyed. It was especially enjoyable during the hot summer months.

I arrived at Cable Gap Shelter shortly after 9 pm, ending the day with twenty-two miles. This was a new personal record that beat my old one by almost nine miles, but it was not without consequences. My feet had paid a heavy price for this victory in the form of blisters and soreness. I'd been so excited to reach this shelter that I'd disregarded my own well-being. I was almost positive that I'd catch some of my companions there, as I was looking forward to emerging from the darkness of the woods to a roaring fire and the surprise of everyone there. However, it didn't play out like that.

Since it was after 9 pm, that meant it was past hiker midnight and everyone was asleep. It was dark and quiet at the shelter when I arrived, so no one was awake to talk to or share my accomplishments with. It was an anticlimactic ending to a climactic day for me. I didn't know who was at the shelter and tried not to make too much noise as I made camp. I would later find out in the morning that I'd caught up with DSOH, while Coma, Laser, and Muzzle remained ahead and War Story remained somewhere behind.

Right after my twenty-two-mile day, I walked onto Fontana Dam on April 18th. Fontana was more or less a resort town that doubled as the southern gateway into the Smokey Mountains on the Appalachian Trail. While setting up camp on the side of the enormous Fontana Lake, I met another hiker by the name of "Apocalypse." He had a heavy set build and turned out to be quite an interesting fellow. All he was carrying was a big black duffle bag that he switched from shoulder to shoulder as he got tired, as well as a gigantic red thermos that he kept hanging from the duffle bag. He was also carrying an enormous Bear Grylls Machete and the matching Bear Grylls Knife on his belt. He looked very out of place and somewhat comical compared to other hikers with their expensive gear and fancy back packs.

I talked with him for a bit and learned that he used to own a sailboat that he lived on while sailing up and down the east coast. He said he didn't have a car and that whenever he needed supplies, he would anchor the boat and swim to shore. He mostly fished for his food and only went ashore when he absolutely needed to. He said that he did this for nearly two years before it ran aground during a storm and was destroyed. Shortly after losing his sailboat, he decided to hike the Appalachian Trail with only the belongings he was able to salvage.

As we continued to talk, I found out that he had led quite the interesting life. He'd owned an online business, but had also been a short notice stand-in for professional MMA fights when somebody dropped out before an event. The guy had seen and done it all and was living life by his wits and doing things his own way.

When I first saw him, I had thought to myself, "This guy ain't gonna make it." However, after talking with him for a while I realized, "How can this guy NOT make it?" Apocalypse was one of those people that didn't care what others thought. He was going to do his own thing, his own way. He just had this sureness about him. Like no matter what unexpected thing happened to him, he still had it all figured out. I admire the hell out of people who think like that and are still able to make life work for themselves.

At this point in the journey I was still susceptible to the "what would people think?" train of thought, when in all actuality it should be: "Who cares what other people think!" You should do your own thing your own way, and as long as it isn't stepping on someone else, then to hell with other people's thoughts and opinions of you. It's easy enough to say, but harder to practice. We can never seem to completely pull ourselves away from worrying about what other people think. Whether it's the car we drive, the clothes we wear, or how we carry ourselves in public. So much of everything we do revolves around what we think is expected of us, as well as what's socially acceptable and the opinions of others. I hoped to rid myself of this kind of thinking while I was out there.

I would intermittently run into Apocalypse out on the trail up until the beginning of Virginia. I never saw him again after my first week in that state. Whether he ever finished the trail or not, I have no idea...

While in Fontana I received a phone call from my girlfriend. Another one of my worst fears had been realized. My little canine princess, Katana, was not getting along with the Weiner dogs or the Chihuahua, causing her parents to make the decision that she had to go. The only problem with that scenario was that she didn't have anywhere else to go. I was the only option left, so Katana had to be dropped off to me as soon as possible. Of course this presented another problem on my growing list of problems, as I was a stone's throw away from the Smokey Mountain National Park that had a strict "No dogs allowed policy."

In the end I was left with only one choice. I had until the weekend to cross the entire Smokey Mountain Range and get out of the park so that I could meet my girlfriend and get Katana. That meant I only had six days to traverse over seventy miles of the trail that resided in the Smokey Mountains. This wouldn't have seemed so bad if the Smokies hadn't been billed as some of the most challenging mountains on the entire AT. I was really going to have to push myself if I was going to make the deadline.

Besides the "No Dogs Allowed" policy, the Smokey Mountain National Park also made thru-hikers buy a $20 permit. I'd learned of this only a couple of days before reaching Fontana Dam. On the morning that I planned to enter the park, I found myself trying to find a way to procure a permit. I originally thought I could buy one at the Ranger Post situated at the entrance to the park, but this was not so, as the permit was only available online where you had to print it out. This was a dilemma, as well as a slight annoyance. If you're going to charge money for the show, then you better sell tickets at the door! The Smokey Mountains didn't operate this way, as they only sold their tickets online.

In the end, a few others including myself, ended up calling a shuttle to the ski resort down the road so that we could use their computer and print out our permits. On the way back, five of us caught a ride in the back of a pick-up truck. It was me, DSOH, and three other hikers by the names of Viking, Da Fonz, and Freebird. We all sang "Don't Stop Me Now" by Queen in perfect harmony all the way back (maybe not perfect harmony, but perfect unison).

It was simple moments such as that one that stand out the most in my mind from the journey. Funny enough, it's the smallest things that weren't that exciting or worthy of recounting to other people; even though at the time they seemed like the most important and joyous things in the world to me and those hiking with me. Even in memory-they're still important, and it is times such as those that I realized what the whole journey was about. Living in the moment, camaraderie with your fellow man, and breaking into song when the moment feels right. The smallest things have the biggest impacts on us, and no one else in the world will understand them as profoundly as we did at those moments.

When we arrived back at the trail head, we discovered that a local church had prepared some trail magic in our absence. They'd laid out hot dogs, homemade cake, homemade brownies, chocolate eggs, coca cola, grape soda, jelly beans, Coors Light, cleaning and hygiene products, as well as condiments for the hot dogs. This was the most elaborate trail magic to date!

There was only one thing that put a damper on all of it. Sometimes actual homeless people or bums near the trail will pose as hikers and take advantage of trail magic. I'm not talking about simply partaking in it, which is fine. I'm talking about REALLY taking advantage of it and ruining it for the people that haven't arrived yet.

There were five bums that had been hanging around the lake area since the night before. Not the older ones or professed veterans that you look at and felt sorry for. These were the kind that looked like criminals. Not only did they look like criminals, but they spoke and acted like criminals and were very confrontational with everyone. I'm not saying that all criminals have a specific look, but these guys had a look and attitude that reminded me of a person who was less than upstanding. These guys were a little bit younger, were very dirty in the unhygienic way (not the hiker way), covered in neck and some face tattoos as well as openly carrying large combat knives on their belts and thighs. Their teeth (or the ones they did have) looked as if they were throwing up gang signs. They were loud, obnoxious, vulgar, and stayed awake into the late hours making a ruckus while not taking anyone else into consideration.

To your average person, a hiker and a bum may look the same, but a hiker can always tell the difference. Unfortunately, these Trail Angels (people who provide trail magic) that brought all the food, could not make that distinction.

Once it was all laid out, the bums descended. The unwritten rule for hikers is to take one of whatever is provided. If there is a large selection or quantity, then you might take one of each or one of a couple things, then move on. You have to be considerate of the people hiking behind you that haven't arrived yet and give them a chance to get in on the magic whenever they get there.

These bums just hovered as they ate, and ate, and ate. Three, four, and five of everything! They never left. There really wasn't anything that could be done about it, unless you wanted to get stabbed. One of the bums even walked off with an arm full of Coors Light and disappeared. I think maybe ten hikers at the most were able to partake before everything was gone. Initially there'd been enough food to last the entire day, but instead, everything was gone within an hour. It really was a shame. Those nice people probably had their impression of hikers lowered that day. I ended up leaving early out of disgust, but I hope someone eventually said something and cleared the air.

Since I had no time to waste with my new deadline, I set off towards the Smokies. No sooner had I begun making my way down the road, rain began to fall. As I crossed the "Fontana Dam" dam, a surreal feeling washed over me. Normally you're enshrined by trees out on the trail; your line of sight restricted by how far the trees allowed you to see. While crossing the dam I had a vast expanse of lake on my right and a vast expanse of mountains to my left, in front, and above me. It made me feel incredibly small, a feeling that I loved.

Moments like these became my favorite moments out on the trail. Whenever I was passing over a bald, through a field, or across a barren ridge, I got this immense feeling of smallness wrapped in the realization of just how big the world really is. I embraced the vast openness of these types of terrain as they gave perspective to the grand scale of everything around me. I could look into the distance and see places that seemed impossibly far away, but then be amazed by the fact that I'd already walked from some of those places, or that I would eventually get to a specific area while passing over everything in between. It was awe inspiring, daunting, and confidence boosting all at the same time.

It was a long, slow, and wet three thousand feet up into the Smokies. Besides the "No Dogs Allowed" rule and the $20 permit, the Smokies also had another rule. No camping out in the open. This rule was put in place in an effort to keep bear encounters to a minimum. Hikers were expected to sleep inside the shelters that dotted the trail throughout the park. The shelters in the Smokies were actually very nice; some of the nicest on the entire trail. They were usually built out of stone and had a fireplace inside.

Even though some of the shelters were very nice, I still had two problems with this last rule. The first one was that I had zero intentions of sleeping in any mice infested, germ ridden, snore plagued, fart saturated shelters unless it was an emergency or I was hanging my hammock inside. The second reason was that I was trying to keep my bear encounters to a maximum. I wanted to see as many bears as possible on this trip and I had high hopes for the Smokey Mountains. I spent my first night of the Smokies in my hammock about two hundred feet away from the shelter. I fell asleep to the sound of rain, and not the sound of bears tearing hikers apart in the night.

The next morning the rain had ceased and I was given a gorgeous reminder as to why these were called the Smokey Mountains. From atop the Devil's Tater Patch I could see the world sprawled out before me. As I looked down upon the earth, I felt as though I was actually staring into the sky. A perfectly smooth blanket of clouds shielded the earth from view while only allowing the tops of certain mountains to peek through. It gave me the illusion of floating islands in a sea of clouds. There was a clear blue sky above, snow white clouds below, and a golden sun between them. I had the impression that I was caught somewhere in between two heavens.

Day two in the Smokies almost had me forgetting about how beautiful they were... almost. The terrain was tough, to put it lightly. There were no flat areas; I was either going up or coming down. I didn't see any fauna on my second day, but the flora was in great abundance. Almost everything had been dead and barren from the biting cold of winter up until the Smokies. In contrast, everything here seemed alive.

Blankets of small white flowers called Cancer Root and Hepatica covered everything. Moss also grew like a blanket that covered the rocks, fallen trees, and anything else that was on or near the ground within the confines of the pine groves. All other plants seemed to be in full bloom as well. The difference in the abundance and types of vegetation since passing into the Smokies was staggering. The steepness of the terrain was consistently more severe than anywhere else on the trail up until that point. My knees and ankles throbbed at the end of my second day in the Smokies as I hung in my hammock near the top of another "Siler's Bald." Still, I encountered no bears.

Twenty-three days into my Appalachian Trail Journey and three days into the Smokey Mountains I passed the two-hundred-mile mark. I found it ironic that this mountain range had easily been the most challenging of the trail so far; yet, I was still able to put in my longest consistent miles of the journey. I had completed ten miles the first day, almost eighteen the second day, and over fifteen on the third. Before my new deadline, I never would have thought I could do those kinds of miles back to back. I still hadn't seen any bears, but the deer had been plentiful. They were fearless, allowing me to almost get within petting distance before they took off. I'm sure they must have been aware of their protected status within the park, because they would've been easy game anywhere else.

Besides passing the two-hundred-mile mark, I also summited the highest point on the entire trail. At 6,655 feet, that point was Clingmans Dome. My climb to the summit of Clingmans Dome was a rather interesting one, full of surprises and revelations.

It was fairly hot that morning as I struggled, huffing and puffing, up the side of that huge mountain. I'd been marching through pristine wilderness, sweating my ass off, swatting at insects, and inhaling clouds of gnats that swarmed everywhere. I'd trudged through the beautiful madness of rocks, logs, and insects, beating up my body while risking life and limb to reach the summit of this megalith, when I finally emerged from the wilderness onto a wide, smooth... asphalt path.

This asphalt path was full of tourists, casually dressed, and leisurely walking up to the summit to take in the spectacular views. "THERE WAS A SMOOTH, GRADUAL, ASPHALT PATH ALL THE WAY TO THE TOP OF THIS BEHEMOTH THE WHOLE TIME!?" I screamed inside my head.

Most of the tourists were Japanese and German with a few Americans mixed in. There was a steady flow of people going up and down that I assume lasted all day. Quite the popular spot-it was. I could hear people panting to one another, "Oh boy-that was quite a hike up here wasn't it?" and... "That's our workout for the day!"

I later found out that the asphalt path was less than a mile long and had started in a parking lot full of snack and drink vendors. I wanted nothing more than to yell at these people, "SHUT UP! I've been traversing cliffs, creeks, mud, jagged rocks, drop offs, bug hoards, and hellish inclines all morning and all I had to eat before all of it were skittles wrapped in a tortilla!"

This visual of two different worlds and planes of existence converging on a mountain top was actually quite amazing and eye opening to witness. The "haves" and the "have nots." It gave me a new perspective. More perspective than I feel I'd gained on the journey so far.

People simply don't know how good they have it, even when things seem terrible or difficult. Although I'd chosen to do this hike and live this way temporarily, I understood there were people out there who lived like this permanently, without any choice, while in much worse conditions and circumstances. Any Dick and Jane can say, "Yeah, I know there are people out there who live like that, and I understand and feel sorry for them." I'm sure some people reading this are thinking that same thing. I'll tell you right now, I've been to third world countries and you can see it, sympathize with it, and think you understand it; but in reality, you may not. Not until you've experienced and lived it for yourself. I thought I understood it simply by seeing it, but it wasn't until I'd lived parts of that "have not" experience, that I realized just how much I didn't understand it.

Defecating outside and maybe not having toilet paper. Sleeping outside, not having running water or hot water, not having showers, and being miles from the nearest help. Not having whatever you want to eat every day or possibly running out of food, or not finding water. Not having electricity, not having climate control, and having your feet as your only means of transportation. Dealing with any and all elements whenever they should arise, as well as having limited hygiene products and smelling terrible every day. This only scratches the surface.

I won't pretend to know exactly what it's like for people who are stuck in this lifestyle permanently, but in making this journey I certainly gained a much better understanding. I knew that even though it was the life I'd chosen to live at that time, I still had it better than probably half the people on the planet. I could get a reprieve (for a price) anytime I went into town. I could end any suffering, discomfort, and pain I experienced on any day I chose... but I didn't. I was enjoying the experience and perspective I was gaining on an almost daily basis. The time for personal reflection and the thousands of moments I had each day that belonged to me and only me was intoxicating. The whole experience was surreal, yet at the same time more real than anything in the modern world. Everything around you out there "is what it is" and isn't trying to be anything else. It's simple and honest, which is more than can be said for the "modern" world, where many things are never as they seem, and most everybody wants something from you.

Towards the end of my third day in the Smokies, I saw a very small squirrel climb up a small pine tree that was right next to the trail. It began frantically squeaking and lunging towards me from a small branch. I'd never seen a squirrel quite like it before. It was a deep chestnut red color, and I assumed it was a baby due to its small size. I pushed my luck and tried to reach up and touch the little creature. The squirrel scrambled higher up the tree, all the while squeaking even more frantically. It was adorable.

I continued on into the early evening to complete over fifteen miles and finish the day atop Mt. Kephart, near Icewater Spring Shelter. I still hadn't encountered any bears.

Day four in the Smokies ended up being a zero day. It was freezing cold, raining, windy, and incredibly foggy. I still had two days, not including that one, to get out of the Smokies and I felt like that was plenty of time to finish up the last thirty miles or so. I spent the day inside the large shelter, in front of the fire place, while chatting with other hikers and various tourists. Muzzle and Coma were there too. I watched deer graze near the shelter throughout the day as blankets of fog and rain rolled past.

Around mid-afternoon when conditions had improved a bit, a female park ranger came to the shelter with a reporter and a photographer from Knoxville. They were doing a story on "shelter graffiti." Most of the shelters along the trail have carvings or writings from people leaving their "mark" or "messages" for future hikers to see. The Graffiti goes back years or even decades at some shelters. The reporter asked for my opinion on shelter graffiti and I told him that it didn't bother me. I told them that I thought it gave the shelters a certain character and history in its own way. Of course it could get obnoxious sometimes, but most of the time it was just names, dates, and inspirational thoughts.

During the Ranger and reporter's visit, something comically interesting happened. There was a hiker named "Smoking Bear," who was an upper middle aged gentleman that was incredibly funny and liked to joke around. He had terminal cancer, and according to him, his doctor had only given him a year or so to live. He was calling this journey his "cancer walk."

At one point while the Ranger was explaining how they were trying to eliminate graffiti in shelters, Smoking Bear walked up and remarked, "Oh, you mean this?" as he took out a black sharpie marker and wrote "Smoking Bear/Cancer Walk/2014" on a wooden plank of the shelter. Then he said, "I'll be dead soon, so I don't really care what you do to me." The Ranger and reporter said nothing, and the only thing the photographer did was take a picture. Needless to say, the Ranger let that one slide. I mean what can you do to a man who only has a year left to live?

My fifth day in the Smokies was a day that shall live in infamy as well as recognition for a great accomplishment. The day was beautiful and the terrain quite modest. I had around six miles of very tight ridge walking first thing in the morning. Ridge walking is what it's called when you walk the crest of a string of mountains or hills. In this particular case of ridge walking, the trail was very narrow with a sheer drop on either side.

Around mile three of the ridge walk, I realized that I needed to go "number two" very badly. The problem was that there wasn't enough room on either side of the trail to do it, so I was stuck holding it in. I kept walking... more ridges. I walked faster... more ridges. It was very quickly turning into an emergency. My stomach was starting to hurt and I was getting cramps. The effort it was taking to hold the landslide back and keep the sphincter muscles tight was messing up my stride.

More trudging brought on more ridges as I began to sweat from the stress of it all. "This is crazy!" I thought... "I'm a grown man and I'm about to shit my pants on top of this ridge!" My walk must've looked painfully unnatural at this point. With every step, my legs were practically pressed together.

Suddenly I noticed the drop off on one side of the trail lessen a bit, as there were a number of fallen logs and trees growing. It was risky, but as soon as I saw it, my body subconsciously committed to pooping there and I had no choice! The food baby was about to be born in the next few seconds whether I was ready for it or not. With watery eyes close to tears, I dashed off the ledge and just about rolled down the mountain. I threw my staff, unbuckled my chest strap, threw my water bottle, unbuckled my hip belt, and slung my backpack off as I half-ran; half tumbled down the steep embankment. I grabbed a tree to kill my momentum, dropped my drawers as fast as I could, aaannd... "Sweet baby Jesus!" I felt liberated!

The crisis had been narrowly averted as I squatted there on the steep embankment for the better part of fifteen minutes while holding onto a small tree for dear life. My legs got so tired from the stress of the angle I was holding myself, that I shifted all of my weight and pull to my arms and hands that were hanging onto the small tree. As I did so, and to my absolute horror, the small tree halfway pulled out of the ground. I quickly shifted my weight back to my legs before the unthinkable happened.

If that little tree had uprooted and I'd fallen backwards onto my own pile of poop and rolled down the slope, I probably would've called it quits and gone home. Not really, but I would've thought about it strongly and probably cried.

After the business transaction was done, I realized that my backpack and the toilet paper that was inside of it were quite a distance above me. "Damn it," I thought as I looked at my parcels strewn about the mountainside. I refused to pull up my pants without wiping first, especially out there. With my pants around my ankles, I climbed with my hands and waddled with my feet up the side of the steep slope to get to my pack. I must have looked pretty pathetic. After a few minutes I reached my effects and squared everything away. I gathered all of my things that were scattered across the embankment and continued on.

Even with all the excitement, the day was far from over. I met up with Muzzle several miles later and together we agreed to hike the rest of the way out of the National Park before the day was done. If everything went according to plan, we would only have a couple miles to hike the next morning. Then, we would be out of the park boundary, and free from all the rules and Rangers.

By the time darkness fell sometime after 8 pm, we still had over seven miles to hike in order to reach our goal. Seven miles in the dark, while in a park with over 1,700 diurnal black bears that were recorded to be living within its boundaries. What could possibly go wrong?

For some dumb reason we decided not to use our headlamps. Instead we let our eyes adapt to the darkness as it fell around us. This initially worked fine without any problems; however, once we were under the total darkness of the tree canopy, no amount of adjusting would help you see.

Sometime after 9 pm, while making our way up a steep climb, we noticed four headlamps above our position coming down the ridge headed straight for us. "Who would be going south at this time of night?" we thought. Visions of hog hunters, drug smugglers, and angry rangers flashed through my head. These visions were made all the more plausible by the heightened paranoia that walking in the woods at night tends to give a person. Since we didn't have our headlamps on, there was no way they'd know we were there until they were right on top of us. We laid low and waited...

As they got nearer and nearer, we began to hear a strange sound. That sound was techno music. Yes, whoever they were, they were listening to techno music as they walked through the night. When they were perhaps thirty feet away I flashed my headlamp at them. They stopped dead in their tracks, but the music kept playing. "Out for a night hike?" I called. "Oh no, we were just visiting the fire tower on top of the mountain," replied a voice with a heavy foreign accent. The four headlamps ended up belonging to four middle aged men from Prague, Czechoslovakia. We chatted for a minute before wishing each other safe hikes. It just goes to show that you never knew who you might encounter out there.

We ended up turning our headlamps on shortly after that, mainly because we kept stubbing our feet on the millions of rocks that dotted the trail. It was nearly midnight when we arrived at our destination of Davenport Gap Shelter without incident. This shelter was different from the others because it had a chain link fence with a latched gate across the front. The entire setup reeked of irony. They were locking people in cages to protect them from the dangerous wild animals that roamed outside.

Muzzle was a hammocker like me and we set up on some trees next to the shelter. With sore feet as well as a great feeling of accomplishment, we dozed off to sleep. We had completed a twenty-eight-mile day. All in all, I'd crossed the seventy mile Smokey Mountain range in only four days of hiking. This was a huge improvement over the twelve days it took me to hike the seventy miles out of Georgia, although it felt like quite an accomplishment at that time. Even with our poor decision to hike at night, we still encountered no bears.

After twenty-six days in the Appalachian Mountains, I walked out of the Smokies. It was a Friday on April 24th and I had made my weekend deadline. Not far from the boundary of the park, I met a local man that was picking what appeared to be weeds on the side of the trail. I struck up a conversation with him and found out that he was picking a wild vegetable known as a "ramp." I'd never heard of them before in my life, but he told me they were edible and that you could eat them right out of the ground. He peeled one and handed it to me to try. I put it in my mouth and chewed it up. The first thing that crossed my mind was, "Where have you been all my life!?"

The taste was magical and what I can only describe as a cross between an onion and a clove of garlic, except milder. Ramps looked similar to both as well. The bulb itself when fully mature is usually no bigger than the bottom half of your thumb, although I've found bigger and eaten smaller.

The man showed me how to identify the ramps by their two leaves and also how to pick them without breaking the stalk and losing the bulb in the dirt. He also showed me some "morel mushrooms" and taught me how to find and identify them. He told me the morels could be sold from anywhere between $45 and $250 per pound.

This gold mine of information completely made my day. There was no way I was going to get any miles done now that I would be foraging these tasty edibles every chance I got. Armed with my new found knowledge, I spent over an hour scouring the area and ended up with over one hundred ramps and about a dozen morel mushrooms. I felt like a true wilderness survivor.

Later that afternoon I arrived at the rendezvous point for meeting my girlfriend. It was a hostel called "Standing Bear" and the surrounding property was beautiful. Creeks, bridges, dogs, cats, chickens, goats, fire pits, camping areas, cabins with bunks, tree houses, a little shed that passed as a grocery store, and a full kitchen to cook anything you bought there (mainly frozen pizza, meat, hot dogs, eggs, etc.). I hung out at Standing Bear with Muzzle and Coma for the rest of the day while waiting for my lady and pup to arrive.

There was another hiker there that I'd periodically talked to throughout the journey so far. His name was Jack, and although this sounds like a real name, it was actually his trail name. He had been hiking the trail with his girlfriend and they had both earned the trail names "Jack and Diane" from the song of the same name by John Mellencamp. If there's one thing I learned about Jack during the conversations we had, it was that he loved everything agricultural. He loved to forage, he loved to farm, and he loved to talk about farming. He worked on farms for years before the trail and planned on going back to them afterwards. He was extremely knowledgeable in everything having to do with agriculture and farm science.

I went over and told him about my findings earlier in the morning. He immediately knew what they were and his face lit up in disbelief at the mention of morels. You would think that I'd won the lottery by the look on his face. "Noooo Waaaaay," he said. "You really found those? I can't believe it! That's so cool! I always keep my eyes open but I can never find them!"

Just seeing someone's passion and excitement over something so seemingly insignificant was contagious. His excitement over my findings got me even more excited. So I said to him, "You know what? You would appreciate these more than I would," as I gave him my entire bag of morels. He was speechless. He sputtered trying to say something before he finally said, "This is the greatest thing anyone has ever given me." It's amazing how the simplest things make the biggest differences for some people. It felt so good to hand that bag of mushrooms to him and see his face light up like Chinese New Year. "I'm going to eat these with scrambled eggs in the morning!" he told me. That sounded delicious.

I hung out some more and cooked a pizza while I waited for my sweetheart. She ended up arriving a little after 10 pm, and when she finally pulled up to the farm-like hostel in the middle of nowhere, I was the only one still awake and sitting on a bench near the gravel road. It must have been a very peculiar sight indeed.

We spent the weekend in nearby Newport, Tennessee. The Shoney's breakfast buffet and the local Chinese buffet didn't know what hit'em! With the addition of my dog, I knew that my hike was about to change. Instead of being responsible for only myself out there, I now had to take care of another living creature and watch out for it 24/7. I won't lie, when I first got Katana I was excited to have a new companion, but terrified that my hike wasn't completely in my control anymore. I mean, it was never completely in my control, but now it was even less in my control. She was simply another factor thrown in that could potentially end my hike.

"What if something happened to my dog and I was forced to quit?" That thought scared the hell out of me. Firstly, because I didn't want anything bad to befall my little princess. Secondly, because having to call it quits on account of something happening to her was not a reason I wanted to give for coming back home early. Since I hadn't done any research into actually hiking with a dog, but only into why you shouldn't hike with a dog, I was essentially going in blind. I was going to be completely winging it. This was nothing new, since I'd been pretty much winging my way through life as it was.

Katana is a small dog between fifteen to twenty pounds at the most. I wasn't too worried about her not being able to handle the terrain because I knew that if she couldn't handle something, I could easily pick her up and carry her. I was worried about her getting sick, getting hurt, getting attacked, snake bit, or running away. She had to be on a leash at all times. This constant leashing was something that I knew was going to really stress me out. During our weekend together I fashioned a long leash out of 550 Para-cord. One end was tied to a standard dog leash snap buckle that was attached to her harness, while the other end was tied to a carabineer that was clipped to the chest strap of my backpack. Voila! Hands free dog leash!

I'd seen other people get off trail because of their dogs getting infections from the chaffing of "doggy backpacks" that their owners made them wear in order to carry their own food. I was not about to strap one of these on my little princess. I am almost certain she wouldn't have taken a single step with it on, had I tried. It was up to me to carry all of her things that amounted to approximately four to five pounds of food per week, Front Line Flea and Tick Prevention, and a little collapsible doggy pop up tent that weighed about half a pound. With the addition of Katana and all of her things, I gained about six more pounds in my backpack. The grand plan was to get out there and see what happened. Not too much different from my original grand plan when first setting out on the adventure.

The entire time I was on the trail, Katana and I ran into many other dogs and their owners. Out of all the other hikers that I met with dogs, Katana and I are the only ones I know of, besides one other wolf hybrid that made it to Maine. I tried to keep tabs on everyone else I met, and took note of the reasons for why they slowly dropped off. One dog I met early on forced its owner off the trail when it got an infection from the chafing of its doggy backpack. Another dog attacked a bear in the Shenandoah Mountains and was subsequently mauled and had to get off the trail. Another dog that we met ran away during the night and when it was found the next day, it had an injured leg and was covered in more than 150 ticks. Another dog fell eighty feet from a cliff in Vermont and I don't remember hearing if it survived or not. I never actually met that one or its owner, but I heard about the incident.

The last dog I heard of getting off trail was one that I was actually very fond of. It was a Husky German Sheppard mix that got bit on the face by a rattlesnake in Pennsylvania. The owner couldn't foot the vet bills without quitting the trail.

There were plenty of other people with dogs that got off the trail due to the stress of hiking with one, or simply because they grew tired of being out there. Anything could happen to a dog out on the trail. They could get injured through no fault of their own, or run away. I even heard about two dogs that were chasing each other in front of a hostel that ended up getting run over right in front of their owners as they charged across the street.

Another common occurrence along the trail were hikers adopting dogs. We passed through so many small towns and farm areas that we came into contact with stray farm dogs or shelter dogs quite often. I knew of at least four people that adopted dogs while they were out there. While nothing bad that I know of happened to their dogs, none of them reached the end of the trail with them as far as I know. The added stress of a dog can be overwhelming, and after hiking with one for months on end, I don't know what would drive someone to adopt a dog while they were out there. Maybe out of loneliness or a need for companionship; but I can tell you now, the negatives of having a dog on the trail are equal to, if not greater than the positives. That goes for both you and the dog.

If the dog doesn't want to hike, then you're not going to hike. Not unless you pick it up and carry it. Depending on the size of the dog, this can be very uncomfortable for you, the dog, or both. Dogs have personalities and get bored and tired just like we do. Your dog didn't sign up for this hike, you did. Not all of them want to go on a walk every day, all day, for months on end. It's a special dog that does, and even when you find that special dog, they're still going to have plenty of bad days over the course of a six-month walk. Some of those bad days might fall on your good days, subsequently turning them into bad days. Some of those bad days might fall on days when you actually need to be somewhere. A dog doesn't understand the concept of needing to resupply. When you run out of food for you and your dog and still have twenty miles to the next town when the dog decides it doesn't want to walk, then you're shit out of luck! Even if the dog does want to walk, the terrain might be so difficult that your dog needs your help in order to traverse it. The heat, the cold, rocks, severe inclines, and river crossings are all factors to consider. If I tallied up all of the miles that I carried Katana during the more than five months that she hiked with me, it would add up to a hundred miles or more. There were some days that I carried her for more than ten miles straight.

Not only does hiking with a dog present more obstacles on the trail, but just as many off the trail. No doubt you're going to want to stay at hotels or hostels along the way. You can say that you won't (I did), but I promise that you probably will. Not all of them allow dogs, and some of the towns are so small that there might be only one hotel or hostel in them. If the establishment doesn't allow pets, then it looks like you're going to be camping on the edge of town while your friends live it up in the nice dry room that has showers, cable television, Wi-Fi, and laundry.

If your dog isn't a service dog, then forget about taking it into restaurants, convenience stores, or supermarkets. It's going to have to wait outside. What if there's no one to watch it or there's a bad storm going on? Too bad! Your dog is going to have to sit next to your pack by itself, possibly in the rain while it waits for you to eat or finish buying groceries. Either that or you just don't go at all. While your dog is used to this kind of weather and independence out on the trail, in the eyes of strangers, you might as well be an animal abuser.

When you have a dog on the trail, you can never just make a decision for yourself. You have to factor in your fur baby. I missed out on a lot of different things while I had my dog. I wouldn't change any of it for the world, but I want people to know the facts. I missed out on train rides into bigger cities and I was sometimes barred from using public transportation to get from one place to another in certain towns due to the fact that my dog wasn't a service animal. I have been stranded in towns because I couldn't get a ride and certain public transportation wouldn't allow my dog in the vehicle. This left me with the options of hitch hiking, walking, or paying the exorbitant prices for a taxi. Those were some of the realities of having a dog on the trail.

The positives are companionship, protection, something to have imaginary conversations with (maybe not that positive or healthy), and something that will keep the creepy crawlies away and stand guard in the night. That's about it. Other than that, a dog is going to cost extra money and extra stress. Plenty of people successfully thru-hike with a dog, but there are even more that don't make it. I wasn't sure how my trek with Katana was going to play out.

My first day on the trail with the pup wasn't too bad. She was excited to be with me again and was eager to smell and explore all the new scenery. We had a hard time keeping a good pace so that she could satisfy all of her curiosities. A few miles in we stopped at a steep fast flowing stream that was traveling down a narrow face of smooth rock. I brought Katana up to the edge for a drink, while I climbed up onto the rock in order to reach a better spot to fill my water bladder. When I was just inches away from the spot I was aiming for, my foot slipped on slick moss and I fell straight into the current. I slid down about fifteen feet on my back into a pool that completely submerged the lower half of my body, as well as a good portion of my back. It was only a matter of time before I took a hard fall I suppose. It had taken nearly a month for me to have my first good fall on the trail, but I was to have hundreds more before I reached the end.

Around five miles in, Katana refused to walk any further. We sat for a while to rest, as I shared some of my snack with her. Ten minutes later she was good to go. We did a short day to meet up with DSOH and Coma, as Katana became familiar with her new uncles and they became familiar with her. She slept soundly beneath my hammock for most of the night, but sometime after midnight, she was up wandering around and pulling against her leash. That meant she was pulling on my hammock and waking me up. I leaned out, scooped her up and let her spend the rest of night sleeping in the crook of my arm.

The second day with Katana was a little more exciting as we climbed the mountain of "Max Patch." It was originally called "Mack's Patch" and was a mountain that had its top portion cleared of all trees for cattle grazing in the 1800's. What remained was an enormous "bald," or a mountain or hill top that's devoid of any trees or large vegetation. A bald is normally covered in grass, dirt, rocks, or any combination of all three, but no trees. The best part about a bald is the views they offer. Nine times out of ten, you will be rewarded with a 360-degree view of the landscape around you. For this reason, Max Patch, at close to 5000 feet is dubbed the crown jewel of the AT.

Upon reaching the summit I quickly found out why it earned that name. The first thing you notice about Max Patch is the seemingly perfect manicured grass. It's like a soccer field on the top of this mountain. The grass is so soft that you can walk or even run around frivolously in bare feet. The next thing you'll notice is the view. The summit of Max Patch is situated in such a location, that on a clear day, you can see almost the entire Smokey Mountain range curving away from you, back to the south. You can see exactly where you've come from on one side and exactly where you're going on the other. This was another one of those moments that I lived for out on the trail. Again, feeling how small you were, and yet knowing that it didn't matter because you were going to conquer the distance no matter what.

DSOH, Coma, and I laid up there for nearly two hours relaxing, sunning ourselves, and playing with Katana. Then we had the bright idea to unclip her leash and see if she would still hang out and play. The second she realized that the far end of her leash wasn't attached to anything, she tore off across the bald, picked up the trail, and began running north. Relaxation time was over as I hopped up and started sprinting after her in my bare feet. It was over a quarter mile before I was able to catch up and step on her leash. The only bright side to the whole situation was that she ran in the right direction. "At least she knows which way we're going," I said to DSOH and Coma upon our return.

It was a little after the one-month mark out on the trail that I discovered the cause of the "thump" noises that I'd heard nearly every single day out there. I was sitting on a log, taking a break with a local day hiker when I heard the noise. I perked up and turned to the day hiker, "Did you hear that?" I asked. "Yeah, it's a ruffled grouse," he replied casually as he continued eating his snack. "I'll be damned!" I thought. "They sit on a log and beat their wings really fast to attract mates or get mites off their feathers," the day hiker added. The guy seemed like he knew his stuff, so I took him at his word and decided to research it later.

I couldn't imagine that a bird, smaller than a chicken was generating all of that noise and vibration. I still have no idea how far the sound carries, but it always sounded like the same distance every time I heard it. The sound never seemed to get any closer or further away. The only thing I could really imagine was that I bet they tasted delicious.

Katana was adapting quickly but still having trouble in some areas. She absolutely abhors water and acts like a cat in the sense that she will go to any lengths to avoid getting even her paws wet. We crossed countless small creeks, streams, and run offs every day and she dealt with each one in her own dainty way. She flat out refused to be the first one to cross any body of water. I always had to make my way across before she even attempted. Then if there wasn't a wooden plank, she would cross in one of two different ways. Sometimes she would back up to get a running start before taking the biggest leap she could muster, attempting to clear the body of water in a single bound. Sometimes she made it, sometimes she didn't. The second way was rock hopping. This one was by far the most comical.

She would take little leaps between the un-submerged rocks, being oh so careful not to let her paws slip anywhere near the water until she reached the other side. She made it look very dainty, but every now and then she would slip off and land in the shallow water. Once her feet got wet, it was game over. Her dainty little water crossing attempt turned into an all-out scramble for the safety of the shore; leaping and running simultaneously while trying to spend as little time as possible with her feet in the water. Once she made it to the other side, she got this relieved, but proud look on her face and began to snort, shake and roll around on the ground, trying to get all the water off her fur. It's the funniest thing you've ever seen!

She excelled on the uphill climbs. With her small frame and low center of gravity, she made short work of just about any climb. When we went up a steep incline, I'd stop for a few seconds to let my legs stop burning. While I was stopped, she would continue to pull against the leash for several seconds before turning around to give me a look that unmistakably said, "Come on Dad! What's the hold up?" I'd then look back at her and say, "Yeah, yeah, I wish I weighed fifteen pounds, had four legs, and wasn't carrying a fifty-five-pound backpack!"

One night there was a bad storm and I was able to hang my hammock inside the shelter where we stopped. I was with DSOH and he decided to sleep on the shelter floor. I tethered Katana to one of my hammock straps, put out her food and water, and then went to sleep. I'd been using the bottom half of two Gatorade bottles as her water and food dishes.

The next morning began relatively normal until DSOH went to put on one of his boots. As he put his foot in, he was startled and pulled it back out. He turned his boot upside down as over two dozen chewed up IncrediBite Dog Kibbles fell out. Apparently, an industrious shelter mouse had discovered Katana's improvised food bowl. Then one by one, throughout the night, had stolen the kibbles and stored them inside of DSOH's boot. Some guard dog Katana was! She couldn't even protect her own food from a mouse. It just goes to show how nature will use anything you leave or don't leave behind, in one way or another.

Hot Springs was the next town we came to in North Carolina. The trail passed straight through, going right down Main Street and the heart of downtown. I think every business in the whole community was situated on this one street. Hot Springs was a quaint little hamlet nestled in the mountains with a population of barely five hundred people. Let me add, five hundred very nice and wonderful people.

When we arrived in Hot Springs a local husband and wife opened their home to us. Actually, Muzzle was the first one to arrive in Hot Springs with terrible shin splints in the middle of a storm, and they had originally opened their home to him. Through familiarity and kindness, they then opened their home which was dubbed "The Lippard Residence" to the rest of us. It ended up being quite a little gathering, with seven of us in total staying at the house. It was me, Muzzle, DSOH, Coma, War Story, Jack, and Diane.

War Story had been hurting. He had metal rods throughout one of his legs as a result of the injuries he sustained in Iraq. His knees were also killing him and he was having a lot of trouble keeping up the pace that we'd been maintaining. Not wanting to be left behind, he had "Yellow Blazed" ahead to Hot Springs to catch up.

Yellow Blazing is a term that refers to someone who skips sections of the trail by hitchhiking or driving around them to other towns or sections. People can earn the name "Yellow Blazer" if they do this a lot and it's normally frowned upon in the thru-hiking community. You didn't want to be branded a yellow blazer. Yellow blazing is also referred to as "Bill Brysoning" amongst thru-hikers. If you've ever read the book "A Walk in the Woods," then you'll know what I mean.

Even with the negative connotations, some people don't care about being branded as Yellow Blazers, and rightly so. There is nothing wrong with a Yellow Blazer that freely admits to doing so. It's their hike and they can do whatever they want. It's the ones that deny yellow blazing even when it's painfully obvious they do, that irks most thru-hikers. It makes you feel like they're getting paid the same wages as you, but for half the work. You know they're going to go home and tell everyone they "did it," when they and everybody else knows full well they didn't. They're taking away from the accomplishments of other people. This shouldn't matter, but when you think about the amount of suffering that you endure on this adventure, it kind of automatically hits a nerve.

The nagging question amongst thru-hikers is, "How much can one yellow blaze before not being considered a thru-hiker anymore?" Many would say that if anyone yellow blazes even once, then they're ineligible. Personally, I don't try to tell people if they're thru-hikers or not. If YOU think you're a thru-hiker, then it doesn't matter what other people think. I personally stay focused on my own hike and walk past every single white blaze that marks the trail.

War Story had yellow blazed once before and met us in Fontana Dam. This was the second time I'd arrived in a town to find War Story had gotten there before me, even though I'd been well ahead of him on the trail. I understood his reasons though. We'd all known each other for a month and had become very close. He didn't want to hike without his friends and we thoroughly enjoyed his company as long as he slept at least a hundred feet away from us every night due to his massive snoring problem. There was nothing wrong with him skipping ahead to be with us. If he didn't have a problem with it, then we didn't have a problem with it. He wasn't hiding or denying anything like many other hikers you met out there.

There is a common saying out on the trail and within every major hiking community. That saying is: "Hike Your Own Hike" (HYOH). It means you shouldn't worry about what other people are doing. Focus on yourself and deal with your own problems, unless someone asks you for help with theirs. It also means that you shouldn't let other people affect you, or tell you how to hike your hike. You're out there for your own reasons and as long as you are getting what you want out of your hike, then it doesn't matter what anyone else is doing. Don't let others influence or dictate how you hike the trail. That being said, be honest about how you hike the trail and no one will care one way or the other.

Meeting War Story ahead of us in towns became a pattern. We would hike out of a town and War Story would keep up for a couple of days. Eventually the pains from his past injuries would get worse the more he pushed himself, causing him to fall behind. Then as we came into the next town, he'd already be there and have everything scoped out. It became sort of a system. He would know where the best deals and meals were without us having to figure it out for ourselves.

The days we spent in Hot Springs were some of my fondest early memories from the trail. We spent two days at The Lippard Residence. That wasn't the last name of the older couple that lived there, but the name written on a sign that was staked in the front yard. The older couple that opened their home to us was named "Ike" and "Sally" and the property they lived on was gorgeous. Situated on the banks of Spring Creek, Sally kept the grounds well-manicured and teaming with flowers, as well as other garden delights. There was a vegetable garden, a gazebo, and stone steps leading down to a stone terrace next to the wide and fast flowing Spring Creek.

Fishing has always been an enormous part of my life. It's my therapy, and back home in Florida if I'm not working or sleeping, I'm usually fishing. It helped keep my mind off my crazy work schedule, as well as keep me sane. I dabble in many different types of fishing, but mostly salt water. I used to work on Deep Sea Fishing boats as a teenager and I'm also an avid pier fisherman, shark fisherman, bow fisherman, and kayak fisherman. Everything I do is either catch and release or catch and eat. If I'm not eating it, then I let it go. I am not a trophy fisherman. I do it purely for sustenance and the therapeutic effect it has on me.

Knowing that I was going to be missing around six months of fishing time back home, I knew that I at least had to try and do some fishing out on the trail if the opportunity presented itself. I had brought a spool of 6 lb. fluorocarbon line, a few rooster tails, panther martins, and spoon lures with me. Also some flies, salmon eggs, small hooks, and a couple of bobbers. I didn't bring a fishing pole or a reel, because I didn't have licenses for every state, so I didn't want to look too conspicuous. I figured that doing it all by hand made up for not having a pole or a license, by presenting a greater challenge. I don't really consider myself much of a freshwater fisherman, but I was dying to get some fishing in!

I really missed fishing a lot, and hadn't gotten a chance until Hot Springs to do some. Not long after arriving, I made my way to the creek and decided to try my luck at hand lining rooster tails for trout. The current was fast enough that I could use it to my advantage. I held the free line and the lure in one hand and the spool in the other hand. Then I spun the lure around 360 degrees faster and faster until I let it fly on the cast. The lure shot out fifty feet into the strongest part of the current. That was exactly where I wanted it. I was fishing right on a bend in the creek, so there was a calm area on the edge of the fast moving water as it rounded the curve. The lure was pushed to the edge of the fast water and the slow water as I slowly hand lined it in. The current helped to keep the lure high in the water and also give it the appearance that it was being worked in much faster than it actually was.

This is going to seem unbelievable, but I kid you not, to my utter astonishment I hooked and landed a small trout on my first cast. I was amazed! I didn't think I had a chance in hell of catching a trout while hand lining a rooster tail, let alone on my first cast.

What was even more amazing was that I really consider myself a terrible freshwater fisherman as I hardly know anything about the finer points of trout fishing. I was totally winging it!

I continued my new technique and within the span of twenty minutes I'd landed two more trout and lost another one while I was pulling it in. On what would end up being my final cast, I was slowly retrieving the line hand over hand when I received my strongest, most violent strike yet! So violent in fact, that it stripped the line back out of my hand and ripped the spool out of the other as all of it disappeared into the dark waters of the creek. "I guess I'm done fishing," I thought sadly. Not that sad though, because I still had three other tasty trout! I cleaned them down at the river, then took them back up to the house and put them in Ziploc bags before placing them in the fridge.

Everyone was amazed that I'd actually caught something. Catching those fish in such a primitive manner earned me the new nickname "Mayor Grylls." This was a play off the famous TV survivalist Bear Grylls. I don't think they realized that I was secretly just as amazed as them. I was determined not to eat the trout while in town; I wanted to instead pack them out and have them as a special meal, cooked over an open fire in the woods.

On the second day at the Lippard House, we all did chores for Ike and Sally to show our gratitude for their hospitality. Jack and Diane helped turn over the mulch pile and also did some gardening and pruning. Muzzle and DSOH helped set up a rope and pulley system to hang plants on the front porch, while Coma, War Story, and I helped fix old furniture that was falling apart.

Besides doing chores and helping out around the property, I wanted to give Ike and Sally a gift as well. I had a couple hundred ramps that I'd collected over the past several days before getting to Hot Springs, so I cleaned and peeled them all down at the creek before giving them to Sally as a thank you gift. She was delighted at the sight of them already being washed and peeled. I don't think ramps were very expensive in those parts, but they are very seasonal and can be a huge pain to wash and peel in large numbers.

During that second day at The Lippard Residence, War Story made a famous batch of lasagna that in later days would be missed and remembered as the best lasagna we ever had. Jack and Diane also made a delicious Apple Crisp dish that was so good, Sally asked them to make another one. She took the second batch in a giant Pyrex dish to a local town function. I don't think I ever felt as much a part of a town as I did in Hot Springs. Those were the golden days when everything still felt new and we hadn't quite perfected our routine or adapted to the trail yet. Although we all felt like hot shot thru-hikers, the reality was that all of us were still very wet behind the ears.

On the day that we hiked out of Hot Springs, I packed out three trout and a squirrel. I'm gonna leave out the story of how I procured the squirrel, but let's just say that the people in these rural mountain towns are huge hunting enthusiasts. I took full advantage of a small caliber rifle that was loaned to me from a local for the very reason of hunting squirrel. So with squirrel, trout, and a few left over ramps in my pack, we all climbed out of Hot Springs eager for the night's feast.

We crossed the French Broad River and made our way up the steep climb that led us back into the mountain wilderness. I would find out several weeks later that a thru-hiker fell off a cliff on that climb out of Hot Springs. With all of the loose shale rock and precipitous curves and overlooks, this was not hard to believe. You constantly heard news on the trail about the misfortunes and accidents that befell other hikers out there. Whether it was animal encounters, falls, or confrontations with questionable characters, you were always hearing something. News traveled surprisingly fast on the trail.

Probably one of the best animal encounter stories I heard out there was from a hiker that I met in Virginia. He was one of the few hikers that had their trail name changed late in the hike. His first trail name was "Bagge" (pronounced Baggy), until it was changed to "Skunk Bite." The hiker formerly known as Bagge was sleeping under his tarp, when a skunk invaded his shelter and bit him on the toe for absolutely no reason whatsoever. The skunk was presumed to be rabid, and Skunk Bite was then forced to endure Rabies vaccinations every several days for multiple weeks. The funny part was that he had to keep returning to the same doctor's office to receive them. Not wanting to miss out on any hiking, this resulted in Skunk Bite doing A LOT of hitchhiking between the office and wherever he kept leaving off on the trail. I don't know how the guy did it, but he was a master of finding rides.

I ran into Skunk Bite off and on up until Vermont. I last saw him in the city of Rutland where I believe he became such good friends with some locals he met, that he ended up staying there and getting a job. I think he mentioned something about finishing the rest of the trail the next year.

Once we stopped and made camp on the top of Spring Mountain, we all took on different duties. Jack and Muzzle set about making a fire while Diane worked on sautéing the ramps and some other vegetables. I found the sticks that were to be used as spits and skewers while also sharpening and fashioning them accordingly. DSOH and Coma collected wood to help keep the fire going and War Story collected water in his plastic three-gallon bladder for all of us to share.

When all was said and done, we had one squirrel skewered on a stick being manually roasted over the fire. Two trout balancing over the fire while skewered on a spit, and one trout splayed open on a flat rock over the embers. It was a beautifully delicious sight and our metamorphosis into true blue mountain survivors was almost complete.

Less than a half hour later we had our mountain feast. It was slightly ironic that most of the wild fixings had been obtained in or near a town, but that's just the way it goes. The trout was moist and delicious as the bones peeled right out and I also ate the skin. The squirrel was amazing and dare I say... a bit nutty. It was nutty with a hint of chicken flavor. I know that sounds cliché as hell, but that's what it tasted like. The chicken flavor most likely came from the chicken Ramen spice pack that we seasoned it with, so go figure.

All in all, everyone loved it. It wasn't meant to make us full, it was simply a small meal for us to share and enjoy as a trail family. The squirrel disappeared in minutes as we fought over the small morsels the little creature had provided us with. I felt like I could check an experience off my bucket list. Live, forage, and hunt off the land. CHECK!

My prowess and obsession with finding and picking ramps became the butt of many jokes out on the trail, all in good humor of course. It became a game for my small circle of hiking companions to randomly start a sentence or ask me a question that left out a key word that rhymed with "ramp" for me to figure out. The exchanges went a lot like this - "Hey Mayor Grylls, what do you call those things for wheel chairs when they can't go up a set of stairs?" Me: "Ramps." "Hey Mayor Grylls, when it's dark and I need some light, I turn on my...." Me: "Lamp." "Hey Mayor, sometimes I call my grandfather...." Me: "Gramps." It went on and on and became a game out on the trail and in camp to try and come up with new ones.

Before all the jokes and rhymes were over, I was branded with yet a third nickname. They began calling me "The RAMPaging Mayor." This was because I was always on a rampage through the forest to find those little garlicky-onion gems. There was almost never a time during the span of nearly a month that I didn't have ramps stuffed into my pack. You could smell me coming from a mile away if the wind was right.

I chopped them up, sautéing them in my pot, then mixing them with my pasta sides and even sautéing small chunks of pepperoni to mix in as well. It really gave me something to look forward to at the end of the day and I was beginning to feel like a back woods chef.

Routine was everything out there and everyone had their own. You had a routine for the morning, a routine for lunch, and a routine for the evening. Everyone had their own rituals out on the trail, but they didn't always stay the same. They changed and evolved just as we did.

Every morning I would wake up and usually have a cold breakfast. I didn't like cooking in the morning because the extra time and clean-up was a nuisance to me. I wouldn't eat first, but I would choose what I was going to eat and then set it aside. Then I'd roll up my food bag and place it on the ground. Next, I'd pull all the gear and clothing out of my hammock pockets and place them in the main nest of the hammock. Then I'd stuff all my clothes and sleeping bags into their assigned dry bags, then toss them on the ground with any other miscellaneous items. After my hammock was empty, I'd fold it up and compress it into its stuff sack. Finally, I took my atlas straps off the trees and rolled them up. Once everything was in a nice pile on the ground, I'd put it all back into my pack in whatever order and sequence it belonged, before sitting down and enjoying whatever it was that I'd chosen to eat for breakfast. Breakfast was usually a couple Honey Buns or Cosmic Brownies... you know, stuff that's terrible for you. Then I'd go through my hygiene routine with my easily accessible toiletries kit. I'd gotten to the point where it took me less than ten minutes to break camp and hit the trail.

Throughout the day, I would take multiple snack breaks. No set times, just whenever I got the hankering to stuff my face, which was practically every half hour. Snacking would normally take place while I was still walking, or during five to ten minute breaks that usually occurred at pretty locations or difficult stretches. Lunch was usually more drawn out, lasting from anywhere between half an hour to an hour. Some people cooked their lunch, but most ate it cold. My lunches normally consisted of larger versions of my snacks. Things like cheese, bagels, candy bars, tuna packets, tortillas, peanut butter, mixed nuts, and more Honey Buns or Cosmic Brownies; nothing overly fancy.

Dinner time was a time that some people lived for out on the trail. It was the last shred of civilization that some people felt they had left. I saw people that went all out on cooking their dinner every single night. It didn't matter how long or rough their day was, they were going to prepare a fancy feast, no matter how long it took them. I never understood this because I'm not picky at all and I could care less if my food is hot or cold. I could eat any type of food, at pretty much any time of day, at any temperature. There was no breakfast, lunch, or dinner specific foods in my book. It's all food and I eat all of it just the same.

When the moment came to put my pack down for the final time that day, the last thing I wanted to do was labor over cooking a meal and cleaning my dishes. The fanciest I ever got was Ramen, Instant Mashed Potatoes, and Pasta Sides. Sautéing ramps and pepperoni was a novelty and a short lived occurrence for me out on the trail. At the end of the day, my dinner usually consisted of whatever I had for lunch. As a matter of fact, after less than two months on the trail, I actually gave up cooking altogether. Once I'd made it to Virginia, I can count on two hands the number of meals I cooked before reaching Maine. When I got to New York, I sent my pot, stove, and fuel back home. I didn't want to deal with the hassle or extra weight anymore. When the day was over, all I wanted to do was sit around a fire with other hikers and relax a while before going to bed. No cooking, no mess, no clean up...just good company and conversation.

The routine of setting up camp at the end of each day was also a unique experience for each individual. Some people would have dinner before they did anything else, pulling their food and cooking items out as soon as they put down their pack. I didn't do it that way. The first order of business when rounding up on my final location for the day was to stake out my camp spot. I would survey the trees and surrounding terrain, then pick out the most convenient or beautiful spot in regard to water sources, bathroom areas, or views.

After settling on a location, I would then set up my atlas straps on the chosen trees before pulling my hammock out and getting it hung. After that, I pulled out all of my clothes and sleeping bags, then dumped them in the main part of the hammock. I put everything into their assigned pockets based on the likelihood of how much I might need them during the night. I put food and water in the same pocket, while gloves, beanies, and base layers went into another pocket. My down jacket and rain shell jacket were placed into yet another in case I got cold and needed some extra layers during the night. Then several other items were put into other pockets in the order of most important to least important. Everything was within easy reach, without me ever having to leave the nest. I always left my backpack clipped to the hammock strap nearest the tree. If it rained, then I would clip it to the base of the gathered end of my hammock so that it stayed beneath the overhang of my rain fly. I had a system and a purpose for everything.

I never ate dinner until everything was set up. This was because once I'd eaten, I didn't want to worry about setting up or missing out on prime real estate. I wanted to be able to eat and crawl into bed if inclined, maybe even eat while in bed. I was a creature of habit and enjoyed having a routine. The entire process of making camp was usually much faster than breaking camp, as I could be completely set up and lying in my bed within five minutes.

It was around the time of Hot Springs that I'd begun to feel the subtle symptoms of some kind of ailment. It started with the lymph nodes in my neck becoming swollen and very sensitive. This was the first symptom and only symptom for nearly a week. I couldn't figure out why only my lymph nodes were hurting and nothing else. I was positive that it was a prelude and a warning to something much worse that was developing.

It would hurt the most in the mornings and evenings, with the worst of the pain subsiding throughout the day. As if by clock work, when evening would approach, the sensitivity would get so bad that it hurt to chew, swallow food, and even talk. I did my best to ignore the discomfort and hoped it would go away on its own as I continued my way through North Carolina.

It was on May 3rd that a couple of new trends were born out on the trail. One of them was good and the other was not so good depending on who you asked I suppose. It was a hotter than usual morning, and I'd been making my way over and through boulder fields, Rhododendron thickets, and small rock scrambles (a scramble is an area of terrain that is too steep to walk or hike up, normally requiring hand over hand climbing to safely navigate). Katana had been handling it all very well and I'd only needed to pick her up once on a six-foot drop that I didn't want her to leap from.

At one point early in the morning, as we were making our way past a thicket of Rhododendron, a bird suddenly shot out right in front of Katana. She pounced on it before my brain could fully process what had happened. With her butt in the air, she kept her paws and chest pinned down on top of the unfortunate creature. Then as she tried to maneuver herself to see her prize, the bird felt the weight come off, seized its chance, and took off with Katana leaping into the air after it. Thankfully, she missed the second time.

I was relieved not to have the blood of some un-edible creature on my hands. I wasn't sure what kind of bird it was, but I assumed it was a species of small song bird. Katana once again gave me that happy-go-lucky, tongue hanging out of the mouth "glance" that said, "See what I can do Dad?" "Yes little dog, I saw it. Why don't you catch a turkey next time so we can actually do something with it?"

We continued slowly through the rocky terrain and caught up with DSOH late in the morning as he was taking a break on a rocky overlook. I joined him, and while we sat and discussed the day's terrain and worked out a place to stop that evening, an idea came over me. Not so much an idea, as a vision. It suddenly dawned on me that this rocky overlook was a perfect spot for a "Pride Rock, Lion King" moment.

On the off chance that you might not know what a "Lion King" moment is, I'll explain. At the beginning of the original animated Lion King movie when Simba (the lion cub) is born, Rafiki (a baboon) takes him out to the edge of Pride Rock and holds him out, facing the savannah for all the animals to see while bowing to their future king.

Upon seeing the rocky outcropping and experiencing my vision, I knew that this was something I'd needed to do my entire life. I gave DSOH my camera to immortalize the moment, then got up, seized the little princess under her arms and offered her up for all of Appalachia to behold! Secretly, I think she loved it. She didn't flinch and had this regal look on her face while all the while holding her paws out as if to say "Yes! Behold me!"

So on that fateful day a new trend was born… "Lion King-ing!" From that day forth it would become a tradition that anytime I came across an epic cliff, overlook, waterfall, view, or rock; I would take a few moments out of my day to add to my collection of Lion King Photos. Unfortunately, there were many times in the future that I was alone and unable to have a photograph taken, so those spots have to live on in memory. I received mixed criticism over my lion king photos, with some people insisting that I was needlessly putting my pup in danger. All I can say is that there wasn't a chance in this universe that my 200 + pound frame was going to drop my stationary, 15-pound dog with my hands entwined in her harness and wrapped around her entire body. In reality, I never actually held her over any ledges in the first place, only next to, and in front of them. The rest was camera angles.

The temperature got warmer and warmer as the day drew on. This day had the warmest temperatures I'd experienced so far on the trail. It was probably only in the 80's, but still hot enough to make going up and down over the many climbs that much more challenging. The temperatures had been fairly erratic lately, as it was that time of year up in the mountains when winter/early spring temperatures hadn't quite left, and late spring/summer hadn't quite arrived. You didn't know what temperatures you were going to encounter on a daily and nightly basis.

I was at the bottom of one of these many climbs when Katana once again refused to walk any further. I sat down and poured her a bowl of water to give her a break. We sat for around ten minutes before I stood up and tried to start up the hill again. Still she refused to walk. I looked down at her, and she looked back up at me. This was to be a battle of wills. "Katana, you know we can't stop for the day yet," I said to her. She continued to look up at me with a defiant expression. "F-YOU!" I imagined her saying. "Katana, the sooner we get where we're going, the sooner you can eat dinner and go to sleep." Still the princess looked up defiantly with that "F-YOU!" look.

I will freely admit that I talked to my dog like some kind of crazy person. I would talk to her and make up responses on her behalf and then respond to those responses that I'd manifested for her. Essentially I was having a conversation with myself. A dual personality just like Gollum from Lord of the Rings, except that one of my personalities thought it was my dog. I'm sure one could come up with some name for a brain dysfunction or disorder to define this mental state, but I already have. I called it, "bored as hell walking in the woods with your dog every day."

I decided to be a little more assertive. I began to walk and pull on her leash at the same time. She immediately dug her back legs into the ground and refused to move or even be dragged. I turned back, but now she wouldn't even look at me. "Katana... Katana... come on." Her body was squared up to me, but her face was turned looking somewhere off to the side pretending I wasn't there. It was funny, pathetic, and sad all at the same time. "Where was the unconditional love to follow thy master to the ends of the earth?" I thought to myself. It was nowhere to be found on this day.

Reluctantly, I walked over and picked her up. I cradled her for a minute and told her how disappointed I was with her attitude. Then I lifted her over my head and set her across my shoulders like some kind of furry scarf. She was just the right size and balanced perfectly up there while leaning against the top of my pack. Her face hovered inches from my face, and I turned my head to look at her. Her mood had definitely improved. She was smiling once again and looked ridiculously comfortable on her new perch.

She had won the first battle of wills between us. She learned that day that I could be beaten. What she also learned was that riding beats the hell out of walking, and for the second time that day a new trend was born. The trend of Katana riding on my shoulders practically anytime she wanted to. I eventually learned how to reason and compromise with her, but the final solution to this battle of wills would not be found for nearly a thousand miles.

As the days began to stay consistently hot, I learned that Katana didn't like to walk between the hours of noon and 3 pm. I don't blame her because I didn't either. I tried to remember that she was wearing the equivalent of a "Down Jacket" that she couldn't take off. More of a "Fur Coat" I suppose, but that's too literal of an analogy.

I tried to stay very in tune with Katana's break needs. Sometimes we would hide in the shade for hours in an attempt to beat the hottest part of the day. Then we'd make up our miles by hiking through the early evening, or hiking into the night. The hot days became a great excuse to night hike.

It was around this stage of the journey that I began to forge a very strong friendship with DSOH. He had his Master's Degree in Business and his undergraduate in Classical History. He was a wealth of information on everything pertaining to national and world history, more so than anyone else I've ever met. The things he knew and the little details that went with them boggled my mind. This was fantastic because I loved history. We would spend the better part of some days walking along together and discussing anything and everything about the people of old. We would discuss and debate what the ancients would think of our journey, as well as how they would handle it themselves. We would discuss the meaning of "honor" and "character" and how the definitions had changed from back then to our present day. We would also debate and construct battles between leaders and empires that existed at different times, and try to decide who would win based on tactics and weapons technology of their own unique time periods. This was greatly entertaining and passed the time as well as the miles rather quickly.

The types of conversations and discussions you can have with people when there aren't any distractions would astound you. With nowhere to be and all day to have them, conversations out on the trail took on a whole new meaning and depth. In this age of technology where everyone is plugged in, it's all too apparent that people have never been more disconnected and out of tune, as well as touch with each other. While out on the trail, walking or sitting around campfires, I'd never had so many deep and meaningful conversations with people in my entire life. This connection I built with people on an almost daily basis was perhaps one of my favorite and most memorable aspects of the entire adventure.

Through our many conversations and debates, I learned that DSOH's favorite ancient civilization was the Romans. He liked them because of their ability to adapt and adopt the tactics and technology of other civilizations. They learned from other's successes and blunders. "It's what made them great," he said. According to his very educated opinion, Genghis Khan was the single most brutal warrior in all of history that had the best chances of coming out on top in a battle with any other great figure from the sands of time. I didn't know enough to really argue any of that, but I still had fun playing devil's advocate nonetheless.

In the time since the Smokies, the trail had skirted in and out along the border of Tennessee and North Carolina. There were never that many signs to tell you which state you were in, but you knew that you were bouncing between the two. I was a day away from my first Tennessee town when my lymph node soreness developed into a painful, hacking cough.

CHAPTER 4: TENNESSEE

"Feeling like Hell, Walking Through Paradise."

When I first reached Tennessee, the biggest difference most evident from North Carolina was the abundance of ramps. You could walk for mile after mile and find them everywhere. I couldn't pick enough of them. I wasn't even one day into the main part of Tennessee before I couldn't strap anymore ramps to the outside of my pack. It was about this time that I realized I had a problem. I was addicted to foraging and needed a major intervention!

I could think of only one way to help overcome my addiction. I made up my mind to give away all the ramps I had in my possession. That night I distributed every last ounce of ramps to other hikers, while also teaching them how to identify and pick them for themselves. With any luck, the people ahead of me would wipe them out before I got to them.

I made the decision to only pick enough ramps each day to add to my dinner. Any more than that was unhealthy as well as overkill. In the end, by imposing my own "self-intervention," I was able to cut back on my foraging by probably 80%. This was a small victory for my hiking pace as well as my bodily odor.

The day before arriving in the town of Erwin, I ran out of dog food. I'm sure Katana felt like this was a blessing, because I had to improvise. For a day and a half, Katana's meals consisted of peanut butter tortilla burritos... and she was CRAZY about them. It was nice seeing her so happy with this new change of diet, but I couldn't help feeling like a bad parent. It was like giving your child candy for breakfast, lunch, and dinner. You feel good because it makes them happy and they love you for it, but at the same time you feel horrible because you know you're responsible for possibly causing some future health issues. At least that's how I felt about the whole situation. I didn't have an option though, as it was feed her tortillas and peanut butter, or nothing at all. I felt like the first option was the lesser of two evils.

The descent into Erwin was a gorgeous one. It was mid-morning as I made my way down Temple Hill with the sun rising over the mountains in the distance. I stopped at a rocky outcropping and was rewarded with a picturesque view of the Nolichucky River as the sun's rays reflected off the surface like streaks of gold and silver. I sat with Katana and breathed it all in for close to twenty minutes. During that time, I observed a hawk lazily riding the updrafts below me. I'd seen plenty of hawks and buzzards riding the updrafts above me in the past, but never had I enjoyed the perspective of seeing one from a higher vantage point.

Although whatever sickness that ailed me was now in full swing, Erwin still holds some of my fondest early memories of the trail as well. This was because so many people that I met at the beginning of the trail never made it all the way. There were many friendships that had begun, but were suddenly cut short due to people dropping off the trail. It was during the early days that the congregation of familiar faces were at their largest, liveliest, and most fun. You looked back on those days fondly because most of the people in those memories didn't share many more with you after those times.

Upon walking into Erwin we found War Story already checked in at the local hostel called "Uncle Johnny's." Somewhere between Hot Springs and Erwin, Muzzle had disappeared and gotten off the trail. I never saw where he got off, and never got to say goodbye. He claimed it was because he'd been accepted into Columbia University, however, he never replied to any of our texts so I can't be completely sure. He was the first person we lost from our original family of six.

Erwin was located on the banks of the Nolichucky River, which was a hub for tubers, kayakers, rafters, and fly fishermen. It also turned out to be a good location for an excuse to have another zero day, because I couldn't get enough of swimming in that river! The stretch of river that we camped on was more than a hundred feet across with a fairly strong current that could sweep you away in seconds if you weren't careful. The section of the river to the east of where the trail crossed over a bridge, turned out to be a fantastic hangout/camp spot. It was hotter than two goats in a pepper patch, and the river offered some much needed relief from the sweltering heat.

At the very center of this section of river was a large rock protruding from the rapids that I very much wanted to reach. Since embarking on this adventure, I'd tried to take full advantage of every moment with spontaneity. Swimming in a fast flowing river like this was a first for me. I examined the course I'd have to take in order to reach the rock without being swept past it, or into it. There was quite a large "eddy" behind the rock that I could use to my advantage. An eddy is an area of calm water that is protected from the current by the protruding bulk of a rock, or any other large object in the water. The current would be almost non-existent for some distance beyond the rock, until it got so far away that the split currents joined back up and resumed normally. I concluded that I needed to start at a point parallel to the rock and swim diagonally towards it. I needed to cross the current and reach the eddy before it pushed me too far and washed me away to who knows where... downtown Erwin I suppose.

I waded out as far as I could without the current sweeping me off my feet; which ended up being about knee deep. When I could walk no further, I crouched down and dove out as far as I could into the current and began "freestyling" as hard as I could. Within seconds I was a hundred feet down from the rock, but still within the farthest reaches of the eddy. The current wasn't completely dead in this spot, but weak enough that I could stand in the belly deep water and walk back towards the rock. When I reached the rock, I climbed up to the cheers of my fellow hikers back on shore.

After several minutes of enjoying my victory and relaxing in the sun, I decided it was time to go back. Against my better judgment, and to the jeers and calls of my peers, I did a front flip off the rock and back into the eddy. Honestly it was more of a back flop because most of my back hit the surface when I landed.

It hadn't occurred to me at the time, but getting back was going to be a lot harder than the swim going over. When swimming back, the eddy had been there to save me from the momentum of the current. On the swim back I had nothing to slow the push of the water. As I swam across, I was soon in water that was too shallow for swimming. I tried planting my hands and feet onto the rocky bottom in an attempt to stop my downriver momentum, but it didn't work even a little bit. The current just rolled me over and over, pushing me along the smooth rocks in the shallow water. It wasn't until I turned my entire body to face completely up river and jammed my feet down that I was finally able to stop myself from being swept away. Unfortunately, this technique also wrenched my toes in the rocks and ripped one of my toenails halfway off. Despite this little hiccup, the pain was outweighed by the feeling of victory and relief at knowing I was still alive.

After this initial crossing to the rock, myself and other hikers would make multiple trips to and from this rocky island oasis. As a matter of fact, the rock ended up becoming a hot spot to lie on and sunbathe. The eddy also provided one of the only calm areas of water that was actually deep enough for swimming. Unfortunately, quite a few toenails were lost when crossing back over to shore; it was an imperfect system.

Over the next two days, DSOH, Coma, War Story, Jack, Diane, and I camped out along the river with several other hikers. I was unsuccessful at fishing in the strong current even when trying to toss my lure into the calmer waters of different eddies. Whatever luck I didn't have in catching fish, I found in catching a brown water snake that I discovered in a shallow pool near my hammock. I chased it through the shallow water for over ten minutes before I was finally able to grab hold of it. After confirming my suspicions of it being a brown water snake, and not a water moccasin, I let it go.

It was a nice relaxing couple of days that I badly needed with my worsening health condition, but on our third day in Erwin we decided to hike out. The local hostel offered to "Slack Pack" us twenty miles. Slack Packing is a term that hikers use when they hike with an almost empty or "slack" backpack. It's much more comfortable due to the relieved stress off your back and leg joints. Not to mention you can walk at a much faster pace while doing more miles in a fraction of the time it would take with a full pack.

There are two different ways to slack-pack; one being slightly less stressful than the other, although this first one is the most common. Since I thru-hiked north, we will use north as the direction in this first example. Let's say I'm at point "A" on the trail and Point "B" is twenty miles ahead of me to the north. I would leave the bulk of my gear at point "A," then have someone with a vehicle drive me up to point "B." After getting dropped off at point "B," I would then hike south back to my gear at point "A." Once reunited with my gear at point "A," I would be driven back up to point "B" on either the same day or the next day before continuing north with a normal pack from there. That's the way that most people slack pack. It involves the most driving, but the least amount of time constraint. This is because there's usually no deadline for you to hike back to your gear that's normally stored at a hostel or some other guarded establishment.

The second way to slack pack is the more stressful way. You start at point "A" while someone drives your gear north to point "B." Point "B" is usually a spot where some form of road crosses the trail. Sometimes it can be another town, but most towns aren't close enough to each other to be reached in a single day, even if you slack pack. Once you've determined point "B," you are then told that you have to be there by a certain time in order to rendezvous with your driver and collect your gear. If you're not on time to point "B," then one of three things can happen... One: Your gear gets left on the side of the road awaiting your arrival and hopefully no one takes it, depending on how busy the road is and where your gear gets left. Two: your driver waits for you to get there even though you're late and they're pretty pissed off/annoyed when you do finally arrive. Three: Your driver steals your gear when you don't show up. I've never heard of a driver stealing gear, but it's certainly plausible depending on whose slack packing you. In most cases your driver will wait for you to arrive, or there will be some sort of instruction/back-up plan to where the gear will be stashed in the event that you're late.

When we decided to slack pack, we went with the second option. We wanted to minimize the headache of extra driving and also didn't want to get stuck in Erwin for a third night. So we left our packs at the Hostel at 7 am and were given instructions that they would be dropped off at a road crossing twenty miles north. The driver said if the first person wasn't there by 6 pm, that they would be leaving the packs in the woods near the road but out of sight. We officially had eleven hours to walk twenty miles and recover our gear.

It seemed like an easy task at the time, but ended up turning into a terrible state of affairs. All I took with me for the twenty-mile day was my two liter Gatorade bottle, my filtering bladder, my water filter, my cell phone, my money, and a few snacks in my pockets. I'd eaten a large pizza and calzone all to myself the night before, so my plan was to coast off the extra calories stored in my body. I was going super light with everything besides my

Gatorade bottle fitting easily into my pockets. Unfortunately, this ended up being a very bad idea.

The morning of the twenty-mile slack pack, I woke up feeling nauseas with an almost constant hacking cough. I managed the first nine miles fairly quickly and without too much trouble by 11 am. Then the entire day fell apart on me. As noon approached, the temperature rose into the 90's and water became very scarce. I was completely out before long, with nowhere to refill for nearly four miles.

Shortly after noon, Katana quit on me and refused to walk anymore. I wasn't even a little bit upset. I knew it was burning hot and neither of us had water. I picked her up and set her on my shoulders. We moved at a snail's pace for the next four miles while taking lots of five and ten minute breaks. Believe it or not, everyone else was actually still behind us. They'd stopped at an earlier road crossing to wait on some promised trail magic. A local trail angel had promised a keg of beer to be delivered to that road crossing at 2 pm. Despite our time crunch, everyone decided to wait on it. I had no interest in beer that day due to my nausea and coughing, so the duty of reaching the packs first and watching over them automatically fell to me. The only problem was that I felt like crap and my pace had slowed to a crawl. I continued feeling worse as the day went on, putting myself in danger of missing the 6 pm deadline.

At close to 3 pm I finally made it the nearly four miles to a water source and collapsed after drinking almost three liters. Katana probably drank a half liter. I was exhausted with a headache and still hacking up yellowish green phlegm. I laid down in some weeds near the small spring at the base of Unaka Mountain and passed out with my head on my pack while the flies and mosquitoes buzzed around me like some kind of corpse.

I later found out that the spot where I took that nap near the spring was where a group of hikers had been held at gun point back in 2012. The area was called Beauty Spot Gap and the hikers had been camped for the night when a man drove up a remote dirt road and claimed to be a game warden. He held them at gun point and searched them all for money and other valuables. The hikers immediately knew he wasn't a game warden; simply a regular guy strung out on drugs or alcohol. When the man let his guard down and turned his back, one of the hikers leveled him with a punch to the side of the head and wrestled the gun away. They hog tied him with Para cord and called the cops. It was a happy ending to a potentially deadly situation.

When I finally awoke from my nap amongst the weeds it was 4:30 pm. I was alone, with no one else around as I nearly panicked. I still had almost eight miles to go with only an hour and a half until the deadline. People were counting on me to get to those packs, if anything happened to them, I would be held responsible.

I felt worse when I awoke than when I'd fallen asleep, but there was no time to waste. I needed to start making good time as I began tackling the steep Unaka Mountain. Katana wouldn't walk, so I was forced to carry her up and over the more than one-thousand-foot climb. I was utterly miserable. On any other day with my backpack, I would've stopped miles ago and called it a day due to my misery and exhaustion. On this day, without my pack, I didn't even have the option to stop if I wanted to. I had nothing to camp with because all my gear was at the road.

When I finally reached the top of Unaka Mountain, I was taken aback by an incredibly beautiful pine grove. This was one more thing to be upset about at the time, because I desperately wanted to stop and camp there. I dragged on through the pine forest carrying Katana while hoping that I wouldn't keel over. The deadline of 6 pm came and went as I still had over three miles to go. I hoped beyond hope that all of our packs and gear would still be there.

Shortly after 7:30 pm, as dusk was approaching, I finally rolled into Iron Gap and reached the road; our packs were nowhere to be seen. My heart sank as I began searching frantically along the road to see if they were hidden somewhere, but still I couldn't find them. It wasn't until I came up over the side of an embankment near the road that I found Diane, as well as all of our packs, safe and sound in a reasonable camp spot with a fire already going. The relief I felt at that moment was indescribable.

Diane had also decided to forgo waiting on the beer keg and had left the road sometime after me. She stumbled across my lifeless, sleeping body and passed by not wanting to wake me. This was very considerate of her, however I wish I would've known, because it would've saved me a lot of panic and feelings of guilt when I realized I wasn't going to make the deadline. Luckily, in the end it didn't matter and everything worked out fine. I learned my lesson about slack packing that day, and right then and there, I made the executive decision to NEVER slack pack again. I would never let myself be on someone else's schedule while on this adventure.

Some people slack pack every chance they get, while some even slack pack more of the trail than they hike with a full pack. That's just not my cup of tea. I went out there to live on a whim and have the freedom to stop whenever I got tired, or whenever I reached a place that was so beautiful that I couldn't possibly pass it up. You don't have that freedom when slack packing. You have a set destination, as well as a set amount of miles that you have to complete on someone else's schedule. It has its place when you need to be somewhere by a certain time, or if your joints are killing you, but when you do it just to do it, as often as you can, I wouldn't even call slack packing "hiking." In my own personal opinion, it's just "slacking."

Each day my sickness grew worse. I was hacking so much that it was giving me headaches. On top of that, my rib cage and chest felt bruised and sore. My lymph nodes and throat were so swollen and tender that it hurt to talk or even take deep breaths. I lost my appetite and even when I could eat something, I didn't want to because swallowing food felt like swallowing broken glass. If you'd asked me at the time, I would've told you that I was surely dying. The whole predicament was a vicious cycle. As if I didn't feel bad enough from my symptoms, the lack of food was making me even weaker. The bitter irony was that I needed rest, but the only way I could get it was to continue punishing myself by walking until I reached the next town. Only then would I be able to relax away from the elements and seek medical attention.

Katana seemed to notice and sympathize with my severely weakened state and began to cooperate more. This was a life saver because I honestly didn't know if I could've carried her when I could barely carry myself. As I would soon find out, when circumstance dictated, I could do pretty much anything...whether I wanted to or not.

May 10th was my 42nd day on the trail, as well as another day that I thought might be the death of me. I was still in the clutches of whatever evil was attacking my respiratory system when I had no choice but to tackle Roan Mountain. Roan was more than a two-thousand-foot climb that I thought might put the nail in my coffin.

Roan Mountain itself is actually quite famous in more ways than one. Firstly, it is the location of the highest shelter on the entire trail at 6,194 feet. Secondly, it's famous for its location of being situated smack dab in the middle of overlapping "ley lines." Ley lines are an invisible grid of energy that encompasses the earth. The significance of the power they are said to possess is really more theory than hard fact, but here is what that theory is based on. People believe this grid of ley lines that encompasses the earth connects important and sacred sites such as Stonehenge, the Great Pyramids, the Great Wall of China, and many other monoliths, megaliths, and natural wonders.

The curious thing is that if you plot these sites on a map, many of them can be connected by straight gridlines. Where the lines intersect is where these structures and natural wonders can be found. They are believed to be areas of high energy. What kind of energy? I personally cannot say. As I mentioned, Roan Mountain lays smack in the middle of two of these overlapping ley lines, and as a result, many people make spiritual type journeys to the summit. The summit itself is not hard to reach, because there is in fact a nice paved road that goes straight up to the top. On this day however, I wouldn't be using or even seeing the road, except for crossing it once at the base of the mountain as I made my way up.

The ascent of Roan Mountain began quite gradually, and in my head I was excited to be climbing a mountain that was famed for its "energy." Part of me wanted to feel like maybe my body would draw from this energy and feel better as a result. Unfortunately, this was not to be the case. Although there was plenty of energy to be found around this mountain, it was not the spiritual kind. At least not today, and not the kind I was looking for.

The rain began about two miles into the climb while I still had another two miles to reach the summit. The rain came down harder and harder as I climbed higher and higher. Heavy fog rolled in as the trail began to swell with puddles and mud. Not long after the fog, deafening crashes of thunder began to sound all around me. The gradual climb disappeared and turned into treacherously steep rocks. Each step was onto another rock that was three to four times higher than your average staircase step. As I climbed still higher, the temperature dropped and the wind increased as the trees got smaller. I developed a headache that soon turned to nausea. The steps didn't seem to end as I continued my ascent. Katana was soaking wet and shaking, but still she kept on without demanding to be picked up.

I got so dizzy that I collapsed a half dozen times on the rocks, with my head spinning, and almost unable to stand. I had never felt my own mortality so strongly until this day. If I hadn't already been sick, I would've said this mountain was trying to kill me with its evil "ley line" dark energy. I ran into DSOH huddling under a pine tree while trying to put more layers on in an attempt to fight the cold and wind. I stopped briefly to inform him that we were both probably going to die, before continuing my stumble up the mountain.

I felt as if I were in a dream bordering on a nightmare. Here I was in one of the more "high energy" places of the world, amidst an epic lightning and rain storm nearly 6,000 feet above the earth with my brain swimming inside my skull. I don't really know how to put the feeling into words, but it didn't feel real. It felt like too many things were happening at one time for me to focus on, with all of it made more eerie by the knowledge of superstitions surrounding the mountain. The side effects of my illness were feeding my paranoid brain, while my paranoid brain fed the side effects. It was a downward spiral.

When I finally reached the summit, I still had another half mile to reach the shelter. It was an easy half mile over relatively flat but rocky ground, and as soon as I got there, I clambered inside and collapsed. I stripped off all my wet clothes and put on dry ones, then plopped down in a corner and huddled there. I fed and watered Katana and tried to eat an Alfredo Pasta Side. I got half of it down before I couldn't take another bite. DSOH joined me and also ate a meal. We hunkered down for nearly two hours as the storm raged on outside. I was freezing, hacking, and wanted nothing more than to get down from the top of that mountain. As sick as I felt, and as much as I wanted/needed rest, I didn't want to be up there. I wanted to be down and off that mountain at all costs. I don't really have an explanation for why, but everything inside me wanted to NOT be on that mountain.

Then, even more suddenly than it started, the storm stopped. I walked out into the meadow that is the summit of Roan Mountain and looked up. Blue skies as far as I could see. "This place is weird," I thought to myself. I wasn't wasting another moment on the top of that mountain, and made up my mind to make a run for it. That meant descending Roan and completing another five miles to the next shelter where the next water source would be. DSOH assured me that he would catch up later as I took off.

The trail down the north-facing side of Roan was a mall walk compared to the south side. I made great time and was thankful there wasn't a repeat of the rocky climb I'd endured on the way up. When I reached the bottom of Roan, I began the gradual climb across Round Bald and Jane Bald. By the time I'd reached Jane Bald, the sky had darkened with storm clouds once again. The storm clouds mixed with the setting sun made for another fantastic sight. I lay down in the grass of Jane Bald and watched the clouds wash over me. I was half taking a break and half trying to duck the strong winds that were driving these new clouds across the landscape.

I started moving again with Katana leading the way as rain began to fall once more. It started off as a drizzle before turning into a hard downpour. Shortly after the heavy downpour had begun, the wind shut off, leaving the clouds hanging stagnantly above me, with the rain falling straight down. The sound of falling rain without the background noise of wind rushing past my ears or rustling the trees, was a peaceful one.

I reached the top of Grassy Ridge Bald just as darkness set in. Darkness has a habit of sneaking up on you in a storm. This is especially true when the clouds block out the ambient light that is usually left over when the sun sinks below the horizon. At the top of Grassy Ridge Bald, I still had two miles of downhill to reach my goal of Stan Murray Shelter.

I pulled off my pack and began digging around for my headlamp as the rain fell heavily around me. I kept everything in my pack meticulously organized so that I could find things easily, even in the dark. My headlamp was one of those things that stayed in a small pocket all by itself in order to make it even easier to find. On this day, it wasn't where it should've been. I couldn't find it and suddenly remembered that I'd packed it inside my hammock earlier that morning while breaking camp. I wasn't about to unpack and unfurl my hammock in this rainy mess and get my shelter soaking wet, so I made the decision to chance the darkness with my unaided eyes.

As fast as I dared, I made my way down the soaked and muddy trail while straining to see the white blazes painted on the trees. The water and mud was so heavy on the ground that I could no longer make out the trail beneath my feet. Everything on the ground looked the same, as there was no longer a definitive path. All I could do was squint through the curtain of rain in an attempt to keep track of the blazes.

More than once I hit an extra slippery patch of mud that would send me surfing down the trail on the soles of my shoes. Tripping over rocks and sticks, I tried to guess my speed and estimate how long it would take me to reach the shelter. It finally materialized out of the rain and darkness nearly thirty minutes after my estimated arrival time. I'd begun to think that I might have passed it in my haste and nearly total blindness. Jack and Diane were there when I arrived and the glowing headlamp of DSOH showed up nearly forty minutes later.

We were pleased to have the place to ourselves and not have to struggle for space within the shelter. It was a hell of a day getting up and over Roan Mountain and the rain continued for most of the night. I hung my hammock inside the shelter before falling into a troubled sleep of hacking coughs and a burning throat.

The next morning, I awoke feeling weaker and worse than ever. Fortunately, this would be the last day that I felt this bad. I couldn't eat anything, but forced myself to chew up a few Mini Snicker Bars. I only had to make it ten miles to reach a road that would take me into the town of Roan Mountain, TN. I didn't make it three miles before I collapsed on a large rock while going up Big Yellow Mountain. My head was spinning and I barely had the strength to keep up a steady walk.

I laid there on the rock in the sun with Katana for almost two hours while taking naps off and on. DSOH stuck with me the entire time. He'd been feeling under the weather before I had, except his symptoms hadn't progressed or gotten as bad as mine. We finally pushed on over the lightly wooded grassy hills, and at the clearing of Little Hump Mountain we had somewhat of a surprise.

Two hunting dogs emerged from the woods with radio tracking collars around their necks. The Hounds looked emaciated and one was covered in what smelled and looked like human feces. The horrifying part was that the dog covered in feces seemed to want the most attention out of the two. It kept trying to get close and rub up against us. If it wasn't for the fresh shit that covered most of its neck and shoulders, I would've been happy to give this pup some attention. Since it was a walking ball of sewage and fur, I tried to keep it at bay with my walking staff.

Katana was freaking out, so I was forced to pick her up and carry her so she wouldn't try to attack them. Hunting dogs such as these were nothing to be trifled with. They're a rough bunch that normally lead hard and violent lives of scrapping with one another, as well as wild animals. Katana wouldn't have stood a chance against either of them. This was the last thing I needed in my present state of health, but I had no choice. Thankfully the two hounds seemed to be oblivious to Katana's presence and didn't try to lunge at her. They fell into line behind us and ended up being our personal little shadows for over six miles as we tackled a 1,400-foot climb across Big Hump Mountain, then down almost 3,000 feet to the road leading into the Town of Roan Mountain.

I was very familiar with these types of hunting dogs and tracking collars. They were fairly common in the panhandle of Florida where I live. These dogs were used in big packs to track and run down bear, deer, wild hogs, and other game. The collars weren't so much a way to ensure the recovery of the dog as it was to ensure they found whatever it was the dog had run down. The dogs were usually not companions to the hunters, just tools they used to hunt game. Individually, the dogs were nearly worthless to them. Back home it was common to see hounds such as these lying dead or wandering the sides of rural roads and highways with their radio collars still on. With their sad state of health, I could tell these hounds weren't the kind being lovingly looked after. They had probably just gotten lost on a hunt.

All in all, it took us nearly thirteen hours to complete the ten miles in our state of sick-weakened, dog-toting nausea. Upon reaching the road, there was an older man waiting in a beat up old pick-up truck. "Ye found muh dogs," he said as we walked up. "They found us," I replied. "They been lost fer two days and I been tracken em' on my computer. I couldn't get to em', but when I saw em' makin their way down that stretch-of-trail, I figgered they was followin some hikers and I came to cut em' off at the road." "One of them has shit all over it," I informed him. "I'm glad we could help out in getting them home safely," DSOH added. The man thanked us and threw them in the big steel cage that took up most of the back bed of his pickup truck. We parted ways and that was that. At least the man had cared enough to pick them up, or maybe it was just because they were in a convenient location. Obviously he'd been watching them for a couple days on his computer, but the man could have easily hiked out there and found them sooner himself instead of waiting at the road.

DSOH and I ended up calling a shuttle to a local bed and breakfast in town as we both settled in for some rest and relaxation. I was in bad need of some TLC, as it'd been a VERY rough couple of weeks in the North Carolina and Tennessee mountains.

I tried to improve my appearance by shaving my neck to make my budding beard look a little bit neater. Although it still wasn't very long, it was the longest I'd ever had it. For the first time in a long time, I took a really good look at myself in the mirror. I looked like shit. A complete stranger was looking back at me. I couldn't recognize who this person staring back was, and it really troubled me. I didn't look well at all. Even if I hadn't been sick, I still wouldn't have looked well. I think it was the fact that I didn't look anything like the person I did when I began the trail. I felt like I was seeing myself for the first time in over forty days, and I tried not to think about how much my appearance bothered me.

The next day I scheduled an emergency appointment at a local walk-in clinic. I also took the opportunity to run some errands around town while I was at it. Roan Mountain was an incredibly small, but beautiful, little town. There really wasn't much to it, but it had everything necessary to be self-contained. Two gas stations, a small super market, one local eatery called Bob's Dairyland, one Subway, a pharmacy, an emergency clinic, a barber shop, a small auction house, and a few other small businesses from what I could see.

DSOH and I made our way to Bob's Dairyland for lunch, and it was at this fine establishment that I enjoyed the best burger I've ever had in my life. It was called the "Holy Cow Burger," and I only hope that I remembered all of the things that were stacked on this holy burger of divine cows. It was made with three beef patties, while each patty had bacon and I believe two or three different types of cheese between them. It also had onions, tomatoes, lettuce, fried onion rings, and some kind of manwich chili that was sandwiched in between the bottom patty and the bread as well. It was quite the spectacle to behold. Too large to be eaten in bites, you had to attack this thing systematically by taking it apart. In later days, I would always tell south bound hikers not to miss out on the Holy Cow Burger at Bob's Dairyland in Roan Mountain, Tennessee.

After the big burger, DSOH walked back to the B&B while I walked back to the Clinic. The doctor diagnosed me with a severe upper respiratory infection that was in danger of developing into pneumonia. He gave me Augmentin to fight the infection and a bottle of liquid codeine to help with the sore throat pain, as well as help me sleep at night. As I walked out of his office, his parting advice to me was, "Good luck and don't be operating any vehicles or walking near any cliffs after taking that codeine! Only take it at night!" To which I replied, "Roger that Doc!"

By the time we left the town of Roan Mountain, I was already feeling 75% better. With my current resupply, I had enough food to get me through to the next planned stop of Damascus, over seventy miles away. This was a significant location because Damascus was the first town in Virginia. For some reason Virginia felt like a milestone in itself, and I was very excited to be getting so close.

That first night out of Roan it rained hard. Rain seemed to be the name of the game through that stretch, as it seemed to visit us at least once a day. That night however, the rain didn't bother me. Armed with my liquid codeine, I slept like the dead.

The next day DSOH and I put in almost nineteen miles. It seemed the closer I got to Virginia, the more Rhododendrons I saw. They were everywhere throughout that section and they were just beginning to bloom. The Rhododendron thickets grew so abundantly that the trail passed through tunnels of them for miles. This is why the section of trail from North Carolina all the way through Virginia was nicknamed the "Green Tunnel." I couldn't get enough of walking through the tunnels of Rhododendrons; they gave me the sensation of entering some sort of secret garden.

Towards the end of our long day we descended what looked like a vertical rockslide into Laurel Falls. This was the biggest waterfall that I'd seen since leaving Amicalola Falls in northern Georgia. It was huge as well as breathtakingly beautiful, and if it wasn't for the fact that daylight was nearly gone, I would've certainly gone for a swim in its dark pools.

We made our way along the trail as it turned into a thin rocky ledge that skirted the edge of the river and the side of a cliff. With the river on our left and a sheer cliff wall on our right, the ledge felt like something out of an Indiana Jones movie. We finally stopped for the day at the base of a mountain named Pond Flats, where we settled in for another night of torrential rain and thunderous lightning.

The next day marked the beginning of a three-day slog in complete solitude for me. DSOH left me at the base of Pond Flats Mountain to go into the town of Hampton in order to catch a ride to an event happening in Damascus that he didn't want to miss. He invited me to come with him, but I stood firm on my resolution to not drive anywhere. I promised him that I would see him there before 8 pm on the 17th of May, and that I would be walking into Damascus on my own two feet. We parted ways late that morning in the drizzling rain as I made my way up Pond Flats.

Without fail, as the morning progressed and I climbed higher and higher, the rain intensified and lightning crashed all around. Katana was un-phased. She was hardening into a rock solid trail dog and finally coming into her own. I was also coming to terms with constantly being wet. It seemed like as soon as I would get my shoes dry from a previous downpour, it would rain again, putting me right back where I started. My soggy feet couldn't catch a break.

As I climbed this volcano of a mountain in the raging storm, squishing along in my wet shoes, I felt this inner peace and joy wash over me. I just felt really good. I was in a happy state of mind as my body was feeling much better since starting the antibiotics. I broke into song, and not just any song, but songs that I actually knew the words to. I kept singing the same two over and over again, trying to drown out the crashes of thunder and rain all around me. I sang "Enjoy the Silence," by Depeche Mode, and "Mad World," by Gary Jewels-probably ten times each. How those songs fit into the situation, I'm not sure, but they were stuck in my head for the rest of the day.

As I finished my climb over Pond Flats, I reached Watauga Lake at the bottom of the north side. Had it been a beautiful day, I could've easily seen myself staying a day or two at this "would be" gorgeous location. Unfortunately, with all the recent rain, the lake was completely flooded and the sandy beach that usually resided there was completely submerged. I pushed on as temperatures quickly dropped and the afternoon grew late. With the combination of freezing cold and being soaked to the bone, I lost my momentum and called it a day at Watauga Lake shelter, after less than eight miles.

I warmed myself up with a bowl of instant mashed potatoes mixed with bacon bits and gave Katana a good portion of what was left at the bottom. We were the only souls there, so I strung my hammock across the inside of the shelter. I decided I would make up for this short day with a longer one the next day. I still had over forty miles to reach Damascus and only two days to get there by the time I said I would.

On day two of my solitary sprint to Damascus, I got a late start around 9:30 am. It was a gorgeous day with a deep blue sky awash with fluffy white clouds, and even though the air was cold, the sun was strong enough to keep me from needing a jacket.

The worst part of waking up in the morning after spending the previous day walking in the rain, is putting your wet clothes on all over again. You've just spent a nice, warm, dry night in your shelter, but now you have to put your freezing wet clothes back on. Why? Because there's no way they're going to dry if they're stuffed inside your pack, and there's no point in getting clean, dry clothes all sweaty or wet if it rains again. So you're forced to put your freezing garments back on in attempt to get them dry.

I must say that the worst part of this routine is putting on your wet socks and shoes. There is nothing worse and more disheartening than slipping your warm, dry feet into a dirty, freezing, soaking wet sock, then shoving them into an equally wet and freezing shoe. Like removing a band aid, the best way to do it is fast. Get it over with and get moving in order to kick start the drying process.

I walked several miles along the perimeter of Watauga Lake thoroughly enjoying myself and taking in the gorgeous lake views. All was well and I was without a care in the world until I smelled the stench of death. I began to look around in an effort to find the source. I knew it was big because it filled such a huge area of air. My eyes finally fell upon a murder of crows that were crowding and feeding on something down in the large rocks by the shore of the lake. Try as I might, I couldn't see what it was they were feeding on between the rocks. I ended up choosing not to investigate and instead continued on. I wish I had, because it later bothered me not knowing the source of that foul stench. I only hoped it wasn't a human body laying down there.

I continued on for a while longer before arriving at the large Watauga Lake Dam. It's incredibly eerie and unnerving to come across large manmade structures devoid of any people. You knew there were hundreds of people here at one time to help construct it, but now they were gone. The entire area looked abandoned, as there was nothing more than a giant dam in the middle of nowhere with not a single soul in sight besides myself and my dog. I once again felt small and alone.

The view from the dam across the lake was mesmerizing. Puffy clouds hung low in the sky as I took advantage of the gorgeous foreground and made my way onto a large, strategically placed rock that was just to the side of the dam. From atop that rock I took the greatest number two of my young life. You usually have to squat, hover, or hang onto a tree to do business out there, but every now and then you can find a log or a rock that's just right to sit on while you pinch one off. I couldn't have asked for a better view, while sitting down going number two. I even took a picture of the landscape to commemorate the moment.

As I walked along enjoying the chirping of the birds and other natural sounds, they were suddenly interrupted by the sound of distant thunder. I tried to look as far beyond the trees at the distant sky as I could manage. I could see a blanket of darkness coming my way. "Not again!" I thought. I couldn't catch a break! I kept moving knowing that I still had a lot of distance to make up. Strangely, I hadn't seen a soul on the trail since parting ways with DSOH.

Although I came out on the trail for solitude and getting back to nature, I saw people almost every day out there. Be it other thru-hikers, section hikers, day hikers, or people just doing different things along the trail, there was always someone. To not see anyone at all in the middle of spring seemed downright strange. Apparently everyone was at the "Trail Days" event in Damascus and not on the trail.

Very soon the dark clouds were upon me once again. The rain hadn't begun yet, but I was ready for it at any moment as the darkness thickened around me. "Damn it, and my shoes were almost dry!" A drop hit me...then another... and another. The drops started bouncing off me and landing on the ground. It was about the time that the fourth drop bounced to the ground that I realized they weren't drops at all, but small balls of hail. As long as they stayed small and continued to bounce off me without soaking my shoes, it could hail all day for all I cared. Getting pelted with hail was better than getting soaked.

It began to fall heavier and heavier until the ground was covered in small chunks of ice. "This isn't too bad," I thought. The balls of ice were starting to build up in Katana's fur and she kept looking back at me as if to say, "What is this stuff?" The hail fell steadily for fifteen minutes before it turned into a mixture of hail and sleeting rain. My luck had run out, but it's like we always said out there, "No rain - No Maine!"

I was soaked again in a matter of minutes as it continued to come down. I walked in that mess for close to forty minutes before I finally broke down from the freezing temperatures and wind. Once again my hands had gotten so cold that I couldn't unbuckle the straps on my pack. I wrestled with them for far longer than it should've taken before I finally freed myself from my backpack prison.

It took me nearly fifteen minutes with my frozen hands to set up my rain fly. Once the fly was set up, I crawled underneath with Katana and laid there trying to warm my hands enough to get the rest of my hammock hung. As I laid there against my soaking pack, with Katana huddled against me, I couldn't help but feel incredibly down trodden and beaten. The last several days had been wet and miserable. Walking in wet shoes day after day was destroying my feet, while the calluses that I'd suffered and worked so hard to build, were soggy and peeling. I tried to find some humor or anything positive in the situation in order to pick myself up. I couldn't find anything. The only thing I could think of that was positive, was that it would make a good story somewhere down the road once I'd overcome it. Misery only added to the cumulative experience of the adventure that would ultimately sculpt me into a stronger, more resilient human being.

I believe the ability to view the agony and discomfort of a miserable and painful situation as a character building and physically strengthening experience. It is what separates the mentally tough from the mentally not so tough. The ability to recognize that in the long run, one's suffering can be nothing but beneficial in the future when confronted with similar situations. Where many might crumble and quit, others see the bigger picture, persevere, and ultimately become stronger. That's not to say that there is anything wrong with those who do quit. It's perfectly natural not to want to voluntarily subject yourself to pain and suffering. However, even though some don't quit, that doesn't mean they don't still think about it. We all have our limits for when we'll say - "NO MORE!" I simply hadn't reached mine yet, and neither had all the other people that still remained on the trail.

In the end, the hail, sleet, and rain forced me to quit... for the day. After hiding under my rain fly for a good twenty minutes, I caved and called it a day in the middle of the afternoon. I couldn't take any more rain and freezing cold. I finally managed to get my hammock hung and stripped down out of my wet clothes. I climbed into my warm nest, pulled the little princess in out of the cold, took a swig of codeine and drifted off to Lala-Land. Before I fell asleep, I couldn't help but realize that I hadn't done nearly enough miles that day, and that I was left with over thirty to complete the next day if I wanted to make the deadline I'd given myself. This truly was going to be a sprint to Damascus.

I got up early and ready to rock on the third day of my Damascus sprint. This was going to be a day for the books! Little did I know, it was going to be a day for the books in more ways than one. I was completely out of food besides some M&M's that I still had left over. That was all I had to power this huge day - two handfuls of M&M's.

Once again, I climbed out of my cocoon and put on my freezing wet clothes and shoes from the day before. There was a light mist hanging throughout the forest and the air was heavy with moisture. Although it wasn't raining, it might as well have been for all of the drops of water falling from the trees. I hit the trail moving fairly quickly with Katana chomping at the bit ahead of me, pulling against her leash.

We were less than three miles into the morning, making our way through an exceptionally long Rhododendron tunnel, when we emerged from the other side to a loud shuffling noise in the leaf litter to our right. I turned my head towards the source of the commotion to see a small bear cub no more than fifteen feet away scamper to the base of a small tree and begin scrambling up. My first thought upon seeing the cub was... "SHIT! ...where's mom?" All of a sudden I heard a crashing sound on my left! I spun around just in time to see a second cub charge across the trail directly in front of me and scramble up the same tree as its sibling. My second thought was... "OH SHIT!! WHERE'S MOM?!" This was quickly turning into one of the nightmare situations that you read about preceding every bear or animal attack. Getting between a mother and her offspring!

I stood frozen in place holding Katana back. She was standing rigid, in hyper alert mode, watching the cubs in the tree, but not making a sound. I scanned the forest frantically looking for any sign of the mother. At the time of the cub encounter I'd felt like I was going to be tackled by a mother bear at any moment. My adrenaline was surging as I was sure this was about to end in blood. After several seconds that felt like an eternity, the mother finally made her presence known.

A head popped up from behind a stack of boulders about fifty feet past the cubs and looked lazily, if not annoyed, in my direction. "Ohhhh, there's MOM!" Now that I knew where she was, I slowly backed away into the Rhododendron tunnel again. Katana came right along with me. As I backed away, the cubs scrambled back down the tree and ran to their mother. Almost immediately she got up and began walking slowly down the embankment to the left before disappearing into the forest below. "WOW!" I declared out loud, and gave a long whistle.

That had been an incredibly intense moment. For the next two hours I was riding high on adrenaline and thinking about all the scenarios in which it could have turned out differently. All in all, I counted myself extremely lucky. I'd been hoping for a bear encounter with no luck for over a month and a half, and when it finally happened, I ended up getting much more than I bargained for. My bear tally went from zero to three in just one morning. If I didn't see another bear for the rest of the journey, that would've been fine by me. The trail however had other plans, as it was going to throw quite a few more bears in my direction before I reached my final destination.

I pushed on at a blistering pace, my feet screaming the entire way. I was bound and determined to make my deadline, and the adrenaline rush from the bear had done nothing but help me. The terrain was moderate and the miles ticked by. It was on this day that I crossed my first of many cow pastures of the journey. Over the decades, farms had sprung up along the trail as land was bought and repurposed. The trail would either be re-routed or the land owners would allow it to pass through their property. This was the case for just about every cow pasture encountered. You were walking across private property and needed to respect it.

I'd never walked through a cow pasture up until this point in my life. Cows are very large creatures, and I will admit that being in a fenced in area with them was a little unnerving for me. Most of them were in fact cows, but there were several bulls with full sets of horns mixed in with them. The adults paid almost no attention to me, but the young calves were very curious. They were getting up and walking towards me from all over the pasture. This was making Katana nuts. She had never seen creatures this large before and it was causing her to run around in tight circles, jumping about and acting like a rabid animal. I couldn't get a handle on her. She looked like she was incredibly excited and wanted to play. During all the bedlam of her running around and me shouting at the calves to go away, she landed herself right in the middle of a huge cow patty. Did I really expect anything less? The answer is no. I now had a little dog with cow poo up to its little elbows.

We finished making it across the pasture without being trampled into submission by baby bovine and hopped over the fence stiles at the far end. The cow crisis had been averted as man and dog escaped back into the wild. The little princess got an icy bath at the next creek we came to, and the world felt right as rain once again.

As I trekked on as fast as my legs could carry me, I couldn't help thinking how awesome it was going to be to finally reach Virginia; I'd heard so many things. Out on the trail you were always running into people with second-hand, or even first-hand information about areas of the trail and terrain ahead of you. When you first begin hearing this info, you take it as gospel because you don't know any better. One thing that people always said about Virginia was that it was flat and easy.

Virginia accounts for nearly six hundred miles and a quarter of the entire trail. It's the longest state of the entire journey, and everyone you met that had hiked there before said it was a cake walk. After all the madness I'd hiked over and through, I wanted to believe this information so badly that I actually did. I convinced myself that Virginia was going to be all downhill (figuratively of course), and that once I was there, this hike was in the bag. Oh yes, the great plains of Virginia... I was ready for them!

I tried not to focus on the pain of my feet literally falling apart in my shoes. Instead I focused on how great it was going to be to see my friends again. This three-day solo sprint had really done a number on me physically and psychologically. I felt like the best medicine for it was going to be a new state and familiar faces. I was so absorbed in my own thoughts and moving so quickly that I almost missed the sign that read "Tennessee/Virginia State line"; "Damascus, VA 3 ½ miles." A feeling of joy swelled up inside of me as I snapped a picture of the sign.

"Woo Hoo! I'm a Virginian now!" If only I would've known that Virginia was going to chew me up and spit me out onto the rocks of Pennsylvania, I might not have been so excited.

CHAPTER 5: VIRGINIA

"Everything We Heard Was a Lie!"

I stood on the trail, just behind the tree line on top of a hill overlooking Damascus. I could hear live music playing in the park down below. The trail itself wound its way through the heart of Damascus, snaking through residential neighborhoods, parks, bridges, and downtown before paralleling Laurel Creek and fading back into the woods along the Virginia Creeper Trail. It was just after 7:30 pm, and I'd made it over thirty-three miles that day to arrive in Damascus before the deadline I'd given myself. I never had to carry Katana once, making this a new level of achievement for both of us. We'd broken the thirty-mile mark together, but as with most victories out on the trail, it wasn't without its consequences. My feet were mashed and mangled. I could feel the bottoms sticking and peeling off the soles of my shoes with each step. It wasn't going to be pretty when I finally took them off.

I made my way out of the tree line and towards the road that went straight through a quiet and pleasant looking residential area. No sooner had my feet hit the asphalt; I heard a voice call, "Are you a thru- hiker?" I looked over to see a woman and several other people standing on the large back deck of one of the houses. "Yeah, I'm just finishing a thirty-three-mile day," I called back, unable to hide the pride and excitement in my voice. "Want a burger?" the woman replied. I looked at her unsure of whether I'd heard correctly, "...please!" I replied after a pause of disbelief and surprise. "Come on up!" I went up and left Katana tethered to my pack in their front yard.

They invited me inside and told me not to worry about taking off my shoes. After cleaning up in the bathroom, I came back out to find that they'd prepared a smorgasbord of goodies for me. Not only did this family give me a burger, but also a full plate of macaroni, potato salad, green salad, sausage, bread, beans, and a glass of locally brewed beer. "It just can't get any better than this!" I remember thinking.

You don't often find trusting and kindness like this in the world anymore. Strangers inviting strangers into their homes to have dinner with them is practically unheard of in this day and age. It felt amazing to be on the receiving end of such kindness, but somehow I knew that the feelings they got from providing the kindness was stronger than the gratitude I got from receiving it. It was on this day that I realized I wanted to experience that feeling as much and as often as I possibly could. I wanted to do good things for people I didn't know and watch the surprise and appreciation wash over their faces.

Before I even finished dinner, the woman set a plate full of peach cobbler, brownies, cookies, cupcakes, pudding, and cake in front of me. I thought I was supposed to pick one, but she informed me the entire plate was for me. "Have I died and gone to heaven?" I'd woken up starving that morning with over thirty miles between me and my next meal. It had been a long and hungry day, but the trail and the kind people who dwelt near it had provided once again.

Come to find out, while talking with the family on the back deck, I learned that the woman and her husband had thru-hiked the entire trail back in 1995. They told me it was an incredible journey I'd embarked on, and that it had changed their lives in more positive ways than they could possibly tell me. Hearing this was incredibly uplifting, and when we finally said our goodbyes and parted ways, I was floating on a cloud. The only thing keeping me rooted on this earth was all the food that was now in my belly.

I found DSOH, Coma, Jack & Diane, Viking, Lobster, Dancing Feather, Grizelle, Baguette, Bangarang, Da Fonz, Free Bird, and War Story on the outskirts of town camping behind a baseball field. I was so relieved to find them and call it a day, that words can't even describe my elation. When I told them about my epic feat, they coined the term "Mayor-thon" almost immediately. The only thing that surprised me was that this hadn't been thought of sooner because it just seemed so obvious. The play on words for my name never seemed to end.

A good portion of the bottoms of my feet peeled off with my socks when I finally took them off. The bottoms of my toes had developed soggy blisters that were now trying to slough off, while the pad of my foot just beneath my toes was in rough shape. The skin had completely separated from the base of my toes and was now creating an open pocket of skin that stretched all the way down to my mid foot. My feet looked like death and felt just as bad. After coming down from my adrenalin high of finishing such a big day, the pain in my feet was really beginning to set in. There was no way that I could hike out the next day. My feet needed some serious recovery time. Before climbing into my hammock and going comatose, I spent about half an hour with my feet propped up next to the fire in an attempt to dry them out some.

I took a zero in Damascus the next day and resigned myself to hobbling around, exploring the small town. At the "Blue Blaze Café" I partook in my first eating challenge of the adventure. It was a pancake eating challenge, and if there was one thing in this world that I was good at, it was eating pancakes and chicken wings. I knew I had to make an attempt on the record. The current champ that was pictured on the wall with an empty plate and victorious smile was a rail thin guy that had consumed nineteen of the almost plate sized pancakes. It always seems to be the skinny guys that held the eating records, the Kobayashi types.

I settled in for the long haul and placed my first order. DSOH sat next to me and offered his coaching skills. "If you listen to every word I say, you can do this Mayor." The pancakes came out in threes. I devoured the first plate no problem. The second plate was set in front of me minutes later. That wasn't fast enough. I put in my reorder before the waitress's hands had even released the flapjack platter. I put down the next three without even batting an eye. The third order came out just as I was finishing the last couple bites of the second order. "This was more like it." Three quarters of the way through my third plate and I could feel my breathing becoming stressed. "Focus!" DSOH said forcefully, "Don't think about the pain!" he added. I silently nodded and grunted through a mouthful of pancake.

Then there was a delay on plate number four. "Where is it?!" I thought. "I can't just sit here and let this food settle! I need to keep a constant flow of pancakes going into my body in order to be victorious!" I began to silently panic as I felt the food getting heavier in my belly with each passing moment.

Finally, the fourth plate arrived. I tore into those Johnnycakes like my life depended on it! As I neared the halfway point of the stack, my pace visibly slowed. "Start drinking water with every bite!" DSOH commanded. I complied, but the mixture of pancake, syrup, and tap water just wasn't doing it for me. It was in that moment that I realized I was but a mere amateur and not a pro. You might say that I'd bitten off more than I could chew.

I entered that pancake contest thinking that I'd already won. Halfway through my eleventh pancake, my jaw muscles turned to cement. My body was telling me "No more!" My brain had physically shut down all of my eating muscles in order to save me from myself. A pro could've overridden that shut-down; however, overconfidence does not a pro make...

At the end of it, all I could say is "Thank you brain!" If it hadn't been for the valiant, subconscious efforts of my brain that day, there surely would have been a hot cake explosion from somewhere in my amateur, competitive eating body. I finally conceded defeat maybe two bites into my twelfth pancake. I felt like I'd let everyone down, especially Coach DSOH. I really wanted to have a picture of us on that wall celebrating the victory together. Maybe next time...

The day after the eating contest I ran into Schweppes and Laser in downtown Damascus. It was the first time I'd seen Schweppes since rolling my ankle and saying goodbye on my fourth day, and the first time I'd seen Laser since the NOC. The two of them had been hiking together since the Smokies, and had spent quite a few zero days in Damascus relaxing. That was the only way I'd ever caught up to them.

Jack & Diane called it quits in Damascus, citing job commitments they had to get back to. We were all sad to see them go, but by this point in the game, we'd gotten used to seeing familiar faces leave the trail.

We set out from Damascus early that afternoon. It was me, DSOH, Laser, Coma, Schweppes, War Story, and the Princess. It was like a reunion from our first days on the trail when we all met at Gooch Mountain Shelter. It felt damn good to have us all together again. My feet were still killing me, as the skin on the front pad of each foot felt as if there was a large, smooth stone wedged underneath it. Every step I took sent an uncomfortable feeling of pressure into my feet and up to my brain. It was painfully distracting. We took a short day of less than six miles, and I was able to catch a trout while hand lining in a creek near the trail. That night it fell off my skewer and into the ashes as I cooked it... I ate it anyway.

Two days out of Damascus we stumbled upon a hauntingly gorgeous pine grove on the far side of Lost Mountain. There were plenty of pine groves along the trail but there was something remarkable and unique about this one. It was captivating and drew me in, we all felt it. This was one of those places you didn't pass up. Even though it was only mid-afternoon, we were all in consensus to stop and camp as we made our way to the center of the pine grove to scope things out. The forest floor was blanketed by years of pine needle accumulation, as well as dried pine branches that had fallen over time. You couldn't ask for a better spot; cool, dark, and protected, with plenty of fuel for a fire.

We cleared out an area, dug a shallow pit, and built a large fire ring out of stones we gathered nearby. Eagle Scout Laser set about making the fire while the rest of us gathered felled pines and collected logs to form benches, encircling the perimeter of the fire ring. When the work was done, we had created one of the best camp sites I'd seen on the trail up until this point. We dubbed it "The Fort." You couldn't see the campsite from the trail, but if you stood up, you could just barely see the tops of people's heads as they walked by.

Shortly after settling in, we noticed there was actually a large beehive a short distance away from our camp. We spent the rest of the afternoon and evening laying around the fire on the soft pine straw, talking about anything and everything. When the sun finally disappeared, the darkness within the grove was absolute. We fell asleep that night to the humming of thousands of bees overhead and the snap crackling of our dying fire.

May 21st was my 53rd day on the trail, as well as another pivotal and painful one. It was the day that I entered the Grayson Highlands; an area famous on the trail, as well as the United States for their wild ponies. Nobody owns them and no one takes care of them. They all live up there grazing and reproducing, with no natural predators, while droves of people visit the highlands every year to photograph and pet them. Due to all the visitors, the ponies can be overly friendly and nippy at times. They're quite accustomed to people and could almost be described as tame. However, the second you forgot they were wild; you could end up with a pony bite.

Something I will admit about myself is that I don't much care for large animals. Cows, horses, llamas, camels, or anything else big enough to step on me, trample me, or knock me over. This all stems from a childhood incident where a horse charged down a hill straight into me, knocking me clear off the ground and a good twenty to thirty feet further down the hill. Ever since then, large animals have always made me nervous. Ponies are very close to being in this large animal category; the only thing keeping them in the gray zone was the fact that I stood quite a bit taller than most of them.

As I made my way up the rock ridden trail and emerged onto the highlands, right away, I saw at least twenty ponies spread out over the terrain in front of me. They spotted me as soon as I spotted them, and almost immediately, no less than a half dozen ponies began to approach me. "Great," I thought.

I was going to be perfectly happy getting some pictures from a distance, but these rambunctious mini mustangs wanted to investigate me for food. I stood my ground and kept Katana's leash short. I had no idea how she would react and I was really worried about her getting kicked or stomped because her small frame wouldn't be able to handle it. One of the ponies that came up to investigate had a foal that was so young it still had part of its umbilical cord attached.

The foal, shakily and curiously walked right up to Katana without any fear. They stood there - nose to nose, looking at each other for the better part of ten seconds. It was the most adorable thing I'd ever seen in my life. I managed to get several pictures and even a video of the encounter. The mamma pony stepped in for a closer investigation of Katana. With the presence of the larger animal, Katana turned her attention to the mother. The mom stuck her muzzle under Katana's belly to smell her and gave a few abrupt nudges. Katana didn't know what to do! She just looked at me confused and slightly worried with her ears halfway pinned back and a look that said, "What are these creatures Dad?"

While Katana's attention was focused on the mother, the foal had taken it upon itself to examine Katana's butt. When the Foal's nose touched Katana's petite hind quarters she must have jumped five feet in the air! I almost died laughing. After the butt sniffing incident, Katana was frantically trying to keep all the ponies in front of her - within clear sight. She kept turning and spinning in an attempt to keep track of them all as they continued to hover.

I spent about an hour walking amongst the herd of ponies while taking pictures and petting the ones that allowed it. They were beginning to grow on me as I became more and more comfortable with them. I managed to escape without any bites or kicks and my faith in medium large animals was restored.

Other than the beauty of the wild ponies and gorgeous landscape, the Grayson Highlands were for the most part a rocky death trap. It was easy to see why these ponies were trapped up there. Any attempt at trying to get down from the highlands would surely result in the death of a pony through a broken leg or neck. Hell, it almost resulted in the death of me, as half the time you were boulder hopping or picking your way over the jagged rocks that covered the ground. It was on this rough terrain that I managed to catch up with my other companions. The irony of the day was that after making it through the worst of the rocks unscathed, I let my guard down and ended up having another accident on a relatively easy descent with relatively smooth ground.

I was descending a short but steep slope that had a small creek running through at the bottom. I was nearly halfway to the creek when I set my foot on a log in an attempt to steady myself as I stepped down. The log wasn't sturdy, and as I shifted my full weight to the foot that was planted on it, the log rolled ever so slightly, putting me off balance and causing my bad foot to slip onto the ground below. The toe of my shoe caught the ground first as I came over and down on top of it. My foot folded the wrong way beneath me while inverting at the same time. I heard and felt a pop, then a crack, before hitting the ground hard.

I've broken my ankle before and torn just about every ligament and tendon there is to tear in it, however the pain from this misstep was worse than any of the accidents before. I felt myself almost go into "pain shock" as I became light headed and then sick to my stomach. I have an enormous tolerance for pain, but this was pushing it. The worst part of the whole situation was that the creek at the bottom of this slope marked the five-hundred-mile mark of the trail heading north. "Happy five hundred miles to me!"

I sat there for several minutes while taking deep breaths and examining my ankle. DSOH, Schweppes, Laser, and Coma helped me up and offered to carry all my gear for the next half mile, until we could stop. I asked them to take Katana, but told them I had to prove to myself that I could still carry my pack and that my hike wasn't over. They were reluctant and called me stupid and prideful. Maybe I was, but I made it that half mile with my pack on, while barely able to limp the entire way. If it hadn't been for my staff, I wouldn't have made it.

When I finally reached the clearing that we were aiming for, I took off my shoes to find that my ankle was the size of a cantaloupe. It was severely swollen on both sides and even the top, with the top harboring most of the pain. At the time I truly believed that my fibula was fractured in some way. The pain, as well as my ability to walk was even worse than when I'd completely broken it as a teenager. I never got X-Rays while I was out there, so I'll never know, but my personal opinion/experience was that it was fractured with undoubtedly torn ligaments and tendons. Words cannot express how angry I became in this moment. To have made it so far, just to have a second small misstep end everything. The anger, rage, and frustration built inside of me to the point that I thought I might stand up and scream.

Within a short period of time of feeling my frustration rise, another feeling of calm washed over me as the anger turned to something else. I suppose the best word to describe that "something" would be "resolve." It was another moment like the one I had down at Lance Creek. I once again told myself, "It doesn't matter what's wrong with your ankle, you still walked another half mile with a full pack, and even though it hurt like hell, you still did it." I decided once again that I could hobble the rest of the way to Maine if I absolutely had to. I felt much better once these thoughts were running through my head. They put me at ease and allowed me to relax. There was no sense in continuing to be upset. It was done and over with, and now it was simply another obstacle that had to be worked through and overcome like any other.

As luck would have it, there was another intense storm that evening. The rain poured, the thunder crashed, and the wind howled as I spent a restless and painful night lying awake in my hammock fighting for space with Katana.

In the morning I popped 1,200 mg of Ibuprofen and wrapped my ankle tighter than a drum with an ace bandage I got from Coma. The plan was to make it eight miles to the next road crossing, then hitch a ride to a hospital.

I started out at a painfully slow limp, almost unable to bear any weight on my right foot. However, once my hiking medicine kicked in, I was able to push myself a little harder. If there is one thing I hate in life, it's feeling my own mortality. When I feel it, I want to defy it and prove to myself that whatever is trying to hold me back, bring me down, or hurt me... CAN'T. Even though that train of thought can cause more pain and damage in the long run, I can't help it – that's just the way I am.

I think "adaptability" is one of the most important qualities an individual can possess, especially when it comes to hiking the trail. If you don't know how to adapt, then you better learn to adapt! Bend and flow with your circumstances, don't let them break you.

After a while I figured out the least painful method of stepping, then improved upon it. Before long I was going at my normal pace and even tried to push faster. I can't take all the credit; the pain killers were a major factor.

I crossed yet another vast, open section of highlands, the sort of openness that I now lived for. The wind was unforgiving, as the highlands are infamous for their strong winds and unpredictable weather. The gusts of wind over that stretch of plain were so powerful that I was forced to dig my staff into the ground beside me rather than in front, lest I be blown over.

The eight miles to the road passed in a blur of 1,200 mgs of Ibuprofen. When I got there, I found Coma had already procured a ride to the hospital for me. I was feeling so good mentally and physically in that moment (thanks Ibuprofen!), that I thanked Coma and the couple offering me the ride, but politely declined. I told them I was going to grit it out and attempt to finish the twenty miles that everyone else was shooting for that day, while proving to myself that I could do this even with my injury.

The way I figured it, the pain would never hurt as bad as it did on the second day, and each day would be less painful than the one before. If I could bear the pain now, then I could bear it all the way to Maine if I had to. Dumb logic, but that sort of thinking had gotten me over five hundred miles thus far.

The rest of the afternoon went off without a hitch, but sadly, we lost War Story on that day. His legs were giving him too much trouble and pain, causing him to fall behind one last time. He decided to catch a ride into town, rent a car, and drive home. We lost a fourth member of our trail family and the second of our original six.

That night as we camped on the side of a hill, Schweppes gave us some good news. Our token ginger just so happened to be from this area of Virginia, with his grandparents, as well as his parents living near the trail. He informed us that eleven miles from our current position was a road that his grandmother was going to pick us up from. She was going to take us back to her house and feed us a home cooked meal before driving us to his parent's house about thirty minutes away to stay for the night. I for one couldn't wait! Not only for the treat of a delicious home cooked meal, but for the rest and relaxation that my ankle desperately needed.

It's funny how being out on the trail hardens you. The longer you're out there the tougher you get. Your skin gets tougher from the elements that constantly batter it, while your mind gets tougher from dealing with the pain of struggling against the elements. This new ankle injury was orders of magnitude worse than the first one; however, I'd managed to go as far in one day as it had taken me to go in three days after my first injury. What had changed? ...My tolerance for pain? ... My mental resiliency? ... My level of fitness? The answer is- ALL of it. The trail was making me stronger and tougher in every possible way; even when it felt like it was doing just the opposite.

The next day when we reached the road, we found several other hikers already waiting there. One of them was named "Leondros" and the other's name was "WoodChopper." Leondros was a nineteen-year-old kid from Germany that had come over to hike the trail. I'd met him several times early on, and he'd been hiking with Schweppes and Laser for as long as I'd been hiking with DSOH and the others. He was to join us on our trip to Grandma's house.

"Leondros" was his real name, as he hadn't accepted any other name on the trail. Try as we might, we could never get anything to stick. Much later on I learned that he accepted the name "Nobody" as his official trail name. Go figure.

WoodChopper was a guy that all of us had met only a day or two previously. I can honestly say I don't really know anything about the guy other than the fact that he was extremely talkative and liked to hike right on your heels while he talked about anything and everything he wanted to talk about.

While sitting at the road waiting for Schweppes' Grandma, it became very apparent that WoodChopper was going to invite himself along on this side trip. This was very presumptuous of him indeed, as no one had invited him, and he had no history with our group. Not to mention he wasn't very polite and had offended several members of our little group the day before with his strong opinions on sensitive subjects; the kind of subjects that were usually avoided in group settings when you didn't know who your company was.

After convening in a private huddle, we elected DSOH to break the news to WoodChopper. We watched with anticipation at how DSOH would handle the situation. He walked over and sat down next to WoodChopper, leaning forward, looking at the ground with his hands together and forearms resting on his knees. He sat like that for a good minute before he did anything else. Like a father about to give some worldly advice to his naïve son, he turned to Chopper and said, "Hey bud, Schweppes' Grandma is going to be here soon." He let that statement sink in for a moment as WoodChopper looked at him with an expression that read, "I know; why are you telling me this?" DSOH then followed up with, "She's going to be here soon and I'm afraid there just aren't enough seatbelts in the vehicle if you know what I mean...sorry."

"Ouch!" I think we all instantly felt bad as the disappointment crept across Woodchopper's face. For a second, the guy looked like he might cry. Regardless, the deed was done and Woodchopper hiked on. Of course we all gave DSOH a hard time and ragged on him for being too harsh on Woodchopper, saying that he'd made him cry and it was all his fault. The truth of the matter was that we were all secretly relieved and thankful that DSOH had done the dirty work for us. The proceedings of this entire predicament sort of went against the spirit of the trail, but if it hadn't been for the guy's attitude and track record for how he communicated with fellow human beings over the past several days, we would've been more than happy to have him. If it hadn't been for DSOH stepping up and putting things plainly, the following days would have surely been filled with some awkward, as well as tense moments. I never saw Woodchopper again after that day, but I would find out months later that he broke his foot in Connecticut and got off trail.

Soon after Woodchopper hiked away, Grandma Schweppes picked us up in her truck and whisked us away to her beautiful homestead. The grounds were breathtaking and sat on river front property with an enormous pasture in the front, with huge sections of land on all sides of the house. Crop gardens on one side, underground naturally cooled storage cellars on another, bees for honey, flower gardens, field houses, and an enormous elevated back deck with a tree growing up through the middle that overlooked this perfectly manicured slice of heaven.

For lunch we enjoyed an amazing ham, fried chicken, biscuits, homegrown salad, cranberries, green beans, corn on the cob, macaroni with real cheese, homemade sweet tea, homemade lemonade, honey sticks, banana pudding, and homemade cake. In my mind, I couldn't imagine the day getting any better. I ate until I was nearly sick, and after lunch we piled into the truck once more and made the half hour drive through the countryside to Schweppes' parent's house.

With a haze of endorphins floating around my brain from the good food sitting heavy in my belly, I felt as if I were in a dream while riding in the back of the pickup truck. Cruising through what I can only describe as a mountainous paradise, I could feel myself getting lost in this lifestyle. Life was so simple in that moment, with the smallest things making me happier than I'd ever been in my entire life. Less had finally become more.

This day and age, so many people over-complicate their lives to the point of ludicrousness. I couldn't see myself ever going back to my life of over consumption and over indulgence with the ambition to acquire "more." When you simplify, you learn to be happier with less. It's a happiness that trumps every other happiness I've ever experienced thus far in life.

We arrived at the house to find that Schweppes' parents had quite a plot of land as well. They too had river front property and Doug and Missie were incredibly hospitable as well as entertaining. Doug told us all about the hunting, fishing, and trapping he did around the area, and I won't lie - I was a little envious. "Let's go fishing now," I said to Doug. "Let's go!" he quickly replied. He leant me a rod and we made our way down to the river.

In the window of about half an hour, Doug made me look like an amateur with his six trout to my one trout. I will argue that he had home field advantage and that if we were back in Florida doing some salt water fishing, it would've been a different story. However, I concede defeat fair and square.

Later that evening we had deer BBQ for dinner and spent the night sitting on the front porch talking about life, the trail, and everything in-between. Hiking, fishing, home cooked meals, good company, and good conversations. It was one of those perfect days that I still often think about.

On day two at the house of Schweppes we couldn't bring ourselves to leave. Doug and Missie had been so welcoming and told us all to stay as long as we'd like. They really didn't have to do much convincing. Doug took Coma and I to the post office where I mailed home about nine pounds of cold weather gear and other miscellaneous items that I no longer needed. This was a huge weight off my back, literally and figuratively.

Later that afternoon, Doug informed us that we'd been invited as guests of honor to a dirt track race in the next town, by one of his friends that ran the track. I'd never been to a dirt track race and had no idea what to expect. Well... I'll tell you now, you should expect FUN! There were several different classes of cars that were racing, but what it boiled down to was a mixture of racing, drifting, bumper cars, and fist fights.

Before the races even started, the announcer called our names over the speakers and wished us all a safe hike; an unforgettably kind gesture. The next four hours were filled with nachos, popcorn, hot dogs, corn dogs, burgers, and the roar of deafeningly loud engines. This was how the second day at the house of Schweppes concluded.

We planned to hike out on the third day but ended up staying again. I wasn't complaining, as my ankle needed all the extra rest it could get. It had gotten very stiff over the last several days and was still swollen and tender. In the mornings I could hardly stand on it, but as the day progressed and I continued moving around, it would loosen up and feel much better. Each day was an improvement over the previous one.

The main entertainment on that third afternoon was guns, and it was Leondros' time to shine. Leondros spoke very good English with a deep voice and an accent like Arnold Schwarzenegger, although he didn't have Arnold's twang. He was very thin, not very tall, and the most noticeable thing about him was his enormous calves. We always joked that his calves needed their own backpacks. Our humor was mostly lost on him, but he was still a good sport. He told us that back in Germany he was very outdoorsy and had taken many survival courses but had never fired a weapon before in his life. So what does Doug do? He breaks out an AR-15 and we head down to the river.

It's not every day that you get to see a full grown, deadly serious, German man shoot a high powered military grade weapon as their first firearm ever. I was ready for the magic and didn't want to miss it for the world!

Leondros expended the first half of the clip in slow single round bursts. "I like this," he remarked in his deep German accent through the shit eating grin that was now frozen on his face. He then expended the rest of the clip in a lightning fast rapid fire burst. I've never seen a smile so big in my entire life. That little German man couldn't wipe the smirk off his face for the better part of the next twenty minutes.

Now Leondros will probably become an arms dealer, a mass murderer, or just that guy you know that owns way too many guns... and it's all thanks to Doug. Regardless of what the future held for Leondros or Germany, you could tell that a box of worms had just been opened. It was a beautiful and magical thing to witness. You might even call it...trail magic.

After blowing out our ear drums, we chilled out some more. Who knew that doing nothing could be so much fun? We made up our minds that we had to hike out the next day no matter what...

Virginia had been a pleasure so far, as it was living up to all the things people had said about it. It had been easy, beautiful, green, and relatively flat. A mystical land filled with wild ponies and hospitable strangers that soon became like family. The only bad thing that had happened so far was my compounded ankle injury. Missie had given me a heavy duty ankle brace that I was now wearing religiously. I'll go ahead and say it right now. If it wasn't for the extra support and protection of that brace, I would've surely rolled my ankle over and over again (more so than I ended up doing in the future), until my foot finally torqued off and I was forced to go home or crawl to Katahdin.

Yes, southern Virginia certainly was a pleasure. There were virtually no sharp climbs, only rolling hills, rhododendron tunnels, and cow pastures. The rhododendrons were now in full bloom as they added an extra aspect of beauty to the overall landscape.

A not so good change that I noticed after entering Virginia was the presence of ticks. Throughout the entire trail, they seemed to be the thickest in Virginia and Pennsylvania, all but disappearing when I got into New Jersey and the states further north. Maybe it was the time of year, or maybe it was just our geographical location, but the ticks made their presence well known soon after reaching Virginia.

Anytime your legs brushed against any kind of heavy grass or tall vegetation you could almost bet that you would find a tick crawling on your shoes or legs. It required an extra dose of hyper vigilance in order to catch them before they attached. It became a ritual to check ourselves after emerging from any kind of heavy vegetation, and also to check each other's backs at the end of each day. Lyme disease was a very real threat out there and the culprit for taking more than a few people off the trail.

Throughout the entire adventure I had maybe a little over a dozen ticks attach to me, and several hundred that I caught and brushed off before they attached. The ones that did attach had done so in various places. You almost never felt them crawling on you, and if you didn't physically see them, then you didn't know they were even there.

The majority had attached to my shins and calves with several getting on my thighs, and one even getting on my upper, inner thigh. I also had one attach to the webbing in-between my index and middle finger, another in my armpit, one on my stomach, one attached to my jaw line inside my beard, and one that had managed to nestle into my hair and attach to my scalp. The one on my scalp prompted me to shave my head later on in Waynesboro. I couldn't bring myself to shave the beard, so I settled for just my head.

Despite having these ticks attached to me, I never got Lyme disease, although other people weren't so lucky. Many hikers got it and were able to treat it early on and continue hiking. A hiker named Powerhouse, whom I would later hike with for some time through New Hampshire and Maine, was one of them. Others that didn't catch the disease early on would sometimes pay a heavy price later. One hiker developed a rare case of Lyme disease that affected his heart and respiratory system. Sadly, it was incurable, causing him to be stuck with heart issues for the rest of his life. He ended up getting off the trail in Massachusetts, and ironically, I believe his name was Superman.

The worst I personally saw was a female hiker named "Finn" that developed bilateral facial palsy from her Lyme disease. The entire left side of her face was completely paralyzed, causing a lazy eye lid, and allowing her to only talk out of the right corner of her mouth. I knew Finn from Virginia all the way to New Hampshire before I never saw her again. Despite her ailments, she still pressed on and managed to finish the entire trail. Of the people who develop Facial Palsy from Lyme disease, 92% spontaneously recover on their own after several months. I assume she later made a full recovery after the trail.

Without a doubt, dogs had it the worst. Even with flea and tick prevention, Katana still had close to a dozen ticks on her at the end of each day that I would groom and pick off. Luckily I would catch most of the ticks crawling up her legs while she was walking in front of me. I could easily spot them contrasting against her golden red fur, allowing me to stop and pluck them off before they had a chance to burrow deeper into her coat and attach. Still, many more would get past my observation as I found them attached in various places each night. The most I ever picked off of her in one sitting was twenty-two. I can't imagine how bad it would've been without the flea and tick prevention.

On one particular evening, we were walking through a beautiful, large, treeless meadow and getting ready to call it a day. The meadow was probably a hundred yards across and lined with an almost impenetrable forest of pines, oaks, and other trees with vines and creepers tangling them all together. We stopped at the edge of a huge cow pasture that we couldn't see beyond to the other side. The majority consensus was to stop and camp on the edge of the pasture. That was all well and good for them because they had tents, but the forest around the meadow and pasture was so thick with trees, vines, and thorns that I couldn't even find an area clear enough to hang my hammock; so in the end, I improvised.

I could've slept on the ground out in the open, but once you've slept in a hammock, you will never want to sleep in anything else ever again (usually). The entrance to the cow pasture was an open gap of about twenty feet, between two fence posts. Sunk into the ground between the posts was a special grating that kept the cows from crossing. People and vehicles could walk or drive across with no problem, but if a hoofed animal tried to walk on it, that animal would find itself in some serious trouble.

I tediously strung my hammock between the two fence posts with my butt hanging mere inches above the grating. My atlas straps, as well as the fence posts were stretched to their absolute limits. With my irrational fear of large animals, this was less than an ideal spot for me to hang. In my mind, I was one more obstacle for the cows to get past, should they attempt to stampede out of their pasture that night. I couldn't help but imagine a cow coming over to investigate the object hanging on the opening to its pasture, then biting my head while I slept. Stupid, I know.

When darkness fell, I beheld one of the most remarkable sights I've ever seen before or since. Maybe it was unique to this location, or maybe we were simply in the right place at the right time. I'll never know unless I go back. The meadow and surrounding forest came alive with hundreds of thousands, if not millions, of fire flies. Thousands blanketed the field while even more blanketed the trees from their base all the way to the top canopy. As far as the eye could see in every direction, fire flies covered everything. It looked like nature's ultimate light show. Nonstop constant flashes, sweeps and darts of golden light, all night long as the fire flies danced and flew to some unheard rhythm.

I attempted to take pictures and video, but in the darkness my phone wasn't sophisticated enough to capture the light show as it was meant to be seen. Only human eyes would be capturing the memories of this night. I drifted off to sleep to the sounds of cows calling in the distance and the golden light of fireflies dancing overhead.

The morning after the fireflies proved to be quite a surprise. Upon opening my hammock canopy, half a dozen orange daddy longlegs spiders fell on top of me. They must've been having a party up there or waiting to ambush me, but regardless of their intentions, a short battle ensued over control for the inside of my hammock; I won by a land slide.

Laser offered to walk Katana that morning and without hesitation I agreed. He left camp with Katana approximately half an hour before I did. I felt my free time to think, as well as the potential for my mind to wander, had increased tenfold.

As I made my way across the enormous cow pasture, chipmunks ducked and dodged across the trail into their little burrows. I saw chipmunks every day out there; they were a constant on the trail. They were incredibly quick, and you only saw them briefly before they disappeared down their strategically placed tunnels.

I was making my way along when one of the chipmunks darted out in front of me. I didn't think anything of it at first, but then I noticed he was still running about fifteen feet into the grass. He looked frantic as I realized the little fella had lost track of his burrow. Now was my chance!

I began chasing him as he took off through the pasture, zig-zagging in an attempt to dodge me. He soon ran himself into some thicker longer grass that drastically slowed him down. I was able to catch up and use my staff to fold the longer grass over top of him, pinning him under the longer blades. Now that I had him in this grassy prison, I reached down and carefully picked him up by the loose skin behind his shoulders. He went a little crazy on me for several seconds but was unable to bite me. He did get a few good scratches before he finally relaxed and hung there placidly in my grip. DSOH caught up and took a quick picture before I set him back down. The chipmunk seemed quite surprised at his sudden release, as I'm sure he'd accepted that he was to be my meal at some point or another. Once he realized that he was a free chipmunk, he scampered off, no worse for the wear, with a cool story to tell his chipmunk friends. He was lucky Katana hadn't been with me, or it might have ended differently, had she gotten hold of him first.

Later on that same morning it began to rain again, light but steady. I decided to take a break and sat down on a log amidst the light deluge and relaxed. Sitting there, as droplets of water fell all around me, my mind began to wander as it only could without the presence of Katana to distract me.

A huge crazy looking wasp began to hover in front of my head about three feet away, for nearly ten seconds. It just hovered there while staring me right in the face. "Why the hell is it looking at me like that?" I wondered. It seemed so unnatural. What if it was some kind of remote controlled insect camera that was spying on me? Or what if insects are actually little biological cameras put here by aliens to monitor us? I mean there seemed to be about a million damn insects that appeared to serve absolutely no purpose other than annoying the hell out of people and getting in their business. It would almost make more sense that they were tiny little alien cameras put here to observe us, rather than being an integral part of the natural world, right? I don't know, but this thought genuinely consumed me for nearly fifteen minutes as I was sitting there.

That evening we were caught in another rainstorm of biblical proportions and ended up hunkering down near a stream. It poured all night and late into the next morning, and it was nearly 11 am before we were all up and packed.

DSOH, Coma, Leondros, Schweppes, Laser, and I were all standing in a circle discussing the rendezvous point for the evening when something incredibly random and fantastical happened. We heard voices coming down the trail... multiple female voices. We waited for maybe forty seconds, when suddenly, from around the corner emerged seven college aged girls and one older gentleman. We stood there dumbfounded. You don't see that many girls out there, let alone seven at once, and after an epic rainstorm none the less.

They walked right up and greeted us, as well as offered us fruit. I felt like I was either dreaming or in some kind of weird, low budget porno that was set in the wilderness. The plot being, "A bunch of dirty male hikers get lucky with a bunch of young babes lost in the woods." I was ready for the old guy to pull out a camera and start filming.

As it turned out, they weren't a bunch of Porn Star babes lost in the woods, but a bunch of young biologists out with their professor doing some research and giving fruit to any hikers they happened upon. This was very kind of them as we chatted and answered questions for several minutes. Katana ended up being the real star and focus of conversation. I know the other guys hated me for all of the attention that was turned towards my dog, as well as the multitude of questions that were shot my way. "Sorry guys – should've brought an adorable little fox dog with you!"

We soon parted ways as the biologists turned back south the way they came and we continued northward. That day Leondros and Coma got ahead of the rest of us, and although it was a little while before we saw Coma, I never saw Leondros again. I would later learn that I'd come very close to catching up with him several times throughout the adventure, but it never played out. To my knowledge he did finish the entire trail.

At this point in the journey I'd begun experimenting with many different types of food out on the trail. I'd become bored fairly quickly with pasta sides, instant mash potatoes, tortillas, peanut butter, and plain tuna packets. As I write this many months later, I can't even look at peanut butter, tortillas, or pasta without gagging. I truly burnt myself out on those items by eating them every day, multiple times a day, for months.

It will amaze you the types of things that we religiously keep refrigerated and throw away if left out for even just a few hours. Here are some fun facts about foods that we refrigerate. Almost every type of condiment says to "refrigerate" after opening. I think that's more of a disclaimer to cover their ass, because in my opinion, you don't have to refrigerate them at all. They are fine at room temperature, backpack temperature, outside temperature, whatever! If you leave that ketchup, mayonnaise, or spicy brown mustard out on the counter, don't worry about it, it didn't go bad.

Another thing people religiously put in their fridge is cheese. An unopened vacuumed sealed block of cheese is good for weeks in a backpack while being put through a myriad of different temperatures. Yeah it might get a little soft and sweaty, but the way to combat that is to buy hard and extra sharp cheeses. It will get a little soft, but it's still very good to eat. The sharper the cheese the better! Even once it's been opened, cheese is good for over a week without being in a refrigerator. You leave the cheese out for a day, it starts to sweat and people say "Ewww, it's gone bad; I have to throw it away!" Well, I have some news for you, it's cheese, it's already bad. In order for cheese to become cheese, it had to start off as milk and a few other things and then be left out to age and go bad. If your cheese gets mold on it, then simply cut off the moldy parts. Unless your block of cheese becomes a giant block of mold, I guarantee that no matter how sweaty, soft, or moldy it gets, you can still eat it or eat around it.

Hot dogs are good for over a week in your backpack, however they'll never last that long before you roast them over a fire. They don't have to be in a refrigerator constantly, and the same thing goes for bacon. Bacon will be good in your pack for several days, but I highly doubt it will last even that long.

Now let's move on to milk. Yes, milk will go bad and curdle if not kept cool. This posed a problem for me out on the trail because I loved milk with my cereal. I tried a little experiment early on in Southern Virginia and bought some powdered carnation milk, as well as a giant two-and-a-half-pound bag of colossal berry crunch, then strapped to the outside of my backpack. I must've looked like a real class act with a giant bag of cereal hanging off my pack.

That first night with the cereal and powdered milk was revolutionary as I camped near a spring that offered icy cold water. I filled my pot, dumped in some powdered milk, mixed it all together and added some cereal. BEHOLD! Ice cold milk and cereal atop a mountain in the middle of nowhere! If I thought I'd been living before, I was wrong. You haven't lived until you've enjoyed an ice cold bowl of cereal in the middle of the woods. To make a short story even shorter, those two and a half pounds of cereal lasted me only that night and the next morning. From the time of my first bowl, it was all gone in less than ten hours; eight hours of which I was asleep. I regret nothing.

Besides the cereal kick that I was now on, I was hopelessly addicted to sugary foods. This happens to many, but not all of the people who do long distance hiking. As the universe would have it, the lightest, cheapest, and most calorie dense foods are the ones that just so happen to be the worst for you. Since I was not made of money and there were no money trees growing in the Appalachian Mountains, I couldn't afford to eat dehydrated meals every night, or beef jerky, and protein bars all day. No, my socioeconomic standing would not allow it, so I made do with what I could afford. What I could afford was diabetes inducing foods like honey buns, cosmic brownies, whoopee pies, oatmeal cream cookies, Oreos, M&M's, Skittles, mini snickers, Paydays, and other candy bars. Yes, sugar was my master and if I didn't have it at least a dozen times a day, I became very "Hangry" (So hungry that I became angry).

I've seen and done some crazy things for food while out on the trail. "Germs" and "expiration dates" no longer held any meaning and the "five second rule" became law. Actually it became more of a suggestion. I've dropped things in the dirt and without a second thought, picked them back up and eaten them; sometimes brushing off the dirt and sometimes not. It just depended on how dirty the dirt was at the particular location of the incident.

I've witnessed more extreme cases of this, as I have personally seen people pick food up off the trail and eat it after not knowing where it came from or how long it'd been sitting there. I once watched a guy sit down on the side of the trail and pick skittles out of the dirt and eat them one by one. They weren't his, he just happened upon them as he was walking along. This is the kind of tone that life takes on for some people out on the trail. I would never go to the extreme of eating food I found lying on the ground, but if it was my food or someone else's that I saw fall, I had no reservations in salvaging and eating it.

Katana was a master of food salvage. My little dog had turned it into an art form. Sometimes she would steal food right out of people's hands and laps if they weren't careful, striking like a snake. Despite the liberties she took with other people's food, she was always respectful of mine. She would never attempt to take anything out of my hands. However, if it hit the ground, that was another story. Katana didn't care if your food hit the ground by accident or on purpose, because as soon as it was on the ground, it was in her domain. If you still wanted it, then you better hurry up and grab it before she did. One prime example of this happened while in Massachusetts.

I'd just come off a recent town excursion and full resupply, so my food stores were high and I was eager to start eating some of the weight down. I stopped atop a mountain and took a break for lunch. I was going to have a nice salami and cheese bagel sandwich with spicy brown mustard. Even though she had her food, Katana still sat next to me, watching me intensely as I prepared my meal. I don't know how it happened, but while cutting a slab off my fresh, one-pound block of cheese that was worth its weight in gold to me, the bulk of it shot out of the wax paper and hit the ground. I didn't even have enough time to yell the word "Shit" before she pounced on it and ran off into the bushes. I couldn't believe what had just happened. The thought of eating salami bagel sandwiches without cheese for the next several days was enough to make me cry. Besides a cheeseburger that she snatched from some poor sod later on in New Hampshire, that was the biggest and best food salvage maneuver Katana ever conducted.

May 29th was my 61st day on the trail as I was pushing towards the small town of Bland, Virginia. All in all, it was about a twenty-two-mile day that I was shooting for. This was all fine and dandy except for the fact that DSOH, Schweppes, and myself had screwed around on breaks so much that we'd gone barely ten miles by 4 pm. Laser was well ahead of us, and we still had over twelve miles to go with only a few hours of daylight left. All of us were more or less out of food, so if we wanted to have a good meal in the morning, we'd have to make it to Bland that night. We made up our minds to grit out the last miles and make it to Bland that evening... no matter what.

To add to our predicament, it was once again raining. At this point in the game, rain didn't bother me anymore. It was another aspect of daily life that I was now accustomed to. One thing that did bother me though, was that the miles in Virginia just didn't seem to add up. After two months on the trail, most people had figured out their pace pretty well. Without even looking at a map, you could accurately guess how far you had gone based on the amount of time you walked at your particular pace. When all you do is walk every single day, you get pretty damn good at calculating your distances over time, even when factoring in breaks and slower uphill climbs. Despite our growing expertise with distance over time calculations in our head, Virginia was throwing a wrench into these calculations.

Miles seemed to tick by slower when you checked your estimations against the land marks on your map. I swear there are two hundred extra miles of trail that are lost and unaccounted for in the state of Virginia. You never got where you wanted to go in the times it usually took to reach other places before and after Virginia. The numbers were just off. It became a joke when talking about distances, to double check with the person if they were describing "Virginia miles" or "standard American miles." When you said this, other hikers knew what you meant (usually).

So on this particular rainy afternoon, as I was running behind on my nonexistent schedule, I was delivered a good dose of "Virginia Miles." I set out in the rain ahead of Schweppes and DSOH at a blistering pace. I was tearing the trail up quicker than I could ever remember tearing it up previously; even faster than my Damascus sprint. I was eating up the miles and crapping out footprints.

I finally reached a landmark and checked it against my map/guidebook. According to my guide, I only had another six miles to go in order to reach the road into Bland. "No biggie, I could knock that out in less than two hours and make it just after nightfall," I thought to myself. I continued on in the soggy conditions once more, all out, nose to the grindstone as I kept going…. and going…. and going. Almost two hours at my fastest pace and still I hadn't reached the road. "What the hell?" I thought. I was exhausted and knew that I should've been there by now, or at least close enough to hear cars or something. I kept going at a moderate pace for another hour and found nothing. By the first thirty minutes of that hour I was annoyed. Another thirty minutes after that hour and I was seeing red.

I sat down on the side of the trail and looked at my guidebook again. I hadn't misread it. I should've been there by now, but here I was an hour and a half after my projected arrival time and still no road. For some reason I pulled out my bag of Mini Snickers and began devouring them furiously. I was eating them so fast that my breathing became labored. I couldn't tell you why I was taking feelings of aggression out on my food, but I was. I even got pissed while my snickers were making me feel better, because I realized that I was affecting my health and well-being by eating so many, so fast. I think I ate over twenty before I ran out. This was just one more thing to be annoyed about. "No more Mini Snickers." They were my favorite snack that made me feel better when I was feeling down or tired… and now they were gone.

It was long since dark, and after another half hour of moderate walking, I was ready to give up or have a blow-out. "I-just-want-to-get-where-I'm-going-and-go-to-bed!" I could've stopped anywhere and hung my hammock, but this had turned into a battle of principle. I'd made up my mind to get somewhere, and now that I was in a frustrated and vulnerable emotional state; nothing was going to make me feel better until I got where I was trying to go. I was chafed, exhausted, wet, and snicker-less. It was a very volatile situation, a ticking time bomb.

Thankfully, I finally reached the road before the bomb exploded. It was dark as the trail dead ended into the asphalt. Usually the trail picked back up on the other side, or just down the road, but always within sight, even in the dark with a headlamp. Not this time. This time I couldn't see a blaze anywhere. This was just befitting the mood I was already in. I looked left down the road... it was downhill and looked as if it went towards civilization and food. I looked to the right... all I saw were trees. "Well.... I'd seen enough damn trees today," I thought to myself as I turned left and began my road walk.

After less than a mile, it became apparent that I was going nowhere, as the road began to parallel a somewhat busy highway. My "annoyance meter" was pretty much broken, as it had gone off the scale quite some time ago. All I wanted was to lie down and go to sleep, but now I was in the middle of a road that was in the middle of seemingly nowhere. There was a virtually sheer, one-hundred-foot cliff of shale rock on my right, and little island cliffs of shale rock about forty feet high on my left that were separating the road that I was on from the highway. There were little breaks in the cliffs on my left where other roads branched off to allow people to merge on and off the two roads.

As I was silently brooding, deep in thought, and about to give up and begin walking back to the trail, I heard a voice yell my name from up above that nearly caused me to jump out of my shoes. Hearing my name called from that direction was the last thing I ever expected. Looking up to the left, I saw Laser standing on top of a rock island approximately 100 feet long and dotted with miniature pine trees. The kind of small trees you might see in parking lots in the areas that divide up parking sections, but slightly bigger. "What the hell are you doing up there?" I called to him, more relieved than upset from being scared shitless. "I don't know," Laser replied. "I just got tired of walking and climbed up here... it's pretty cool." "Can we camp there?" I called back. "I think so," was the reply.

Laser showed me the way onto the rock island and helped pull Katana up as I climbed over the shale. Once atop the rocky island I realized that Laser was right. This place was pretty cool. It was like some kind of Nature Island Oasis in the middle of two urban roads. Indeed, there was a spot for my hammock, as well as a spot for Laser's tent. The rain quit a short while later, affording us an opportunity to build a small fire with baby pinecones and small pine branches. It was a seriously amazing location. A steady flow of people passed below us on the highway, with no idea there were two individuals on an epic trek across the nation encamped right above them. I imagined myself living up there for the rest of my life, only going into town at night to scavenge for food in order to survive. That would never happen, but those were the kind of crazy thoughts that this little spot brought to mind; sort of like a desert island in a sea of concrete... where I would try to survive.

I stayed up until 11 pm waiting to see if DSOH or Schweppes would pass by, but they never did. Hopefully they were smart and camped out on the side of the trail, but either way they were missing out on a pretty unique camping experience. According to my map, I went twenty-two miles that day, but that was definitely a load of shit. It was probably closer to an extra four miles on top of that twenty-two. I fell asleep that night to the sounds of automobiles and thoughts of mini snickers.

Bland turned out to be pretty bland after all. As fate would have it, I did go in the wrong direction the night before, and Laser and I ended up backtracking. Then we walked almost another two miles before an elderly gentleman in a pickup truck finally stopped to take us the last half mile to town. As far as food and resupplies went, they had a Dollar General, a Subway, and that was about it. DSOH and Schweppes had camped by the trail the night before, then rendezvoused with us at Subway. I took advantage of the free Wi-Fi to update my blog, and after two bacon and egg sandwiches, one large meatball sub, and one large double meat, double cheese, tuna sub that the sandwich artist couldn't even close, I was all set to go. Oh, and I grabbed one more meatball sub for the road.

We set about trying to hitchhike using the "active hitching" technique. Within about ten minutes a middle aged man pulled over in an SUV. "I know where you're goin, hop in," were his first words to us. We loaded our packs in the back and climbed in. I got in the front seat, so I was in charge of small talk. I hated small talk because I wasn't very good at it; however, I always did my best when the responsibility fell upon me to make conversation with the strangers that picked us up.

Once settled in and on our way, I initiated small talk. "Thanks for the ride; do you do much hiking yourself?" I asked. "I've done some; this bitch that cleans my house will drop me off and fucking pick me up sometimes. Fuck, I'm retired thirteen years ago and I've got some spare time to do it." "WHOAH!" I thought. This was the first thing he said to us after getting in the vehicle. Despite this strange first exchange, he ended up being a nice enough guy, but didn't seem to know how to talk to people. He cussed like a sailor but put all his cusswords in awkward parts of his sentences. It was a very strange, if not humorous, five minutes back to the trailhead.

Since we had gotten a late start, we only hiked about nine miles before making camp. After getting set up, we later discovered a rotting deer carcass next to our camp while gathering fire wood. Cause of death, who knows? Luckily the stench never wafted into our shelters.

Later on in the journey, I would hear of a hiker who came across a freshly deceased deer. Whether it was killed by predators or died of natural causes, I don't remember. I do remember (as well as hearing first hand from a person who was there) that the hiker removed a leg from the deer and packed it out until he made camp later that evening. He and half a dozen other hikers then enjoyed a feast of deer leg roasted over an open fire. I would've loved to partake in that campfire meal.

Another highlight of Virginia was a spot called "Dismal Falls." This was where we caught up to Coma. Dismal Falls was not on the main trail and required a side trail detour of about three tenths of a mile. Those three tenths were well worth it, as Dismal turned out to be one of my all-time favorite spots on the entire trail.

Dismal Falls resided approximately twenty miles north of Bland, and was a camping Utopia. Everywhere you looked were picturesque spots to camp. The falls themselves were also exceptionally beautiful. The drop was maybe a little less than twenty feet, but the falls were wide and dramatic. At the bottom of the falls was an icy swimming hole filled with trout, horny heads (look similar to a carp), and overhanging rocks to sit on. The top of the falls was nothing but smooth limestone rock that offered the perfect area to lie out or soak in the shallow, moderately fast current. I did some swimming, some laying, some soaking, and some fishing. All of those were successful except for the fishing because I couldn't find a good spot to hand line.

Besides not catching anything, I did notice quite a few freshwater mountain stream crawfish...big ones! I switched modes, as well as tactics, and went on a crawfish rampage. Before I was done wading around upstream on top of the falls, I'd procured around forty mud bugs. I boiled some water and added the only seasonings I had; Garlic Salt and Louisiana Hot Sauce. It took me about thirty minutes to boil them all in small batches, but they turned out pretty damn good if I do say so myself. I shared them with my hiking family, plus a few other hikers that happened to be enjoying the great natural beauty of the falls.

The next morning, I made the decision to remain at Dismal another day. It was just too relaxing, too beautiful, and too much like a vacation from my vacation to leave so soon. DSOH, Laser, and Schweppes all hiked on. Coma and another hiker named Space Ranger stayed at Dismal with me.

Space Ranger was a guy in his mid-thirties from Indiana who'd gotten his name from the blissfully distant and distracted look that he always had on his face. You could often run across him sitting atop a rock on the side of the trail, staring up at the trees while smoking a cigarette, completely oblivious to anyone or anything else around him. He always seemed to "appear" places, as you never saw him arrive anywhere. One moment he was nowhere to be found; the next moment he was standing right next to you. He would just "space-ranger" his way around as we liked to say. He was a quiet guy of few words-more of a listener than a talker, who rarely contributed to campfire conversations. Despite being a very reserved individual, his presence was always readily welcomed and appreciated by all. You couldn't help but smile and be in a good mood whenever and wherever he popped up. That was the effect he had on people; he was that person that everyone was glad to see, no matter the place or circumstance.

I'd known Space Ranger from my earliest days in Georgia, and I hiked as well as camped with him all the way through New Hampshire. I lost track of him in Maine, but he did complete the trail and was victorious in his Appalachian endeavor.

After another lazy day, I decided I would attempt another crawfish boil. As the sun disappeared behind the mountains and darkness crept in, I donned my headlamp, grabbed a plastic bag and began wading upstream. Crawfish are more active at night, and almost immediately I began finding them creeping along the smooth bottom of the stream.

There were two colors to the smooth rocky stream bottom; a light beige color and a dark green. The beige was slicker than snot while the dark green had a good grip for my bare feet. I was a couple hundred yards upstream from the falls and our camp, combing my way back and forth across the stream, collecting crawdads as I found them.

While wading across a dark green patch of rock in a fast flowing section of stream about ten inches deep, I unknowingly hit a beige patch. With zero warning, my feet shot out from under me and into the air. Before I made land fall, I was looking at my feet silhouetted against the night sky. I came down hard on my back with a splash and a thud. My headlamp was knocked clean off my head, and my bag of dinner knocked out of my hands. The current pushed me down stream about ten yards before I managed to pop back up and begin chasing my still shining headlamp and bag- O'-crawfish. I caught both of them in a calm pool of water around two feet deep further downstream. I called it quits after that little episode and waded back to camp. I still had fifteen crawfish left in my bag that I boiled up and split between Coma and Space Ranger. I have to say that a crawfish boil in the woods is tough to beat.

I said goodbye to Dismal Falls the next day on June 2nd. My other companions had mentioned the day before that they were possibly going to stay at a Hostel thirteen miles past Dismal. The Hostel itself was called "Woods Hole Hostel" and besides being a lodge for hikers, it was also a self-sustaining little farm. It was located half a mile down a dirt road that branched off from another dirt road that bisected the trail. It was literally in the middle of nowhere and I doubted that my buddies would still be there.

After a somewhat leisurely hike through multiple rhododendron gardens and pine groves, along with one huge climb up an unnamed mountain, I finally reached the dirt road to find Coma laying on his pack taking a break. "The Hostel is just down that way, right?" I asked him. "Yup, but I'm not going down there, I'm going to push another five miles," Coma replied. I thought for a moment and said, "Well, it's only half a mile. I think I'll run down there to get a cold drink, then run back up and meet you." Coma responded, "Mayor, you know if you go down there you're gonna see our buddies and wanna stay." I gave it some more thought. "Nah, I bet they pushed on; I'll leave my dog and pack up here with you as insurance that I return," I answered. "Fair enough," he said.

I quickly made my way down the dirt road, practically salivating at the thought of drinking a cold soda. I got to the bottom of a small descent before rounding a corner onto the property. BAM! There was DSOH, Schweppes, and Laser all sitting in hammocks and rocking chairs on the front porch of a wooden bunkhouse. "WOW, Coma called that one!" I thought to myself. "Oh Mayor, you made it!" They exclaimed in half mocking sarcastic voices that really meant, "We've been lounging around relaxing all day while you've been sweating your ass off in the wilderness." "I thought you guys would be gone by now," I said. "Nope, we're staying another day," Laser answered. "Come up here and have a cold soda, they're only fifty cents," Schweppes added.

Fifty cents; that was the cheapest soda I'd encountered on the trail so far. I never drank soda EVER before the trail, but sugar is a harsh mistress once you let her grab hold of you. I drank four Dr. Peppers in less than ten minutes before I started feeling guilty. Coma was up there with my pack and my dog, awaiting my return. Laying in a hammock while drinking sodas and reading books seemed so much better than hiking another five miles in the humid heat.

"So are you going to stay?" Laser asked. "My stuff and my dog are up at the trailhead with Coma," I replied. "Well, go get it!" DSOH remarked. "I'll tell you what, if one of you runs up there and gets my stuff and my dog, I'll stay and buy you two sodas." Being the sprightliest and most energetic of all of us, Laser immediately agreed and took off up the road. He left so fast that I forgot to send a soda up with him to give to Coma. I felt really bad.

Woods Hole turned out to be a great pit stop on the trail. The environment was cozy and home-like, while the couple that ran it emphasized family values and traditions. The dinner was all home grown and home cooked with lettuce and veggies from the garden, meat from the farm raised pigs, homemade dressings, home baked bread, and rice from an Amish Market. It really hit the spot. DSOH, Schweppes, Laser, and I concluded the evening playing a friendly card game of "Bullshit" that Laser ended up winning.

The next morning the skies looked threatening as Laser left early at 6 am while the rest of us hung back. I didn't know it at the time, but I wouldn't see Laser again for weeks. I'd known that he had to meet his parents by a certain date somewhere, but I'd always assumed that we'd make it there together. We waited for most of the morning, but the rain never came. We were just looking for an excuse not to hike and spend some extra time at Woods Hole, but at 11:10 we hit the trail. At 11:20 it began to pour. It couldn't have happened any other way.

Pearisburg was the next town in our sights, and the last town before a long stretch with nowhere decent to resupply until the town of Daleville. The twenty-mile stretch leading into Pearisburg, especially the last ten miles, was some of the most gorgeous Rhododendron tunnels that I can remember seeing. They were almost constant, only broken up by meadows, cliffs, and rocky carapaces that overlooked the Virginia countryside for more miles than I could count.

Pearisburg was a medium sized town that had everything you could possibly want in a place to live. It had plenty of eateries and a big supermarket. What more could you need? After resupplying at the local "Food Lion" grocery store, we noticed a "Good Will" store in the same plaza.

Now before I go any further, let me explain some things about the trail, and what it does to your average thru-hiker.

The longer you stay on the trail; the less social norms will matter to you. What kind of social norms? Mostly appearance and bodily functions, but there are other subtler norms that you adopt and abandon throughout your journey along the trail. For now, I'm going to focus on appearance and bodily functions. In the civilized world, a lot of energy and focus is put on your appearance. People stake their lives and careers on it. In the "real" world there are certain expectations of how you're supposed to look when you go out in public. The more time you spend on the trail, the less this matters.

Out there in the woods, there's no one to impress and no one to judge you. The only people you'll see are your fellow hikers, and they don't care what you look like, or what you wear. It's when you get past this attitude of judging people by their surface appearance that you're able to genuinely get to know someone on a deeper, more personal level. This is why relationships formed on the trail are so strong.

In the material world you miss opportunities to forge friendships and meet people because of appearance, social, and socioeconomic standings. Examine your friends that you have in the real world right now; many of them probably dress similar to you, as well as have similar affiliations, interests, and hobbies. On the trail, stripped of all your comforts and everything you own, everybody you meet is the same yet simultaneously unique. Everyone you come across is just another sweaty, smelly human being that's having the same rough day as you. This allows you to meet and talk to people that you would otherwise never speak to in any other setting. You will meet people from every walk of life that will amaze you with their life's stories and be amazed by yours.

You learn not to care about your appearance, because you realize that appearances don't matter. It's the people underneath them that matter and every single one of them has a unique personality and story. On a less serious note, allow me to explain what happens when people stop caring about their appearance.

Firstly, you grow lots of body hair... everywhere; men and women alike. You don't wash your clothes and you don't care what kind of clothes, if any, you wear. You start seeing some crazy combinations of outfits, and believe it or not, a lot of people will hike in their underwear/undergarments. When it's ninety something degrees in the middle of nowhere and no one is watching anyway, it doesn't hurt to knock out some miles in your compression underwear or super short shorts. The only time this becomes a spectacle is when the trail fashions overlap into the towns. You lose all your shame and humility out on the trail, and it's not uncommon to enter a town during the summer and see a male hiker wearing a kilt, a sundress, or just his boxers or compression underwear. Women might wear crazy sun hats, dresses, leotards, or just their underwear and a sports bra. Sometimes townsfolk will give you some funny looks and maybe even get offended, but most of them understand and laugh it off. It's like having a free sideshow in your town for a few months out of every year.

Another social norm that's abandoned out on the trail and sometimes at the wrong time in town is one's own bodily functions. Farts and burps are a natural part of life. Everybody does it; men, women, children and the elderly alike. Most people would not be caught dead farting out loud in public or even belching loudly in public. On the trail, no one is going to judge you and everyone understands. Guys and gals fart and belch freely around campfires and while hiking. It's a natural part of life, and nobody says anything or gives you a hard time about it out there. It's pure freedom.

You get so used to this freedom of farting and belching as soon as the need arises, that you sometimes forget where you are when you do them. More than a couple of nine times I've been walking in a supermarket, browsing the aisles for cosmic brownies when I've let horrendously loud farts loose without even a second thought, only to realize a split second later that I'm surrounded by non-hiking strangers. I think the embarrassment lasts about .7 seconds before I forget about it and continue shopping for my sugary delights.

So there we were, right outside the Pearisburg Goodwill Store when DSOH, Schweppes, and I decided to have a look-see. When we finally emerged from Goodwill, we'd given ourselves a fashion makeover worthy of our own TV show. We'd all bought button down Hawaiian style t-shirts and goofy hats to go along with them.

Mine was bright red with white Hawaiian flowers all over it and a gray baseball cap that simply read "Cockerhams" across the front. I looked like a cross between a pedophile and Johnny Depp from "Fear and Loathing in Las Vegas." I looked like pure money (NOT!)

DSOH had a brown shirt with yellow pineapples all over it and a cream colored straw hat. He looked like a younger version of Dr. Hammond from "Jurassic Park."

Schweppes had a blue shirt with waves and other designs all over it along with a matching blue sailor's hat. He looked like Popeye's younger, flamboyant, ginger brother.

We were quite the sight to behold in our new hiking getups and all the townspeople let us know it. After breaking down all of our food to its simplest packaging and fitting it into our packs, our snazzy little posse made its way to some woods on the edge of town and called it a day.

The next morning, we heard from several locals that some severe weather was coming our way. The sky looked perfectly calm and beautiful at the moment, so Schweppes and I decided to hike out in our new attire while DSOH and Coma stayed behind. Schweppes and I hiked together for most of that day. At one particular time early in the afternoon, I was walking several paces ahead of him while in the midst of conversation. Schweppes was talking when he suddenly cut off and I heard what sounded like a woman's shriek. Startled, I spun around just in time to see a four-foot black rat snake quickly finish slithering across his foot. We'd surprised the snake and it had shot down off the embankment to our left in an attempt to make a downhill getaway. I glanced back up at Schweppes, giving him a look. He grinned,

113

slightly embarrassed, before saying, "I'm not scared of snakes' bro, but that caught me off guard!" Despite his womanly shriek, I believed him.

We pushed up over a few big climbs and eventually hit a ridge that was more or less flat, albeit very overgrown and infested with ticks. The vegetation was thick and brushed against most of our body for many miles at a time. It was on this ridge that I witnessed two dung beetles rolling a perfectly spherical ball of dung. It was as smooth as a marble and unlike anything I'd ever seen before. I honestly didn't even know there were dung beetles around those parts, as I'd only seen them on TV, and even then I believed they were only in Africa.

As the afternoon drew on, I slowly pulled ahead of Schweppes. I had the impression that I was on a plateau. About twenty yards to my left was a sharp drop off, as well as a view across the landscape far below. On my right was what looked almost like a subtropical forest, thick and overgrown, but more or less flat for as far as I could see through the trees and vegetation.

I was in my own little world as I made my way through this overgrown Virginian wilderness, when I heard a loud grunt and a very loud crash ahead of me on the right. I looked over to see a large black bear that I would estimate at close to four hundred pounds, barreling full speed through the underbrush about seventy-five feet in front of me. He shot across the trail and towards the edge of the ridge as I stood there with Katana, frozen, watching. I'd never seen a bear run so fast in my life. It looked terrified, as if I was the absolute worst thing that could've possibly happened to it. The bear hit the edge of the ridge at full speed and kept right on going. No sooner did it vanish over the side, I heard a sound like a tree snapping, then the sound of a large rock rolling and smashing over other rocks. The sound continued until it was too distant to hear any longer. "Did I just make a bear kill itself?" I wondered. I'll never know, but hopefully it was ok, and will continue to steer clear of humans. The bear tally was now at four...

All afternoon I saw no sign of the severe weather the locals had warned us about. "Maybe we walked out of its path, or the weather report was wrong," I thought. The sun disappeared and darkness fell as I continued hiking, with Schweppes somewhere still behind me. We'd agreed upon a stopping point, and when the light had finally faded, I still had over four miles left to go.

In the dark, while under the thick canopy, I was unable to see the sky. That was how the storm snuck up on me. There was no noise or distant thunder. One second it was a calm, cool night; the next second it was buckets of rain. The heavy rain came first; I could handle that no problem. Then it got heavier and heavier as the winds began to pick up. Over a matter of minutes, gusts of wind in excess of thirty and forty miles per hour were sweeping across the ridge. As the wind howled, whipping rain and leaves across my face, the lightning and thunder began. It certainly was shaping into an epic storm, but still I kept walking.

The trail became a puddle as I strained against the darkness and thick foliage to see the white blazes with my headlamp. For the better part of twenty minutes, I made barely any progress as I tried to make certain that I was still on the path; all the while the rain and wind intensifying around me. It reached the point where the rain was so heavy and had blown across my vision so violently, that my headlamp was reflecting off the curtain of water. I could no longer see more than several feet in front of me. I stopped to assess the situation. I looked down at Katana as her sopping wet little body looked back up at me, clearly inquiring, "We stop here Dad?" "Yes little dog, we stop here."

I bushwhacked off the trail and attempted to clear out the vegetation between some trees in order to pitch my rain fly and hang the hammock. I cleared out some dead branches and other vegetation in order to make room for Schweppes's tent in case he made it as far.

Fifteen minutes after I'd begun clearing out the spot, I saw a headlight bobbing down the trail through the rain towards me. "I'm glad you stopped!" Schweppes called over the howling wind and rain. "I was close to stopping myself, but I figured since you were in front you would've stopped first and waited," he added. He was right. It took twice as long to get set up while trying to fight the high winds, but eventually we got situated and hunkered down for the evening. The storm raged all night and into the morning as I lay in my nest with Katana nestled up against me.

The temperature plummeted sometime in the early morning hours and continued to stay cold well into mid-morning. When I finally got moving and climbed out of the nest, it was close to 11 am and a light mist still hung throughout the forest. I'd left my soaking wet clothes hanging on my hammock straps the night before, but with the high winds they'd been blown to the ground.

I went through the standard routine of putting my freezing wet clothes back on. I put my Soffe running shorts on first after shaking them out, then set about wringing out my shirt and socks. Not thirty seconds after putting my shorts on, I felt something crawling on my leg. At this stage in the game, little creatures crawling on you were commonplace, so I thought nothing of it at first. After several more seconds, I nonchalantly glanced down to see what it was. My eyes widened in horror as they beheld a large brown spider with a fat abdomen emerging from the left leg of my short shorts in the very high, upper thigh region. What an unpleasant surprise this was. I slowly and calmly reached my right hand down and gave that spider the most powerful flick I've ever mustered in my entire life. The spider flew off with such velocity that he left a few legs behind. Regardless of the spider's ultimate fate, the coast was clear, the family jewels were safe, and another crisis had been averted.

As the days began to feel more and more like summer, with more consistently warm days and fewer cold snaps, the animals began to make themselves known... especially the snakes. I was now seeing at least one snake, if not multiple snakes per day. I've always been fond of snakes and as a child and young teenager I would catch them and keep them as pets before letting them go a short time later. Actually, to say that I was "fond" of snakes is an understatement. I was obsessed with snakes as a youth! Steve Irwin was my hero and I had aspirations of becoming a herpetologist from the age of seven until my teens. My days were consumed with searching my backyard and neighborhood for snakes well into my mid-teens. It was only when I got my driver's license and discovered "girls" that my obsession with these reptiles took a back seat. Although I do not absorb myself with the world of snakes and other reptiles any longer, they still hold a very special place in my heart and childhood memories. Even as an adult, I can't resist capturing a snake every time I come across one, if only to relive the excitement and boyhood wonder of my youth once again.

As far as snakes on the trail go, the usual suspects are normally garter snakes, brown water snakes, and black rat snakes. You wouldn't even notice the garter snakes unless it was out of the corner of your eye, as they slithered off the trail and disappeared into the undergrowth. If you spot one sitting motionless on the side of the trail, then hats off to you and your good vision. I came across many that laid motionless on the trail and didn't flinch, even as I stepped over them.

The black rat snakes were a little more conspicuous. These bruisers can be found anywhere from a couple of feet long to over six feet long, in rare cases. Once again, you normally won't see them unless you keep a wary eye out, or you noticed one as it shoots off the trail to get away from you. Quite often you could spot them sunning themselves in the middle of the warm trail. I couldn't tell you how many garter and rat snakes I caught and released while out on the trail; it became substantial over time...passing the time.

Some other species of snake that you might run into on the trail, although less common, are the eastern milk snake, timber rattlesnake, and the copperhead. I was lucky enough to run into at least one of each of those three species as you will find out later on in my adventure.

On one particular snake catching day in the stretch between Pearisburg and Daleville, I caught a rather large black rat snake that was nearly five feet long. He shot across the trail as I was carefully making my way through a thicket of stinging nettles. I lunged forward and was able to grab him by the tail and then maneuver my grip to the base of his head. He was a very thick bodied and healthy looking rat snake, and as I examined him, I noticed his entire body was covered in white scars that contrasted heavily against his jet black silky skin. These mountains were crawling with chipmunks, and I could only make the educated guess that "chipmunk" was probably his main source of food out there. He probably earned those scars in the depths of the chipmunk's burrows where he tracked them down and subdued them. Those little rodents had some serious teeth and claws. This snake was an old warrior; if he could talk, imagine the stories he'd have behind all those battle wounds.

Just imagine for a moment what it would be like if you had to navigate pitch black tunnels beneath the earth in order to catch your meals with nothing but your physical strength. It's frightening to think about. We don't give our animal friends enough credit for the lives they lead until we try to imagine ourselves in their position. Only then will you find the respect for these creatures they undoubtedly deserve.

Another animal that I became quite familiar with in the Virginia wilderness was a little bird called a "Whippoorwill". They were usually heard in the evenings, at night, and sometimes the early morning. These were time periods that a person would normally be asleep or trying to be asleep. These little demon birds are hell bent on keeping the entire forest up all night long. You will enjoy the call of the Whippoorwill for about ten seconds before you begin looking for a gun.

It may sound ironic for me to say that right after going on a spiel about respecting our animal friends, but this bird is an exception. They call it a "Whippoorwill" because the call it makes sounds exactly like it's saying "WHIPPOOR-WILLL," but in a whistle. Oh it doesn't stop there, because they don't just whistle it once. They whistle it over, and over, and over again in rapid succession for minutes on end. "Whippoorwill, Whippoorwill, Whippoorwill, Whippoorwill, Whippoorwill, Whippoorwill, Whippoorwill, Whippoorwill" over and over again, all night long with only a couple minutes in between every bout of its maniacal whistle. I won't say it's impossible, but it's definitely incredibly difficult to drift off to sleep with one of these whistling devils perched nearby. On more than one night I've found myself wildly hurling sticks and stones into the darkness screaming "SHUUUUT UUUUUP!" like some kind of mad man. Oh yes, the soothing sounds of nature.

Recounting the torturous call of the Whippoorwill was something that I did quite often after the trail. Most people had never heard of one, let alone heard one. When I encountered somebody unfamiliar with the call, I would almost always look up the call online in an attempt to give them a better understanding of what it sounds like. Even playing over the speakers of an electronic device, in broad daylight, when I hear the call, my eye begins to involuntarily twitch...

In early June, Laser was somewhere way ahead, Coma was somewhere way behind, while DSOH and Schweppes became my main hiking companions. It was around this time that we began to learn that all the nice things we'd heard about Virginia were lies. Well, not completely, but the greatness and flatness of Virginia had been very much exaggerated. Every day became full of arduous climbs. BIG climbs! 1,000 feet, 1,500 feet, 2,000 feet, 3,000 feet; not a day went by without at least one or two enormous climbs. We had entered the land of "Switchbacks."

A switchback is a term that refers to the zig-zagging turns that the trail would make up the side of a mountain. Switchbacks look like the trail a skier leaves when carving back and forth down a steep slope in an effort to control their speed. The trail will cut diagonally up the side of a mountain for a couple hundred feet, then sharply "switch back" in the opposite direction for another couple hundred feet before switching back again, and again, and again; so on and so forth until you reach the summit of the mountain. The sole purpose of the switchback is to even out the climb and make it more accessible to more people. Yes, switchbacks add many extra miles to the journey, but without them you would be stuck going straight up the mountain while tackling any steep rocky areas head on.

What it really comes down to is picking your poison. Do you like doing extra miles over long and arduous climbs that vary in steepness? Or do you like getting it over with and possibly having to climb hand over hand while risking a fall to your death by going straight up? Well you can't really pick, but you can decide which one you like more. Either way, it's going to be whatever the trail wants it to be.

On this particular day we'd tackled several very large 1,500 foot and higher climbs. We were aiming for an area on the map that was labeled "Audie Murphy Memorial Monument." Audie Murphy is recognized as one of the most decorated service members in American history. He was a WW2 hero that was killed in 1971 at the age of forty-five in a small private plane crash on Brush Mountain. This crash claimed the lives of four other people including the pilot of the aircraft. The memorial monument was subsequently placed at the top of Brush Mountain in commemoration.

At the time we were planning to camp there, I had no knowledge of the history. None of us did. All we knew was that Audie Murphy was a decorated war hero. We didn't know that he'd died in a plane crash on that same mountain. I originally assumed the memorial was placed there because it was maybe near his hometown, or it was an area that he'd spent time at during his youth or as an adult. I had no clue it was the place of his untimely death.

We reached the memorial just in time for sunset. The memorial itself was covered in numerous small stones that were placed as mementos of his service by the countless people that had crossed paths with the place. We left our own small stones around the memorial plaque and proceeded to watch the blood red sun sink dramatically behind a distant ridge of mountains. Then we set up camp about a hundred yards down the trail from the memorial. The trail was wide and level enough to offer a convenient spot to camp, so Schweppes pitched his tent while DSOH opted to cowboy camp on a mat with only his sleeping bag. There was no one else around at that time. I climbed about twenty feet up a steep embankment before finding two suitable trees to hang between. We built no fire as we crawled into bed with the darkness.

For some reason on this night, I couldn't get to sleep. At around 11 pm I was wide awake in my hammock, staring into the darkness of my cocoon. As I lay there, I heard the "crunch, crunch" of small pebbles being treaded upon as someone made their way down the trail. This was nothing new; hearing people pass by in the night was a semi-frequent occurrence out there, especially during the summer days. The strange thing was that I heard the steps stop on the trail directly down from my hammock, but somewhere between DSOH and Schweppes. I heard some rummaging in gear, then silence. At this point all of my senses were heightened and my adrenaline was pumping. I was completely tuned into the situation and thinking that someone was snooping around or trying to steal from us. Nighttime thieves did exist on the trail, and I kept waiting for either DSOH or Schweppes to wake up and catch someone... but nothing happened.

Then I heard the footsteps crunching loudly on the leaf litter as they made their way up the embankment towards my hammock. Closer and closer they came as I could hear each individual step. I was beginning to get very worried. "Why was Katana not barking or at least getting up to investigate?" I thought. The steps stopped directly outside my hammock on my right side before walking a complete circle around me and stopping right in front, where they'd started.

Whoever it was...just stood there. Feeling thoroughly scared, I weighed my options. I could pretend to still be asleep, or confront the noise. I chose action! I slowly moved my hands through the darkness to the zipper of my hammock canopy above my head. Once the zipper was firmly between my thumb and forefinger I forcefully pulled it down while simultaneously forcing myself out of the opening and yelled "HEY!" as loudly and intimidating as I possibly could. Nothing and nobody was there.

I flipped around and looked at Katana. She was in her same spot, behind my hammock, curled up in a ball looking at me with a worried but sleepy expression. "Is everything ok?" DSOH called up. "NO!" I yelled back. "Someone was just walking around over here and going through yawl's gear." DSOH had been asleep for the entire ordeal and Schweppes had too. In fact, Schweppes had fallen asleep with headphones on while listening to music, causing us to physically wake him up in order to recount what happened. Upon further inspection, no one's gear was missing.

Katana certainly hadn't moved, because I would've heard her leave the spot behind my hammock to go down the hill. Not to mention her leash wasn't long enough, and I had heard the steps long before they came up the leafy embankment. I was positively freaked out! The steps had stopped right in front of my hammock, and every single one of my senses had been tuned into it. I could picture in my head where the source of the noise was physically taking place during every moment of the encounter. When the noise stopped, it never moved from the front of my hammock. So, logically it should have still been there when I threw open my canvas, but it wasn't. I've never believed in ghosts in my entire life and I'm not going to try to convince anyone that this might have been a ghost. All I can say is I know what I heard and experienced that night and I can't even begin to explain it. It either happened the way I heard it, or it was all in my head. Since I don't believe that I'm crazy or that I was dreaming, I am personally inclined to believe that it happened.

As if that night hadn't been strange enough, I finally awoke in the morning to find more than thirty millipedes covering all my gear. You see millipedes nearly every day out on the trail, but never that many in one spot. They were all over everything; my hammock straps, my backpack, and my shoes that were under the hammock. There were two inside one shoe, and another one that managed to crawl inside my sock (which was stuffed inside my other shoe.) I'll give you two guesses as to how I found the one in my sock. Yeah, I was cleaning smashed millipede out of my sock for about two minutes that morning. Very strange spot - that memorial was, and it changed my outlook on a few things. Once I'd done some research and learned about the plane crash, this entire series of events seemed even stranger. Or maybe they made more sense...

Not too long before getting to Daleville, we finally reached McAfee's Knob, the most photographed spot on the entire Appalachian Trail. What makes it so famous is the drop off, or should I say the illusion of a drop off. When you first walk up to McAfee's Knob, the first thing you'll think is "WOW! What a view!" The second thing you'll think is, "This looks nothing like the pictures I've seen." That's assuming that you've ever seen a picture of McAfee's Knob in the first place. In pictures it looks like a narrow slab of rock sticking out over a drop-off that appears to go down for literally thousands of feet. This is an illusion and so is the rock slab that seems to be jutting out over the side of the cliff. It's simply a trick of the camera. If you position your photographer at a certain angle on another ledge, the resulting photograph is spectacular. In reality, you're sitting or standing on a normal cliff ledge with the tops of trees almost directly beneath you. This doesn't take anything away from the spot however, because the view is without a doubt one of the most open and dramatic views in all of Virginia, and most of the south. The visibility must be over a hundred miles out across Catawba Valley and beyond on the right day.

I took this opportunity to take the most epic Lion King picture of the entire journey. I picked up the princess, walked to the edge of the precipice, planted one foot on the edge and one foot back behind me and held little Simba up for all of Catawba Valley to see. "All that the light touches are yours Simba," ran through my head. This picture captured one of my most prized and treasured moments from the trail. It was truly a masterpiece.

The rest of the late afternoon and early evening was spent traversing a beautiful ridgeline, where I was fortunate enough to see quite a strange sight. While I was procuring water from a spring, I noticed a deer about fifteen yards away, standing there, staring in my direction. That wasn't the weird part however; the weird thing was that one of the deer's eyes was dangling out of its socket and hanging loosely against the side of its head. It was a creepy looking deer, but I felt bad for it.

I told many people of this encounter afterwards and only one person gave me an explanation. That person was a hunter that said he'd seen it several times over the course of his life, and had even shot one with an eye dangling out. He said the cause of the eye ball popping out was the work of a tick. The deer that reside in these parts of the country are so completely covered in ticks that sometimes one will attach deep in the corner of the deer's eye. As the tick sucks more and more blood, swelling up bigger and bigger, it eventually pushes the deer's eye right out of its socket. This sounds horrifying and yet another reason to be thankful for opposable thumbs.

I made it to the Tinker Cliffs just as the sun was disappearing beneath the horizon. These cliffs were approximately six miles past McAfee, and I liked them much better than the Knob. From the edge of the cliffs you could see all the way back to McAfee and the entire ridgeline that you'd just traversed. In the fading light, the ridgeline looked so beautiful and peaceful. The trees gave it a very smooth and tranquil appearance, but I knew better... I knew that beneath those trees lay a path strewn with jagged rocks and short but sharp climbs. I liked the view from above the trees much better.

I should have camped up there on the Tinker Cliffs. There was a gorgeous, flat, grassy area dotted with trees and twinkling fireflies that would've made for spectacular camping. Not to mention the sunrise I would surely have enjoyed the next morning. Unfortunately, the forecast had called for rain that night, and even though the skies were beautiful at the moment, I wasn't about to make the same mistake again. Mother Nature was an excellent teacher - I was done camping on the tops of mountains and ridgelines during rainstorms. Instead, I decided to head for a creek that was more than a thousand feet below.

As I made my way down the mountain and through Scorched Earth Gap in the darkness, I periodically scanned the sides of the trail with my headlamp looking for eye shine. As a loose rule, the eyes of non-threatening animals reflect green in false light, while predator's eyes reflect yellow. During the course of my descent, I counted more than five different pairs of green eyes looking back at me. The deer were out in force that night.

I neared the bottom of the mountain, came around a sharp curve in the trail, and was suddenly greeted by a cluster of eight green eyes staring back at me. They must have been a good sixty yards ahead, but I couldn't make out the terrain or shapes of the animals at all, even with my headlamp turned to its brightest setting. It looked like a blanket of blackness with four pairs of eyes looking directly at me. Three pairs of those eyes were grouped close together while the fourth pair seemed to be sitting a good bit higher off the ground than the other three. My initial impression was three baby bears and their mother. "But the eyes are green!" I said to myself. I began whistling and calling in the direction of the eyes. They didn't move, but one pair out of the lower three began to bob up and down quickly while remaining fixed on me. This only troubled me further, and after perhaps five minutes of making noises in an attempt to get the eyes to move away, I decided to approach them. I hoped against hope that the eye shine rule held true.

As I got nearer and nearer, outlines began to develop around the eyes and they all turned out to be deer. The pair of eyes that appeared to be quite a bit taller was nothing more than a deer standing several feet higher on an embankment behind the others. I felt like a fool, but I was secretly very relieved. I made it to the creek at close to 10 pm and settled in for the night. I would hit Daleville the next day in the early afternoon.

CHAPTER 6: VIRGINIA - Part 2

"Now the Fun Begins!"

Daleville was a nice reprieve. I spent two days there, while my mother, aunt, and my aunt's boyfriend came to visit me. It was the first family I'd seen in nearly three months. Sadly, they could only stay for a few hours, as they had made a detour while on their way to a family reunion in another part of Virginia. My mother was quite taken aback by my blossoming beard and the weight I'd lost. It was nothing to write home about, but at the time it was the most facial hair she had ever seen me with. It was also the longest my hair had been since my early teenage years, not to mention I was about thirty pounds lighter. As a token of trail magic, my mother took me, DSOH, and Schweppes out for lunch, and then paid for a hotel room before saying goodbye and continuing on their own little road trip adventure.

Undoubtedly, the best part about the hotel was the pool. I hadn't swum in a pool for what seemed like forever. I spent most of the day lounging around, drinking a few PBR beers that I got from a local gas station. Then things took a turn for the worst... sort of.

As I was standing near the edge of the pool, engaged in conversation, DSOH bull rushed me in an attempt to push me in. Growing up around pools and water my entire life, my reflexes for this type of assault were quicker than lightening. As he rushed me, I grabbed a hold of his forearms and fell back with the momentum of his charge while twisting at the same time. Everything that followed happened in the span of less than three seconds. As I feinted back and twisted, DSOH realized that his plan had backfired and that he would be the one ending up in the pool instead. As I twisted further and tossed at the same time, he let out a very quick "NO- I HAVE MY WALLET ON ME!" and for a split second I tightened and held my grip on his forearms as this sentence processed through my brain. "Wallets can get wet," I quickly reasoned as I released my grip and allowed him to continue his new trajectory. "I-MEANT-CELL-PHOOOONE!" he cried as his feet hit the water and the rest of him disappeared beneath the surface. "Whoops," I thought. That was a rookie pool mistake. You never attack someone next to a pool if you have any kind of water sensitive device on you.

Unless the element of surprise is completely in your favor, you have to factor in the risk that you may yourself be tossed in, or at the very least taken in with your victim.

So this was how the first cell phone died. I felt bad, but ultimately it was DSOH's fault. Since our cell phones doubled as our cameras, they were one of the most important pieces of electronic equipment we carried. His wasn't insured, so the incident ended up setting him back quite a few hundred dollars in order to replace it with a phone of equal camera quality.

The story of the pool incident would be retold many times after this day, but with quite a different spin from DSOH's perspective. Anytime he told it, he had to inject some of his dry sense of humor into it. In a nutshell, his recounting of the proceedings would describe me as being a tyrannical bully with a lifelong hatred and track record of picking on nerds. He would go on to say that my final words to him before maliciously tossing him into the pool were, "Fuck your cell phone! Nerds suck!" and also that the entire episode was actually a nerd hate crime initiated and perpetrated by me alone. For good measure, he would add that as he resurfaced, I put my foot on his head and pushed him back underwater. While this version was hilariously funny to hear him tell, it was far from what actually happened, as I was the real victim that was forced to bear the guilt of his murdered cell phone.

On the day that I left Daleville, I left very late in the morning while DSOH left early in the afternoon, and Schweppes left the earliest at 6 am, gaining a very large lead on us. Six miles out of Daleville I stopped at a shelter to get some water and take a break. It was a very hot day and much of the hiking had been through cow pastures that offered no protection from the sun. One of the pastures had actually been home to an overly curious donkey that had attacked several people earlier that day. I never had any problems, but I learned of the incidents later on in the shelter's log.

At this shelter I met a couple that was in their late thirties or possibly early forties. I have no idea who they were, and I don't believe they were thru-hiking. What seemed obvious was that they were strung out on something, and were either very drunk or very high; possibly a combination of both. The man was having a mini melt down because he'd found a tick attached to his leg earlier that morning. He was going on and on about needing to get to a hospital to be tested for Lyme disease. If he was so worried, I don't know why he was wasting time sitting at that shelter. The nearest road was only a couple hours away. His freaking out about the tick wasn't the most annoying aspect of the situation however. He kept saying the same things to me over and over.

He would look at me and say in a slow, drawn out, slurred speech, "Hey... hey maan... can I tell you somethin maan?" Me: "Sure." "You have a beeautifuullldawgmaaan." Me: "Thanks." Every word he said was over pronounced and slurred together. He must have told me that I had a beautiful dog about seven times before I wrapped up my filtering process and moved along. My parting words to the couple were, "I wouldn't worry about Lyme disease, I think ticks are the least of your worries right now."

As the day and evening wore on, a storm rolled in and I decided to make camp a little early before it hit. DSOH did the same, consequently ending up somewhere behind me, while Schweppes remained somewhere ahead. The three of us were scattered across the trail.

I again hiked alone for all of the next day. It was exceptionally hot, and as a consequence, I ended up carrying Katana for quite a few miles. It was a hard day that had me very chafed by its end. I'd put in over twenty miles and was trying to wrap it up at a shelter called "Bryant Ridge," as it was labeled in my guide. I waded across a small stream and came up over a berm to see what appeared to be a huge house or small mansion through the trees. "What a remote area to find a mansion," I thought to myself.

As I drew nearer, I realized that the front of this mansion was completely open. Then it dawned on me, "WOW, that's a shelter!" This was the biggest, nicest, and most elaborate shelter I'd ever seen on the trail. It looked like you could fit close to forty people into it. The structure was three stories tall with lofts, benches, seats, and platforms, as well as giant hooks to hang your gear to keep out of reach of mice. There was also a fancy privy (outhouse) off to the side. The forecast had called for rain that evening, so I was happy to have a shelter large and sturdy enough to hang my hammock within, so as to avoid setting up my rain fly.

As I entered the front of the shelter, I noticed another man sitting on a bench. No sooner did I notice him; I was startled out of my skin by a demonic growl bellowing out from a corner of the shelter. I looked over to see an enormous, close to two hundred pound, Irish Wolf Hound. "HO-LEE SHIT!" I said under my breath.

Imagine an animal that was bred to operate and make decisions independently from its master over long distances. Now imagine that animal being capable of running down a wolf, then being able to kill it once it caught it. That's what an Irish Wolf Hound was bred to do. One look at one of these monsters and you'll believe that they are damn well suited for that task.

I've never had a fear of dogs and I've always felt that in the case of an attack I would be more than capable of defending my life against any dog with nothing but my bare hands and will to live. When I looked at that Irish Wolf Hound, I saw an animal that could probably kill me at will, and kill Katana with one shake of its head. In Katana's eyes, she was twice as big as this brute and had no problem attempting to confront him. This was the exact reason that I decided NOT to stay in the shelter that night. I hung my hammock a couple hundred feet away and pitched my rain fly, then thought nothing else of the situation for the rest of the evening.

It was approximately 2 am when my eyes opened wide awake for seemingly no reason. My senses came to me as I realized it was steadily raining. "Why am I awake?" I thought to myself. I laid there for a moment, staring at the ceiling of my canopy wondering why I'd awoken for apparently no reason when my stomach began to rumble and tighten uncontrollably. It was instantly an emergency. I threw open my canopy, hopped out, frantically rummaged through my pack for my bathroom kit and took off for the Privy. Most people would never recount or admit what I am about to tell you because of the embarrassing and gross nature of it, but it was completely out of my control. It's an experience that I can now look back on and laugh at, even though there was not a damn thing funny about it at the time.

As I tried to awkwardly run through the rain, I was only fifty feet short of the privy when I quite literally lost complete control over the muscles below my waist. My legs buckled beneath me, and as I began to fall, I threw my shorts down as far as I could. I landed against a slight embankment as the flood gates opened. There was nothing to hold onto and no strength or control in my legs to stand up. I just laid there, collapsed and crippled on the ground, as the worst diarrhea experience of my life unfolded. It was all over my cheeks, my lower back, my legs, and calves, even on my feet. I laid there in my own puddle of disgust, horror, and discomfort for the better part of two minutes before the worst was over. Then I shakily stood up and made my way to the privy.

For the next hour my body completely drained itself in every way that it could. I was sweating profusely, fighting cramps, puking, and crapping. At the time I honestly thought that I might be dying because it certainly felt like it. Looking back, I would recall this as the moment that I felt my most helpless while out on the trail. At no other time while I was out there did I wish that I was back home more so than in that moment. I just wanted someone to be there for me. I was beyond help out there and almost to the point of being unable to help myself. I was scared and didn't know how much worse it would get, or for how much longer.

When it was finally over, I cleaned up the mess in the privy and buried the excrement on the embankment, but didn't have enough paper to clean myself. In the cold rain that had now slowed to a drizzle, I made my way down to the stream. I stripped down and settled myself onto the rocky bottom of the stream and set about cleaning. The water was freezing, making the entire experience even more miserable. By the time I made it back to my hammock, it was almost 4 am; I fell asleep almost immediately.

The morning after the great crap-scapade I felt weak and my joints hurt. I was also dizzy with a severe headache. I lay in my hammock all day, drinking as much water as I could and forcing myself to eat any snacks that I could stomach. DSOH caught up around 3 pm and stayed with me for an hour before pushing on to the next shelter that was over two thousand feet above me and nearly five miles away. Not a terribly steep climb, but a long one.

Despite still feeling weak and nauseas, I made the decision to attempt some miles. I slowly packed up camp and began making my way up Floyd Mountain. Almost immediately I wished I'd just stayed in my hammock. I ended up having to stop every fifteen minutes for about five to ten minutes. The only thing that kept me from pulling over and making camp again was imagining the feeling I would get from climbing Katahdin. I thought about all the challenges I'd already been through and how utterly fantastic it was going to feel to summit that mountain knowing everything I had overcome, including this. I kept getting goose bumps every time I thought about touching the sign on the summit of Katahdin. Those thoughts were the only thing that kept me going. When I finally reached the next shelter, it had taken me over four hours to go those five miles. I didn't even care about how long it took, because I'd done it, and now I could sleep once more.

I was nearly 300 miles into the state of Virginia and 760 miles into the entire trail when I started feeling the monotony of the journey. I was so tired of Virginia. I was ready to start entering some new states and feeling like I was actually going somewhere. These feelings I had were products of a well-documented condition known as the "Virginia Blues." With more than a quarter of the entire trail residing in this state, it was easy to get discouraged by the seeming lack of progress. I felt like I'd been out there for a lifetime, and when I tried to remember life before the trail, it seemed much longer than a mere 78 days ago. It felt like a whole other lifetime ago. I was still enjoying myself tremendously, but I was really feeling the grind - mentally and physically.

Summer was just about in full swing as I made my way closer to the "bump in the road" town known as Glasgow. The days were hot and arduous; causing Katana to make my life difficult on an almost daily basis. Although it highly aggravated me on the inside, I did my best not to project anger or frustration towards her when she refused to walk any further. It was almost like clockwork. As soon as the sun got high in the sky and we'd reach an incline, she would sit down in the middle of the trail, refusing to walk. It was ALWAYS before a climb. I would never give in right away, but first let her rest a moment before attempting to lead her up again. Eight times out of ten, she would dig her hind legs into the ground in protest, then lay down when the pressure came off the leash. I would then go over and attempt to stand her up in an effort to pet and coax her forward. Like a little kid that's reluctant to go somewhere, she would let her body go limp so that I couldn't even stand her up. It was when she played this card that I normally gave in and slung her onto my shoulders. That little dog had me wrapped around its little paw.

Many of the dogs I ran into out there looked as if they were wasting away. They all lost weight and began to take on a pretty emaciated form. Not all of them, but many. Katana was doing just the opposite. Her breed was made for this, and that little dog was packing on muscle like it was her job. Through her chest, arms, and shoulders, Katana was getting buff! When she stood facing you head on, you could see every muscle in her forelegs and shoulders outlined through her thick fur. Towards the end of Virginia, she weighed twenty pounds or more; up from the fifteen or so that she weighed when she first came out. It was good for her to be getting in such good shape, but killing me to add twenty pounds to my already too heavy pack on those long up hills. Once at the top of the climbs she would always be game to start walking again on the downhill. This was very considerate of her...

On a blistering hot day, I had been carrying Katana off and on for quite a distance. I was trying to push twenty miles in order to reach the town of Glasgow, and I'd been leap frogging with Viking all day. Leap frogging is when you pass someone on the trail, then they pass you later on. This can go back and forth over the course of a day, depending on how many breaks you or the other person took. I would catch up to Viking and pass him while he was on a break, then he'd pass me every time I took a break or had to carry Katana.

I was getting close to thirteen miles into the day when I reached a very steep climb on a mountain called "High Cock Knob." Don't ask me where the name comes from, that's just what it was labeled. True to form, when Katana realized we were about to be going up a steep climb, she refused to go any further. Not wanting to waste any more time getting into town, I picked her straight up without any argument. As I was slinging her onto my shoulders, she somehow managed to catch my neck, shoulder, and upper chest with two really hard kicks that scratched the hell out of me. I cursed at the pain, as well as her out of character squirming as I finished putting her across my shoulders and thinking nothing else of it. Once across my shoulders, she relaxed and soon had the stupid grin that she always wore when getting a free ride.

In order to reach the road that lead into Glasgow, I had to cross the James River Footbridge. It was the longest "foot traffic only" bridge on the entire trail, and it was a tradition for hikers to jump off this bridge into the James River. This would normally be right up my alley, but as I approached the bridge, another hiker informed me that three other people had been fined over $200 each for jumping off the bridge earlier. Apparently wardens watched the bridge from some hidden location on the shore and looked for jumpers on busy days. Since it was a Sunday, the river had its usual light crowd of fisherman, kayakers, and rafters. The wardens kept a vigil watch; as soon as you jumped, they show up just in time to write you a ticket as you're climbing out of the water. I wasn't about to risk forking over that kind of money, so I passed.

Viking and I were able to catch a ride with a young female day hiker into Glasgow after about twenty minutes of failed hitchhiking. We had a pizza at the only eatery in town called Scotto's, then set up camp on the edge of a large field that the town had actually designated for thru- hikers specifically. After getting my hammock set up, I took a load off and sat around a small fire that was already burning. Through campfire talk, and the trail grapevine, I learned that Schweppes had been there the night before. I also learned that his father and younger brother had met up with him and were going to tag along for nine days or so.

DSOH was still behind me due to the fact that he had met a female hiker that he was spending time with, and as a consequence was going at a slower pace. It was also while sitting around this fire with perhaps a half dozen other hikers that I noticed the small gold chain that I always wore around my neck was gone. I had worn that chain non-stop since I was fourteen years old. It was a gift that was left to me in my grandmother's will when she passed away. I'd always worn it, only taking it off during sporting events in my teenage years. As soon as I realized it was gone, I felt a depressed hopelessness wash over me.

I tried to think back to where I could've lost it and the only thing that came to mind was Katana scratching my shoulders and neck when I lifted her onto my shoulders. This was the only instance that I could think of where it could have possibly come off. Of course it could've come off anywhere, but I could only remember that one event as being the most likely catalyst. I mentioned my loss to maybe three or four of the hikers that were there and said nothing more about it. It took a little while, but I resigned myself to accepting the loss. It was a very small, thin chain, and I highly doubted that anyone would ever spot it lying on the overgrown, leaf littered ground. Even if someone did find it, the chances that they would try and find the owner were extremely slim. I quickly accepted the inevitable reality that I would never see it again.

I woke up in a puddle of sweat the next morning as the temperature was already in the mid 90's. I decided to get some chores done, do some laundry, then hike out in the early evening when temperatures would be cooler. DSOH arrived mid-morning as I was walking to the local Laundromat. I garnered some strange looks from the old ladies there while I was lounging around in only my Soffe short shorts, reading Cosmo and Seventeen Magazine while waiting on my laundry. This was the first time I'd ever picked up these magazines in my life, and I won't lie, I picked them up because of the attractive women on the front cover. I had nothing else better to do while I was waiting.

Another huge game changer took effect in Glasgow while I was there. This was the place that I would experiment with Tupperware in my pack. I'd been storing all of my cosmic brownies, honey buns, oatmeal cream cookies, and cheese inside of a dry bag. This always resulted in completely smashed and sometimes pulped food. There comes a time in a man's life when he has to put his foot down and say "NO! I will not eat smooshed cosmic brownies any longer!" That time for me was Glasgow.

Tupperware completely revolutionized the food aspect of my hike. It was a little awkward, but in the end I got it to fit ergonomically inside my pack. For nearly the rest of my hike I enjoyed pristine sugary snacks and unsmooshed cheese. I no longer had to eat pop tart dust, and instead enjoyed crisp pastries in all of their un-smashed glory. If you can fit a one or two liter rectangular Tupperware into your pack without minding the extra ounce of weight, then I highly recommend it. Your hiking constituents will be terribly jealous of the "right out of the box" appearance of your food.

The first couple of days out of Glasgow were painfully brutal. The heat was unforgiving, the bugs were out in hoards, and the climbs had been huge, steep, and rocky. Throughout Virginia (and Pennsylvania as I would later find) there had been a type of large black fly that would follow you for miles if you let it. These big bruisers of a fly would buzz loudly while doing touch and goes on the back of your head, so much that it was enough to drive you insane! They never made a solid landing while you were walking, and it was nearly impossible to swat one in the middle of a "touch and go." The only way to get rid of them was to calmly stop in your tracks, then hover your hand about eight inches from the back of your head...and wait. The fly would eventually make a solid touchdown directly on the back of your head, giving you a chance to end its flying career. You had to be quick or they'd dodge your slap, leaving you with a stinging and rattled head, as well as an undead fly. Then the task of luring the fly back into a false sense of security would start all over again.

It was on a hot morning, after having dealt with flies like that, when I came to the summit of Bluff Mountain at nearly four thousand feet in altitude. On this summit was a small memorial plaque that read: "This is the exact spot little Ottie Cline Powell's body was found April 5, 1891, after straying from Tower Hill School House on November 9th; a distance of 7 miles; aged 4 years, 11 months." I sat next to the memorial for a few minutes and reflected on what it said. A four-year-old child had climbed up here, and this was the spot where he had succumbed to the elements or starvation. I thought about how difficult it had been for me to climb up to this spot even with a cleared trail, and how back then there wasn't one. How a four-year-old child managed to climb up there over that terrain and thick vegetation is beyond fathoming. The longer I sat there, the more I thought about it. "Why did he climb up here?" "How long did he wander around before he finally got here?" "How long was he here before he died?" I had so many questions that could never be answered by anyone but little Ottie. He had been missing for five months before they finally found him. No doubt his body had been covered by snow and only revealed to the world once spring had arrived and melted the snow. It's sad, intriguing, and eerie being at the spot where it happened. Such a tragic story, little Ottie Cline's was.

It was later that afternoon, as I made my way down Rice Mountain that I crossed paths with two young women that were headed south. When they were perhaps a hundred feet away from me, one of them called, "Hey are you the Mayor?" "How did you know that?" I called back. "We were told you wear American flag shorts and have a little fox dog," she replied. "Someone found your necklace; a hiker named Rodeo has it and is trying to catch up with you." My jaw dropped. This information floored me. I'd lost the necklace who knows how many miles back. "How was this news reaching me from people that were ahead of me and going in the opposite direction?" I wondered.

It turned out that some plant biologist found my necklace, gave it to a forestry worker, and then the forestry worker gave it to the hiker named Rodeo. Rodeo had arrived in Glasgow and asked around if anyone had lost a gold chain. Somehow, someone was still there that remembered me mentioning it and told her that it was mine. The forestry worker somehow learned that Rodeo had found out the name of the owner and their description, then gone up the trail and informed any south bounders to relay the information if they came across me.

"WOW! This trail is magical!" I thought. I didn't think I would ever see the chain again, and certainly not through a crazy series of events such as these. I thanked them and pushed on. How crazy it was for my chain to be found in such a manner; however, it would be some time before I would finally get it back.

Not too far from a road leading into the town of Buena Vista, DSOH would become very sick from dehydration and end up taking a few days off to recover. I sat at the road with him for some time waiting on a shuttle that he'd called to pick him up. I was very close to going in with him, if only to take a break from the brutal heat and enormous climbs, as well as to make sure he was alright. In the end, I wished him a speedy recovery before pressing on through the Virginia summer.

Leaving DSOH that morning had put me in a less than good mood. It was the combination of bugs, heat, thirst, grueling climbs, and then watching my good friend leave in a weakened state while not knowing if I would see him again. Not to mention, I had a three-thousand-foot climb just beyond the road I'd been sitting at. I was depressed and tired, but gritted out the long climb up Bald Knob Mountain just the same. After a couple hours of climbing up Bald Knob and Cold Mountain, I was even more downtrodden. On top of that, I was out of water. There had been no water on the climbs, and when I finally did find the landmark for a spring, it was nearly half a mile off the trail. Since there was no water for miles after this source, I was forced to make the side trip.

A funny thing about us thru-hikers is that even though we are on this epic long distance trek of thousands of miles, we don't want to walk any further than we have to. Earlier in this book I'd mentioned "sideways miles." If a water source or a shelter resided off of the main trail, it was referred to as a sideways mile. As a rule, most people didn't like to do more than two tenths of a mile to any water source or shelter off the trail. Three tenths was pushing it; that was normally on the very edge of what most people were willing to walk sideways (if it wasn't leading into a town). Half a mile was a huge side trip. That meant that you were making a one mile round trip, sideways walk. That's about twenty minutes if you walk at a quick three miles per hour, not to mention whatever time you spend at the halfway point on your round trip. Yes, you can kill close to an hour in sideways hiking while procuring water and not get anywhere. There's nothing you can do about it, because it's a necessity, as well as another aspect of hiking the trail that you have to accept. However, just because you have to accept it, doesn't mean you have to like it.

Upon discovering that I had to make this long round trip for water, it put me in an even worse mood. I left my pack, with Katana attached to it, on the side of the main trail beneath some trees. Then I began making my way down the side trail. A couple hundred yards down the trail I noticed a man sitting under a pine tree about twenty yards or so off to the side. I could tell immediately that he wasn't a thru-hiker, so it was strange to see him sitting in such a random out of the way spot. He didn't look at me, so I ignored him and continued on. I filtered and drank a couple liters of ice cold spring water before beginning the walk back.

As I was passing the man once again he turned and called, "Do you think the clouds will come out and block the sun for a bit?" I thought this was a funny question. I told him that I didn't know and asked him why it mattered. He replied, "I burn very easily and don't want to get Melanoma again." As he said this, he pulled up his sleeve and preceded to show and tell me all about the scar from where they removed his first case of Melanoma. He said he wanted to get back to his car that was down by the road leading into Buena Vista, but was afraid to be out in the sun for too long. As a result of his "sun phobia," he'd been sitting under the trees for a couple of hours. I told him he would be just fine and that he'd be under the shade of trees mostly, with just a few seconds of sun exposure at a time. He wasn't convinced.

This guy was wearing a huge sun brim hat, long sleeves, long pants, and boots. The only part of him that was exposed to the sun were his hands. He was definitely more than adequately protected from the sun, yet here he was hiding under this tree like some sort of creepy vampire. I tried to assure him that he would be just fine leaving right now, but he made it very clear that he was going to wait a little bit longer until the sun went down some more. Before he tried to show me his scars from his second bout with Melanoma, I politely started on my way back to Katana.

When he was perhaps fifty feet behind me, he called "Wait!" I turned around not completely sure of what he could possibly have left to say. "Do you want this knife?" he said while waving a large, opened, folding knife in the air at me. I didn't say anything, instead giving him a look that said, "If I come over there to get it, are you going to stab me with it, skin me, and then use my skin as an umbrella to shield you from the sun?" I think he realized how strangely he came across , and quickly closed the knife before adding, "I just found it sitting here, you can have it." "Sure," I replied. He tossed me the knife and I thanked him for the gift before continuing on again. "The strangest things always seem to happen to me," I thought to myself as I walked away. Boy was that the understatement of the year as I would soon find out later on in my journey.

After the vampire encounter, I continued my trudge across Tar Jacket Ridge, still depressed, still tired, and still sweating bullets. A couple miles later, I came to a dirt road that was most likely a service or fire road. On this road I found two large coolers and a short note explaining that it was "Trail Magic" left by a thru-hiker who completed the trail in 2012. I opened the first cooler to find that it was full of Gatorade. It must have been left the day before, because the ice had turned to slush and those babies were as cold as Antarctica! I can say with complete honesty, that the blue Gatorade I consumed at that spot was the single greatest drink of liquid that I've ever had in my entire life. Never had a cold drink tasted so good to me before. The positive psychological affect this had on me was unbelievable.

The other cooler was full of candy bars, Twinkies, and Moon Pies. This simple gesture turned my entire day around. I was suddenly in high spirits as a wave of happiness and light-heartedness washed over me. I ended up crushing the rest of the day. Before stumbling across those coolers, I'd only gone five miles before noon. After a short break with the trail magic treats, I ended up knocking out twenty-three miles before darkness fell, singing and whistling the whole way. I must have looked like a real happy-go-lucky candy ass to any unseen observers, but who cares?

It was moments like finding coolers full of drinks and snacks left out in the middle of nowhere that made me appreciate the little things in life. Allow me to try and put this into perspective. When I ran into trail magic like this, or when I was in town for the first time in nearly a week and about to have a sweet tea, a slice of pizza, or any one of the small things that we would normally not think twice about in daily life; a special feeling would wash over me. I can only describe that feeling as being exactly like the feelings you would experience as a child on Christmas morning or waking up on your birthday, except stronger. Out here you don't get that feeling only twice a year. You get it every time someone performs a simple act of kindness, or when you get a dose of something that you otherwise could've had at any time back in the "real world." It's addicting, humbling, and eye opening. It makes you appreciate what you had before the trail and makes you want to never take such simple things for granted ever again.

That evening, shortly after 8 pm, I reached a shelter near the top of a mountain called The Priest. As I rolled in, I discovered Schweppes, his dad, and his younger brother were already there. It had been over a week since I'd seen him. We caught up as I enjoyed hearing about the trials and tribulations of his father and brother during their first several days on the trail. It all sounded vaguely familiar to my first days.

It was on this night I learned that Schweppes had made the conversion to hammock camping. His younger brother had brought a hammock to sleep in and subsequently not liked it; unbelievable! So Schweppes leant him his tent while taking the hammock, and was now "sold" on hammock camping. Another ground dweller turned to the dark side.

The next morning, Schweppes' dad and brother left earlier than us. After finishing the rest of the climb up The Priest, we began a long four-mile descent back towards level ground. At the bottom of The Priest we caught up with the Schweppes' duo at a state road near the Tye River, just before another three thousand foot climb up Three Ridges Mountain. We weren't going to catch any breaks that day, as the terrain was bent on killing us. In the end, Schweppes' dad and brother decided that their feet were hurting too much to make the distances we needed in order to get into the town of Waynesboro before running out of food. They planned to stay down at the road and attempt to hitch a ride to another road that was ten miles ahead, then hike another twelve miles or so and meet us at a shelter later that night. This meant a long day over some hard terrain for Schweppes and me, but we were confident we could handle it.

It was hotter than twenty hells, but we were lucky enough to have a good breeze blowing that day. We began the three-thousand-foot climb at a fairly quick pace, and around 2.5 miles in we stopped at a shelter called "Harper's Creek" to get some water. On the path to that shelter we encountered a huge rattlesnake that I identified as a "timber rattler." It was sitting right on the path next to a large log. If I hadn't spotted it first, Katana would've reached it about fifteen feet ahead of me. This was extremely lucky since I was usually looking down at my feet, trying not to trip half the time. I pulled Katana back, took off my pack and tethered her to it. I made the decision that I was going to catch this snake. I'd caught countless cotton mouth snakes and copperheads back in Florida, but never a rattlesnake. This was going to be a first.

I knew I couldn't leave the snake near the shelter where people walked and had dogs with them on a daily basis. I also knew that I couldn't simply carry it around and relocate it somewhere else. Before I even approached the rattler, I made the decision that I would harvest it for food. I knew they were supposed to be great to eat, but I'd never tried one. In fact, I'd never killed a snake before in my life, and this was a decision that I didn't take lightly. It was made with the safety of other hikers and their pets in mind. I also rationalized that if someone else came across it, they would probably toss a rock or log onto it, then kick it off the trail... wasted. I felt that eating it would be a far more ethical and respectful thing to do.

Obviously I could've dropped a rock on it or smacked it with my staff, safely killing it and then eating it instead of catching it by hand, but that seemed so dishonorable. I truly do have great respect for these creatures, and felt the only way I would kill it was on an even playing field, where it had an equal chance to get me if my skills were unworthy. Call it crazy if you want, but it made perfect sense to me at that time.

I approached the rattler slowly as I reached out and used my staff to uncoil it. It remained still and did not rattle. Those were the dangerous ones; the ones that didn't let you know they were there. As I pinned its head with my staff, it began to rattle but still remained motionless. My heart and my adrenaline were pumping, but the snake's docile behavior up until this point had succeeded in lulling me into a false sense of confidence with a lowered guard. I had gone through these motions hundreds of times before with other snakes. "This is going to be just like any other snake," I thought to myself. I reached down without hesitating and grabbed it just behind the head. Instantly and unexpectedly the snake began to thrash around violently! So hard that it nearly broke the grip I had behind its head before I completely tightened it. I grabbed the body with my free hand in an attempt to restrain it further, and briefly, it yanked my arm around before I managed to get complete control.

I hadn't expected this snake to be so strong. Since rattlesnakes are not constrictors, I didn't anticipate such a violent reaction with so much power. The rattler's thrashing was stronger than any non-venomous snake I'd ever caught in my life. Katana was going crazy behind me, barking and wailing frantically. I don't know if she was worried about me or just wanted to get to the snake. What was apparent was that the sound of the rattle seemed to have some kind of instinctive effect on her, because she was acting more frantic than I'd ever seen before.

Schweppes pulled out his knife and I asked him to hold the body while I made the cut. He refused, and I didn't blame him. Not wanting a repeat of the thrashing, I knelt down and put my knee on the body of the snake. I took the knife in my free hand and quickly separated the head from right behind where my grip was. I let go of the head, but held onto the body as it thrashed around wildly. The decapitated stump automatically struck at my hands repeatedly where they were holding onto the bulk of the snake. It was unnerving and difficult not to instinctively drop it while it was striking me, but I knew the body was harmless without the head. I buried the head off

133

to the side trail before we continued the rest of the way to the shelter. I went down to the creek and began cleaning.

I cut down the belly from stump to tail. Then I grabbed the esophagus at the top of the stump and pulled all of the entrails out in one motion. They were all in a membrane encasing, so they came out together in one piece fairly easily. I returned my focus back to the stump and pulled the skin away from the meat. Once I had freed a good flap of skin from the muscle, I gripped the chunk of skin and peeled the entire thing off like a sock. Three minutes after my first incision, I had a clean, pinkish white chunk of snake meat. Not a tough job at all; almost easier than filleting a fish. I washed the meat in Harper's Creek before putting it in a spare Ziploc bag. Now we had dinner! Measuring the skin against my staff, we found that the rattler was well over four feet long. That was pretty large by rattlesnake standards.

As we pushed on and finished the climb, we soon realized it was going to be a day of snakes. I caught another black rat snake that measured almost six feet long. That was the biggest one I ever caught over the course of the entire trail, and after taking a picture, I released him as we continued hiking.

As the afternoon progressed, it became apparent that our plan to meet Schweppes' family members was going to be more difficult than we anticipated. The trail became a boulder field for miles, slowing our progress dramatically. We hiked until nearly midnight before calling it quits atop Humpback Mountain. We never caught Schweppes' father and brother but managed to rack up more than twenty-three miles over the nasty terrain.

I built a large fire and enjoyed a late night (or should I say early morning) meal of rattlesnake. I seasoned him with garlic salt, wrapped him around a medium sized tree branch, and roasted him over the fire. The rattler turned out fantastic! The texture and taste was that of calamari and beef ribs. That's only my opinion, as someone else may have a more accurate description of rattlesnake flavor and texture. After dinner, all that was left was a bare snake skeleton sitting in the embers of a dying fire. I passed out shortly after eating, feeling exhausted, full, accomplished, and slightly guilty.

When I awoke the next morning, I smelled like a mixture of cooked rattlesnake, sweaty armpits, and ammonia. It was not a good combination. I packed up and left camp early while Schweppes was still asleep in his hammock. About four miles into the morning I came across Schweppes' dad and brother. They had just finished packing up their tents and hadn't made it to the meeting point of the previous day either, falling short by several miles. I spoke with them for a while and recounted the story of the rattlesnake before continuing on.

I made it almost twelve miles and reached the road into Waynesboro just before noon. There was a small parking lot on the side of the road near the trailhead where a woman was taking a bicycle off the back of her compact SUV. I tried an indirect hitching method. "Excuse me Ma'am, do you think you could point me in the direction of town?" "Yes, it's right down this way," she said pointing left down the road. "I would give you a ride in, but I've only got an hour to do this bike ride and I'm kind of in a hurry." "Oh no problem, thanks for the info!" I replied.

At that moment as I was turning away, she opened one of her back doors to get something and Katana spun around and jumped in. "No Katana, we're not riding with her, we have to find another ride," I said in a voice that you might speak to a young child in. I pulled her out and when I set her on the ground, she kept straining against the leash in an attempt to get back in the SUV. "Awwww," the woman crooned. "You know what; your dog won me over, hop in!" Bingo! Katana was pulling her weight once again and scoring me rides. I didn't have it down to a science yet, but further north, I would use Katana and her cuteness as a strategic method for gaining rides in and out of towns.

Waynesboro was an eclectic little town, and for as small as it was, they had an array of stores that might surprise you. The most surprising being an indoor Porsche dealership. I walked around town for a bit and had lunch at a huge Chinese Buffet called "Ming Tree." This buffet would later become the buffet that all buffets and other eateries were measured against on the trail. After Waynesboro, when asking for a review of a restaurant from hikers already in town or coming out of town, the exchange would usually go something like this: "Hey buddy, how was that buffet in Bennington?" "Oh it was pretty good, but it was no Mings!" "Gotcha! Thanks!" Yes, Ming Tree was the finest eating establishment ever established for eating near the trail. I spent the better part of two hours in there trying to stuff more and more sushi and honey chicken down my esophagus.

After the eating affairs were all in order, I looked for a place to unwind. I ended up checking into a Comfort Inn, which was a much needed reprieve. My blog needed to be caught up, not to mention I'd been killing myself with long days in the brutal heat, over the most challenging terrain Virginia had thrown at me so far. I wanted to at least take one zero day while I was there. From Daleville to Waynesboro I felt as if I'd been put through a ringer. That stretch was the toughest stretch in all of Virginia and the entire trail for me up until that point, and I was in dire need of some rest and relaxation.

Later that afternoon, Schweppes and his family members rolled into the hotel. Since they were only slotted to hike another two days, they were set on making the most of it, and planned to hike out the next morning. I didn't know how I felt about that because I really wanted to hike with them, but I also really wanted/needed the extra day to rest. In the end, after some pleading and convincing from Schweppes, he changed my mind to hike out with them the next day. We would be entering the famous Shenandoah National Park...

CHAPTER 7: VIRGINIA-Part 3

"Whippoorwills, Bears, and Snakes - OH MY!"

We got a very late start leaving Waynesboro the next day. We called a shuttle to take us back to the trail and the driver turned out to be an overweight older man in a huge, beat up, yellow truck that was kind of a rude jerk, but I think that might've been his sense of humor. The first thing he said to us when we climbed into his truck was, "I don't want to know your trail names or your real names, y'all smell bad and I don't like ya." Great introduction, right? The drive back to the trailhead was awkward and filled with brash remarks from our driver. Like I said, I don't think he was trying to be intentionally rude, I just think he had a backwards sense of humor and didn't care if anyone understood it. Since I have somewhat of a flippant sense of humor at times myself, I could understand where the guy was coming from and tried to overlook it.

When we reached the trailhead, the sky was already darkening with storm clouds as the wind picked up and that familiar rainy smell permeated the air. "This is my last chance," I thought. "I can still go back into town and have a relaxing day to myself." I went against those thoughts and decided I would stick with my friends. We were required to fill out some paperwork before entering Shenandoah National Park, and had to carry a permit with us that proved we had registered our presence.

Shenandoah National Park was described as the easiest and most enjoyable hundred-mile stretch in all of Virginia. It was the "Disneyland" of the trail. It was also described as having the best maintained trails and the most bears per square mile out of any other park in the country. I believe the ratio was said to be one bear per square mile throughout the entire park. When I first heard this, I thought it was a gross exaggeration, but as I made my way across this wooded "Disney" paradise, I learned that it was quite possibly an understatement.

We set out together, the four of us maintaining a nice straight line while going at a moderate pace for about twenty minutes. I soon became restless with our slower pace and informed them that I would meet them at the first shelter that resided eight miles into the park. I pulled ahead and began maintaining a quick 3.5 miles per hour. Not ten minutes after leaving them, the sky exploded. Once again it was raining as hard as it ever had out on the trail. For about five minutes I was immensely frustrated with myself for not staying in town. Then I did what you have to do in order to not lose your mind out there... I accepted my predicament and moved on.

As I was going across a small field of very jagged rocks, I tripped and began to fall. Usually when I tripped out there, I was able to catch myself with my staff, but on this occasion, I wasn't catching anything. As I tripped, I threw my staff out and away from me while putting my hands out to catch myself. Had I hit the more jagged rocks that surrounded me, my hands and other body parts would have been split wide open. Luckily my hands fell on relatively level rocks as I landed in a push-up-like position, jamming my wrists and jarring my elbows violently. My right elbow that had recently undergone surgery the previous November, pinched and throbbed with shooting pains for hours after the fall. Needless to say, I was once again in a bad mood. My elbow would end up becoming sensitive and bothering me for weeks after this day. So much so, that I would end up switching my staff to my left hand for most of the day in the coming weeks, in an attempt to avoid the pinching sensation that I was now getting from pushing off with my right.

After three hours of slogging through the monsoon, I finally reached the shelter. I set up, stripped off my wet clothes, and climbed into the nest that made everything feel better. I pulled out my cell phone and kindle to check any messages and began some light reading. Upon checking my phone, I saw that I had a text from Schweppes. It read, "Hey man, after the rain started we turned around and went back to the hotel. Sorry." "WHAAAAAT!" I screamed half in my head and half out loud. That's what I should have been doing! Relaxing in a nice climate controlled room, not sitting in deplorable weather conditions, sucking farts in my own personal fart dungeon. They had convinced me to come out with them, then abandoned me to the rain Gods. I was again upset for maybe two minutes before I shrugged it off and began reading my book.

I managed to read more than three, five hundred page novels throughout the course of my adventure, plus two or three smaller books with two to three hundred pages. Most of my reading was done at night, while lying in my hammock, but I also logged many hours during lunch breaks, or breaks at beautiful locations throughout the day. One thing I found strangely ironic about my choice in literature was that it was all Sci-Fi. Most people read Sci-Fi in an attempt to escape reality and get away from it all (I know I do); at least while your mind wanders the confines of the book. Here I was on this epic journey that was quite literally getting me "away from it all," yet I was still reading books that were metaphorically taking me away from that. I always chuckled whenever I thought about it; "Would I ever be far enough away from it all?"

Day two in the Shenandoah Park proved to be quite eventful. The trail was easy, well graded, and the surrounding forests seemed almost sub-tropical at times. There was a lot of moisture in the air, on the ground, and all over the vegetation. Everything was green and growing thickly. As I made my way along the narrow path surrounded by shrubs and trees, I heard what sounded like a hiss above me. I looked up to see an adolescent bear that was thirty feet up a huge basswood tree to my immediate left. It looked to be maybe a hundred pounds, hanging onto the upper boughs looking down at me, hissing and clicking its jaw. If it had just kept quiet, I never would've known it was there. I began removing my pack in an attempt to reach my phone, to take a picture. No sooner did I have one strap free, the small bear began to slide down the tree very quickly. I realized this was my queue to leave, so I slid the strap back on and began walking briskly away with Katana in tow. The Bear tally was now five...

As I continued on through the pleasant backcountry, I couldn't help but think of my luck at having seen five bears on the journey so far. "That's a respectable number to encounter," I thought to myself. The trail through much of Shenandoah was for the most part mundane. You never realize how entertaining the sharp climbs and rocky terrain can be, even though most of the time you hate them. The obstacles give you something to focus on, as well as something to set your energy and will against. Walking on a flat featureless trail, although easy, can get very boring. You simply run out of things to think about, and you've already exhausted every song that you know after walking for nearly nine hundred miles. The trees, as well as the scenery beneath them can only be gawked at and admired for so long. Unless it's something truly unique or remarkable, it all begins to look the same.

While coming down a slight decline that zig-zagged unnecessarily, as it "switch backed" its way down, I came around a corner and found myself within spitting distance of two large black bears staring each other down. There was a large male close to four hundred pounds and a medium female under two hundred pounds going face to face. The male kept grunting and bluff charging the female while she held her ground. This was all happening less than thirty feet off the trail right before my eyes! I was mesmerized as the bears took virtually no notice of me. The bluff charging and the vocals went on for several minutes before the female retreated maybe ten feet up the trunk of a large ash tree. It was only once she was in the ash tree that I noticed there were three very small cubs clinging to different branches at varying heights of that same tree. Now it all made sense. The male was trying to get to the cubs and the female was defending them.

As the female clung to the side of the big tree, the male then turned his attention to me. I can't tell you why, but I wasn't afraid. Unbelievably, Katana wasn't even paying attention and had actually laid down. The foliage was a little high and I don't think she even had a view of the bears in the first place.

I slowly took my pack off and placed it on the ground. I crouched down keeping my eyes and head fixed on the bear as I felt around for my phone in the small front pocket of my pack. As I stood back up, the male began to click his jaws at me, but wouldn't move. I took several pictures and began recording a video. I figured if I was going to be attacked by a bear, then I might as well capture it on film. As the video started recording, the big male turned and walked away only a couple seconds in. As he disappeared into the underbrush, I turned the camera towards the female who was mostly focusing on her cubs up in the tree, but giving me sideways glances every now and again. For maybe ten minutes I stood there watching and taking pictures before moving on. The bear tally was now at ten...

Later that evening I reached a shelter without any further bear excitement. The shelters in the Shenandoah National Park are no different from the shelters anywhere else on the AT, but here they insist on calling them "huts." Just like the Smokies, it's forbidden to stealth camp, as you're expected to sleep in or near the huts.

I had dinner which consisted of a can of chicken and dumplings, as well as a can of corned beef hash with Sriacha on it. This was yet another new food phase that I was in. I'd taken to packing out cans of chicken and dumplings, corned beef hash, potato soup, chicken corn chowder, beef stroganoff, as well as a multitude of other canned goods. This trend lasted only a few weeks, but was another nice change of pace, along with the cereal. I think my breaking point with the cans, was how heavy they were to pack out. I always took to stomping them flat after they were empty, then shoving them into a heavy duty Ziploc bag that I always carried as my trash bag.

I climbed into my hammock completely overjoyed with all the bears I had encountered that day. I honestly couldn't believe my good fortune, but no sooner was the sun behind the mountains that I heard an all too familiar whistle. "Whippoorwill, whippoorwill, whippoorwill, whippoorwill," began to incessantly drone on. Over the course of the next half hour, no less than six others joined in, as overlapping calls of "Whippoorwill" penetrated the night. I can tune out one of them, maybe even two if I'm really tired, but six was impossible! There was no rhyme or rhythm to any of it. It was non-stop chaotic whistling. This was one of the few Whippoorwill nights that had me up in arms, screaming into the darkness while hurling rocks and sticks. It was a long and nearly sleepless night.

Day three in the Park found me sitting at a Wayside for a good portion of the day. As I mentioned earlier on, one can count on the National Parks to be quite capitalistic, and Shenandoah was no different. The original Appalachian Trail used to traverse the entire ridge of the Shenandoah Mountain range, but when they realized the trail across the ridge would be more profitable as a road that they could charge people to drive on, they re-routed the AT to skirt around the sides of most of these mountains, while turning the old one into a road called "Skyline Drive." Wait, they didn't stop there! There are car camping campsites, RV campsites, camp stores, and these fancy snack bar restaurants called "Waysides." These Waysides usually require a little sideways hiking to get to from the trail, but besides the camp stores, they're for the most part the only places to get food on this 100-mile stretch of trail. Needless to say, you end up paying tourist prices for everything. A burger for $10, fries for $4, bags of chips for $3, and Ramen noodle soup for a $1 apiece. They have you trapped in this park until Front Royal near the end, so you have to pay their prices.

I had been in contact with Schweppes, and we agreed to meet at the first Wayside in the park. It was going to be a short seven-mile day for me, but a twenty-mile day for him to catch up. I had zero cell reception at this Wayside, so I was forced to wait... and wait... and wait. I sat at the Wayside for more than six hours while spending a small fortune on French fries. Finally, the Wayside closed and there was still no Schweppes. For the second time in three days I'd been snubbed at a rendezvous point. Now I was six miles from the nearest shelter with less than two hours of daylight in a bear infested forest.

I retraced my steps up the half mile long and very steep side trail that I'd taken down to the Wayside. When I finally merged back onto the AT, the sun was already low in the sky. Only a couple hundred yards from where I merged onto the AT, I reached a rocky overlook on the left side of the trail that had a great view of the forest below and the sinking sun. I took off my pack and got my camera out while leaving Katana tethered to it. I detoured off the trail once again and walked about eighty feet over rocks to the edge of the precipice. I took it all in and snapped a few pictures before turning around to head back to the trail.

As I began to make my way back, I immediately noticed a rattlesnake tightly coiled under the ledge of a rock that I'd just stepped over in order to get to the edge of the overlook. "WOW, you couldn't have written that into a horror movie any better," I thought. Knowing this was probably a high traffic area, I felt that I at least needed to relocate the snake off the outcropping. I took several pictures, then used my staff to pull the snake out of its crevice. As I did so, I noticed another Rattlesnake six feet away under another rock that I'd walked by in order step over the rock that the first snake was under. These things were everywhere! I lowered the snake with my staff over the precipice and onto a lower tier of rocks, then went over and did the same with the second rattler. Neither was as big as the first one that I encountered, but they were still good sized specimens. I spent a few more minutes looking around to see if there were more, but couldn't find any. After all the fun and relocations, I was hiking once again. The rattlesnake count was now at three.

The trail was smooth for the most part, but still had several moderate climbs over small hills. For the first time in a long time, I was actually nervous about possibly being caught in the dark. There were so many damn bears here, that I didn't want to bump into one in the dark. When the light was all but gone, I began to whistle as I walked. This was always my favorite method of making my presence known. It was casual, nonchalant, and to the average person nearby would seem like nothing more than a fellow out for a jolly evening walk; and not someone scared of running into unwelcome nighttime creepy crawlies and such...

I finally reached the shelter in the almost pitch black of night to find several familiar hikers whom I hadn't seen for quite some time. We caught up for a bit and I recounted the tale of the rattlesnake before Waynesboro. "Which shelter?" they asked. "Harpers Creek," I replied. After telling them which day I was there, they informed me that they had been there the day before me, and a man had been "life-evacuated" out by helicopter after being bitten by a rattlesnake he was trying to remove off the trail. "No way!" I thought. There was a damn good chance that I had eaten the rattlesnake that bit someone. I don't know why this intrigued me so much, but it made the harvesting of the rattlesnake seem that much more justified. That snake had gotten his revenge on people before he had even needed to get revenge, and before I had unknowingly harvested him as food, consequently avenging his victim.

During and after the trail, I tried to find some proof of this incident online but couldn't. Were the other hikers pulling my leg? I don't know. Maybe it never made the news or didn't get reported. I would like to think they were forthright in our conversations, given the seriousness of the topic.

Not long after the stories and catching up, we decided to make a fire. A few of us donned our headlamps and went into the surrounding forest to look for fallen branches and logs. I had probably ventured less than fifty yards past the creek that snaked by the shelter when I heard a crash and a thud. I looked up just in time to see a bear of maybe a hundred pounds hit the ground as it slid out of a tree and then took off running, maybe fifteen feet in front of me. "It's just raining bears out here!" I thought to myself. That little guy had been sitting up in that tree like some kind of ninja, watching the shelter area while waiting for everyone to go to bed so it could investigate. What a sneaky bear! I never did run into Schweppes; he never made it in that night. I had no idea what happened to him, but what I did know was the bear tally was now eleven...

On day four in Shenandoah I decided I was going to knock down some miles and try to get the rest of Virginia over with. I had been doing small miles for my first three days into the park in an effort to let Schweppes catch up. I hadn't seen nor heard from him, so I decided to make a sprint for Harpers Ferry, West Virginia. Harpers Ferry is the unofficial halfway point of the entire trail. It resides just over a thousand miles from Springer Mountain, and a little less than a hundred miles from the numerical half way point of the trail. I knew that getting to Harper's was going to be a huge morale boost.

So, I began day four on a mission, a mission to finish up the rest of Virginia as quickly as possible. It turned out that there would be all kinds of trees, rocks, and nature to look at that morning, and around five miles into the day, I turned a corner and came face to face with another bear. This one was sitting in the middle of the trail about seventy feet ahead of me. As I came around the curve, he gave me a startled look, sprung to his feet and began casually walking northward on the trail. He was maybe two hundred pounds, but I didn't even break stride upon seeing him. I kept right on walking. He lumbered seventy to a hundred feet in front of me for over a minute before I started to speed up. When he finally noticed that I was still behind him and closing the gap, he took a sharp right turn off the trail and broke into a faster gait. When I reached the spot where he turned, I looked over to see that he was maybe fifty yards away and had resumed his casual walking pace. The bear tally was now at twelve...

The bears in Shenandoah seemed to be very accustomed to humans. Every bear reaction I'd gotten so far had been one of indifference or fright; on almost every encounter the bears had done whatever they could to avoid me. This was really beginning to desensitize me to bear encounters. My first bear encounter back in Tennessee had been heart pounding, scary, exciting, and surreal all at once. Every encounter after that, although unique, had not evoked the same feelings, or at least not the same intensity of feelings. With each new encounter, the bear lost a little bit more of its fearsome aura and gained the image of a gentle, opportunistic giant that simply wanted to be left alone as humans encroached more and more on its habitat.

Over the course of the day I traversed more than seven mountains and encountered many other day hikers as I crossed the skyline drive multiple times. By 7 pm I made it to Big Meadows Campground and completed over eighteen miles. I was getting low on food and decided to make a pit stop at the campground's camp store where a handful of other thru-hikers were already enjoying some cold drinks and snacks. I joined them as we conversed over the day's obstacles and bear encounters. I spent nearly an hour at the camp store drinking Gatorade after Gatorade until a car pulled up in front. It was a car camping campground, so this was nothing out of the ordinary. Then the last person I would've ever expected to see at that moment emerged from the car. It was "Laser Pussy!"

Up until that moment, I'd been sure that he was more than a hundred miles ahead, and that I might not see him again. He began hiking ahead of us way back at Woods Hole Hostel in order to meet his parents by a certain date in Buena Vista. I hadn't seen him in almost a month, but it turned out that he had gotten sick and took four days off to stay with his brother who lived in the area. He was getting back on where he left off when we ran into each other at the camp store. What were the chances he would get back on this huge stretch of trail at the exact same place that I was taking a break, at that exact same moment? I'm telling you, I was beginning to think this trail had a mind of its own.

People that have lived around the trail for their entire lives or had thru-hiked it before would always tell you the same thing. They would say the trail took on a life and culture of its own, and that it was almost a living thing. I took this mostly as "BS" in the early days, but the more time I spent out there, the more truth I found in it. Unbeknownst to me, there was a lot more magic to come. There were even ways of bending that magic to your own will. There was a saying out there... "the trail provides." You never quite understand it until you've been out there and truly needed "something," only to get that "something" or have it happen to you right when you needed it most. I can't explain it and I haven't met anyone else who can, but if you've hiked the trail or spent any amount of time near it, then you know what I mean. Synchronicities out on the trail were commonplace and unexplainable. They had meaning, but you could never figure out how or why they happened.

Laser and I hiked together for another mile and a half to the next shelter. As we were walking, talking, and catching up on current trail happenings and events, we were interrupted by a loud crashing on our right. We both looked over without skipping a beat as the biggest bear I'd seen so far began sprinting away from us before quickly disappearing into the thick vegetation. This bear was huge! I would estimate it at close to five hundred pounds or more. We only saw it for maybe six or seven seconds before it was gone, but the bear tally was now thirteen....

142

I had learned a couple days earlier that when DSOH got sick, he shuttled out of Buena Vista and into Waynesboro to recover. He resumed the trail just outside of Waynesboro on the day that I was hiking into it. He planned to come back and finish that brutal section later. With the bigger miles I did that day, I knew I couldn't be too far behind him. I figured if I put in more big miles the next day, then I could possibly catch up.

Day five of the Shenandoah stretch was another snake day. Laser hiked ahead of me for most of the day as the terrain was for the most part flat and easy. I kept grinding the miles out all day, and as the afternoon began to pass into evening, I caught up to Laser near a beautiful rocky outlook. A gorgeous view across the valley revealed a storm that was sweeping across the landscape in our direction. We debated for a moment whether it would hit us or skirt by, but concluded that it would just miss us before continuing on.

We hadn't gone far from the overlook, when Laser, who was keeping a good pace directly in front of me, abruptly slammed to a halt and yelled, "SNAKE!" It was another rattlesnake lying across the middle of the trail that Laser had come within half a stride of stepping on before noticing it. The well camouflaged creature blended in perfectly as its colorful scale patterns broke up its outline amongst the leaf litter. Once again, I couldn't resist attempting to capture it. Laser pleaded with me to leave it alone, saying that he didn't want to watch me die, but in the end pulled out his cell phone and recorded me capturing the snake. This one put up the same fight the first one did when I grabbed him, but this time I was halfway expecting it. After subduing the rattler, I walked it a short distance off the trail and released it into some vegetation. It would probably be back soon enough, but at least it was out of harm's way for the time being. The rattlesnake tally was now four...

Not long after the rattlesnake relocation, the bottom fell out of the sky. Our prediction had been wrong as we marched another two miles in the pouring rain before coming to a clearing and picnic area with a large pavilion. Under the pavilion we found none other than DSOH himself. He'd taken cover just before the rain and was toasty dry next to a fireplace at the center of the structure. Of course no sooner did we take cover under the pavilion, the rain stopped.

After half an hour of hiding beneath the pavilion, a Korean family began setting up for a BBQ at a designated grilling area some fifty yards away. "They picked a hell of a time to have a picnic," we joked. Not long after they'd begun cooking, and to our complete surprise, the father of the family came over and invited us to eat with them. We graciously accepted the offer and followed the man back to the grill.

This amazing family literally cooked us POUNDS of "Korean Bacon" as they called it, along with Kimchee and a spicy noodle soup. More amazing kindness on the trail, and the last thing any of us expected on a rainy evening at a remote picnic area in this national park. That night we slept near the pavilion as I hung my hammock in some trees at the edge of the clearing. It had been another twenty-mile day, but no bears had been sighted.

Despite the lack of mammals from the previous day, Shenandoah found me counting bears again on day six. DSOH hiked out before sunrise, while I hiked with Laser for most of that beautiful day. Before I go any further I will let you in on a little known secret about me. That secret is that I am a Lord of the Rings super fan. Not a super fan in the sense that I dress up on Halloween, get together with other nerds, or dress up for movie releases. I'm a super fan in the sense that these books were an enormous part of my childhood. They played a huge part in sculpting my future interests, ideals, and desires for adventure. I know more details about The Lord of the Rings, as well as the Tolkien Universe than MOST people who claim to know a lot about the Tolkien Universe, and I have proven it in many an LOTR debate.

Laser and I had been discussing various subjects throughout the morning that the two of us were interested in. Laser was into video games and technology, while I was into science fiction, fantasy, fishing, and bow fishing. My love of Sci-Fi and Fantasy overlapped his love of video games and technology. So when he finally asked me to enlighten him on some of the history of Lord of the Rings and Middle Earth, what ensued was a two-hour long lecture as we walked across the Shenandoah Mountains.

I began with Eru Iluvatar, Ainulindale, the great songs, and the shaping of Arda and Middle Earth; then the creations of the Valar, Maiar, and the corruption and deceit of Melkor, who later became known as Morgoth. Next, I spoke of the awakening and sundering of the Elves, the Petty Dwarves, and the creation of Men. I followed that with the three great ages of the Years of the Lamps, the Years of the Trees, and the Years of the Sun, as well as the sub ages within them. I told Laser of the War of Wrath during the first age of the Years of the Sun and Melkor's top Lieutenant Sauron, and how he resumed Melkor's evil plan after Melkor had been thrust through the door of night into the timeless void. I captivated Laser's imagination with tales of how the entire region of Beleriand was sunk beneath the Great Sea because the land was so scorched by dragon fire as to be uninhabitable.

I recounted the great men of Numenor and Sauron's surrender, as well as the brainwashing of these great men. Such was Sauron's influence that the entire Island of Numenor had to be sunk beneath the sea by Eru, lest they reach the undying lands in the Utterwest. I concluded the fictional history lesson with the forging of the great rings, the War of the Last Alliance, the War of the Ring, and the beginning of the fourth age of the Years of the Sun. I enjoyed fielding his questions, and I think my enthusiasm was contagious. I only hoped that I'd recruited another Tolkien fan.

Needless to say, the miles flew by... and as they did, I captured a small garter snake that was maybe six inches long. I handed it to Laser who decided to keep it as a "trail pet" for the day. We named the snake "Shannon" and gave her the last name "Doah" - very clever of us, I know. We passed Mary's rock to the west, climbed over Pass Mountain, then crossed through Beahm's Gap before we reached Elkwallow Wayside, where we met DSOH and enjoyed some cold drinks and snacks. Life was good as we enjoyed the hot Virginia day in a beautiful national park, answerable to no one but ourselves, with nowhere to be. It was a utopian afternoon and the last time the three of us would be together for quite some time.

As 6 pm approached and the sun sunk lower in the sky, I decided that I wanted to get my twenty miles done for the day. I only had another six miles in order to reach twenty, but DSOH and Laser had resigned themselves to staying in the woods near the Wayside. When I told them I would be pushing on, they replied, "It's already the end of the day, just stay here." I countered, "All the wildlife comes out in the early evening when everyone else is off the trails. This is the best time to hike!" I bid them good night, then pressed onward up Hogback Mountain.

As I began the first leg of the six-mile stretch, my first animal encounter was to be a box turtle crossing the trail. Not overly exciting, but it was a start. Not fifteen minutes past the tortoise, I walked upon a mamma bear and three of her cubs. The cubs immediately scrambled up a huge birch tree while the mother laid down somewhere behind it. They were in no way, shape, or form interested in me. I attempted to watch them for several minutes but didn't have a good view and moved on.

As I walked at a brisk pace, I observed the fireflies scattered across the ceiling of the trees and hovering above the vegetation; absorbed in their golden dances and flashes of Morse Code. I always thought fireflies were at their most enchanting during the twilight hours. Instead of being random flashes of yellow light against a dark and featureless backdrop like they were at night, in the early evening they became a magical addition to the already enchanting landscape that surrounded you. I loved it... I couldn't get enough of it.

I was so consumed by my observations of the fireflies, that as I ascended a slight switch-back climb, I almost failed to notice the large black bear that sat in the middle of trail just above me. I got very close before I noticed him, but surprisingly, I saw him before he saw me. I stopped and crouched down, observing him through the low hanging branches of a tree that stood between us. He was preoccupied with something; upon closer inspection I noticed he was fumbling with a shredded food bag. There was no food in it, just the empty bag. After several seconds I gave a loud whistle. The bear perked up and looked around but still didn't see me. I gave a longer whistle, and when the bear's eyes finally noticed me, he immediately got to his feet and sauntered away. As he wandered off, I proceeded my walk in the same direction.

I got to his spot and picked up the shredded yellow, "Sea to Summit" dry bag. The bear had stopped a little over a hundred feet away and was once again sitting down, going about his bear business. I tried to take a picture, but it came out as a black blob that didn't even resemble a bear due to the distance and thick vegetation. I picked up the shredded food bag and continued on. The bear tally was now eighteen...

I finished the rest of the climb up Hogback Mountain, then a short trek across a wooded ridgeline before reaching my stopping point. It was to be my last night in the Shenandoah National Park. Schweppes, DSOH, Laser, and Coma were behind me, and only friendly strangers lay ahead. My body was beaten down, but with the end of Virginia in sight, my spirits were soaring once again. I only had to keep up twenty mile or more days, for another three days, in order to reach Harper's Ferry and the end of Virginia.

On one of my first days in Shenandoah National Park, I ran across three young guys in their twenties headed south. I stopped and chatted with them for a bit and learned they were doing a huge southbound section hike from the top of Pennsylvania to the bottom of Virginia. They told me horror stories of the Pennsylvania rocks and all the copperhead snakes they had encountered. We talked for the better part of ten minutes while standing in the middle of the trail, but before parting ways, one of the guys had an interesting piece of advice for me. He told me that when I finally left the boundaries of Shenandoah, I would reach a shelter by the name of "Tom Floyd." He said less than a mile past that shelter would be a small weathered looking wooden sign that was easy to miss if I didn't keep an eye out for it; on that sign was the engraving "4-H." He concluded that this sign marked a small path that would lead to something good, but refused to tell me what that "something" was. He simply told me to follow it and I wouldn't regret it. I thanked him for the strange advice, but didn't give it much thought afterwards.

My seventh day and last morning in the park was a gorgeous one. There wasn't a cloud in the sky, making everything around me appear sharper and more vivid. Not even twenty minutes into the morning, a small bear scurried away from me into the underbrush on my left. I gave him a passing glance without stopping. Bear tally...nineteen.

With only a couple miles left in Shenandoah, while climbing Compton Peak, I saw my last Shenandoah bear. It was another adolescent that took off into the trees as soon as I came into view. I had seen twenty bears so far, sixteen of which were in that national park. I wasn't sure if it made me proud or indifferent; the novelty of bear sightings had worn off. Seeing so many bears in such a short time had taken a great deal of the excitement out of bear encounters for me. I had resigned to the conclusion that the only way I would be able to feel excitement around a black bear again was if it was chasing me. When I did finally cross over the park boundary, the difference in trail quality was night and day. Less than a hundred feet from the small boundary sign, the smooth trail turned into jagged rocks and a tricky rock scramble right off the bat. Perhaps the easy, smooth terrain of the national park was boring at times, but my knees sure enjoyed it. As I scrambled over the rocks, reflecting on my stint through Shenandoah, I suddenly remembered the sign the section hiker told me about. I stopped in at Tom Floyd shelter for a short rest and a snack before pushing on with a weary-eye open for the sign. The south bounder had been right; if I hadn't been looking for it, I would've missed it.

Across from the "4-H" sign was a narrow leaf covered path leading straight down the side of the mountain, perpendicular to the AT. Not knowing how far I had to follow it, I almost dismissed it, but in the end, curiosity got the best of me. I began following the path and was perhaps a half a mile into it, contemplating turning back, when I began to hear the distant screaming and laughter of a great number of people. I continued on, my curiosity peaked even more. As I got closer and closer I heard the tell-tale sounds of a diving board and people splashing. A deer spooked out of a thicket of bushes as I pushed my way through them to emerge onto the top of a small hill overlooking what I can only describe as an upscale summer camp/lodge area. Several hundred feet below was an enormous fenced in pool that was filled with kids and their parents. To the left of the pool was a lake with floats and other toys, and all along the path, as well as the road down to the swimming holes were fancy cabins and lodges. "WOW! This little oasis was just sitting out here. Why wasn't it in my maps or guide?" I thought to myself.

I walked directly down to the pool, went straight up to the front desk and said, "I'll take one pool session please!" Four dollars later I was in. Katana had to stay tethered to my pack out front, but the people at the desk told me they would keep an eye on her. I left her with food and water, then made a beeline for the pool.

I decided to do some "Streamlining." What's Streamlining? It's wrapping multiple tasks into one task in order to save time while maximizing efficiency. I began streamlining fun, bathing, and laundry into one task. I took turns wearing my different clothes and jumping into the pool. I jumped in the deep end and sunk myself to the bottom where I would shake out my shirt and shorts in an attempt to remove the superficial sweat and dirt from them. With the great abundance of little children there, I'm sure there was no shortage of urine, band aids, and who knows what else in that pool, so I didn't feel guilty. Thank science for chlorine!

It was shortly after laundry, bathing, and swimming that I noticed they had a snack bar. Cash in hand, I almost skipped over while trying not to break the "NO Running" rule. What I discovered upon reaching the counter almost made me weep for joy! $1 slices of pizza, $1 bottles of Gatorade, $1 ice cream cones, ice cream sandwiches, and $1 hotdogs. Words cannot express the gratitude that I felt for the south bounder in that moment. I spent over $20 on every single one of those items. I ate until I could eat no more, as I took full advantage of this Oasis of cold drinks and good old American roughage.

I stuck around for two hours before I began heading back to the trail. If I hadn't been set on my twenty mile days, then I probably would've camped next to that pool and took advantage of it for another day.

I was well on my way once again, several miles from the "4-H" sign when I had my final encounter with Virginia bears. While climbing up a large hill I spotted ANOTHER small bear of about two hundred pounds, crouched on the hillside next to the trail, a short distance above me. He seemed to be intensely focused on something as he took no notice of me. I kept walking, but gave a loud whistle. He looked up quick before spinning around and taking off further up the hill. Not ten feet from where the bear had been, a small fawn appeared, then briskly took off along the side of the embankment. "What the hell?" I thought. I hadn't even noticed the fawn before. The bear and the fawn were either buddying it up, or that bear was about to kill it. I didn't see the fawn's mother, as it was definitely small enough to still need one. In a way, I felt like I'd given the little fellah a small extension on life by startling the bear away.

I later researched that new born fawns were a source of food for bears in the spring. While this one was not a new born and knew how to use its legs, it certainly would've put its young legs to the test with that bear on its heels.

As I continued up the hill, I kept running into the little bear. It almost became like a game. I would continue climbing higher up the hill until the bear would notice me; then he would spook and run another couple hundred feet further up before sitting down again. Then I would reach the spot where he was, and the process would repeat. This went on for ten minutes before he finally skirted the side of the hill.

Towards the end of the day I encountered two woodchucks that ran across the trail in front of me. At first I thought they might be badgers and believed they were for quite some time before seeing another one close up. It was standing next to a privy and I realized in hindsight they weren't. I ended up calling it quits just under the twenty-mile mark at a shelter full of boy scouts. I still had around fifty miles to go in order to reach Harper's Ferry and I was determined to get there within the next two days. The bear tally was twenty-one…

June 28th was my 91st day on the trail when I awoke from my hammock slumber with a ravenous hunger. I hadn't had a re-supply since Waynesboro more than a hundred miles back, and as a consequence, my food stores were very low. I ate very small snack foods for every meal. As I sat in my hammock, I examined my guidebook and map, looking for a good place to end the day. While going over the elevation changes and looking at the features of the terrain ahead of me, my eyes fell on the words "Bear's Den Hostel." I flipped another page and began reading up on this "Bear's Den Hostel." As I did, a couple of trigger words caught my eye. Those words were "Open Kitchen," "Pizza," and "AYCE Pancake Breakfast."

By God, all of those things sounded so good! I wanted them all right now, but that wasn't going to happen. I was going to have to work for it. After some simple math, I came to realize that the work I was going to have to put in was about twenty-nine miles' worth if I wanted to get there that day. If I didn't make it there on that day, then I wouldn't be able to stop in the next day for a pizza dinner or a pancake breakfast, because the timing wouldn't match up and I would be on a collision course with Harper's Ferry. I wanted it all! I wanted to double dip. I wanted my Bear's Den pizza and pancakes, and my Harper's Ferry BBQ and ice cream; but the only way to make it work was to reach Bear's Den that night and Harper's Ferry the next.

There was only one problem with my master plan to obtain all of these foods in the order that I wanted to obtain them. As if twenty-nine miles wasn't far enough, Bear's Den resided on the far side of the infamous "Virginia Rollercoaster." What's that you ask? The Virginia Rollercoaster is a thirteen-mile stretch of constant up and down climbs. First, it takes you sharply up hundreds of feet before dumping you down hundreds of feet.

Next, it immediately takes you up hundreds of more feet before dumping you back down, then does it again, and again, and again. It's nothing but a steep, constant up and down trek of rocks, dirt, and roots for thirteen miles straight. The average rise and fall of the climbs was between three hundred and five hundred feet. Not only was it a difficult stretch, but I was doing it as the final thirteen miles of an already almost thirty-mile day. The thought of pizza and pancakes was making me feel bullet proof that morning, so naturally, realistic thinking was the last thing I was worried about. In my hunger obsessed mind, the Rollercoaster was only going to make the pizza and pancakes taste that much sweeter. Shortly after plotting my destination, realizing there wasn't a moment to lose, I put my nose to the grindstone.

Once again I was eating up the trail and crapping out footprints. Katana was all about it and wasn't giving me a hard time at all. I had Pizza/Pancakes on the brain and I think she was channeling those brain waves. It was onward through Manassas Gap, past Trico Tower, and over Whiskey Hollow Creek when I suddenly came to a screeching halt at Ashby Gap. Someone had left a twenty-four pack of Yeungling Beer on the side of the trail, a couple miles from the start of the Rollercoaster. SOMEONE had good taste! That beer was exactly what I needed even though it was the same temperature as the hot summer day.

After some carb-loading, I kept on at my blistering pace and began to notice that someone had drawn faces with a black sharpie pen on the white blazes of the trees along that stretch. The white blazes painted on trees and other objects can be as close as ten feet, a couple hundred feet, half a mile or even over a mile in between each other. As I went further and further on, I first noticed a placid smiley face on one of the blazes and thought nothing of it. Then a smiley face with a mischievous expression passed by. The faces were becoming entertaining and motivating as they built up the suspense. Next, a smiley with vampire fangs went by. "Very foreboding," I thought. As I came to one last blaze that was right before a drop off, it had a smiley with its mouth open in an "OoOoOoH" expression as if it was just about to go down the first drop of some ride. I smiled, thinking of my pizza and pancakes as I took off down the hill.

I conquered the first climb on pure adrenaline, the second climb on sheer will, and the third climb on determination and defiance of my tired beaten body. Halfway up the fourth climb, I collapsed. I was dehydrated and physically crashing. To make matters worse, I was practically out of food with which to fuel myself. I drank the rest of my water, which amounted to less than half a liter at this point, and forced myself to eat a couple of mini snickers and peanut butter cups. I sat for a while, letting the food settle and the sugar absorb into my blood stream. Ten minutes later I was ready to rock. "Pizza dinner, here I come!" The sun was getting low as dusk set in when I began round two with the rollercoaster. I continued to crush the climbs one after the other until the light was all but gone.

It was dark when I stopped in at a shelter just off the trail to see if there were any familiar faces. There weren't any. However, I ran into two men that were surprised to hear how far I'd come that day and how much further I still intended to go. I told them I was hell bent on having pizza that night and pancakes in the morning, but when they informed me that the kitchen at the hostel closed at 9 pm, I almost screamed. It was just after 8 pm and I still had three more climbs with a little over three miles to go. I took off faster than I can ever remember going before. I never slowed down once and developed a stitch in my side before finishing the first mile. I began to wheeze as I power walked over everything in front of me. As I pushed myself harder and harder through the pain, it became less about the food, and more about completing the challenge of getting there on time. In all actuality, I was making myself sick due to the level that I was exerting myself, subsequently killing my appetite.

When I finally knocked on the door it was 9:07 pm. It was after the cutoff, but I felt that seven minutes would be of no consequence. Surely whoever was in charge would be swayed by my epic quest and allow me to pop a frozen pizza in the oven. A pizza that I only wanted as a reward at this point, as I would probably end up bagging and packing it out for the next day anyway. Nevertheless, pizza had been a main reason for the death march, so I wanted one regardless of whether I was going to eat it right away or not.

Bear's Den Hostel is owned and ran by the Appalachian Trail Club (ATC) and the Potomac Appalachian Trail Club (PATC). All profits are put towards maintaining the local stretches of trail and there's usually one caretaker that lives in the house and oversees all operations. The hostel itself looked like a giant stone mansion on the outside and maintained the same appearance on the inside as well. You have the option of renting an individual room or staying in the bunkroom.

When the caretaker, who was a young guy maybe in his mid to late twenties, opened the door… all I could ask was, "Is the kitchen still open?" "No it's not," he replied. "Man, I just hiked twenty-nine miles through the Rollercoaster to get here; do you think I could please pop a pizza in the oven really quick?" "No, sorry, the kitchen closed at nine, but I can give you some sodas and you can go down to the bunkroom and take a shower; it's on the side of the building around there," he said in an airy tone with a slight smirk, while pointing to my right. I tried to stifle my disappointment and annoyance before replying, "thank you." I paid the man before making my way around the side of the building to find the bunkroom completely empty. This was a pleasant yet not unexpected surprise. With a caretaker as rude and cocky as this guy had come off during our brief exchange, it was no wonder nobody wanted to stay there. It was "no dogs allowed," so I scouted out an area with some trees and foliage near the bunkroom and left Katana with food and water before going inside.

As I pulled my soaking wet shirt off, my eyes and nostrils began to burn. I'd been sweating what smelled like pure ammonia. In all my hurry to get to Bear's Den, I had over exerted my body and allowed myself to become severely dehydrated. I showered, put my laundry in, drank as much water as I could, then passed out almost instantly.

The next morning, I awoke early and went up into the main house. Not a soul was awake, but there was a huge bag of Bisquick pancake mix, a griddle, some Pam and a few other odds and ends on the counter next to a sink. I guessed it was self-serve AYCE pancakes, and I wasted no time in setting to work. I made pancakes for forty-five minutes straight, eating them as I cooked more. The pancake mix only required water, so it was a fairly quick and easy process.

I finished up and went back downstairs without seeing a soul. I checked the hiker box out of curiosity and found six Mountain House dehydrated meals. I had been out of food, but now the trail was providing once again. Who throws away Mountain House meals? Those things are like six to eight bucks a piece, sometimes more. I managed to score two chicken teriyaki meals with rice, one pack of scrambled eggs with ham, one lasagna meal with meat sauce, and two chicken and rice meal packs. It was my lucky day! I packed them up and hit the trail.

A "hiker box" is something that exists along the entire trail. You can find them in every single town along the trail, and usually quite a few of them. They're nothing more than a container filled with items that have been discarded by other hikers. You can find food, gear, fuel, and a variety of other miscellaneous items in these little treasure boxes. You never know what you'll get. Almost every single establishment that houses, caters, or shelters hikers will have a hiker box somewhere on the premises. These establishments are usually hostels, certain hotels, outfitters, and sometimes private residences that frequently take in hikers, but sometimes you can find them in less likely places. If you get to a hiker box at the right time, you can sometimes stumble across incredible findings in regards to gear and food. It's a shining example of "one man's trash is another man's gold."

My twenty-one-mile day into Harper's Ferry went by leisurely. I was hurting pretty badly from my almost thirty miles the day before, so I took my time. I knew I was getting to Harpers one way or another that day, so I wasn't in a huge hurry. One mile past Bear's Den, I reached a sign nailed to a tree that simply read "1000." I'd finally reached the one-thousand-mile mark, and damn did it feel fantastic!

I hadn't really felt like I'd accomplished anything until I reached that 1,000-mile marker. Finally, in the quadruple digits, I felt like a true veteran of the trail and not so much of a wannabe anymore. "I'm really going places!" I thought.

Many hikers often argue over how and when you can call yourself a "thru-hiker." Some say you're not a thru hiker until you summit Katahdin, while others say you're a thru-hiker just for attempting it. I say you're a thru-hiker until you quit. From the moment you set foot on that trail to attempt a thru-hike, you are a thru-hiker. If you make it all the way to the end without quitting, then you're a thru-hiker for the rest of your life.

I stopped and ate two of my Mountain House meals for lunch and took a little nap for close to an hour. A little further past where I took my nap, I passed a man who was maybe in his thirties, going in the opposite direction. He was wearing jeans and walking very funny. "A day- hiking rookie," I surmised. I knew that gait the second I saw it. That was the walk of a man who was dealing with severe ball chafing. We didn't exchange any words, but I gave him a nod that offered my sincerest condolences and sympathy.

I hammered the last nine miles with the soles of my shoes, and the mountains were a little less tall that day and every day afterwards due to my pounding footsteps. I cruised down Loudoun Heights, leaving Virginia and entering West Virginia before skipping across the enormous bridge spanning the Shenandoah River and finally gliding into Harpers Ferry. "Now I need to find some BBQ…"

CHAPTER 8: WEST VIRGINIA & MARYLAND

"Crazy People and Puppy Freedom"

Virginia/West Virginia State Line Crossing Potomac into Maryland

Harper's Ferry was founded in 1763. In 1783, Thomas Jefferson visited and declared the area "...perhaps one of the most stupendous scenes in nature." The town was named after a Quaker colonist by the name of Robert Harper who established a ferry transport across the Potomac, consequently making the town a starting point for settlers moving into the Shenandoah Valley. Located on the confluence of the Potomac and Shenandoah Rivers, the town of Harper's Ferry certainly is nestled in quite the beautiful location. Today it remains a historic national park where you can find many old buildings from the time of its earliest development in the 1700's.

The first thing I noticed walking into Harper's Ferry was the view. A gorgeous view overlooking the Potomac and Shenandoah Rivers, rocky cliff faces, and tree covered mountains. A train bridge leading into a tunnel that was drilled right into the side of a mountain gave it sort of a "Wild West" feel. As I skirted the side of the hill I was on, I came across "Jefferson's Rock." This was the rock that Thomas Jefferson stood upon when he first laid eyes on Harper's Ferry and declared it "one of the most stupendous scenes in nature." I passed old churches and other historical buildings before making my way to the bottom of the hill where I found the main strip and food vendors.

When they call Harper's Ferry a town, it's not really a town in the traditional meaning of the word. People do live there, but I would define it more as a tourist attraction than an actual town. On the main strip at the bottom of the hill is a continuous line up of BBQ, ice cream, and seafood vendors, as well as some restaurants. Every single one of them was exorbitantly over-priced. It was a budgeting hiker's nightmare, as there was nowhere to resupply unless you caught a ride across town or into another town. The resupply in Harper's Ferry was so limited and expensive, that it was more economical to hold out for another town to buy food.

As I walked the strip, I window shopped for a place to eat. I had been told to at least have ice cream and BBQ while I was there, because it was what Harper's Ferry was famous for. I stopped at a vendor and ordered two scoops of vanilla ice cream and a Dr. Pepper that cost me nine dollars. "What is the world coming to?" I thought. That highway robbery put a damper on my mood, but what did I expect?

I continued up the road further before finally spotting a thru-hiker at a restaurant. The hiker was sitting on the front deck, while eating and drinking a beer, and seemed to be the establishment's only customer. I didn't recognize him, but out on the trail and in towns, no fellow hiker is a stranger. We all talk to each other as if we've been friends for years. "How's the food?" I called up to him. "It's good!" he called back. "And the price?" I added. "It's pricey, but there's a 20% hiker discount." That was all I needed to hear. If there was a discount, then that meant it probably went from being overly pricey to just a little pricey.

I went up and sat down at a table across from him and introduced myself. His name was "Gumby." He was a tall skinny guy, maybe in his mid-twenties like me. I ordered a full rack of smoked ribs and a Yeungling Summer Wheat from the female waitress. The ribs were fantastic, some of the best I've ever had. While Gumby and I sat there enjoying our meal and beer, a man came out of the restaurant, pulled up a chair at our table and began chatting.

The man's name was "Stan," and he informed us that he was the manager of the eatery and his best friend was the owner. Stan looked to be in his early to mid-forties, and had long, sandy blond hair. He had that California Surfer look, and the Cali surfer lingo, but without the valley boy accent. He turned out to be a very intelligent and charismatic individual, chatting away about anything and everything under the sun. He was one of those people that could have a conversation for hours without you ever needing to talk in return. As long as your attention was on him and you nodded and made little comments when he paused to see your reaction, then he could talk for days if you let him.

So Stan kept on and on and very soon turned the subject to religion. He told us he'd read the Bible and the Qur'an, as well as a half dozen other religious equivalents to those holy books. He seemed to be incredibly well read, as well as one of those people that was self-educated and knew more about a religion than most of the people that followed them. After going on and on about backgrounds, histories, similarities, and parallels of a multitude of religions, he finally confessed, "I'm intrigued by all the religions, but I tend to lean more towards the dark side." As he said this, I thought to myself, "This just got interesting." I raised my eyebrows at this last statement as if to say, "Please do go on!" And OH did he ever...

He went on to say that he was a "major" believer in the paranormal and magic, particularly dark magic. His hero and favorite character in all of history was Aleister Crowley. Crowley was a famous occultist, ceremonial magician, poet, painter, novelist, and mountaineer from the late 1800s until the mid-1900s. You may remember Ozzy mentioning him in a certain Black Sabbath song entitled "Mr. Crowley."

Stan went on and on, and I only wish that I had brought a tape recorder with me, because I can't possibly recall all the crazy things he said. Then Stan dropped a bomb by informing us that he was an "ordained Priest of Satanism" and that he could ordain us if we wanted to be Satanic Priests too. That little piece of info was a show stopper. Stan continued on, but very soon after the Satan Priest confession, Gumby announced that he had to go. As he asked for his check, a little problem arose. The restaurant wasn't accepting cards and Gumby didn't have any cash. His bill was over thirty bucks after his discount and there weren't any ATM's around. He was screwed, and Satan Priest wanted to get paid.

They tried to figure something out for about five minutes, as promises of coming back the next day to settle the tab were not going over well. As the situation became more and more awkward, I finally stepped in and told them that I would take care of it. I always kept extra cash on me for this exact reason. I asked for my check as well, and in the end I paid almost seventy dollars for the two of us. Gumby thanked me profusely and headed out. I was about to do the same, but Satan Priest insisted that he give me a beer, "on the house" for my generosity. If there's one thing I know, it's that you never turn down a free beer, even from a Priest of Satan... so I accepted.

He gave me an IPA called "Snake Dog." I'd never heard of it before, and with 7.1% alcohol content, I was ready for it to taste like shit. In the end, I was very pleasantly surprised as Snake Dog became my new favorite beer that night. Satan Priest was weird, but he had good taste! As I drank, he kept talking. Sometimes he talked about music, sometimes about magic, and sometimes about haunted areas in the town and the surrounding countryside. He talked about having séances in old houses and abandoned caves up in the mountains. He talked about hiking, nature, girls, drugs, religion, the paranormal, everything! He kept giving me beer after beer for free, so I kept sitting and listening. You only meet someone this colorful, strange, and charismatic maybe a few times in a lifetime and I was determined to soak up every bit of the encounter.

Besides being incredibly talkative, Stan was one of those people that claimed to have a "friend" for just about anything you could possibly need or want to do; or a friend that was the best in the world at one thing or another. He claimed to have a female friend who played the guitar better than anyone else in the world. Another friend had the best voice, and yet another that could play the violin and the piano unequal to any other human being on the planet. This went on until it was nearly midnight. The streets were empty and the entire town seemed abandoned as everything was shut down. Even the lone waitress of the restaurant had gone home. It was a ghost town, with not a soul in sight. I was about to politely excuse myself and go look for a place to camp when an individual came walking down the road beneath the yellow street lamps.

Stan pointed to the man and said in a low voice, "That guys crazy, he thinks everyone is trying to poison his drinks and food with bleach. He gets the cops called on him all the time." "Crazy?" I thought. "Look who's talking!" Initially I assumed that Stan was telling me this and pointing the guy out so that I knew to avoid him when I eventually left, but this was not so. As the man passed by the front deck, Stan yelled at him and motioned for him to come up. "REALLY?! You tell me this guy is crazy and then invite him up here!" I thought to myself. Just let the crazy man pass by, no need to antagonize him!

Crazy guy turned and came up on the deck. "Wonderful." I thought. They began talking as if they were longtime friends. I didn't see that coming, but I also wasn't surprised by it. They talked for a few minutes as Satan Priest expressed his concerns for Crazy Man's wellbeing. I learned that Crazy Man was known as the "Jolly Green Carrot" in the local area. I honestly couldn't tell you why. Everything was going calmly and smoothly until the Satan Priest says to Crazy Man, "You know you're fucking crazy, right?" This prompted me to think... "Now why in the hell would you go and tell a crazy person that they were crazy, right to their face?" That's the last thing you say to a crazy person! That's like the biggest crazy person "No-No" ever!

Upon hearing this, Crazy Man began to flip out. "YOU KNOW WHATS CRAZY?! YOU KNOW WHATS CRAZY?!" he screamed. "WHAT'S CRAZY IS HOW CRAZY NON-VIOLENT I AM!" As crazy man screamed this, he grabbed Satan Priest in a bear hug. Whether this was truly a hug or an actual assault, I can't be sure, but Satan Priest didn't take it well. "GET THE FUCK OFF ME YOU CRAZY SOCIALIST FUCK!" Satan Priest yelled. "I'M A FUCKING BLACK BELT, I'M GONNA BEAT YOUR ASS!" he screamed as Crazy Man held him in the bear hug. Then Satan Priest shoved Crazy Man off him and proceeded to physically beat him up and off the front deck of the restaurant and back into the street. Crazy Man broke free and ran down the street, screaming with his arms flailing wildly. "That escalated quickly," I thought to myself.

Throughout the entire episode, I'd sat in my little plastic chair with Katana underneath me, watching the antics unfold. I won't lie, I was very entertained. When the scuffle went into the street, I grabbed my pack and Katana before making my way down the stairs. I told Satan Priest "thanks" and that I was going to go find a place to camp. He shook my hand and wished me well on the journey. "Watch out for that crazy fuck," he added as I walked away.

I picked up the white blazes that led through town and followed them across a huge footbridge that stretched over the Potomac and into Maryland. "Three states in one day!" When I finally reached the other side, I was exhausted, slightly drunk, and wanted nothing more than to pass out. The surrounding forest was as thick as hasty pudding and I couldn't find a place to hang my hammock. There were a couple of medium sized trees beneath the bridge that I managed to get a good hang between, right on the banks of the Potomac River. "Even if it rained, I'll be dry under here," I thought. In my inebriated haze, I felt clever.

Not twenty minutes after setting up and drifting into a light sleep, I was violently awoken by what sounded like possibly the world exploding and breaking apart. After several moments of panic stricken horror, I realized that in my drunken, exhausted state, and being in a hurry to go to sleep, I'd hung my hammock directly beneath a train bridge. The footbridge had paralleled the train bridge, and where it connected to the Maryland side of the river was actually a crisscrossed intersection for trains. One set of tracks crossed the river before disappearing into a tunnel on the side of a mountain, while the other set paralleled the river.

Not wanting to pack up all my stuff, I decided to stay put and grit it out. All night long, approximately every half hour, an enormous freight train would go shrieking overhead. I don't know if you've ever stood under an old bridge as a train passed over top of it, but if I had to describe the sound, I would describe it as what I imagine the end of the world would sound like. It was a long night, but I was determined not to let anything get me down.

Needless to say, I didn't sleep too well that night. I managed to sleep through most of the train racket, but there were several exceptionally loud ones that managed to pierce my dreams and wake me up. I awoke the next morning to the talking of several bicyclists sitting on the path that was at the start of the footbridge. I poked my head out of my hammock as they pretended not to see me until I loudly announced, "Good morning gentlemen." They looked at me, nodded uneasily, then rode away. I loved looking like a homeless bum that lived under a bridge...

I went back across the Potomac into West Virginia in an attempt to find a ride into another town where I could get a proper resupply. My girlfriend had booked a hotel for me in the nearby town of "Martinsburg," so my first task of the day was to figure out how to get there.

At this stage of the journey I was used to people fawning over Katana. Everywhere we went she was met with copious amounts of attention. People always said the same things and asked the same questions. "What kind of dog is that?" "A Shiba what?" "Is it a boy or a girl?" "How old is she?" What's her name?" "Oh, she looks like a fox!" "Is that a fox?" "How is she handling the trail?" The list went on and on. Much like hiking questions, the Katana questions were always the same, only by now I'd learned to use them to my advantage.

I found a nice open area on the side of the main strip and sat down in the grass with Katana next to me. I waited patiently for not even five minutes before a young lady stopped and said, "Cute dog! What kind is it?" "A Shiba Inu." "A Shiba what?" "Inu." "Oh are you a hiker?" Hook, line and sinker. "Why yes ma'am, I am! Me and the fox dog here just passed the 1,000-mile mark and it just so happens we're trying to find a ride into Martinsburg." "I can take you there, I'm about to pass right by Martinsburg" she replied. "Suhweeeet," I thought. That was easy. I'd have been there all day if it wasn't for Katana.

Turns out the young lady had just gotten back from watching the Soccer World Cup in Brazil and was now on her way home to Pennsylvania, after driving back up from a friend's place in Texas. She drove us to the hotel, but check-in wasn't until 3 pm, so instead she dropped us off at a nearby Wal-Mart that was half a mile down the road. She even gave me some snacks and drinks before she left. I thanked her and also informed her that she was officially a trail angel.

I was once again a stranger in a strange land. The only difference being that this strange land wasn't a trail town, and there weren't any hikers anywhere. The people here hadn't even heard of the Appalachian Trail. In their eyes, I didn't look like a long distance hiker making a personal and spiritual journey across the country, or a hiker that was tired, beat up, and far from home. No, in their eyes I looked like a homeless bum wearing an American flag loincloth.

I didn't want to leave my pack or Katana outside unattended, so I threw them both in a cart and walked in. I laid my goose down jacket on the bottom of the cart so that her feet wouldn't slip through. She sat perfectly calm and quiet in the buggy as I stacked boxes of honey buns and cosmic brownies all around her. That's one of the wonderful things about Katana. Even though she can be hyper and disobedient, she doesn't make a sound unless it's very, very important. Also, when you sit her down or pick her up, she doesn't move a muscle. We were in stealth mode throughout our entire foray in Wally World, as nobody even noticed her. If they did, no one said anything.

I ended up walking back to the hotel and was able to check in early. Schweppes finally rolled into Harper's that day and also found a ride out to Martinsburg. We shared the hotel room and got all our laundry taken care of. I always felt bad for the cleaning lady that had to clean up after a room full of hikers. Not because we left a mess (which we didn't), but because the room smelled like a rotting bog of sweat and grime. Not only did we stink, but our gear stunk even worse, and the smell seemed to linger anywhere we went.

The next day was a humbling lesson on the "real world." After checking out of the hotel, we had to find a ride back to Harper's Ferry about twenty miles away. We knew it was going to be tough, since there were very few people familiar with the trail in Martinsburg. Also, hitchhiking was illegal in West Virginia, so we couldn't go sticking our thumbs out on the busy roads around there. We decided to find a high foot traffic area and let Katana do the work for us.

We decided to sit at the front entrance to Wal-Mart in an attempt to strike up a conversation about Katana and the trail while simultaneously hinting about our need for a ride. It was a brutally hot day in the mid to upper 90's and Katana wanted no part of it. I couldn't get her to sit in front of the bench with us, as she kept crawling underneath it and lying down. She wasn't being a team player, but once again I couldn't blame her. No one stopped to talk with us, and nobody we talked to would give us a ride. Before long, an employee came out and informed us that if we didn't leave they were going to call the police.

We relocated to a Buffalo Wild Wings just up the street and decided to have lunch. I left Katana out front attached to my backpack, in the shade of the building's large overhang with some food and water. Out on the trail and within trail towns, people frequently stopped to admire and commend Katana for being able to keep up on this journey. Sitting outside in the shade with food and water in this off trail town, everyone that walked by gave angry looks and shook their head. Some people went as far as coming inside to inquire who'd left their dog outside in the heat. I had to explain myself more than once that she wasn't some fragile house dog, and that she lived with me in the wilderness, exposed to the elements 24/7. Not to mention that she'd walked more miles in the last several months than they probably had in their entire lives. I made it very clear that sitting out there was a "break" for her and that we dealt with much worse conditions while climbing up and down mountains all day, every day. Besides, where was I going to go? I didn't have a house nearby, the restaurants didn't allow pets inside, and I wasn't rich enough to afford a hotel room for every second that I wasn't on the trail hiking. These people just didn't get it, and the response that I got from most of them was, "What's the Appalachian Trail?"

Even though we were freshly showered and laundered, the fact of the matter was that we still looked rough. It was very clear that the employees of Buffalo Wild Wings wanted us out. Even though we kept ordering drinks and small meals, they kept trying to usher us out and bring us the check. They must've asked us if we were ready for the check eight times in the course of a little over an hour that we were there. It was incredibly annoying and very eye opening. Was my money not as green as everyone else's? They finally got us by saying Katana couldn't stay outside the restaurant any longer, forcing us to leave.

This day was a huge lesson in perceptions, as well as a reminder of how judgmental and rude our modern culture could be; I wanted no part of that. Long story short, we never found a ride and had to call a shuttle, which arrived three hours later. We got back to Harper's in the early evening and camped on the shore of the Potomac, far away from the apocalyptic train bridge.

My third day in Harper's Ferry was the hottest day I could remember on the trail. I recall someone mentioning that it got up to 107 degrees in some areas, but I couldn't confirm that for sure. There wasn't a chance in hell we were going to hike out in that heat. I would later learn that many hikers that were on the trail that day ended up with heat exhaustion and more than a few people passed out or had to seek medical attention. We decided to lay low in Harpers and let things cool off a bit. We hunkered down in a train station waiting room with several other hikers in an attempt to beat the heat. We enjoyed the amenities of AC, bathrooms, running water, and power outlets, what more did we need?

At the train station I ran into a female hiker named "Stardust" whom I saw off and on since meeting her at Woods Hole Hostel back in Virginia. She was a cute blond with a great sense of humor that could hold her own with the guys. She could also hold her own in the hiking arena. She was fast and could hike a thirty-mile day without a second thought. She got her name from some guy that was probably high. The guy had asked Stardust her trail name and when she replied that she didn't have one, the stoner responded with the partial words of Carl Sagan, "We are star stuff; you're Stardust because we're all made of star dust!" So in a weird way the star dust quote made sense because of the theory that we're all made up of star dust. So technically she WAS star dust and the name "Stardust" stuck. Did I lose you?

Our initial meeting at Woods Hole had been rather shaky to say the least. Stardust looked very young, and when I first saw her sitting in a chair outside the bunk room of Woods Hole, the first thing I'd said to her, half-jokingly was, "Is hiking the trail your high school graduation present?" She looked at me for a few seconds before replying, "I'm twenty-three," then got up and walked away.

So Stardust and I had not started off on the right foot, although I'd long since apologized for my initial brashness and we were now on friendly terms. Little did I know, she would become like a little sister to Schweppes and I. Well, big sister to Schweppes, because he was only twenty-two.

Stardust, Schweppes, and I sat together and hung out for a few hours in the train station. The weather that day was strange indeed, and around 4 pm a severe thunderstorm rolled through with hurricane force winds. Trees and tree branches were downed all over the place. The squall had only lasted for a little over thirty minutes, but the destruction was pretty bad. The upside was that it was now much cooler, so we decided to hike out, going ten miles into Maryland before calling it a day.

Only around forty miles of the Appalachian Trail resides in Maryland, and besides West Virginia, it's the shortest state you'll pass through. There is a challenge out on the trail called the "four state challenge" and it consists of crossing from Virginia into West Virginia, West Virginia into Maryland, then Maryland into Pennsylvania within twenty-four hours. Since the trail is only in West Virginia for about thirty minutes, you only have to hike about forty-four miles to complete the challenge. I had initially wanted to do this four state challenge when I first heard about it, but there was no way in hell that I was going to hike back to Virginia in order to do it. I decided that I would come up with my own challenge later on in the hike.

July 3rd was my 96th day on the trail and also the most revolutionary day of the entire journey. How fitting and ironic that it would be on the day before America celebrated its freedom and independence, that I would be celebrating my own personal freedom and independence. I'm talking about my freedom from the umbilical cord that had attached me to Katana for the better part of the last three months.

I was feeling like a gambling man that morning as I walked through the wilds of Maryland, when I decided to see if Katana could finally walk without her leash. Silently wishing for success, I unlatched her lead and let her go free. She looked at me cautiously for several moments before tearing off down the trail at full speed. "DAMN IT!" I yelled as I prepared to give chase. However, I was surprised when she turned around and ran back. With a wild and crazy grin on her face, tongue hanging out, she ran by me again, then made a half circle as she went running back down the trail. She did this several times before I realized that she was simply celebrating her freedom. We had finally reached an understanding...

She walked in front of me, darting back and forth across the trail taking in the smells at her own liberty, and basking in her new found freedom. Anytime she got too far ahead of me, I'd whistle or call her name, causing her to freeze in place and wait for me to catch up. I was so happy I could've cried tears of joy. She finally learned to associate me with survival and knew that if she wanted food, water, and shelter that she had to stick by me. She'd also come to realize that if she wanted to stay off the leash, she had to respect the rules. The rules were to stay close and to "stop" and "come" when I gave the command. It felt like I'd begun hiking the trail all over again. The feeling of not having a dog attached to me at every moment of the day was incredible. It felt like a new chapter. She even learned to stop and wait for me at roads. When we got near a road, she would stop several yards away and wait for me to pick her up and carry her across. In the times that I had her off the leash, she became more like my child than ever before. Instead of sometimes being an extra burden, she was now a constant joy.

Later that same day, we were slotted for more extreme weather. My aunt, who lived in Maryland, wanted to stop by and see me, but couldn't find her way to any of the roads near the trail. It was up to me to get into a town where I had given her directions to meet me. The closest one was Shepherdstown, a stone's throw back into West Virginia. Schweppes and Stardust were to accompany me into town as we met at a fairly remote back road and decided to try our luck hitchhiking. Since there were three of us and a dog, and the road didn't seem too busy, I figured we'd be waiting a long time before we finally scored a ride.

To my utter amazement, the first car to pass by pulled over for us. This was the magic of hitchhiking with a pretty girl. Funny enough, it was a tiny Volkswagen Golf with two elderly ladies that pulled over. After we all crammed in, we were on our way. We introduced ourselves and learned the names of our driver and her passenger. The driver's name was Mindy, but when we asked her passenger her name, Mindy replied, "Oh that's Fatima; she won't speak to you because she took a vow of silence four years ago." "Interesting," I thought. I'd never met anyone that had taken a vow of silence, and it really intrigued me. As expected, Fatima didn't have much to say about it... nothing actually.

We never asked Mindy the reason for her vow of silence, but I wouldn't have been surprised if it was due to the fact that people just didn't have anything good to say these days. We made small talk with Mindy, who asked us about life on the trail. Although Fatima might have taken a vow of silence, I guess that didn't include laughing and giggling. Fatima communicated with Mindy through a series of hand gestures, motions, and lip reading that I couldn't really discern from the back seat.

After a twenty-minute drive we arrived in Shepherdstown, just as it was beginning to rain. Aunt Janet met us at the Comfort Inn and put us up in a room for the night before taking us out to a Chinese Restaurant down the road. It was a very nice reunion; I hadn't seen her in over a year. We spent time catching up before saying goodbye. She got a little emotional during our goodbyes, as she was worried for my safety out in the wilderness. It was nice spending time with her and I was sad to see her go.

Aside from earning my freedom from the umbilical cord of Katana, Maryland was mostly uneventful and boring. That may sound terrible, but when you spend all day, every day in the woods for months on end, not every day is magical, breathtaking, exciting, and inspiring. As the city may become mundane and repetitive, so can walking in the woods beneath the trees. I've said it once and I'll say it again; a boring or bad day in the woods beats the hell out of going to work at a dead-end job. There isn't even a debate there. Even though I was bored out of my mind sometimes, the reality was that there was no place else I would have rather been.

It had been another long, hot summer day in Maryland, filled with mosquitoes, snakes, and black flies as we finished making our way down a suicidal rocky descent. We couldn't help but wonder if the infamous rocks of Pennsylvania were starting early. As the darkness descended upon us, we crossed into PenMar Park, situated right on the border of Maryland and Pennsylvania. It was an enormous park with playgrounds, gazebos, picnic areas, stages for live music, and a gorgeous view of the setting sun across a vast valley of small towns and farmland. We relaxed and chatted with some locals as well as a couple from New Zealand that lingered long after the sun had sunk beneath the horizon. It was almost 10 pm when we finally reached the sign that read: "MASON DIXON." Written beneath that in smaller letters was: "Mason Dixon Line, Maryland/Pennsylvania."

The Mason Dixon Line signified that we were leaving the southern half of the country and entering the northern half. This was another big milestone that I for one, was nervous about. Everything I knew and was accustomed to was in the south, as the north would prove to be quite a different animal. It was a land where sweet tea no longer existed, and instead you were offered Arnold Palmer's or Raspberry Tea. A land where when you ordered a coffee, you were asked if you wanted it iced or hot. Yes, a strange land indeed where the accents were different and the restaurants charged you for refills on everything except water. We had left the land of southern hospitality and entered a region of fast talkers with strange accents that wanted to pump your gas for you. This was going to be quite the new experience...

CHAPTER 9: PENNSYLVANIA

"Where Shoes Come to Die and Hikers Come to Rock On... And On... And On."

Oh Pennsylvania...where do I even begin? It was 230 miles of suck it up buttercup. From my earliest days on the trail, maybe even my earliest research of the trail, I was conditioned and warned to fear Pennsylvania. Or should I say...PAINsylvania. Why so much fear and horror stories surrounding the beautiful commonwealth of Pennsylvania? I'll sum it up for you in three words: Rocks! Rocks! Rocks! The trail is so utterly full of rocks in this state that you literally cannot set your entire foot on dirt for the better part of twenty miles through some stretches.

When I say "rocks," I don't mean nice, big, smooth ones that you can easily walk and hop across as spritely as an elf. I mean sure, there were those kind too; there's every kind of rock you can imagine. For the most part though, they're jagged and sharp, jumbled and tossed around in every which way. They didn't even have to make a trail through many parts of Pennsylvania. All they had to do was paint white blazes on rocks and trees for hikers to follow because there was no need to cut or blaze a path. The level of soreness that your feet will reach in Pennsylvania is worse than what you experienced in your first weeks on the trail.

There was a joke amongst hikers in Pennsylvania, and that joke was that the trail maintainers actually came out with files to sharpen the rocks along the trail in order to keep Pennsylvania painful and infamous. This was of course absurd, but after spending a few days on those rocks, one was left wondering if perhaps it was true. They did seem extra sharp compared to anywhere else. I did some research into WHY there were so many rocks in Pennsylvania and what I found was actually quite interesting.

Thousands of years ago, during the end of the last ice age, the glaciers had begun to melt and slide across the landscape. As these

163

behemoths slid, they shattered and pushed up the bedrock before dumping it all into great big piles that we call mountains on what is now known as Pennsylvania. Then someone decided to make a great big trail across those piles of rocks.

Yes-sir Pennsylvania was different from anything I would encounter along the entire trail. Sure the rocks were bad, but I wouldn't have had it any other way. Pennsylvania rocks are another big reason for why the drop-out rate is so high on the trail. Quite frankly, I think the AT experience wouldn't be complete without them. I hated them at the time, but in hindsight they were character building, and I was a stronger person for having made it across them. Yeah, there were some really rocky areas further north in New Hampshire and Maine, but the Pennsylvania rocks held a special place in my heart. They were the FIRST bad rocks I encountered, therefore leaving the strongest impression. It's like that metaphorical Sheryl Crow song, "The First Cut is the Deepest." That statement couldn't be truer, because Pennsylvania cut me deep!

On my first full day in Pennsylvania, I was pleasantly surprised by the lack of rocks. They were fabled to be the worst in central and northern Pennsylvania, but I'd always envisioned them showing up in some shape or form the second I took my first step into this state. I was wrong however, and starting out, Pennsylvania had been nothing but pleasant. In fact, it felt almost like a vacation. We did twenty-five miles on our first day into PA. The trail was smooth while the climbs were gentle with forgiving descents. It really began to lull me into a false sense of security. "Maybe the exaggerations of how easy Virginia supposedly was will prove to be the same as the exaggerations of how terrible Pennsylvania would be." Many times throughout the day, Schweppes and I would exchange looks and say "This ain't too bad at all!" If only we'd known that we were jinxing the hell out of ourselves.

Katana had been having a blast, and was still reveling in her new found freedom. We'd entered Caledonia State Park earlier that day and it was after 8:30 pm as the later stages of twilight were in full swing. The trail was narrow and lined with many bushes, as well as scattered with a multitude of pine and birch trees. I was coming around a slight bend when I heard a light crashing in the underbrush just ahead of me to the right, but behind some bushes. It didn't sound huge, but it sounded much larger than a squirrel or chipmunk scampering away. I assumed it was a deer or small bear, so I yelled at Katana to "STOP!" To my relief, she obeyed. I grabbed her harness and picked her up.

I was ready for a bear or deer to emerge from behind the bushes and bound away into the early night, however nothing ever emerged and the sounds continued. Whatever was making the noise was still moving, although moving very slowly. Holding onto Katana, I walked forward to peer around the bushes just in time to see a fairly large creature of perhaps thirty pounds, lumber up a tall, thin paper birch tree, climbing claw over claw. "What the hell is that?" I said out loud to nobody, as Schweppes had been a short distance behind me and hadn't caught up yet.

The creature was black and white, and appeared to have very long hairs coming off its body with a black and white bushy tail. It had huge claws on the end of long arms that reached out above it, wrapping around the tree and pulling itself gracefully and swiftly upwards. The head looked strange too, as it was stretched out away from the rest of the body and focused on whatever point it was trying to reach high up in the branches. In all honesty, it looked like some kind of mutant ring tailed lemur going up that tree. My first thought was, "Holy shit! There is some kind of wild monkey hybrid loose in the Pennsylvania wilderness!" I was thoroughly convinced that's what this creature was until Schweppes trotted up next to me and exclaimed, "I think it's a porcupine."

As soon as he said porcupine it all came together as an afterthought, because that's exactly what it looked like. I'd never seen a porcupine in person, much less climbing a tree. Climbing trees just seemed very un-Porcupine-ish. When my brain initially saw what was happening, the word "Porcupine" was subconsciously shoved into the "NOT IT" pile of what it could be. Let me be the first to tell ya, a porcupine doesn't really look like a porcupine when it's climbing a tree.

We went a few miles past the Porcupine and further into the darkness before making camp near a shallow creek. Stardust, the human female walking machine, was about five miles ahead of us. "Take that you wimpy boys!"

My 100th day on the trail was a day of reflection, as well as a day for yet another milestone. It was the dawn of the triple digit days. I thought back and remembered my first day, along with all the nervous excitement of not knowing what to expect. The learning curve had been very steep; trying to remember everything I'd ever read about the trail and practiced before going out there. Everything that I was so nervous about back then had become second nature and part of everyday life. Nothing was forced or remembered anymore because it all came naturally now.

I could remember my first day on the trail and the emotions I'd felt as if it were only yesterday. It had been my first day down a path of transformation. Trying to remember times before the trail felt like remembering events from a separate life; a life that wasn't mine anymore...a life that didn't have direction or purpose. It's hard to explain and I'm afraid that I can't articulate nor describe it accurately enough to convey the full feeling.

Being out there had taught me the purpose of life, or at least my own purpose to life. To be clear, the purpose wasn't long distance hiking. The hiking gave you the clarity of mind that helped you realize and understand the purpose. The purpose is happiness in simplicity. Life is about being happy for as much of it as you possibly can. To embrace true freedom and the freedom to do what you want, when you want. It's about the freedom of not always being on someone else's schedule and living to please and meet other's expectations. You only have one life, and its ending one minute at a time. Don't let all of those minutes' tick by or belong to people that don't truly appreciate them. If you're not happy, then what's the point? Figure out what makes you happy, then do everything in your power to make it your reality.

Forget about the social norms and ideals that constrict us on a daily basis and tell us to fall in line and do things a certain way. You realize that life isn't about buying and acquiring more things. Things like the hottest fashions, the fastest cars, the biggest houses with rooms full of gadgets and a garage full of toys. If that makes you happy, then so be it, but it will never be enough because you'll always want more. Life is about simplicity and experiences. It's about having the things you need in order to survive and be happy. Things like food, water, shelter, good friends, loved ones, and great memories. Anything beyond that is a bonus and should be viewed as such. Life and living is simple; we are the ones that complicate it.

Once we stray beyond the simple foundation of happiness and get caught up in all the extras, then we begin to take the foundation for granted and the extras no longer make us happy...for long. Relax! Slow down and enjoy the little things. Sit down and watch the sunset while contemplating the amazing fact that every human being and living creature that ever existed on this planet has looked upon that exact same sun and possibly wondered the same things as you. Realize that at the end of your life you can't take all of your things with you. All you will have is the people you love and the memories of your life; shaped the way you lived and made them. Focus on acquiring experiences and memories, not things.

Another fantastic coincidence of day 100 was that I reached the numerical halfway point of the trail at 1,093 miles. You couldn't help but soak that in. "I just walked 1,093 miles and ONLY JUST reached halfway!" It certainly was mind boggling. There was a large sign erected at the halfway point to commemorate the location. I set Katana on top of it and snapped another one of my favorite pictures of her from the journey.

Not five minutes from the halfway monument we ran across another rattlesnake. Rattlesnake number five. I spotted it stretched out across the trail a good forty feet ahead of us and called Katana to a stop. I took off my pack, pulled out her leash and tethered her to it once again. Schweppes was right behind me watching the entire time.

I didn't get twenty feet from this snake before it began rattling. I had already done this four times before and was ready to do it a fifth time. The serpent continued to rattle as I approached, but did not coil. He was a big snake, even bigger than the first one. I dropped to a knee and pinned his head with my staff...the snake didn't flinch. In fact, he stopped rattling all together. This was completely backwards from all of my previous encounters. As I knelt beside the snake, one hand on its body and the other hand about to grab it behind the head, a strange feeling came over me that I can't explain. The snake was calm, but I had a really bad feeling. I knelt there looking at him, and could feel him looking right back at me. I began to feel uneasy and not the least bit excited for the first time in my life during a snake capture. After a few more moments I let go of him, stood up and lifted my staff. The snake coiled and sat there staring at me.

This snake had some kind of invisible mojo that exuded "Don't mess with me!" Some would argue this is the quality of all poisonous snakes, but I've never gotten that feeling with one before. It was very strange. I scooped him up by his coils with my staff and walked him across the trail into the woods before releasing him.

I kept thinking about what had happened as I continued walking along. "Did I just get psyched out by a snake?" "Was this a special case or was I losing my nerve?" The only way I'll ever know is to capture the next poisonous snake I come across. Until then, I can only guess that I've perhaps lost my nerve.

Day 100 wasn't over and still had more in store for me. The halfway point was not far from Pine Grove Furnace State Park. There was a small convenience store here that was home to the "Half Gallon Challenge." It was a tradition for hikers to buy a half gallon of ice cream from this store to commemorate reaching the halfway point. The challenge was to finish the entire half gallon as fast as they could, armed with nothing but a tiny wooden paddle spoon; the kind that's traditionally used for sampling flavors in ice cream parlors. It seemed simple enough, especially on a blistering hot day like it was, and especially after completing twelve miles already.

Stardust had gotten there before us and eaten her half gallon of Butter Pecan sometime in the neighborhood of thirty minutes. Schweppes bought the chocolate and polished it off in fourteen minutes. I made the tactical error of buying Rainbow Sherbet. First of all, it was terrible; second of all, it was filling. I ate only a third of the carton before throwing it away in disgust and defeat to the jeers of Schweppes and Stardust making fun of me. I'd failed my second eating challenge. I was a disgrace to the thru-hiker eating legacy. Now I was just a dumb guy with a cute little dog, no appetite, and one who thought porcupines were monkeys. My reputation was growing!

July 8th was a great day with some crappy undertones. It was "Africa hot" once again when Pennsylvania decided to give us a little taste of what it had in store. The trail cut straight through the town of Boiling Springs, and I was determined to stop for only a small resupply before continuing on. Before getting there, I was forced to navigate through miles of rollercoaster climbs that were covered by a maze of rocks. They weren't jagged rocks however, but huge, lumbering, semi jagged ones that you had to pick your way over and leap across like a sprite. They were an inconvenience, but it could've been much worse. It was during the course of this rollercoaster rock maze that I gave myself a new temporary injury.

While taking a huge step down from a large rock onto a smaller, narrow rock, I miscalculated my foot placement. I came down too fast and didn't get enough of my left foot onto the smaller rock. I only got maybe half of the front pad of my foot onto the rock as I came down heavy and hard with the weight of all my gear. I simply didn't have enough strength in my foot to cushion and support the landing as well as the extra weight I was carrying. The force bent my foot so far back that my toes nearly touched my shin. I heard a "POP," as I slid to the ground and landed on my feet. My ankle pinched and throbbed intensely for several minutes. It didn't hurt to walk, but when I stopped to do range of motion exercises, the top of my ankle hurt so bad that I couldn't "dorsiflex" (flex my foot and toes upwards) my foot without wincing. This was unfortunate, however inconsequential, because all I cared about was that I could walk. Nothing else mattered to me.

The pain this injury caused lasted for weeks. Ironically it didn't hurt when I was walking, but only when the weight was taken off my foot and it hung there loosely. As a result, it hurt mostly at night as I lay in my hammock. The pain would randomly wake me up in the middle of the night if I unconsciously rolled into a wrong position.

I met up with Stardust at the bottom of the last rollercoaster and walked a couple miles through corn fields with her. As we reached the outer limits of Boiling Springs, the trail turned onto a road and we soon found ourselves walking through town.

While going over a small bridge, a woman slowed to a stop next to us in her Toyota Camry. "Can I buy you two lunch?" she asked. Having never had anyone say something like this to us yet, we both gave her a surprised look and said "Sure! Thank you!" I thought she was going to pick us both up and take us somewhere to eat. Instead, she stuck her hand through the window, handed us two twenty dollar bills and said, "Here you go! There's a café just ahead and a pizza place not far from there. Welcome to Boiling Springs!" She then pulled away as we gratefully thanked her for her kindness. This was a first for me on the trail. No one had ever pulled over and given me money to eat before. My faith in mankind and my opinions of Pennsylvania had never been so high!

Boiling Springs was a gorgeous little town that was centered around an enormous crystal clear pond that was filled with fish and fed by a large spring on what I would deem the north side of town. The park surrounding this pond was like something out of a painting. Strangely, I found myself envious of everyone that had the privilege of growing up there. The people were so friendly, the town so small, and the scenery worthy of the highest praise.

Stardust and I waited for Schweppes near a gas station for nearly an hour before he arrived. He was dehydrated and thought that he might have Lyme disease. He had pulled a tick off his shin the other evening and was now letting paranoia get the best of him. It was better to be safe than sorry, so a local resident gave him a ride to a nearby clinic where he was tested and found to be perfectly healthy. He was simply dehydrated, but also had water in his ears for some reason.

Schweppes and Stardust decided that they wanted to stay at a local lodge called the "Allenberry." I only wanted to resupply, eat some pizza, then move on to camp somewhere. In the end they decided to stay, while I decided to get a bite to eat and move on. As I went in search of the pizza place, I forgot to get my half of the $40 from Stardust. I wasn't worried about it because she could put it towards a meal for her and Schweppes.

It was mid-afternoon when I found the local pizza place called "Anile's." The parking lot was empty. I left Katana near the front entrance with food and water before going inside. As I passed through the front door,

168

the first thing I noticed was a man sitting behind the counter with his feet propped up and reading a magazine. "How you doin?" he said in a thick New York accent as I walked in. My first thought was, "This guy looks exactly like the actor, Robert Davi, from the late 1980's early 1990's." My second thought was, "I bet this guy makes a damn good pizza!"

I took a seat and ordered my standard large pepperoni and sweet tea. "We don't have sweet tea, just lemon tea and iced tea," was the waitress' response. "NoOoOoOoO!" I screamed in my head. I'd forgotten I was no longer in the south and sweet tea didn't exist anymore! "I can bring you some sugar to put in it," she added. "Oh no thanks, I'll just have a water." It's just not the same unless the sugar is dissolved in the tea when it's hot. Sweet tea is one of those things I didn't compromise on.

Upon finishing the most delicious pizza I'd eaten on the trail thus far, the waitress came up and informed me that someone had anonymously paid for my tab and also left a box of dog treats for Katana. "Boiling Springs, you guys are amazing!" Boiling Springs ended up having the highest "kind deeds to time ratio" of any other town I ever came to. The sign leading into that town should read "Boiling Springs, the friendliest place on earth!"

I left the restaurant and began walking back across town to pick up the trail again. On my way, no less than five people pulled over to warn me that a severe storm was approaching and that I should take cover indoors. It was incredibly kind of them. However, I mistakenly let my now overconfident thru-hiker attitude get the best of me. I should've taken cover, but I'd walked in plenty of severe storms already and I was fairly certain this one would be no different.

I hit the trail to find that it was completely flat as it paralleled more corn fields. I knocked out two miles before I heard the sounds of distant thunder. I strained to see above and beyond the trees in an attempt to spot any incoming weather. As I squinted through the canopy back towards the south, I saw them... clouds as black as night coming my way. They looked terribly ominous contrasted next to the blue sky, prompting me to look around in search of anywhere decent to set-up and take cover. Once again the woods were too thick with vines and shrubs to hang my hammock. I hurried on in search of a suitable spot as the constant roll of distant thunder mocked and fueled my increasingly fevered state. I finally spotted an open area more than a hundred feet off the trail through some thick vegetation. With reckless abandon I crashed through all of it with Katana hot on my heels.

I reached the trees in the little clearing and quickly set up my atlas straps before attaching my hammock. It took me less than a minute and a half to get my hammock hung correctly from the moment I pulled out my atlas straps. I then pulled out my rain fly and began to loop it around and attach it to the first tree. I got it secured in less than thirty seconds. I hurried across the gap between the two trees and began to loop it around the second tree. I had it looped but not tied when a dark shadow washed over me. I looked up to see the midnight black clouds overhead. There was an eerie calm and silence for a few seconds as I heard the first raindrops begin to hit the uppermost leaves of the tree canopy. Then without warning, a wall of wind slammed into me followed by horrendous stinging lashes of rain.

The cord for my rain fly was ripped out of my hands as the tarp flew into the air, tethered only by the first tree. My hammock shot into the air as well, the slack where it had sloped lazily towards the ground had now been reversed so that my hammock was out of reach above me. Leaves swirled everywhere and branches fell to the ground all around me. I could hear the snapping sounds of trees as they toppled to the ground, while the larger branches hit the earth with loud cracks and thuds. The sounds of their impacts penetrated the howling wind. The cacophony of sounds from the chaos was deafening, and I would be a liar if I said that I wasn't frightened. I was almost certain that a falling tree or branch was going to kill me.

I couldn't do anything about my hammock or rain fly, so I rushed back over to my open pack and began to furiously stuff everything back into it while pulling my pack cover over to protect it from the rain. It was no use, everything had happened too fast. The strongest winds subsided in less than ten minutes, leaving only a severe rainstorm. I eventually got control of my shelter and managed to get my rain fly up.

My hammock was soaked, forcing me to use my clean dry clothes to mop up the inside before I could lay my sleeping bag in it. The whole ordeal had been a nightmare! I couldn't remember feeling so annoyed and frustrated since the night I had shit all over myself. This wasn't quite as miserable as that, but it was close. The locals had warned me that a severe storm was coming, but they had failed to mention it would be a hurricane. I don't blame them at all because it was my fault and my fault alone for my predicament. When the worst of the storm had calmed down, I heard the sounds of many sirens and emergency vehicles buzzing around town in the distance. I counted myself lucky.

Early on in Pennsylvania the terrain had been relatively flat and forgiving. Having over a thousand miles under our feet had brought our hiking stamina close to rock star levels. We could do huge miles on a daily basis over the southern Pennsylvania terrain if we wished. Distances that used to take us several days to traverse would now only take us one or two big days if we wanted to push it. With this capacity to cover much larger distances, the travel time between towns subsequently became shorter. We could hop from one town to the next in a day or a day in a half; it all depended on how hard we wanted to exert ourselves, as well as how many breaks we took throughout the day.

On the morning after the storm, I awoke to find there were trees and branches blown down all over the trail. Some trees were bigger than the ones I'd hung my hammock between the night before, reinforcing how lucky I was. I linked up with Stardust who actually ended up passing me early that morning. Go figure. I left to get a head start, and then she ends up passing me early the next day. She informed me there had been a town-wide blackout; trees had blown down on the streets and some power lines had been knocked over. Not to mention there were several automobile accidents as well. It was definitely not a storm to have taken lightly.

170

Stardust and I put in twenty-five miles that day by 5:30 pm. That was the most miles I'd ever completed that early in the day. Stardust was a slave driver of a hiking companion. I think we took four five-minute breaks the entire day. Luckily, the terrain was very flat, with the exception of two moderately big climbs. It was mostly walking through farmlands, pastures, and along rivers. Anytime you walked along a river you could count on the terrain being relatively level.

We walked through seemingly endless fields of daisies and wildflowers as Pennsylvania showed off its "lighter" and more "colorful" side. It was in one of those daisy fields that Stardust snapped another one of my favorite pictures of Katana. The little dog had gotten ahead of us and I'd called her back. In the picture, Katana was trotting towards us on a straight away surrounded by white daisies, a blue sky filled with wispy white clouds, and a huge smile on her face. It looked like a scene from "The Wizard of Oz."

Towards the end of the hot day we stopped at Hawk Rock and took in a spectacular view of the town laid out before us and the great Susquehanna River. This town was called Duncannon and the trail once again passed straight through it. There really wasn't a whole lot in Duncannon, but it struck me as an old town that was trapped in the wrong era. I liked it.

We had arrived in time for a dinner (that we had no previous knowledge of) being held at a local church. It was arranged specifically for thru-hikers. There was spaghetti and meatballs, salad, drinks, brownies, doughnuts, and homemade ice cream. It was a fantastic way to end a long sweaty day, and Schweppes was lucky enough to arrive about an hour behind us and still partake.

There was one other attraction for hikers in the town of Duncannon besides the hiker feeds put on by the church. That attraction was an infamous old hotel called "The Doyle Hotel," but it was always referred to as simply "The Doyle." This hotel was famous for being bad. It wasn't supposed to be fancy, comfortable, or hospitable. It was simply a trashy, run down, ugly building that served amazing food, and it was tradition for thru-hikers to stay there. It was four stories tall, and by all accounts, from the outside looked like a haunted house.

As soon as I checked in and began making my way to the top floor, I was instantly reminded of the house on Paper Street in the movie "Fight Club." It looked EXACTLY like the inside of that house - I kid you not! It had spider webs, peeling paint, and dead bugs in my room. There was no air conditioning, no bathrooms, and only a small fan. There was one communal bathroom for each floor, sort of like a boarding house. One of the most notable things about my room was the smashed bug on the wall that was smack dab in the middle of a dirty boot print where someone had ended its life. It was funny because no one had even tried to clean it. It was obvious that the rooms weren't cleaned and that a conscious effort was actually put into letting them look bad.

To be perfectly honest, I loved it. I loved novelty stuff like this. This place wasn't parading as something it wasn't. It was advertised as a dump, and that's exactly what it was; if you didn't like it, you didn't have to stay.

171

One thing I hadn't expected was for the bed to be very comfortable, but it was. I've stayed in plenty of average to upscale type hotels and condominiums over the course of my life, but how many people can say they've stayed in a hotel that was famous for being a shithole? I made a walk-through video of the place, but it didn't do it justice. You had to be there to get the full picture and experience.

That night at the Doyle I slept beautifully! When you live in the woods, anything indoors will do. The next morning, I went across the street to a breakfast spot called "Goodies." It was a little hole in the wall joint with camouflaged painted walls and I liked it immediately. No sooner had I sat down, I was informed of their pancake eating challenge. The challenge was to eat six pancakes and your prize was a free breakfast. No one had ever finished six, because if they had, the challenge would go up to seven. It had originally started at three pancakes, but had been increased up to six over recent years. These weren't your normal run of the mill pancakes though; they were MONSTER pancakes. They were bigger than a standard dinner plate and probably an inch thick. I decided to give it a shot.

The pancakes came stacked in a lopsided tower. I straightened them out and set to work. I got maybe a little more than three quarters of the way through the stack before my brain saved me from myself once again. I tried to do the math on the mutilated stack and figured that I'd maybe finished four and a half of the pancakes. I felt the taste and sting of another food challenge failure for the third time on the adventure. I didn't even want to look at myself in the mirror.

That morning Stardust hiked out earlier than me and I hiked out earlier than Schweppes. I didn't know it at the time, but we wouldn't see Stardust for a couple weeks. She ended up getting poison ivy and took some time off with family. I had a long two-mile road walk through a town that included crossing the great Susquehanna River on a huge busy bridge, before melting back into the forest and a steep climb up onto a ridge.

The pancakes were sitting heavily in my gut as I was feeling the heat of the day only a few miles into the woods. I stopped at a shelter and laid down to digest for a bit. It was at this shelter that I met a funny little character named "Sweet Pea." He was a thru-hiker, or so he claimed. He certainly had the look. This little fellow was missing a few front teeth, giving him a somewhat comedic lisp. I'm not making fun, just building a description.

Sweet Pea seemed to be drunk, high, hung-over, or strung out on something, because he just wasn't making any sense. He kept telling me that he was mad that he'd hiked out of Duncannon so early, because he really wanted a pizza. So I said to him, "We're not too far, go back and get one." "Yeah, you're right," he replied. Wearing the expression of a deep thinker on his face, he was silent for several minutes. Then he began explaining his master plan to me. "I think this is what I'm gonna do," he began. "I'm gonna hike five miles ahead to another road, hitchhike back into Duncannon, get a pizza and then hike back up here and eat it." I looked at him for several seconds while trying to process what he'd just said to me. "Good idea," I replied.

Yes, it was a genius idea! Hike ahead five miles just to hitchhike backwards and then re-hike the five miles out of town back up to this spot while carrying a pizza. You just did fifteen miles of walking today for only a five mile gain to go practically nowhere. Five miles of which you've already done, and another five that you're going to have to do again when you do finally leave this shelter for the second time. I'm telling you, this guy had it all figured out!

He repeated about four different versions of this plan to me over the course of twenty minutes. Each version had him ending up back at this shelter with or without a pizza after either hiking ahead or hiking backwards. I don't know if he was just stupid or on some controlled substance, but whatever it was, I didn't want any... and I hoped it wasn't contagious.

Schweppes caught up with me at the genius' shelter before we pressed on together. We went another seven miles before a bad rainstorm rolled over our position, causing us to make camp early at Table Rock Outlook. This spot will always be another one of my favorite camp spots of the trail. Although the weather was deplorable for most of the time I was there, you couldn't beat the location. It was a beautiful grassy clearing on the edge of a rocky precipice overlooking a vast uninterrupted forest for as far as the eye could see.

When we first hunkered down, we were caught in a thick blanket of fog as the rain poured heavily. When the rain finally shut off around sunset and the fog lifted, we were left with a spectacular double rainbow that was arching over the swath of trees beneath us. The most amazing part of this rainbow was that we were looking straight down on the end of it. It was the first time I'd actually seen the end of a rainbow, and from a viewpoint that was above it no less. Usually they fade away as they get nearer to the ground, but this one was coming right off the tops of the trees directly in front and below us. I couldn't stop taking pictures. This was one of the more beautiful and unique moments that I can remember from the trail.

The next morning, I was awoken by a strange noise; it was definitely a bird by the sounds of it. I peeked over the edge of my hammock to see a grouse standing right on the edge of Table Rock Outlook, its neck outstretched while making a God awful call. It was another beautiful moment in its own way; an animal admiring and calling out over its forested kingdom. I watched it for a few moments and contemplated getting out of my hammock to see how close I could get and maybe procure a meal. In the end I was too lazy and tired, and only wanted to sleep in a little longer. I rustled my hammock canopy with my hands as the grouse turned and looked over. As soon as it noticed my hammock, it crouched, then tucked its head back towards its body as if to become less conspicuous, and then sat there frozen looking in my direction. It was so comical the way it played out that I actually laughed out loud. I laid down and went back to sleep.

Pennsylvania had been quite overgrown since leaving Duncannon. The trail was narrow and congested with vegetation on all sides. Moisture was thick in the air and the bugs were out in force. The bugs mainly consisted of gnats, mosquitoes, and these huge black flies that could bite through your shirt. The big black flies were the worst because you couldn't feel them landing on your clothes. When you did finally feel them, it was a white hot pinch, like they were spitting a tiny pin head of acid onto your skin.

The briar vines with their tiny thorns were bad as well, snagging your clothing, as well as your skin every time you drifted too close, or when the vegetation closed in on all sides. Before long, you'd have thin scratches all over the surface of your arms and legs that stung as the sweat soaked into them. Pennsylvania was also where I began to see a lot of poison ivy. It was tough to identify or even see when moving at 3.5 to 4 mph, with vegetation brushing against you on all sides. I could only hope that I didn't touch it long enough for it to really set in, but of course being covered in sweat didn't help that situation at all.

On this day we were shooting for the town of Lickdale. After checking the maps and the guidebook, we noticed there was a Subway restaurant there, and that the town itself was only 2.5 miles from the trailhead. That was a very walkable sideways distance for getting into a town. The plan was to try and hitchhike first, but if that was unsuccessful then we'd suck it up and walk. It would be a hard twenty-six-mile day, but Subway would make it worthwhile... Subway always made it worthwhile.

Food takes on an entirely new meaning to the average thru-hiker. Suddenly there is no such thing as "healthy" or "unhealthy" foods; the calorie content is all that matters. You can often find thru-hikers comparing similar meals or snacks for the overall calorie content, or the calorie content per serving. Not only was it about calories, but calories versus weight. It was simply uneconomical to carry foods that didn't pull their own weight in calories. That's why you almost never saw people packing out vegetables. Some did, but it wasn't very common. Sometimes your craving for something would outweigh its economic hiking value.

When you're thru-hiking on a budget, life becomes a game of calories. Your body is burning through them so fast, that you can hardly eat enough to sustain it. Your only option is to either eat copious amounts of more expensive foods that are tough to carry in large quantities, or you can eat the smallest, lightest, and more inexpensive foods that have tons of calories. Unfortunately, these inexpensive foods are usually not very healthy for you, causing huge spikes in your insulin levels. Out on the trail, you don't care about any of that. It's simply about putting enough calories into your body to get you to the next resupply station where you can indulge in some of your more desired foods.

I was always torn between my cosmic brownies and oatmeal cream pies. The cosmic brownie was denser and more compact, but had around 100 fewer calories than the oatmeal cream pie per packaged unit. The oatmeal cream pie was fluffier, more fragile, and took up more room, but was lighter. The oatmeal cream pie was lighter in weight and contained more calories than the cosmic brownie, making it the most logical choice. On the flip side, you could fit more cosmic brownies into your pack than oatmeal cream pies. It was a matter of deciding which quality was more important to you. I almost always went with the Oatmeal cream pie when I had both options, but sometimes I chose both.

Most living creatures are driven by hunger, the necessity to obtain food in order to survive. Almost everything that a wild and even not so wild creature does is usually a means to an end in the struggle to obtain food in any manner that it can. Many humans don't have to worry about this, because obtaining food is not really a main concern. It's a secondary concern, because in the modern world you need something else before you can get the food. Humans are driven by the desire to obtain money. Obtain money so they can obtain food, as well as all the other things that we deem important to live and be happy. That is one of the major differences between the majority of modern humans and all other living creatures on this planet.

When you go on a long distance hike that spans many months, it's safe to say that you're not working, so in most cases you're not making money. In theory you should already have the money you need in order to complete your thru-hike in whatever amount of time it takes for you to complete it. With the acquisition of money removed from the equation, food becomes your main focus. You know you already have the money to buy it, so now you only have to get to where it is. Walking becomes your only means to obtain food. The paradox is that walking all day, every day, really builds an appetite. So your only means to obtain food becomes the reason why you're craving so much of it in the first place. It's a cruel and vicious cycle.

Food begins to consume your thoughts, as it becomes all you can think about all day, every day. Instead of philosophizing and trying to solve the major problems of your life and the world, you find yourself in a fierce personal battle over what you want to eat more of when you finally get into town...pizza or wings? The answer is simple, you get both. However, that answer doesn't stay your ravenous, hunger-obsessing brain. You can't stop thinking about it as your brain plays tricks on you by generating smells that aren't even there. I've been in the middle of nowhere, miles from anywhere, when with closed eyes I could've sworn on my life that I smelled Dr. Pepper and pepperoni pizza right under my nose. I could almost feel the bubbles of carbonation popping against my upper lip and nostrils. It's absolute torture.

Food is the only reason that you even HAVE to go into towns. If it was practical and legal to obtain all of your food on the trail, then in theory, you would never have to hike into town. However, that's not how it works out there. The food cravings will make you do crazy things as I've already explained to you earlier on. When you look at the map of a town that's ahead of you and see a restaurant or fast food joint that you like, it all of a sudden becomes your job to get there. You plan all of your days, as well as your miles around it. Case in point, I did almost thirty miles just so I could get a frozen, oven baked pizza that I didn't even get to have. Sometimes you might look ahead and see something that you like in a town that's hundreds of miles, as well as multiple other town stops away. You start making plans now on how to conveniently end up in that town with minimal food stores and an excuse to stay a while. Let me rephrase that, you start making plans to end up there no matter what!

175

Yes, food is the driving factor in almost every trip into town, as well as every crazy decision you make out there. Trust me - the obsession with food that drags you into multiple towns doesn't take anything away from the hike or the overall adventure and experience. It's just another part of hiking the trail. If you want to live in the woods, live off the land, not see any people, and never go into any towns while still hiking somewhere new every day, then the Appalachian Trail is not for you. If you are at a level of survival knowledge that allows you to subsist in a nomadic way such as that, then you should trail blaze your own path into the middle of nowhere and good luck. If that's your thing, then you will be happy and I will be happy for you. If you want to hike thousands of miles, see the countryside, as well as a plethora of American culture, unique little towns, and meet amazing new people while at the same time enjoy your solitude on an almost daily basis, then the Appalachian Trail is for you.

It had been a long and overgrown day when we finally made it to the road that led into Lickdale around 8:30 pm. It was almost dark and I was covered in briar scratches as well as chafing a bit from all the humidity. I really didn't want to walk the 2.5 miles into town unless I absolutely had to. We tried hitching for thirty minutes with no luck; nighttime was simply a lousy time to hitch.

We began active hitching as we walked down the road towards town, and made it maybe half a mile before a car pulled over about fifty yards ahead of us. We ran up to it and thanked them for stopping. They popped their trunk and we threw our packs in before hopping in the back seat. The driver was a woman in her early thirties, and her passenger was a guy that was also in his early thirties. The guy was big and husky, maybe 6'5, didn't have a shirt on, and was covered in random tattoos all over his torso. For the privacy and safety of the people who picked us up, I am changing their names. I will refer to the man as Jack and the woman as Jill, from here on out.

Jack asked us where we were headed. I told him if he could drop us off at Subway, we would be grateful. So we continued east on our way into Lickdale, and once again I initiated small talk. I asked, "Do you guys pick up many hikers?" to which Jack turned around and said, "No, are you guys' hikers?" My first thought was, "SHIT, they picked us up thinking we were bums hitchhiking on the side of the road." My second thought was, "What kind of people pick up other people who look like us in the middle of the night?" This was the first time I'd been picked up by someone who was unaware of the trail or hikers. "Uhh, yeah," I replied. "We're hiking the Appalachian Trail and were nearly 1,200 miles into a 2,200-mile hike." For some reason this information seemed to make Jack's night. "No way! That's awesome man!" Jack exclaimed. Schweppes and I both explained a little more about the trail before Jack insisted that we had to stay at their house, eat some home cooked ribs, take a shower, do our laundry, and sleep on real beds. What an offer this was! It sounded like an amazing idea, so Schweppes and I both agreed, almost in unison.

No sooner had we agreed, they turned the car around in the middle of the road and began heading back the way we came. "Uhhhhh... we're not going to Lickdale?" I thought to myself. Wherever they'd been going that night, they cancelled their plans and were now taking us in a whole new direction. We had no idea where we were going and didn't want to seem alarmed by asking. Besides, it was obvious, they were taking us to their home... wherever home was.

A couple minutes after having turned around, Jack looked back at us and said, "I just got done serving eight years in prison; do you guys need any nug?" "DING! DING! DING! WINNER! WINNER!" was going off in my head (nug is a slang term for Marijuana). "Oh we're good, thanks though," we replied, trying to play it cool. "Well, I got a bunch of different strands and not that dirt weed, it's the good shit from Colorado," he added. "Oh nice, we'll keep that in mind," we replied. The he said, "Do you guys need anything to sleep? I got Xanax, methadone, and some other good shit. I'm bipolar and manic depressive so I got all kinds of psych medicine." It was after hearing this that I wanted nothing more than to open the door and fall out of that car. Fuck my backpack, the trail, this guy, and Schweppes (if he didn't fall out too); I just wanted to get out!

"This guy was bipolar, manic depressive, a drug dealer, AND just got out of prison!?" That was a laundry list of red flags, and we were sitting in a vehicle with a stranger that had every single one of them! We replied, "Oh thanks, but we did like twenty-six miles today, we'll sleep just fine." Jack promptly responded, "Ok cool, cool, you know you guys are some chill ass dudes." ...to which we replied in unison, "Thanks."

It took us twenty minutes going in the other direction from Lickdale to get to their house. Surprisingly, they actually had a very nice home. I guess it goes without saying that the drug business paid well. They had two kids; an eleven-year-old girl and a nine-year-old boy. When we pulled up to their house, both of them came running out. "Who are these people?" they immediately asked. "They're some chill ass dudes that are hiking over two thousand miles and they're going to stay with us tonight," Jack told them. The little girl came up to me right away and asked, "You're not going to murder us are you?" This was ironic because I was about to ask the same question. I didn't even get to reply before Jack snapped, "No! Shut up! Go inside!" They let Katana in as we set about taking showers and getting our laundry going. I found three ticks on me while in the shower.

The kids, although outspoken and assertively curious, were intelligent, obedient, and had very good manners. They were awesome kids. The strange thing was that their parents cursed at them like sailors. Whenever they told them to do something, they would call or refer to them as "Shithead" or "Motherfucker" or "Little Dumbass." I'd never seen parents speak to their kids like that before in my life. Maybe there's something to it, because those were the most well behaved, obedient kids I have ever met.

After showers and laundry were done, we all gathered in the living room. I wanted nothing more than to eat, but no ribs had been brought out as promised. Jack began asking us all about the trail with the kids chiming in here and there. They were the usual questions. Where do you sleep? What do you do when it rains? How do you get food? How do you get water? Do you get scared? Have you had any close calls? Have you seen any bears? What crazy stuff have you seen? Are there a lot of snakes? Do you carry a gun? What do you carry for protection? They were all the standard questions that come to people's minds when they meet someone walking thousands of miles through wilderness.

After thirty minutes of fielding questions and telling stories, Jack got up and left the room. He came back two minutes later with a large machete. I began to go over contingency plans in my head and look for an escape route. "Hey man," Jack began. "I've had this machete for a really long time and it's very near and dear to me, but I can see when someone else needs it more; I want you to have it." "Oh, that's ok, I really don't need it that bad," I responded. In hindsight, I probably should've taken it right away just to get it out of his hands. "Please take it, I want you to have it," Jack replied. "Ok, I'll take it. Thank you so much Jack," I said as I gave in. I stuffed the machete into the side of my pack. At least I was more or less in control of it now.

Jack got up again and left the room. Once again, he returned in a little less than two minutes. This time he had a pair of worn out leather gloves that looked as if they'd seen better days. He then said, "Hey man, I want you to have these leather gloves for all those snakes you been catching." I didn't even try to refuse; I took them and thanked him.

Then the little boy left the room and came back a minute later. He had two enormous "Hulk Smash" toy boxing gloves. "I want you to have these," the little boy said to Schweppes. "I don't need those," Schweppes replied. "Take em!" the little boy demanded. Schweppes didn't even have to reply a second time. "He doesn't need those fucking things, go put them back in your room you little dumbass!" Jack scolded.

We sat for a bit more, but still no ribs were offered. Jack started again, "Hey man, I was looking at your shoes and they're looking pretty worn out. I have a pair of boots you can have." "Oh, I have a new pair of shoes waiting for me at the post office in the next town, I'll be ok," I replied. "Well what if your shoes fall apart before then? What size do you wear?" he asked. "I'm a fourteen," I responded. "Well these boots are a twelve, but you could probably make them work until the next town." Jack just wasn't giving up. He was going to try and give me every little thing that he wanted to get rid of until I had thirty extra pounds in my pack. "I don't think they'll fit, the shoes I'm wearing are barely wide enough for me as it is," I replied. He finally took the hint and left it alone. By now, all I wanted was to go to sleep. It was getting later and later and I'd already accepted that I wasn't going to eat, let alone eat ribs.

Then Jill announced that it was movie time. They chose the movie "Cop Out." Not really a kid's movie, but then again these weren't normal kids living with normal parents. Jack and Jill got into two reclining chairs behind the "L" shaped couch that Schweppes, myself, and the kids were all sitting on. It was nearly 11 pm when they popped the movie in. Since the kids were both sitting next to us, neither of us could lie down, so we were forced to watch the movie sitting up. At one point the little girl got up and went to the kitchen. This was my chance! I seized the moment and laid down while making a mocking face at Schweppes. When the little girl came back and found that I'd taken her seat, she got the hint and went to her bedroom.

Jack broke out some "nug" and began smoking openly in the living room. I've been around recreational drug use throughout my life, and I've found that it's really not for me. That being said, I've never seen anyone smoke so much marijuana in one sitting before in my entire life. Jack was chain smoking bowls non-stop for almost the entire movie. I've never seen anything like it. He was living proof that you couldn't overdose on marijuana.

Midnight came and went. As I lay there, I heard the boy say to Schweppes, "It's after midnight... I can't sleep after midnight... looks like it's just you and me staying up till sunrise." It took everything I had not to burst out laughing, because I knew this was the last thing Schweppes wanted to hear. When the movie finally ended, the little boy got up to put another one in. As he did so, Schweppes laid down in his spot. The little boy also took the hint and went upstairs to his room while Jack and Jill lay asleep in their reclining chairs behind us.

This was one of the strangest hitchhiking encounters I had during the adventure. It was the second time I'd stayed at a stranger's private residence, and the last time I stayed at a stranger's private residence. We'd only wanted food and rest, but got neither. The next morning Jack was late for work and left without us, leaving us to wait on Jill. She got us back to the trail a little after 9 am, but not before giving us Jack's number. They wanted us to call them at the next road we came to and said that no matter how far away it was, they would come get us. It was really very nice of them.

As random and strange as all of this was, Jack and Jill had been incredibly kind to us. We didn't get to eat, and we hardly slept, but their hearts had been in the right place as they had opened their home, as well as their drugs to two complete strangers. It was just unfortunate that their lifestyle didn't jive with our hiking style. They were nothing more than a simple family trying to get by in tough times, and they have my thanks and gratitude.

As we began hiking, I noticed that I was beginning to break out in a rash on my arms and legs; I knew immediately that it was poison ivy. It was just a matter of time I suppose, and one more thing to add to my growing list of miseries out on the trail. I can't say I was even surprised that I got it. In fact, I think I would've been more surprised if I hadn't gotten poison ivy at some point.

Only an hour into the hike it began to rain again. I swear Pennsylvania seemed to have a rain storm at least once a day. I tried to put my pack cover on, but the machete was making it impossible. In the end, I stuck it into the nearest tree and hoped the next person that found it had more use for it than I did. Funny enough, it wasn't too long after that, the trail got so overgrown that I wished I'd had a machete. Figures...

We hiked in the rain for several miles before reaching a shelter and decided to take a break in an attempt to wait out the weather. There were two other hikers with the same idea that were already inside. We hunkered down at the shelter for over an hour before the rain stopped and we moved

179

on. One of the other hikers had made some mash potatoes and was eating them from a bowl as we started to leave.

Perhaps a hundred yards from the shelter, I noticed that Katana was no longer in front of me. I turned around to see her standing in place about ten yards back, frozen, looking straight at me. "Katana come!" I commanded. She looked behind herself, then back at me. "Katana come!" I repeated. She spun around and began running as fast as she could south. I started chasing her, not knowing why the hell she was running away.

She hauled ass all the way back to the shelter, leapt inside, then shoved her head right into the bowl of mash potatoes while it was still in the other hiker's hands, and began devouring them. I would liken it to the situation of when someone is trying to steal your food, or you're trying to claim someone else's and you lick the food and say, "my germs," in an effort to deter anyone else from eating or finishing it. This was pretty much exactly what Katana did.

I was so embarrassed, but the mashed potato guy was laughing his ass off. I apologized for Katana, but he said it was ok because he thought it was hilarious. It was pretty slick of her, and he ended up letting her have the rest. After the mashed potatoes incident, we pushed on to the next shelter and called it a day.

Katana's antics with stealing the other hiker's mashed potatoes was not a new occurrence. She'd actually built quite the reputation as a food thief. It became a bit of a tradition, as well as a game, to give Katana trail names after the foods she stole. Her earliest trail name was "Tortilla." She earned that one in Tennessee after snagging one of my tortillas that had fallen off my knee while I was rummaging for something to put on it. It kind of sounded like the name of a Mexican stripper. Some other names that she earned were: Bagel, Sausage, Bin Laden (because she was a terrorist), Little Dummy, Potato Head, Cheese Head, Katana Dogue (Pronounced like "Vogue" but with a "D" instead of a "V"), and her most famous trail name of all... CatFox. CatFox, because she acted more like a cat than a dog, and of course because she looked a lot like a fox with her colors and features.

Without fail, people would always inform me that she looked like a fox. Although Katana's "foxy features" were so blatantly apparent, people always found the need to remind me of the resemblance, as if I hadn't already noticed, or as if no one else had ever made the connection. If I had a dollar for every time someone came up to me and said, "You know your dog looks like a fox," I could have paid for that hike probably two times over. Lemme tell ya, it got old! The main names that we usually called her out on the trail were CatFox and Katana Dogue.

Besides having fun coming up with new names for Katana, I also had a good time messing with people in towns and out on the trail when they would ask questions about her. I'm sorry, but I got so tired of answering the same questions over, and over, and over again, that I had to find a way to entertain myself. In town on a busy day, I could have a half dozen people stop me within a couple hundred feet and ask me the same five questions over and over again. I try to be polite, but sometimes making things up was so much more fun, and also helped to make the constant stop and go worth it.

The first questions or statements that people would always ask were, "What kind of dog is that?" or "Is that a fox?" or "That looks like a fox!" To the second question, if they were so unfamiliar with what a fox actually looked like that they had to ask this, I would almost always reply with, "Why yes it is!" Then I would continue on with some made up story of how I'd caught her digging in my food bag one night, captured her, slapped a harness on her, then tamed her with tortillas and banana chips, and that she'd been hiking with me ever since. You would be amazed at how many people believed this story.

To the first question, I had many answers. It all depended on what kind of mood I was in when they asked. When someone asked, "What kind of dog is that?" I would sometimes reply "Actually it's a cat; A Himalayan Murr Minx Cat" (I have to give DSOH credit for that one). Unfortunately, I couldn't play that one off for very long and usually had to come clean pretty quick. It was usually only good for a double take or an incredulous look of surprise before they realized I was full of shit.

Other times I would reply, "It's a Foxsky, half fox-half husky." This one would lead to more questions, which would lead me to digging myself a deeper hole. My final explanation would usually be "Yup, she was made in a Petri dish in a science lab and I paid about ten thousand dollars for her."

What finally became my favorite answer when asked this question was, "She's a Russian Curl Tailed Fox." People would believe this without question as I recounted my journey across Russia on the Trans-Siberian Railroad where I found her in chest high snow, eating a rabbit near a train station. People soaked this up with wide eyes and attentive ears. Yes, people WANTED to believe this answer. I'm sure many a stranger went home those nights to be very disappointed when Google responded with: "Did you mean (Fox), (Russian Fox), (Russian), or (Curl Tailed)?" ...before they finally realized that none of those words existed together in that order anywhere but my imagination.

To be honest, it was actually very rare that I let someone walk away not knowing the true breed of Katana. After I'd gotten my surprised reaction and taken the joke as far as it could go, I would come clean and answer all of their questions. It really just depended on my mood and how the person responded to me. I had some really good reactions as you will see later on. Funny and ironic as it was, the less someone seemed to believe my stories, the more I wanted to convince them. Those were the people that I usually left hanging. It was the suckers that soaked up everything I said as gospel that I felt bad for and always came clean with.

It was somewhere in between the towns of Lickdale and Port Clinton that Pennsylvania really showed its ass... or should I say rocks. You try and mentally prepare yourself. You try to imagine just how bad it could possibly be and what it could possibly look like, but nothing ever prepares you for the real thing. Descriptions don't paint a good enough picture and pictures don't do it justice. You have to see it and walk on it for yourself.

One second the path was nice, smooth, hard packed, darkly colored dirt; the next second it was small to medium sized sections of awkwardly shaped, jagged, and pointy rocks. No, the rocks weren't just lying there loosely on the ground. If that had been the case, then someone would've picked them up decades ago and moved them a foot in either direction to the side. These rocks were like icebergs; just the tops of larger rocks that were sticking out of the ground. It was the bigger parts you couldn't see that held them anchored down, keeping you from ripping them up and throwing them as far as you could.

Unless you had little Thumbelina feet, or you'd been a fan of Chinese foot binding, you weren't going to be able to set your feet on, or in between these rocks to save your life. You were forced to walk over them as the awkward points and jags pin pointed the sore spots on your feet with every single step. If your feet weren't already sore, they got sore quickly. Believe it or not, the worst part wasn't walking on them. No, the worst was when you couldn't set your entire foot on a rock, or when it would slip off a narrow jagged part, then get smashed between the rock you were stepping on and another one. It was enough to make you wince, and it would go on for miles and miles. This would happen constantly, speeding up the process of mashing your feet into a sore and blistered mess. You would find yourself going slower and slower when you did finally reach smooth ground, if only to delay your arrival to the next rock field.

It wasn't just the little ones that hurt, but the big ones too. Have you ever seen rock jetties in a harbor? Huge granite boulders jumbled together into a narrow line. That's what the trail would turn into at times, except the rocks were sometimes never big enough to actually walk on top of. You had to pick your way in-between them and along the edges, while your foot got caught in the nooks and crevices like some kind of vice grip. When the rocks were big enough to boulder hop, it was usually HUGE steps up and down that you could feel grinding the cartilage off your knees. You simply couldn't win; you had to grin and bear it, then bitch about it with your buddies at the end of the day, because no one else would listen and no one else cared, besides the ones who endured it with you.

Hiking into Port Clinton became one of the scariest nights on the trail up to that point in the adventure. Schweppes and I had been battling rocks all day, and were looking forward to a little reprieve in town. My poison ivy was in full swing and the rashes were oozing a fluid that would turn yellow when it dried. I had it on my stomach, arms, chest, quads, calves, neck, part of my forehead, and also my genitals. Besides my genitals, the worst place was my upper heel, right on the Achilles tendon and the bottom part of my calf. It was right where my shoe rubbed the skin. All day long as I walked, it would rub and itch so much that I would have to stop and scratch it or try to find ways to scratch it while walking. This usually involved trying to get a quick passing kick with my back foot as it passed my leading foot in stride. Sometimes I'd trip, and sometimes I'd satisfy the itch. I would also try to rub it with my walking staff really quick when my foot was planted on the ground, in-between strides. This was hit or miss as well, because sometimes I would end up stabbing myself in the ball of my ankle, or missing all together. Long story short, that area became very, very raw, and very, very miserable.

I made up my mind on that day that I had to get into town and find some relief for the rashes, NO MATTER WHAT! People on the trail had told me, "Find jewel weed and it will knock it right out!" Well if "Jewel Weed" had been as common in Pennsylvania as ramps were in Tennessee, then I probably would've been okay. Maybe it was, but I was never able to identify it positively. Nevertheless, I had my heart set on something else, something potent. Something I KNEW would take care of it right away. That something was bleach... I needed to get my hands on some bleach.

It was 9 pm when Schweppes and I were only three miles from Port Clinton after already having hiked over twenty miles. The last of the light was all but gone when the wind began to pick up and become thick with that familiar rain smell. "Come on! Please just let us have one day without rain in this rocky horror state!" If the hiking Gods were there, they weren't listening. The wind picked up and the rain fell in buckets. Soon flashes of lightning began to pierce the darkness, while crashes of thunder rolled through the night. It was another bad one, as this storm easily ranked in the top three worst storms that I walked through while out on the trail.

The heavy winds, rain, and lightning mixed with the overgrown vegetation on all sides, as well as the rocky death trap that you could barely see beneath you (due to the darkness and overgrown vegetation), made for a desperate and dangerous situation. Despite the growing and worsening list of obstacles, we knew we were close and that we had to make it that night. We had looked at the elevation profile for the trail leading into Port Clinton, and found the descent to look like a waterfall. On the map, it showed a flat line for a mile before it finally began to slowly curve downwards and become a vertical line that went straight down. We knew it was going to be a very dangerous descent in the dark, especially with the addition of severe weather.

We pushed on and on, but still the trail remained level. "I feel like we've GOT to start descending at any moment!" I called to Schweppes in frustration. "Yeah, I thought we would be on our way down already too!" he called back. When you're in crappy weather, as well as crappy terrain simultaneously, your sense of time and distance seem to warp. You're never going as fast as you think you are, and you're never as far along as you thought. The irony is that you know this in your head, but you still let yourself get frustrated. Getting angry and bitching about it helps the time pass and makes you feel better even though you know you're being ridiculous. Although it's only worth bitching about if there's someone to bitch along with you, listening to your bitching in return. When you're by yourself, you might as well suffer in silence or laugh.

The thunder and lightning had reached a crescendo of an almost constant flashing and crashing of light and sound. It was intense even for someone like me who was used to this sort of thing back in Florida. Katana had long since given up walking and had been on my shoulders for the better part of two miles since the weather began. With the addition of the worsening thunder and lightning, she began to squirm and freak out while on my shoulders. I couldn't get control of her as she was scratching the hell out of me, so I set her back on the ground thinking that she wanted to walk again. This was not the case. Her soggy doggy body stood there looking up at me defiantly, clearly saying, "NO more dad! We STOP here!" I picked her back up and put her on my shoulders where she began to squirm and scratch again. It was when she got a painful kick in behind my ear that I lost it. I completely lost my cool.

I was caught in the equivalent of a tropical storm. I had poison ivy all over my body. I was walking over hellacious rocks while simultaneously bushwhacking my way through vegetation with my hands. I was hurting, exhausted, and balancing a dog on my shoulders all at the same time, and to top it all off, I was less than a mile from town where I could get away from ALL OF IT! Now this little dog was trying to physically stop me from getting there when I was so close. All of these things culminated into one explosion of frustration in an instant.

I picked Katana off my shoulders and held her up under her arm pits facing me in a reverse lion king pose and began screaming. "I'M TRYING TO HELP YOU! I'M CARRYING YOU! WE'RE ALMOST THERE! STOP FIGHTING ME!" The rain poured down as lightning silhouetted the sopping wet figure I held above me. Katana squinted against the rain and my fevered screams as she hung there in suspension. I set her back on my shoulders where she didn't struggle again. I felt bad for doing it, but my point had gotten across. She had felt my emotion and desperation, and decided to cooperate once again. In the heat of the moment, pain, and frustration, I'd lost what little calm and sense of humor I had left for the situation. I'm pretty sure I heard Schweppes laughing behind me throughout our little episode.

As we slogged on, the river of water that we splashed through began developing its own current. I was too disoriented to tell if we were beginning to slope downhill, but the fact that the water was picking up speed around our ankles was very apparent. It got faster and faster until our downward descent became painfully obvious. Then suddenly, the earth just fell away as I was staring down eighty degrees of declination over rocks and dirt. In reality, I didn't see any dirt. I only saw water rushing over rocks on its way to the bottom. In all honesty, it looked exactly like a waterfall. In later days, Schweppes and I would refer to this as one of the scariest nights on the trail while descending the Port Clinton Waterfall amidst a biblical storm.

One cautious step at a time, hoping to whomever or whatever was listening that I wouldn't slip, I made my way down. I had one hand on my staff and the CatFox, one hand on whatever could be grabbed onto, and one foot moving in front of the other. It felt like a lifetime, but eventually we began to see the twinkling lights of civilization through the fog below us. SALVATION! We touched down onto some train tracks and found that the lights were actually street lamps, and that there was a locked train station not far away. In all the rain and low lighting, I couldn't find a white blaze to save my life. We had no idea which way to go, so we headed for the train station where we hid beneath an awning. As we plopped down, the reality of what we'd just been through set in. We looked at each other, began laughing and bumped fists. "We did it! We made it down in one piece!"

After calling a shuttle and making it to the neighboring town of Hamburg, we stopped at a gas station where I bought a gallon of Clorox Bleach. Ooooh I could feel the sweet burn already! When it came to getting some relief, or getting out of the elements for a short while, money became no object. We checked in at the local Microtel where I wasted no time on my bleach bath. I chose not to dilute the bleach at all, instead pouring it over a small wash cloth until it was thoroughly soaked. Then I began to furiously scrub my poison ivy rashes until I'd made sure they were ripped open and the tender gore underneath exposed to the sterilizing power of bleach. OH BABY DID IT BURN! The temporary and excruciating burn was well worth not having to scratch at myself like some kind of feigning crack head for the rest of the night. Was this bleach bath hazardous to my health? Maybe, but so is smoking and driving a car, and I don't smoke and I haven't died in a car accident yet, so I took my chances.

I actually used to work on deep sea fishing boats as a teenager, and every day, multiple times a day, that boat got a bleach bath to wash away the dried blood and fish slime. I constantly had cuts, bites, and impalements all over my body that got bleach in them all day long. I never got an infection, and I never got sick, melted, or had my pee start glowing. I only had layers of skin peel off my hands every now and then, that's all. If that was the worst that happened here, then it was well worth it.

We spent a couple days in Hamburg and Port Clinton taking a break from the rocks and poison ivy. One thing I'd noticed between shuttle rides back and forth from Port Clinton to Hamburg was a huge rocky cliff overhanging the Schuylkill River that separated the two towns. The rock face was covered in graffiti with a huge "peace symbol" painted on the center of the rock near the top. While taking us to the Post Office in Port Clinton, one of our shuttle drivers had informed us that the locals called it "Peace Rock" and that a couple of people had died from jumping off it over the years. When he spoke, all I heard was, "People can jump off it." I had to make up for not jumping off the bridge outside of Glasgow back in Virginia; I saw this as my chance.

Sadly, Port Clinton was as far as my first pair of shoes ever made it. They'd lasted for 1,200 miles of trail, but much further than that if you added up the sideways miles and town miles. They might've lasted another couple hundred miles if I really pushed it, but they never went any further than Port Clinton. The tread was all but completely gone, and they were both split open along the outside edges. The toe areas were gnarled and cracking from the hundreds of toe stubs and foot jams, while the material around the edges were worn out and falling apart. They'd started off water proof (NEVER do long distance hiking in waterproof shoes!!!), but now I couldn't walk through the morning dew without my socks getting soaked due to all the holes torn in them. Quite frankly, I was damned impressed they lasted as long as they did.

My parents had sent me a new pair of the exact same shoes, made by the exact same company, except in the non-waterproof version. I was dying of excitement to put these new shoes on until I realized they were size thirteen and not fourteen. My feet still fit, but just barely. They were constricted on the sides and went numb fairly quickly. I made the ill-fated decision to wear them anyway and try to break them in. I figured my rock hard calloused feet would beat the shoe material into submission. This turned out to be wishful thinking.

On the day we left Hamburg and Port Clinton, the trail passed beneath the highway that connected the two towns, then followed alongside the Schuylkill River before crossing a small parking lot and climbing back up a nameless mountain. "But how do I get to Peace Rock," I thought as the trail turned away from the river and up the mountain. Schweppes had no intention or desire to find this rock, and only wanted to hike. I stood there at the cross roads of the mountain and the river, torn between trying to follow the river on my own or just hiking on. Within minutes, two cars packed with teenagers pulled into the lot. I walked up and asked if they knew how to reach Peace Rock, whereby they informed me they'd come for just that reason. Once again the trail had put me in the right place at the right time. If it wasn't for those teenagers pulling up right then, I never would've found Peace Rock.

I followed the adolescents down a side trail that I wouldn't have even recognized as a side trail because of its paralleled proximity to a guardrail. It eventually branched away from the guardrail and into the forest where it opened onto a rocky beach next to the river. Peace Rock stood about two hundred feet across the Schuylkill in all of its BASE jumping glory. The first obstacle was to swim across the river in order to reach the rock. After the swim, there was a rocky embankment that you had to climb onto once you got out of the river; then climb hand over hand up some more steep boulders in order to reach the highest point of Peace Rock.

There were seven teenagers - five guys and two girls; every single one of them afraid to swim across. "I thought you guys lived here and did this all the time!" I chided at them. "Actually we live forty-five minutes away and we've been here before, but never swam across and jumped off," was the reply one of them gave me. "Great," I thought.

Since I was supposed to be some crazy mountain man that was unafraid of all things nature, and because these were teenagers, I decided to set the example and take the lead. I waded into the river and three of the guys followed suit, while Schweppes pulled out the camera, ready for the magic.

The current wasn't strong at all. In fact, it was barely moving as I leisurely side stroked my way across. My feet finally touched hard rock as I climbed out of the black water. I wished I'd brought water shoes, because it was rocky as hell and killed my feet. I gingerly climbed up the rock face and waited for the teenagers at the top. When they finally joined me, none of them wanted to be the first to jump. Truth be told, I didn't either! This was the kind of thing that I really could've used some local advice on. Where do I jump? Are there any shallow areas, stumps, or submerged rocks? Is the river too low to jump in right now? So on and so forth. One kid who claimed he'd seen others jump before said that they jumped straight out. I looked over the edge, all I could see was black water. I couldn't see the bottom, but then again the visibility had only been about two or three feet on the other side.

I tried to count the positives. At least this wasn't Florida and I didn't have to worry about alligators, giant gar, enormous snapping turtles, or bull sharks coming up the river. The positives stopped there. I didn't want to look like I was hesitating, so I got on with it.

I stepped up to the edge again and looked down. It must have been close to forty feet. The mixture of fear and excitement was strong; I loved that feeling. I would probably only feel it for my first jump, so I might as well enjoy it now. I took a bit of comfort in knowing that this wasn't my highest leap into a body of water. "I didn't die then and I won't die now," I told myself. "Just a nice pencil dive and everything will go smooth." This was the pep talk I gave myself as I stood at the edge. I gave Schweppes the thumbs up to start taking pictures before taking a huge leap straight out.

There is always that instance of panic when your feet first leave the ground and you realize there's no turning back as you quickly think, "This might kill me." That's the paranoid, second guessing, and self-preservation part of you talking. This moment of panic as you first leap is quickly followed by the calm acceptance of knowing you can't do anything about it now. "I'm riding this all the way to the bottom, and whatever happens... happens." It's the combination of those two moments that gives you "the rush." You get scared, then overcome that fear as you accept your fate, as well as the fact that it's no longer in your hands.

WHOOSH! I hit the water with a slight sting on the bottom of my feet before instantly realizing I wasn't dead. Second realization...I have to do this again...and maybe again. I jumped two more times before swimming back across the river, thoroughly pleased with my experience. I tried to convince Schweppes to jump, but he made the excuse that he didn't want to get his only shorts wet before hiking. Good excuse buddy, but it still doesn't trump missing out on an awesome experience like that... while on the journey of a lifetime.

I'd overcome a lot of fears on this journey. Prior to the trail, I would've never walked alone at night in the wilderness, hitchhiked, stayed with strangers, swum 200 feet across a strange river (partly because in Florida our rivers have teeth in them), and I certainly would never have jumped from a height that high without first seeing someone else do it. All of these fears tie into my one ultimate fear that has plagued me my entire life. Fear of the unknown. The fear of what I cannot see, cannot predict, and cannot know has haunted me for as long as I can remember. This journey had taught me to just LET GO. Let go of the fear, let go of the paranoia, and go with the flow. To let the chips fall where they may, not second guess myself, or hesitate. I'd never felt so free before in my life...

CHAPTER 10: PENNSYLVANIA - Part 2

"Still Rock'n Out Harder Than Ever!"

These pictures don't do justice to the actual condition of my shoes or the rocks on the trail.

The "new shoe" situation that I thought I was going to have under control was deteriorating fairly quickly. Not far out of Port Clinton, I realized my feet were no match for the material of my new shoes. My toes and the sides of my feet were getting torn up as the situation became more and more helpless. I'd thrown my old shoes away thinking that I would adapt to the new ones. After about a day hiking in the new ones, if I could've gone back in time to pull the old ones out of the dumpster, I would have. There is nothing worse than being in excruciating pain and knowing that you can't do anything about it for at least a few days. I was forced to suffer through it as the rocks continued to get worse. The rocks combined with my new shoe issues created one of the most unpleasant stretches of hiking that my feet endured out there.

I'd also taken to carrying Katana almost constantly. She could handle the rocks and had no problem going over them, but she was slow. She would pick and choose which rocks to jump on in her usual dainty fashion and I didn't have time for it. For the sake of actually getting somewhere, I would toss her on my shoulders and keep on trucking. She loved it, as I'm sure I looked like some sort of super hero in her eyes. Actually I take that back, I probably looked like a slave in her eyes. A slave sent here to answer her every beck and call. Yeah, that's probably more accurate.

My feet were slowing me down quite a bit, and on a day that Schweppes and I had planned to go big, he got ahead of me, while I fell short. I was sixteen miles into the day when I stopped in at a shelter for a quick break and some water. It was late afternoon, but there were still plenty of daylight hours left. My feet had been killing me, so I popped off my shoes and even went as far as taking off my ankle brace and socks to let my feet air out for a minute. As soon as those socks were off, and my beaten, suffocating feet felt fresh air, I knew I wouldn't be able to put them back on. After less than thirty seconds of internal argument, I decided that I wasn't going to subject myself to anymore rock torture and called it a day. I figured I would catch Schweppes at least by New Jersey, if not sooner. I simply didn't know what kind of big days I could push with my new foot problems. All I knew was that I needed new footwear the second I got into the next town.

In all of Pennsylvania, I think there are two major attractions that hikers talk about as far as sights on the trail. You're never that high up here in old RockSylvania, so the views are never overly spectacular. It's all mostly ridge walking somewhere between a thousand and two thousand feet above sea level, but it's nothing to write home about. The two most talked about areas in Pennsylvania have to undoubtedly be "The Pinnacle" and "The Knife's Edge."

I'll be honest, I was in so much pain and in such a hurry on the day that I reached The Pinnacle, that I walked right by it without even stopping to look. There was a small side trail, a sign, and a huge pyramid of rocks. I passed all of it by, only taking a snap shot of the rock pyramid. I recall my only thoughts being; "Now if only they could use all the rocks on the trail to build one of these pyramids every half mile, then we'd be getting somewhere."

The Knife's Edge was a little more impressive to me. This was something that I enjoyed even though it was quite literally a death trap. I would learn later on in New Hampshire that a boy scout fell and cracked his skull while on The Knife's edge. It really wasn't a place to take children of any age, and if I had to describe it, I would say that it looks like a miniature version of The Great Wall of China. It's a steep pile of rocks and huge boulders that continues on for a couple hundred yards. You have to nearly climb hand over hand to reach the top of it, and once you're there, you better not fall off. The ridge of this Great Wall of Rocks is as narrow as your foot in some places, and at times the rock is so slanted, that unless you have a death wish, you'll probably crawl or crouch to get across, just so that your hands are holding onto something.

If for some reason you do end up falling off one side or the other of this Knife's Edge of rocks...you're screwed. The fall isn't a big one, less than ten feet in some areas, a lot more in others, but it's not the fall that's going to get you, it's the landing. If you fall off that thing, you're not getting back up unless you're being carried on a stretcher or a body bag. The angles and edges of the rocks are such that even a small fall is going to break something.

Fortunately, my crossing of The Knife's Edge went very smoothly. Katana rode atop my shoulders the entire way, and we even stopped halfway across to sit down and have lunch. I got some great shots of her sitting on a narrow slab of rock, staring into the expanse.

Since the encounter with the porcupine and the rattlesnake, there really hadn't been any wildlife in Pennsylvania. I saw garter snakes on a regular basis, but never any deer or bear. The answer to "why" I never saw much wildlife seemed simple. All you had to do was look around while up on those ridges. It was nothing but rocks, with nowhere for a hoofed animal to put its feet. There was really nowhere for anything to put its feet, including humans, as this was the kind of terrain that was well suited for something's belly; this was snake country.

I wasn't far outside the town of Palmerton, while walking through a narrow corridor of bushes with Katana about ten feet ahead of me, when she suddenly stopped in her tracks. Two seconds later she leapt back exposing the biggest copperhead snake I'd ever seen. I had caught numerous copperheads back in Florida, and have even been bitten by a baby one on my pinky. However, out of all the copperheads I've ever encountered, none of them had ever been more than a couple feet long. They usually just aren't a big snake, but this one was huge, pushing three and a half feet.

The second I noticed it, I yelled "KATANA!" very loudly in an attempt to get her to freeze as I lunged forward to grab her harness. The combination of me yelling and lunging for her ended up having the opposite affect that I intended. She got scared and backed straight over the top of the second half of the snake's body. The copperhead had already been in striking position when Katana initially jumped, and remained in that position when she stepped back over it. That was all it took for me to make a move. It took less than two seconds for me to react and take action.

"WHACK!" The staff came down about four inches behind the snake's head, crushing the afflicted vertebrae and rendering everything above that spot virtually void of coordination. I shoved Katana back as it began to writhe uncontrollably. She tried to push past me to investigate, so I snatched the tail of the snake and quickly tossed it far into the bushes. Another crisis averted.

It all happened so fast that it took a moment for the guilt to set in. I'd killed a snake without the intention of eating it. I could've gone back and recovered the body and ate it, but I wanted nothing more than to get Katana away from that area. It all happened so fast, that all I could think about was eliminating the threat and evacuating the area. I felt like I was protecting my child, and that rationalization made me feel slightly better. Still, I was upset about the whole situation for the rest of the day.

I crossed the Lehigh River Bridge a little after 6 pm and made it to the side of a busy highway. There was nowhere to hitchhike safely, as there was no room on the side of the road to stand, and nowhere for anyone to pull over. As I looked east up the hill where most of the traffic was coming from, I noticed a nice little three-way intersection, as well as a store that looked like a good place to stage a hitchhiking attempt. I walked on the far side of the guardrail as I made my way up.

As I drew closer to my hitchhiking destination, as well as the small business, I noticed a police car was sitting in the front parking lot of the building, presiding over the intersection. "Damn!" I thought. Hitch hiking was illegal in Pennsylvania too, and I couldn't do it right in front of the cop. I decided to walk into the parking lot and wait for him to leave. As I got closer to the squad car, the cop rolled down his window and asked, "How far you hike today?" "Eh, about twenty miles," I replied. "Not bad," he said. "You know you're late, most people have already passed through here by this time of year." "Really?" I replied, surprised. "I know there's quite a few more people behind me still," I said. "Well, they're even more late!" the cop added. "You guys will be walking in snow if you don't step it up!"

I decided to take advantage of this little exchange and ask the question that was burning in the back of my mind. "Are you going to arrest me if I start hitchhiking right here?" I asked him. "You're a thru-hiker, I don't think anyone will care," he replied. Since he was the only person I was worried about "caring," this was a good answer in my book. Then he asked, "Where are you trying to get to?" "Palmerton," I replied. "Well, I'm about to head up there and turn around," he remarked. After he said this, there were approximately five long seconds of silence before I replied with much uncertainty, "Are you offering me a ride sir?" "Wellll, I'm not really supposed to... but ya know what, go ahead and hop in back, I'll run you up there real quick!" he answered.

"Hell yeah!" I thought to myself. My hitchhiking bucket list was now officially complete. This one wasn't even on the list, but I was happy to pencil it in. "Hitchhike to town in a cop car, while in a state where hitchhiking is illegal." CHECK! This was icing on the hitchhiking cake as far as I was concerned.

I've had, as well as heard my fair share of crazy hitchhiking stories from other people, but this one was up there with the best of them. The best ones I heard while I was out there, were of one guy getting picked up by an off duty limo driver, and another riding on the back of a motorcycle. I'm pretty jealous of those ones.

I threw my pack in the backseat before tossing the CatFox in too. They really don't leave you much leg room back there, as it was cramped as hell; but still I wasn't complaining. I attempted to take a picture because I knew no one would believe me, but as I raised my phone, the officer politely asked me not to take any pictures due to the fact that he wasn't really supposed to be doing this. Fair enough, I could easily respect that.

While on the way, the officer picked my brain about the trail, and as it turned out, he had dreams and aspirations of hiking the trail as well. He expressed an intense interest to thru-hike the entire thing after he retired from the force. He was an incredibly nice guy and I sincerely hope that he does one day pursue and achieve his dream.

The officer dropped me off at a gas station, and more than a few heads turned as the homeless looking guy with a cute dog exited the vehicle, then casually walked down the street after shaking the police officer's hand. What an awesome guy; if more people would be less rigid and that laid back, then the world would be... a more laid back place, obviously.

I ended up getting a hold of Schweppes and meeting him at the "Jailhouse Hostel." It was a free hostel that resides in the basement of an old police station. There was a basketball court, an indoor shooting range, bunks in the basement, old school showers, and old school bathrooms. The place was amazing, and the perfect sort of old building to do some "urban exploring."

I'd mentioned earlier in my story that the "trail provides." This meant that just when you needed something the most, it seemed to come to you... as if by magic. Some would say that if you thought about something hard enough, you could "will" it to yourself out on the trail, even manifest it in some cases.

Well, something happened in the basement bunkroom of that hostel that changed my outlook on the trail, as well as life in general, forever. I was checking the hiker box for any useful gear or thrown away food that I might be able to use, when I noticed a lightly used looking pair of shoes that had been neatly placed next to the box. I picked them up and looked at them in utter astonishment. They were the exact same non waterproof version of my first shoe in a size fourteen. It was the exact same shoe that my parents had sent me, but one size larger. I couldn't believe my eyes. It's so difficult to find size fourteen anything at a shoe store, as I usually had to order my shoes online. Now here was the exact shoe that I wanted in a size fourteen, just lying around for the taking in the middle of a small Pennsylvania town, right when I needed it most.

Call it divine intervention if you're religious, call it the power of the human mind, or call it a major fucking coincidence, but I was BLOWN AWAY! My entire thought process was altered that day. Everything that I'd ever deemed a "coincidence," or attributed to "good timing," or "good luck" up until that day, all of a sudden seemed a little more purposeful than that. Was I making these things happen just by thinking about them, or was something else at work? Is there an undeniable truth in the theory that people "willed" things to themselves out there? Is "conscious creation" a fact of life and not merely a theory?

I was by no means the first or last person to have things like this consistently happen to them out on the trail, as you will see further on in my story. The shoes were simply the most obvious, yet unforeseen happening, besides my gold chain; but even more obvious things would happen to someone that I was hiking with later on.

After getting settled in at the hostel, we decided to forage for food. There was a "No Pets" policy for the hostel, so I left Katana tethered to a paint can just outside of the basement door leading into the bunkroom. Then Schweppes and I walked a short distance down the street to a 1950's style diner. I was almost done with my meal, when I had an uneasy feeling about Katana. Call it a sixth sense, but I got up from my meal and asked Schweppes to wait for me till I got back. I then headed back towards the hostel.

When I turned the corner and looked down at the basement door, Katana was gone - leash, paint bucket, and all. My stomach knotted up. I began running down the back street while calling her name. Almost immediately, a man down the road called back to me saying, "A small dog just came running down this way dragging a metal bucket before running into someone's yard!" I thanked him and followed his direction. I went between a fence and some hedges before noticing a bunch of people on their back porches and balconies looking in the same direction. "There's a fox dog attached to a paint can that's tangled up in some bushes over there!" a woman called. I walked over and found Katana tangled and hiding in a bush, shaking, with the paint can still tethered to her. I should've checked the paint can earlier, because it turned out that it was empty.

This is what apparently happened when I left Katana outside the door. She'd hung out near the stairs leading down to the basement, when at

192

some point she probably walked to the limit of her tether and dragged the paint can over the concrete ground. The sound it made had probably startled her, making her jump, causing the paint can to make more noise as it dragged over the cement. It only escalated from there; the faster she tried to run from the paint can, the more noise it made, and the more it scared her. If she hadn't gotten tangled in that bush, there is no telling how far she would've made it, or who would've found her and possibly decided to keep her. It was a close call, but ended up becoming something to laugh about in the end. I got her back safely and tethered her to a nice solid hand rail instead.

Leaving Palmerton ended up turning into an awkward situation in itself. Schweppes and I couldn't seem to find a ride out, so we began walking the highway. I didn't want Katana walking on the asphalt, or even that close to traffic, so I put her on my shoulders once again. Not ten minutes into the walk, right before an overpass, a compact SUV pulled over. A woman hopped out and informed me that she hadn't stopped for us, but for my dog, and that we would only be tagging along. "Hey, that works for me!" I replied. Katana was being a team player again and finding us rides.

As we got in, we met another woman in the passenger seat. They were both possibly in their late thirties and very friendly as well as talkative. Then things took a turn for the awkward when the driver set her smart phone in the center cup holder between her seat and the passenger seat. Everything would've been fine, except for the fact that there was a full mug of coffee already sitting in the cup holder that her friend had set there previously. The smart phone went right in. Instantly realizing that she'd just dipped her high tech cellular device into a cup of coffee like some kind of scone, the driver snatched it back out and proceeded to get very pissed off.

"GODDAMN IT!" the driver yelled, "HOW MANY TIMES HAVE I TOLD YOU TO BRING A TRAVEL MUG IN MY CAR AND NOT A CUP?!" She screamed at her passenger. I can only assume they were friends, but they could've been sisters. I don't know, but they looked nothing alike. It's just that I can only imagine someone yelling at a close family member like that, and not a friend. Family usually forgives easier than friends and it's normally easier to go off like that on a sibling. If DSOH would've screamed at me like that when his phone got ruined in the pool, we probably wouldn't have hiked together ever again.

The yelling, chiding, and lecturing on travel coffee mugs and the incompatibility of electronic devices and piping hot liquids went on for the rest of the drive. I think she almost forgot we were in the back seat, because she seemed startled when we had to butt in and let her know that our stop was coming up. I don't even recall a "goodbye" after we'd gotten our stuff out of the back. That poor woman's day was ruined over a cell phone.

The climb out of Palmerton in Lehigh Gap was the steepest and longest scramble that I'd encountered on the trail thus far. It was nearly a thousand feet of mostly hand over hand climbing, and Katana rode on my shoulders the entire way. This terrain warped my mind, but secretly, I was enjoying it. Even though it was incredibly challenging and dangerous, it broke up the monotony that was Pennsylvania. Having to actually think and engage your upper body was a nice change of pace. The fact that the temperature was in the mid 90's again didn't even dampen my spirits on the climb. Once atop the crazy ascent and looking out over Lehigh River and the surrounding towns, I took the time to do my Pennsylvania Lion King pose with the CatFox. It was definitely in the top five Lion Kings for sure.

Not far from the top of the crazy rock climb, I walked through what I will always consider my favorite part of Pennsylvania. The trail became a narrow, smooth path of brown dirt that was free of any rocks, and lined with yellow daisies for over two miles, all the while overlooking the town of Palmerton. I felt like I was dreaming as it was similar to another scene out of "The Wizard of Oz." I couldn't seem to get enough of it. Maybe it was the simple calm and smoothness, like a little patch of paradise thrown in the middle of a rocky hell. I don't recall enjoying myself more on any other stretch of trail in Pennsylvania than I did right there. It simply made me happy inside.

The only negative to this day, was the fifteen-mile stretch with no water. We had camel'ed up before leaving Palmerton, but it wasn't enough. "Camel-ing up" is a term that refers to drinking a bunch of water, but also carrying extra water with you, usually before a long dry stretch devoid of any water sources. We had downed two Gatorades each before we left, and even packed out more than four liters of water each, but still ran out. It was so blistering hot on that day, that we recklessly and uncontrollably drank everything we had. The abundance of rocks, combined with the high temperature, turned the trail into what I would liken to a brick oven; the heat seemed to hit you from all sides, not just from the sun.

With about six miles still to go until the next water source, we didn't want to chance it when we came to a small paved road. We were absolutely parched, and didn't want to take the risk of not finding water at the next source (which sometimes happened); so, for the first and only time on the trip, I hitched a ride into town for the sole purpose of obtaining water. A man in a big white work van that had "Handyman" written on the side, picked us up and drove us roundtrip to a convenience store on the outskirts of some town before bringing us back to the trail. He was incredibly kind and even gave us each a candy bar as we departed.

Our water woes didn't stop there. When we finally called it a day during the twilight hours at a large clearing on the side of the trail, we were out of water once again. The kicker was that the only water for miles in any direction was half a mile downhill, on a side trail from where we were camping. Normally I would've toughed it out and got water the next day from somewhere else, however that wasn't viable, or smart in this situation. I was parched now, and the next source wasn't for many miles the next day. I knew I'd regret it in the morning if I didn't get a drink that night. I had no choice but to get water from this source, which was a one mile round trip, and decided to get it over with that night (instead of waiting till morning). This was aggravating, but unfortunately we living creatures need water to stay alive, so it was a must.

I donned my headlamp as I made my way down the side trail to a weak and trickling spring. I filled my bottles with some water, filtered it, drank it, gathered more, then began my trip back up the hill with eight extra pounds in my arms. As I made my way back up the trail in the near pitch blackness, something huge fluttered through the light of my headlamp and disappeared above me. I quickly looked up as I tried to follow it with my light in an attempt to identify it. "HOLY CRAP!" Hovering ten feet above, while looking straight back down at me was an enormous Luna Moth; the largest moth in North America!

It was a light lime green with a huge set of main wings and a set of secondary smaller wings below them. The smaller wings had streamers that looked like legs flowing off the back of them. Then there was a large dark head with thick antennae sitting atop a fat body. It was literally hovering in place, looking right back at me, as if studying me.

After realizing what it was, I couldn't help but think, "Wow, this thing looks exactly like a fairy!" In the dark, illuminated only by my headlamp, everything about this big bug looked like a tiny winged human being. The head was round, dark, and contrasted independently from the rest of the body much like a human head. The antennae almost looked like a leafy crown or headdress, while the streamers coming off its smaller bottom wings looked exactly like dangling legs. There was also a dark outline on the wings that looked like arms. Its entire charade was incredibly deceiving. In fact, I'm not entirely convinced that what I saw wasn't a crowned fairy of royal lineage or some kind of fairy scout warrior investigating my presence in its forested kingdom.

If you had seen what I saw, then you would probably be on the fence about it too. Logic and my vast knowledge of the animal kingdom (omit porcupines) told me that it was a Luna Moth, but the hopeful and imaginative child that still lived within me, said that it was without a doubt, a fairy gracing me with its magical presence.

After the fairy moth encounter, I went to bed. I couldn't help but be in high spirits since I was only a little more than twenty miles from the New Jersey border. I can't remember any time in my life that I was actually happy to be going to New Jersey. I knew this was probably the first and last time I would feel that way about the Garden State. I drifted off to sleep with visions of green fairies dancing in my head.

July 22nd was my 115th day on the trail and my last day hiking in Pennsylvania...and what a grand day it was! I was so happy that I'd gotten water the night before, because if I would've had to make that one mile round trip first thing in the morning, it certainly would've put a damper on my mood. The only negative about that day, was a horrendous pinching feeling I developed deep in the joint of my right hip. It hadn't been there the day before and I couldn't find any explanation for it.

The rocks were out of control once again, as Pennsylvania wasn't going down quietly; she was going to fight to the last breath. The uneven ground was making my new hip problem worse, and as a consequence, I began to worry. I couldn't find a reason for the pain, as the joint continued to get tighter and tighter, while hurting more and more.

Sometime around noon, Schweppes and I stopped for lunch. About ten minutes into lunch, as we were sitting on the ground, Schweppes calmly said, "Hey Mayor... there's a good sized snake lying right next to my leg and I don't recognize it." I popped up and went over to check it out. Sure enough, no more than ten inches from his outstretched leg was a snake, an eastern milk snake no less! It was very rare to see one during the heat of the day, as they're normally nocturnal and very difficult to find. This was a rare treat and a privilege.

It was about two and a half feet long, and I was able to pick it up fairly easily and take a few pictures. Milk snakes are extremely docile and make exceptionally good pets. Had I not been in the middle of an epic journey on foot, I would've kept this guy as a pet for a short while. I released him a few minutes later and he quickly disappeared under a rock. In the words of Steve Irwin: "Nature Rules!"

Later on in the day, around the fourteen-mile mark, my hip began to hurt so badly that I could no longer walk. I stopped to do some stretches to no avail. Then, in a desperate, last ditch effort, I laid down on a huge, flat topped, rectangular boulder (of which there was no short supply), and let my leg hang limply off the right side. As I lay on my back, dangling my leg freely off the edge, I tried to concentrate on relaxing every single muscle. As I did so, my right leg began to tingle after a minute, then "POP!" Something happened to my hip! I got back up and to my surprise the pain in my hip was completely gone. I couldn't tell you what was wrong to begin with, and I couldn't tell you how it fixed itself; but what I will say, is this was the nicest thing a Pennsylvania rock ever did for me...

There were more pleasant surprises a few minutes later as Viking materialized out of the woods. I'd known Viking and had hiked around him since my first week on the trail. I hadn't seen him since Glasgow around a month and a half earlier, and he was one of my favorite hikers out there. When you first looked at him, you might think he had a scary appearance. People would normally be quick to judge, but the reality was that he was one of the nicest and most considerate people I've ever met in my entire life.

He had long black hair down to his shoulder blades that was shaved into a thick Mohawk that you couldn't tell was a Mohawk unless he slicked all of his hair back. He had a beard that was braided into two forks that reached almost to his belly button, and two rings pierced through the sides of his bottom lip. When I first saw Viking on the trail back in Georgia, I was sure he was some kind of heroin shooting, bat eating, devil worshipping, punk rocker. That couldn't have been further from the truth. He was one of the prime examples of not judging others by their surface appearance.

He was a twenty-six-year-old guy that had earned his name "Viking" for his fierce appearance. He was a very lean and solidly built guy. He was also very spiritual, extremely well-read, and a jack of all trades. In addition to all of that, he was the kind of guy that would do anything for you, even if it inconvenienced him, or wasn't in his best interest at that moment. He ALWAYS put others before himself.

Camping with Viking was always a pleasant experience due to the fact that he was a workhorse around camp. He always built huge fires every night as soon as he stopped for the day. We called them "Viking Fires." If it wasn't raining, he almost always "Cowboy Camped" next to the fire in only a sleeping bag. We had an ongoing joke that sleeping next to the fire was how he "recharged." This was because he stayed up late every night, woke up early every morning, and still pushed big miles every day before foraging every piece of dead wood within a quarter mile radius and building an epic Viking fire. The guy was a machine.

Since it had been so long since I'd last seen him, I had no idea if he had been ahead or behind us. This was another cool thing about the trail and being out there. Everyone is on this narrow line, heading north over this vast distance of terrain. You get separated from time to time and lose track of where people are. If someone pulls a big day, a little day, or a zero day, there is no telling who you might catch up to, or who might catch up to you. You can go over a month without seeing someone while wondering if they're still on the trail, when the whole time they may have never been more than five miles away from you. It's just a matter of how individual hiking patterns match up, and it's really cool to think about if you take the time. You never knew what familiar face was going to emerge from the trees.

The group Viking was hiking with had broken up, with some people having gone home, much like the original group I'd began hiking with in Georgia. Pennsylvania was his home state, and he'd taken some time off to go home and take care of some things. He'd only gotten back on the trail the week before and was just now catching up with us. It was nice to see a familiar face, because Schweppes and I had been moving so quickly since the Shenandoah Mountains that we were in between hiking bubbles and hardly saw anyone.

A "bubble" is what a group or amalgamation of hikers throughout a certain region is referred to. It can span anywhere from twenty to over fifty miles, sometimes more. It's nothing more than an area where a decent number of hikers are all traveling around the same pace and arriving in certain locations within a two to three-day span. When you're in a bubble, you normally saw people every day as you passed them, they passed you, or you saw them at shelters and campsites during the evenings. We had been in a small bubble since just before Shenandoah, until we picked up the pace, subsequently pushing out of it. Ever since Harper's Ferry, we hadn't seen hardly anyone, and the ones we did see were new faces. We were "in-between bubbles," as the traffic out on the trail had been nearly non-existent.

The three of us reached Delaware Water Gap (DWG) that evening, a small town situated on the edge of the Delaware River. Once you crossed the Delaware Bridge you were in New Jersey. However, we had no plans of going any further that evening. We stopped in at a Free Church Hostel that wasn't far from where the trail dumped us onto a road. I didn't sleep inside the hostel, choosing instead to hang my hammock from some trees in the woods just behind the church building. I was getting to the point where I preferred my hammock over just about any other method of sleeping. Beds killed my back, but I'll admit that in the case of a bad storm, or an extra cold night, I'd gladly suffer a bed to take a break from the elements.

The next day in Delaware Water Gap, I had breakfast at a local diner with Viking, before meeting two of my aunts at an upscale restaurant called the "Sycamore Grill" for lunch. I had not seen my Aunt Laurette or Aunt Kim for the better part of ten years. They lived not too far away in New Jersey and Staten Island, and both had taken time to make the drive when I got into DWG. Being able to see family in other states on this trip had been a huge bonus. They treated me to lunch and also left me with a pile of snacks. It was another wonderful "mini" family reunion on the trail.

It was mid-afternoon when I finally said goodbye to my lovely aunts. I made up my mind to stay in DWG one more night, and after speaking with Viking, I learned he was going to hike out that day and try to do ten miles. He said his parents' house was located in the Tri State area, and we would be getting close to it over the next thirty miles into New Jersey. He also mentioned he planned to stop there for a night or two, and we were more than welcome to stay when we caught up. It was a generous offer that we gladly accepted.

Schweppes and I left DWG fairly early the next morning. I was practically dancing as we made our way down the road. We had a short road walk over the Delaware River Bridge that would drop us into new strange lands that weren't called Pennsylvania. I had high hopes, but I'd also been warned that the rocks didn't completely go away in the first part of New Jersey. Anything was an improvement over where we just came from, so we didn't care.

As we began walking down the road through the quiet neighborhood full of unique little houses, I noticed a small bird hopping down the sidewalk attempting to fly. It was obvious the bird was injured. I passed Katana to Schweppes and shuffled down the sidewalk corralling it into my hands. I'm not sure what kind of bird it was, but its color was a darkish mottled brown and it was slightly bigger than a large mouse. Once in my hand, the bird calmed down and looked at me as if to say, "Just get it over with and eat me." It definitely had a tweaked wing.

For a minute I contemplated bringing it with me and making it my trail bird. Just when I was about to make the executive decision to adopt the bird, I noticed a guy in his front yard a couple of houses down. He was a younger guy in his early thirties, and looked like he belonged on the show "Jersey Shore." I decided to appeal to him for help, because I was in a hurry to get the hell out of Pennsylvania and didn't have any other options.

"Excuse me sir, I found this bird in front of your neighbor's yard. It's hurt and can't fly; do you think you could take it somewhere to get help?" The man looked at me for a second like I was wasting his time, then walked over and said, "Sure...I'll take care of it." He took the bird from me and walked straight to his backyard and out of sight. I'd like to think that he got that poor bird some quality help, or at least a home to live out its remaining years, but I have a sneaking suspicion that he might've "taken care of it" in the mafia sense of the phrase. I'll never know. Nevertheless, I left Pennsylvania feeling like a Good Samaritan and avian friend.

CHAPTER 11: NEW JERSEY

"It's Just an Extension of Pennsylvania!"

Border of PA/NJ on Delaware Bridge.

There is only a little over seventy miles of trail in the Garden State of New Jersey, so I wasn't destined to be there very long. This next stretch of the journey had me checking off states less than a week at a time. The prospect of crossing state lines every several days for the next big section had me giddy as a school girl. Pennsylvania had been close to breaking me down, but I'd somehow managed to grit it out.

New Jersey wasn't known for anything exceptional on the trail. However, one interesting fact that I'm sure most people don't know, is that there are more bears per square mile throughout New Jersey than any other state in America. I never knew this little fact until I started hiking. New Jersey was the last place I expected to see any bears. In fact, later on in the journey while in Maine, I heard that a student was killed by a black bear in New Jersey not far from the trail. My black bear "eagerness meter" went up a few more notches without even having to see one. Black bears obviously had a different disposition up north.

I entered New Jersey with high spirits and what I thought was a high level of Karma coming off the bird rescue, but I was wrong. New Jersey got on my shit list almost right away. Not even an hour into Jersey and just across the border of Kittatinny State Park, I was making my way up a gentle slope covered in long majestic blades of grass, minding my own business, when I felt an intense stinging and burning pain on my left calf. The pain was so sharp and intense that I instantly thought I'd been bitten by a venomous snake. In my mind, that was the only thing I thought could cause a stinging pain that strong.

I jumped up as I whipped my head and torso around quickly to look at my calf. A huge black and white ringed wasp was clinging to my leg! I reached down and swatted! The swat knocked its legs loose from my leg, but to my unpleasant surprise, it was still stuck to me by the stinger coming out of its ass. I frantically swatted again, knocking him loose as the bastard nonchalantly flew off! I didn't know if I was more disappointed in getting stung, or the fact that I wasn't able to kill this little insect that had just launched a one-man assault on me.

The pain from the sting came in throbbing waves. It was so intense that I almost had to sit down. I've been stung by more bees than I can count during my childhood, but never in my life has an insect sting hurt so badly. I have even been stung by a small scorpion on the bottom of my foot in Florida, and it didn't hurt nearly this bad. I never wanted to deal with one of those creatures ever again! However, I couldn't help but wonder what was going through that wasp's mind when he attacked me. I decided on, "Welcome to Jersey Asshole!"

Besides highly aggressive and volatile insects, New Jersey didn't start off all too bad. That first day we came to a gorgeous body of water by the name of Sunfish Pond. It was the first pond of that size that I discovered right on the trail and a sure sign of the beauty in New England that was yet to be encountered. It was a bit rocky as the trail went around the west shore of the pond, but it didn't matter. This was a huge change of scenery and a welcomed one at that.

Surprisingly, New Jersey was actually quite swampy through the first section. I didn't have to walk in any swamps, but the trail went around quite a few of them. The telltale signs of beavers were everywhere. Mostly in the form of beaver dams and mounds that you saw rising out of the swampy areas that they flooded for their own purposes. The second sign of beavers were the trees. Most of the trees surrounding these flooded swampy areas were chewed completely or partially down. There were entire groves of trees with the little apple core/hour glass shape chewed right into the base of their trunks, a couple feet off the ground. It looked like a scene from a cartoon, with the trees balancing on the narrow piece of wood that the beavers left them with as some kind of joke.

At one point, while crossing a shallow creek over some rocks, I spotted a small snapping turtle in the shallows. This really surprised the hell out of me, because I thought for sure they were only a fixture in the lakes, ponds, and rivers of the south. What was a snapping turtle doing all the way up here? The answer is they've always been there, as I learned something new on my first day in New Jersey.

The next day we hiked nearly twelve miles before noon into Culver's Gap to meet Viking. Two other hikers would be accompanying us to Viking's house as well. Their names were "Engineer" and "Ski."

Ski was in his late twenties and hailed from Colorado. He earned his name because he previously used to work at a ski resort. For some reason, early on, nobody could ever remember his real name, so they always referred to him as "the guy who worked at ski resorts," thus the name "Ski" stuck. Ski was a lone wolf most of the time. He never stayed in any groups and always preferred to do his own thing, but at the end of the day, he was so well liked that he could blend in with any group, as if he'd been hiking with them all along. Very easy going and fluent in sarcasm, Ski was a great guy to hike next to and converse with.

Engineer was a very intelligent, as well as pragmatic twenty-nine-year-old guy that had gotten his name because he was...well, an engineer. He was an aerospace engineer to be precise. He had become bored with his job, so he quit and came out on the trail to take a break and figure out what's next. Out of everyone I ever met on the trail, I would have to say that Engineer was probably the fastest hiker I ever encountered. I believe he was powered by the pints of whiskey that he religiously kept stashed in his water bottle pockets. The man loved his whiskey, but I have no idea how he didn't sweat it out faster than he could drink it.

This brings me to another interesting thing about the trail; you never know who you're going meet out there or what their personal background will be. I met so many entrepreneurs, PHD's, people with incredible careers and past jobs; folks from different walks of life that I would never have suspected. The irony was that no matter what someone did for a living, we still looked like homeless people out there. You would never guess that someone was rich, a doctor, or a lawyer just by looking at them. The best dressed hiker could have been a retail worker, while the homeliest looking hiker could own their own law firm. You just never knew...and it didn't matter.

One of the funniest stories I remember hearing was from DSOH. He had gone into the town of Gatlinburg, Tennessee with some other hikers when I was ahead of him in the Smokey Mountains. They were eating at a Mexican restaurant, drinking, having a good time and maybe getting a little too loud, when a woman confronted them in a slightly rude manner. The woman was sitting at a table behind them and had leaned back and remarked, "Are any of you people that hike the trail even educated?" This was the wrong table of hikers to address this inquiry. Of course DSOH's response was, "Actually I have a Master's degree in business and an undergraduate in Classical History." While another hiker named "Frisbee," who was an older gentleman, replied, "I have a PHD in Law." There were a few other replies that I can't remember off the top of my head, but long story short, that woman was left speechless as she turned back to her table.

I mean if you think about it, even though many thru-hikers may look like bums most of the time, the majority of them couldn't be further from that stereotype. How many people can take six months off work, have virtually no income, and still pay bills back home while simultaneously paying for their hike? People who have earned the right to be out there in one way or another, that's who.

Yes, the best way to hike is to simplify your life back home so when you leave, you have as few expenses as possible. No debts and minimal bills, that way you can save up faster and leave quicker to pursue adventures like this. I have no desire to be rich, I only want to live simply within my means, and have rich experiences. That's all.

Viking picked the four of us up a little after 1 pm, as Schweppes and I rode in the bed of his pickup all the way back to his house. Viking's family owned a beautiful home in the countryside, and were big time hunters and fishermen. They were my kind of people. Viking's parents, Bob and Kate, were incredibly warm and welcoming. We took showers, did laundry, swam in the pool, and had a few beers. Kate put out a plate that must have had over thirty homemade chocolate chip cookies. For dinner they made venison burgers, zucchini fritters, wild caught salmon, and wild caught flounder. I was in heaven once again.

A plan was formulated that first evening at Viking's house. That plan was to hike every day, but finish each day at a road where his parents could pick us up and bring us back to the house. This was an amazing gesture because it involved his parents dropping us off and picking us up further and further away each day. If Viking wasn't already going to be doing it in order to spend more time with his family, I probably would never have accepted the offer. That was a lot of back and forth driving, but his parents were as selfless and giving as their son. I could see where he got it from.

Day one of using Viking's house as a base point was a good one. Kate had made dozens of blueberry pancakes before we woke up. This was a fantastic first morning send off, and after breakfast, Bob dropped us back off at the trailhead. The rocks were bad, but nowhere near as bad as Pennsylvania. We were moving fast and the miles were ticking by. We knew that the sooner we finished the day, the sooner we could get back for more R & R.

As I was making my way through a grove of very tall white pines, I spotted an albino squirrel. I'd never seen one before and wanted to get a picture. It was snow white all over with beady red eyes that seemed to glow. It ran far up into a tree and I waited for it to reappear so that I could snap a picture. After a short while of waiting on the squirrel, Viking and Engineer caught up to me. "What are you doing?" Engineer asked as I stood there with my head tilted all the way back, looking into the tree. "There's an albino squirrel in that tree and I'm trying to get a clear picture," I replied. Viking was skeptical and said that it was common to see white squirrels around the area, but that true albinos were very rare. He asked if it had red eyes and I replied, "Yes!" Still I could tell he was skeptical.

After perhaps two minutes of staring into the tree, Katana suddenly bolted after something. The squirrel had come down the back side of the tree that was right next to the one we were staring at. Now it was making its way across the ground to another cluster of trees with Katana hot on its heels. Its demon red eyes were glowing plain as daylight as it ran by. "I'll be damned! You were right Mayor, it was an Albino!" Viking remarked. None of us got a picture and the squirrel escaped Katana's curiosity. Nevertheless, it was enough to know that we had seen it.

We passed into High Point State Park and saw High Point Tower rising like the Washington Monument above the trees. This tower marked the highest point in all of New Jersey. All through that stretch, the trail was just as bad as Pennsylvania. The rocks were jagged and plentiful as they gave me a good dose of PPR (Pennsylvania Pain Remembrance). Schweppes even had a little fit of his own, as his feet also felt the pain that we thought we had left behind us.

The last part of the day was spent hiking through open fields of rolling hills, while passing countless streams and small ponds. It was very enjoyable, and New Jersey was slowly creeping back onto my good side. We received word from Stardust that she wasn't far behind our position, and upon finishing our twenty-two-mile day around 6 pm, we waited until she caught up with us. Ski being the one-man wolf pack he was, ended up hiking on. I would continue to intermittently run into him all the way into the beginning of Maine before I finally lost him for good. He would go on to be victorious in completing his Appalachian Quest, and even find love on the trail that would continue to last even after the adventure...

After goodbyes and hellos, we were then whisked back to the house of Viking where we enjoyed a Spaghetti and Venison meatball dinner with garlic bread. We wrapped up the night with a dip in the hot tub where we ate grapes and had a few more beers.

Day two of using Viking's house as a home base was another interesting, albeit painful, day. After a breakfast of eggs with peppers, onions, and other veggies, as well as English muffins with jam and jelly, we were dropped off at our ending point from the day before. The rides to and from the trail were getting longer, and I couldn't help but feel a pang of guilt wrapped in immense gratitude for Bob and Kate for making the drive twice a day.

Literally within two minutes of being dropped off, it began to pour down rain. The rain only lasted for maybe ten minutes, but it was enough to soak everything I was wearing, as well as my shoes. The sun came out promptly after the downpour and once again it was a blistering hot muggy day.

We weren't two miles into the day's hike and I could feel some serious chafing setting in. I don't know if it was a combination of the humidity, moisture, and sweat; but on this day I chafed worse than I ever had on the entire journey. It was so bad, that Body Glide couldn't even save me. Throughout the day I developed a walk that would've made the most saddle sore cowboy weep for me.

Several miles into the day's hike, we hit a road walk in the middle of a residential neighborhood. This road was right on the New Jersey/New York border and apparently dipped into New York for about a quarter mile before slinking back into Jersey and staying there. While walking through the New York portion of the neighborhood, an old man sitting in a beach chair out in front of his garage called and motioned for me to come over. Not wanting to be rude, I complied.

"I'm the New York welcoming committee!" the man proclaimed as I walked up. "Boy do I have a treat for you!" he said. "Creepy," I thought to myself. As I approached him, I noticed a bunch of large vegetables sitting on a table. "Fresh Squash!" the man exclaimed loudly. "Fresh picked from my garden this morning! Please, take three or four of them, they're wonderful!" he added. "Are you kidding me?" I thought to myself. "Is this some kind of sick joke?" It was a kind gesture but I couldn't help but think this was some kind of prank.

Each one of these mega squash probably weighed four to five pounds each. Like I really wanted or needed another fifteen pounds in my backpack. Besides, I don't think I could have made more than one of them fit in my already stuffed pack. To be polite, I picked the smallest one I could find and crammed it in. He was insistent that I take more, but I politely declined citing my lack of extra space. Thanks, but no thanks.

At that moment Schweppes walked by and the old man called him over too. He tried to pull the same squash offer on him, but Schweppes wasn't having it. "Look man, I'm gonna be honest with you… I don't much care for squash even a little bit," Schweppes said in his thick southwest Virginia accent. The old man looked hurt, but came back with, "When you're hungry you'll eat anything." To which Schweppes replied, "Not me man, I got plenty of food." Schweppes was hell bent on not taking any squash or extra weight with him, and in the end he succeeded.

When Stardust walked by, she simply ignored him. Well, actually I don't think she heard him because she had headphones on, but it looked like she ignored him. In the end, I was the only sucker that was conned into carrying a giant squash. I guess nice guys do finish last.

We passed through a bird sanctuary, then onto a wooden boardwalk that stretched for nearly two miles. It was the easiest two miles of the entire trail…literally. The boardwalk crossed through a swampy area full of reeds, with turtles and snakes abounding everywhere. Nine times out of ten, when you looked over the side of the boardwalk, you would see a turtle's head or a snake sitting on top of the algae covered water. There was a lot more reptilian wildlife in New Jersey than I ever would've guessed existed.

We took a break at a Farmer's Market outside the town of Vernon, where we all bought snacks and drinks, and between the five of us, probably spent close to eighty bucks. We sat out front in some chairs with our shoes kicked off, airing out our feet and letting our shoes dry in the sun from the earlier rain. It wasn't long until the manager came out and said, "I'd appreciate it if you kept your shoes on your nasty feet while you're out here."

There were a few other remarks that he made, and he wasn't joking or playing around; the man was genuinely upset about us having our shoes off in front of the building. Not wanting to be around that kind of negative energy, we all got up and left. We were in the countryside, miles from anything urban, and if there was any place where kicking your shoes off shouldn't matter, this was that kind of place. I left my squash sitting in a chair before we left. I figured it would find a better home at the Farmer's Market anyway. This was my first rude exchange with somebody up north.

We wrapped up the twenty-mile day with the hardest climb in all of New Jersey, a mound of dirt called Wawayanda Mountain. This little beast was no joke, as I got lost twice on the way up. It was a jumbled mess of rocks, boulders, dirt, and fallen trees that made it very difficult to keep track of the blazes. There were so many branch-offs and beaten paths that I couldn't seem to stay on the right one. I had also fallen way behind the others due to my chafing situation, and didn't make it to our final pick up point until half an hour after everyone else.

On our last night at the house of Viking, we enjoyed about ten pounds of grilled chicken and Macaroni with real cheese. After dinner we watched one of my favorite movies, "Fight Club." Once you get past the violent overtone of the movie, there are some great lessons to be learned from the undertones. The philosophies and messages delivered in that movie are amazing and ingenious. Especially the messages about "letting go of the things in your life that don't matter," and "the things you own eventually end up owning you." I don't think it gets any more accurate than that.

Kate had a plethora of baked French toast ready for us when we awoke on our last morning at the house. I'd never heard of baking French toast, but I'm now a firm believer that's the only way to make it. We piled into the van and left the house of Viking for the last time. It was more than an hour's drive back to where we left off. To this day, I still can't believe how many times they came to pick us up, but it created an unforgettable experience that became another one of my fondest memories of the journey.

Kate had us all take a group photo together at the trail head to commemorate the moment. I had already met so many wonderful people on this adventure and it was barely halfway over. We didn't make it to the trailhead until almost noon, but we were all in New York before one o'clock.

CHAPTER 12: NEW YORK

"Surprisingly, New York Isn't Just One Big City."

The CatFox with two paws in Jersey & two in New York

The border for New York and New Jersey was marked in white paint on a huge slab of rock in the middle of the woods that you actually walked straight over top of. I took this opportunity to have some more border hopping fun. I placed little CatFox on the white line with her front half in New York and her back half in Jersey. Her dual statesmanship was complete and another one of my favorite Katana pictures was born.

I really hadn't heard too much about New York prior to getting there, but I remember the rumors being that it was "harder than you might think," and that it had more rocks than anyone cared to admit. This was true, New York was quite rocky in some areas, but it was a different type of rocky. There were huge slabs of steep coarse granite that you were constantly climbing up, down, and over. This however was just the beginning of New York; once you got further in, the rocks turned into massive boulders that you had to climb and step over in order to overcome the huge vertical ascents. Not "mountainous huge," but fifty feet here, a hundred feet there, and a couple hundred feet every now and then as well. What made it monotonous was that it was non-stop. New York was a collection of short but sharp brutal climbs that came one after the other. This made it very difficult to keep up a good pace.

One humorous and peculiar occurrence on my first day in New York pertained to a spot in my guidebook marked "ladder." At first, this didn't strike me as odd because there'd been multiple areas named "Ladder" along the entire trail. It usually meant that it was a steep climb and that you would possibly have to use your hands. So that's exactly what I prepared for, a short but steep climb. Imagine my surprise when I pushed through some small, low hanging branches and ran smack dab into a rock face that had an actual aluminum ladder bolted right into the rock. I chuckled out loud at the fact that it literally meant there was a ladder this time.

Another interesting spot that I found marked in my guidebook was the existence of an ice cream shop about half a mile down a road that we reached later that day. If there was one thing about New Jersey and New York that I didn't like, it was the presence of so many damned road crossings. I crossed more roads in those two states than anywhere else that I can remember, besides Shenandoah National Park back in Virginia. It seemed like every five to ten miles you would hit at least one or more roads. This was nice from a resupply (or an ice cream standpoint in this case), but I really felt like it took away from the wilderness experience. If I had one complaint about New York and New Jersey, it would be the frequency of road crossings.

When we finally did reach the Ice Cream store called Bellvale Farms, it was quite the pleasant surprise. The store belonged to a local farm of the same name where all of the ingredients for the ice cream where procured and prepared. This store was in the middle of the countryside, far from any city, but still had lots of people traffic. Their ice cream was fantastic, as was their location. The building sat atop the crest of a huge rolling hill, and the view out across the landscape was gorgeous. There was even a nice picnic area next to the building that overlooked it all. You could see the farm and the surrounding countryside below for as far as the eye could see.

While at Bellvale, I had a bowl of vanilla ice cream, a cone of vanilla ice cream, and a root beer float with vanilla ice cream. One of the employees even asked me if my dog wanted some ice cream. "Can dogs even eat ice cream?" I asked. "As long as it's not chocolate," the young girl informed me. "You're the ice cream expert," I replied as I accepted a small bowl of vanilla ice cream from the employee.

Katana inhaled her bowl of ice cream in less than two minutes, and less than a minute later she threw it all back up. "Yup, ice cream is fantastic for dogs," I thought to myself. It was probably the fact that "ICE" cream, being as cold as "ICE," probably doesn't sit well in a dog's stomach, not to mention a possible "lactose" issue. No sooner had she puked it up, she began attempting to "re-eat" her ice cream. Being the responsible and ever vigilant parent that I was, I covered it up with gravel and moved her to a different spot.

It wasn't long after her puking episode that I had my favorite encounter of "What kind of dog is that?" Schweppes, Engineer, Stardust, Viking, and I were all sitting, enjoying our ice cream when a middle aged man approached me and asked, "What kind of dog is that?" I informed him that she was a "Russian Curl Tailed Fox." Suddenly, my fellow hikers began eating their ice cream a little quicker to conceal their smiles. "Really?!" the man said. I could tell he was completely intrigued. "Yes sir, I acquired her myself while on a trip through Siberia; she had been abandoned by her mother." "Wow!" the man said without taking his eyes off of Katana, and adding, "That's a very beautiful animal." "Yes it is." I replied.

The man began to walk away as my friends tried not to spit up their frozen dairy treat. Several steps from the door to the ice cream parlor, the man stopped and half turned around to look back at me. I met his gaze, ready for whatever he might say. There was a long pause as he looked at me, then to Katana, then back to me. "Russian?" he said with curiosity. "Rrruusian," I replied, while slightly over pronouncing the "R" and "U" and nodding my head down in a semi-dramatic drop at the same time. I even tightened the muscles around my eyes to add to the intensity of the reply. Doing this gave the statement that finality of "I'm dead serious."

The man's eyes widened as if he was hearing this information for the first time. "I'll-be-GOD-DAMNED," he said, pronouncing each word slowly and emphatically before turning and entering the parlor. I turned back to everyone, my eyes wide and my expression frozen in pursed lips, trying not to explode with laughter, but my companions were already losing it. Out of all that information and the little story I'd recounted, the guy had been most intrigued and surprised by the fact that I'd said she was "Russian." That slays me!

For the rest of the journey, it became a joke for other hikers who heard the story to randomly turn to me and say "Russian?" if only to see me do the look and then nod back while saying "Rrruusian." They would then of course recite the man's next lines in their best "serious but surprised" voice. This may not sound as humorous in writing, but out on the trail it was hilarious! There was only one other reaction that trumped or even equaled this one, and it happened later on in New Hampshire.

As we sat there enjoying our cream of ice, we saw a vast storm approaching over the surrounding countryside. It was moving fast and heading our way. We watched the farms and fields disappear one by one as the wall of clouds and water made its way closer. Having no other options to stay dry, we went inside and asked if we could take shelter in the parlor with all our gear. They happily obliged us, as this became one of my fondest memories of sheltering from a storm. I don't think we could have picked a better spot if we tried. We were hiding from a storm inside of an ice cream parlor. Fate had me covered as well as fed with ice cream on that hot stormy day.

July 29th was my 122nd day on the trail and also the day that I decided New York was one of my favorite states. I'll be honest, I hadn't seen that coming. I thought New York would be less than memorable, but I was wrong. I entered Harriman State Park on this day, and New York proceeded to dazzle me with its enchanting landscapes.

Most of the terrain and areas you passed through on the trail were actually quite thick and congested with trees and vegetation. Many times, if there hadn't been a trail, the forest might have been considered impenetrable. This makes it very difficult to stray off the trail if you should desire to do so. In Harriman State Park, the forest was wide open. Red oaks, white oaks, black oaks, hickories, and ash trees were scattered everywhere over a sea of long, thin grass, rolling hills, and islands of large boulders. Lakes and ponds were everywhere as I quickly fell in love with this place. It was so unique to anything else I ever saw on the trail, that it would always stick out in my memory.

When you've been on the trail for as long as I had at this point, you start to eyeball everything as: "a good place to camp"- "a decent place to camp"- "an amazing place to camp"- "a once in a lifetime place to camp"- and, "that will do." The entirety of Harriman State Park ranged from "amazing" to "once in a lifetime" on my camp-rating scale. Not just parts of it, the whole place. I didn't want to ever leave.

It was so gorgeous, we almost couldn't find a place to have lunch, as the spots kept getting better and better. First, we saw a nice grassy hill and decided on that. Once at the top of the hill, we noticed a nice grouping of rocks down in another grassy clearing that had a fire ring. We adjusted course and made for the newer spot. Once there, we looked a little further past and beheld a beautifully placid lake ringed by smooth, rocky precipices and an island in the middle. Lunch location found! We laid up there for nearly two hours, eating and taking naps. I truly did not want to leave, but I couldn't justify stopping this early in the day, plus we had already planned on another special location for the night.

After lunch and naps, we encountered the "Lemon Squeezer" a short distance later. This was a spot where an enormous boulder had cracked and separated from a cliff face creating a narrow passageway that you were lucky to squeeze through with your pack on. Both of my shoulders were scraping the rock as I passed through the fifty feet of crevice. The Lemon Squeezer was not for the claustrophobic! Right after that, was a boulder climb that was so high it involved some very technical climbing maneuvers in order to ascend. New York seemed to have a little bit of everything, as well as a little bit of what other places didn't have.

We were aiming for a location that was six tenths of a mile off the trail that night. We normally wouldn't have given a spot that far off the trail a second thought, but this one was different. This spot supposedly had a clear view of the New York City skyline thirty miles away. This was the closest the trail ever came to New York City... thirty miles.

The final climb of this twenty-one-mile day was up West Mountain. This was easily the hardest climb of the day and possibly the hardest and tallest climb in New York that I can recall. Viking and I were ahead of everyone else and made the climb in the dark without our headlamps. The headlamps finally came on when we reached the summit and side trail that lead to our desired location. On the way down the side trail we encountered a deer that was standing next to some medium sized creature that was low to the ground. I never did identify it before it scurried into the bushes, but if I had to guess, I would say it was a skunk or woodchuck.

When we finally reached West Mountain Shelter, the view didn't disappoint. The Hudson River lay sprawled out before us as it snaked its way across the landscape while New York City sparkled majestically in the distance. You could see the individual sky scrapers perfectly. I managed to hang my hammock between two trees in such a way that all I had to do was roll onto my side in order to have a perfectly unobstructed view of the city laid out before me in all its concrete glory. It was so quiet and peaceful looking from such a long distance out in the woods, atop that mountain. It was a marvel of human architecture and a beautiful sight in its own right. Thirty miles closer, this place was a mad house full of every kind of good and bad chaos that you can imagine; but from atop West Mountain, it was serene.

Initially, I never had any plans to go into New York City, but Schweppes had never been there before and expressed interest in going. It would definitely be a good side trip for him. I had family on Staten Island that we could stay with, so it wouldn't be an expensive pit stop. Our plan was to get into the town of Pawling, then catch a train into Grand Central Station. To tell the truth, I was getting very excited about this trip. I knew it was going to be overwhelming, but it had been nearly ten years since my last visit to NYC. The only question was how will CatFox handle the trains and the hustle and bustle of the Big Apple?

Besides all of the road crossings that frequent the trail in New York, I guess there is one other positive that comes with it, and that positive is Delis! New York has so many Deli Stores that reside on or near the trail, that a new hiking term was coined for this state. That term was "Deli Blazing."

Deli Blazing is when you hike from Deli to Deli while taking advantage of each one. Sometimes it can require a good bit of sideways walking when you tally up all the extra tenths of a mile, but it's well worth it! The food in New York was superior to food in most places, especially anything made with dough or New York tap water. Everyone who's been to New York knows that their claim to fame (reason for great tasting food, especially their pizza) is attributed to their tap water. You may know about the tap water, but how many people know what makes their tap water so good? The answer is hard minerals. Their tap water is laden with hard minerals, which gives their food that extra "Yum."

After descending West Mountain the next morning, we passed into Bear Mountain State Park. The climb up Bear Mountain was something that I can only describe as a pleasant and joyful experience. Not strenuous at all, with plenty of views and some impressive slabs of bare granite rock that were pock-marked like the surface of the moon. Each pock-mark was as big as your fist or bigger and held water from the last rain. I never saw anything quite like it before or since.

Bear Mountain itself had many small areas throughout the climb that reminded me of Harriman State Park. It was another amazing spot that I would've liked a whole lot more with the absence of the road that wrapped around it. Once at the summit, we hit pay dirt - there were three drink machines. I'll tell you what, if every mountain out there had drink machines at the summit, hiking would be a lot more popular.

We hung out by the machines, replenishing our electrolytes, and once again, our timing was impeccable. To my dismay, I ran out of small bills before I was satisfied with my drink purchases. Not minutes later, the guy that stocked the machines pulled up and began unloading carts of soda, Gatorade, and snacks. This kind gentleman gave us every single dented can for free. Of course they weren't cold yet, but they were free...and free always tastes better.

Upon descending Bear Mountain, we entered an enormous park on the shores of Hessian Lake. The trail passed right through the park alongside the lake before going through a tunnel that went beneath a road. Almost directly after the tunnel, the trail literally passed right through a zoo. Thru-hikers were allowed free admittance, but it wasn't your typical exotic zoo. It was a zoo filled with all of the creatures that you could find in the forests of New York. It had foxes, skunks, eagles, hawks, porcupines, snakes, turtles, fish, and various other mammals, reptiles, and avian creatures. The bear exhibit was home to two large black bears in the three and four-hundred-pound range. Subsequently, this bear exhibit also represented the lowest spot on the entire Appalachian Trail at one hundred sixty-three feet above sea level.

Near the zoo we met up with a thru-hiker named "G-Hippie." He hiked the trail back in 2010 and was a member of the hiking group "Riff Raff." Riff Raff is a group you had to be invited into. They were well known to the hiking community on the AT and famous for their hospitality towards current thru-hikers. They provided all kinds of free food and services to help hikers out. What they were also famous for were their parties. Riff Raff worked hard and played hard too. Viking had met G-Hippie in Damascus and G-Hippie had asked Viking to contact him whenever he passed through Bear Mountain Park.

We all piled into G-Hippie's 1970's Volkswagen Van as he drove us downtown into Fort Montgomery by the West Point Army College. He was taking us to lunch, answering questions, and giving inspirational advice. I wish I could remember the name of the pub where we ate, because it was the best Buffalo Chicken Pizza I'd ever had in my entire life! Real fried cutlets of chicken scattered all across the pizza and drizzled with Buffalo sauce. DAMN it was good! We spent a little over an hour at the pub before G-Hippie dropped us off back at the trail head.

From there we crossed the Hudson River on Bear Mountain Bridge where there was a narrow walkway for pedestrians separated from the road by a concrete divider that was waist high and six inches wide. Katana walked on the divider almost the entire way across. Her balance was impeccable and her dainty gait was perfect for the narrow walkway. As cars passed us head on in the opposite direction, Katana was cool as a cucumber while she pranced along. I could read people's lips and wide eyed expressions in the vehicles as they passed by. "Oh My God!" "... A FOX?" "Look at that!" "What is that?" I never knew my lip reading skills were so good until Bear Mountain Bridge.

Once again, not six miles past the bridge and two small mountains later, we came upon another road with a deli in the median. It was called "The Appalachian Deli." It was more of a glorified gas station really, but it had a Deli inside. The little thing that happened here would normally not be worth mentioning except for one major detail; I'd fallen about ten minutes behind everyone due to my new obsession with raspberries. They were growing everywhere throughout this section and were ripe for the picking. No pesticides! Only animal pee and little bugs, aka: "Au Natural."

I knew I was perhaps half a mile from the Deli because I could hear the road. I was getting ready to break through the tree line when I heard the long screech of braking tires followed by a loud crash. "Yikes!" I thought. "Somebody must have been looking at hikers crossing the road and bumped into their fellow motorist!" Turns out a car had rear ended another car at about forty-five miles per hour. One of the drivers had been texting and driving while the other was at a stop light, but luckily they were both Ok. The craziest part of the entire incident (and the major detail worth mentioning) was that the guy who'd been rear ended was carrying two thirty-racks of beer in his trunk. His trunk had been obliterated in the accident and so had the cases of beer. Beer was now oozing out of the smashed trunk of his car and spilling out all over the street. This was the first time in my life that I ever saw a car leak beer after an accident.

Sadly, we also said goodbye to Engineer at this deli. He was going to a wedding in Turkey for ten days and was going to resume the hike when he got back. We all hugged him goodbye as he got into his Taxi and headed to LaGuardia Air Port. We all figured he was fast enough to catch us after a ten-day hiatus depending on where he picked the trail back up. Although he did end up finishing the trail; unfortunately, I never saw Engineer again.

Besides a zoo, the best pizza of my life, a car leaking beer, and saying goodbye to Engineer, this day stuck out in my mind for one other reason. That reason was BUGS! The mosquitoes and other biting insects got so incredibly bad on this particular day, and didn't let up until I reached Vermont.

That evening I was almost running from the mosquitoes as the light faded into darkness. Viking and I picked a stealth spot down in a grove of oak trees that had dead branches lying everywhere. We built a big fire ring from the plentiful stones that were scattered around, and proceeded to build the biggest bug fire I can ever remember building on the trail. The flames must have been eight to nine feet tall at one point. We weren't worried about fuel because we had more logs and branches than we knew what to do with. I set up my hammock about twenty feet from the fire, finding myself in heaven as the mosquitoes bothered us no more. I was free to sit about shirtless without smacking myself two times per second.

After Bear Mountain and slightly beyond, I can say that I didn't much care for the rest of New York, or at least not during the summer season. This was mostly due to the bugs. The terrain wasn't half bad, but the forests had become thick with vegetation and undergrowth. Stopping for water became torture, because the moment you stopped, the cloud of mosquitoes, gnats, and biting flies that followed, caught up to you. You could easily net yourself over thirty bites in the time it took to filter a couple liters of water. It was unbelievable, as I hadn't encountered biting insects this thick even down in the Florida swamps and rivers.

It was August 1st when we road-walked into the train station of Pawling, NY. We were all pretty much strangers to mass transit and public transportation, but we all managed to figure out the train schedule and purchase our tickets to Grand Central Station. I was extremely nervous about Katana not being allowed on the train, because I wasn't sure what I would do if they told me she couldn't come. All I could do was get on and wait until someone noticed.

The train finally arrived around 1 pm as we piled on with a few other locals. It wasn't too crowded and we all found seats to ourselves without a problem. I kept Katana cradled like a baby, where she almost immediately passed out. That was a little known trick with the CatFox, for all her energy, all you had to do was flip her on her back, rub her belly, and she goes out like a light.

The conductor came down the aisle checking tickets as I held my breath. He came by, picked up my ticket, looked at Katana and said, "cute dog," before moving on. "PHEW!" I gave a mental sigh and flashed thumbs up to Schweppes, Stardust, and Viking.

We didn't really have much of a plan as far as getting to Staten Island from Grand Central Station, but originally it went like this: Get on the train to Grand Central, then find a way to the Staten Island Ferry. After the ferry, get to the Staten Island train and ride it to Nassau Station. It was fairly simple and straight forward, with some grey areas in between the different destinations, but we weren't too worried about it. We had just walked over fourteen hundred miles, how difficult could this be?

When we arrived in Grand Central Station, my anxiety levels shot into outer space. There were too many people to let Katana walk, so I draped her over my shoulders. We must have looked like one rough bunch that just rolled in from "BFE," because every single one of us was in dirty, smelly clothes, with dirt on our legs, and carrying huge dirty packs that had little odds and ends attached all over them.

We had Viking with his huge wooden staff that had a giant rock attached to the end of it, making him look like some kind of dark wizard. Schweppes, a red headed, red bearded, Yeti-looking fellow that was wearing all green. Me, a tall, bearded barbarian looking guy that was also carrying a big stick, wearing short American flag shorts, who also had some kind of live, wild fox draped over my shoulders. Then lastly, a cute blonde girl with brown eyes, short shorts, and an equally large pack was hanging out with this motley crew of characters. This was all amidst a throng of people dressed to the nines. We stuck out like turds in a punchbowl, and everybody let us know (with their startled and incredulous expressions), that we looked nothing less than strange.

Having Katana on my shoulders drew hordes of attention to us. People stopped to take pictures and even tried to take them discreetly as they walked by. Everywhere I could hear the whispers and hushed voices of, "Is that a Fox?" "What kind of dog is that?" "These people smell bad!" and "What are those people doing?" Stardust snapped the photo of the century of the three of us standing in Grand Central looking like we belonged in the Scottish Highlands about four hundred years in the past.

When we finally made it up to the surface and arrived in Time Square, it was the same story. I felt as if I was part of the New York City side show. The whispers and exclamations were almost constant. The stares and looks from people were non-stop. At one point I must have had a dozen people snapping pictures of Katana and me, while everywhere people were reaching out to pet her, asking me questions and posing with us for pictures.

I honestly think people thought we were out there for their entertainment and not travelers far from home. I felt like some kind of celebrity or maybe just some strange creature to be looked at and wondered about. I couldn't handle it and Katana was on overload too. There was so much going on that her ears were plopped to the sides, something she never did. I wanted to get somewhere quiet and secluded to regroup; we all did. As I walked, a man tapped me on the shoulder and told me to put my knife away. "They will arrest you or confiscate it if the police see it," he said. I'd completely forgotten! I always kept my belt knife strapped to the outside of my pack for easy access. I stopped and quickly put it away in one of my zippered compartments.

We stopped and sat in some chairs in the middle of Times Square somewhere between the Naked Cowboy, some women walking around in thongs, and a man carrying a sign that proclaimed they were all damned to eternal hellfire. What a freak show! It was kind of sad that everyone thought we were part of it. It was here in time square that we took another priceless picture of the four of us that I like to call, "Filthy hikers in the Big Apple."

I had contacted my cousin Michelle earlier in the day, and she drove into the city to pick us up. This eliminated the logistics of our earlier plan. We met her, and soon I was wondering if the logistics of public transportation would have been a better choice than a private vehicle racing through New York City; cutting off every other vehicle in sight, while dodging pedestrian speed bumps every twenty feet. I was slamming the invisible brake pedal on my passenger side floor board the entire way to Staten Island.

That night my Aunt Tara, Uncle Joey, and cousins treated us to a case of beer as well as some New York Pizza and subs. We showered, laundered, took some shots of Vodka, and passed out. The plan was to go back into the city the next day and see the major sights. Viking had no desire to go since he lived so close to the city anyway, being from the Tri State area. He decided to stay at the house and relax with Katana.

The next morning my aunt got us something that I had been looking forward to - New York Bagels (also known as the best bagels in the world). They're approximately three times the size of your average "other bagel" and nearly 999,485,454 times tastier. I devoured three "Everything Bagels," two of them I ate plain. Why would perfection need anything added to it?

After breakfast, the fun began. The day was a whirlwind of activities and traveling, as I had a laundry list of things that I wanted to check off for Schweppes and myself. Stardust too, but she'd been to NYC before, so the experience wasn't as new. My father grew up on Staten Island and in Brooklyn, so there were places to go, things to do, and foods to eat, as I remembered all the activities he always talked about doing during his youth. My cousin Kristina dropped us off at the Staten Island Train Station shortly before 9 am. Everything that follows is an abbreviated version of that entire day in the city.

We rode the train for about forty minutes all the way to the Staten Island Ferry. Ride the Staten Island Train. CHECK! We caught the Staten Island Ferry after a ten-minute wait. Ride the Staten Island Ferry. CHECK! We got to see the Statue of Liberty on our voyage into Manhattan. See the Statue of Liberty. CHECK! We arrived in downtown Manhattan. "What do we do first?" Walk and see what happens. We immediately saw a "Sabrett" hotdog stand. According to my father, Sabrett is the best hotdog you can get on the streets of New York as long as it's served from "dirty water." He's told me that my entire life, so we all got one. Eat a Sabrett hotdog. CHECK!

"What's close by?" Wall Street, let's go see the Bull. On our way, we ran into a public drinking fountain labeled "New York City Water." My father also told me throughout my life that "New York City tap water is the best water in the world." So I drank some. It was pretty damn good, but I like mountain spring water better. Drink NYC tap water. CHECK! Five minutes later we were at the Bull. Over a hundred people surrounded the inanimate object like it was going to all of a sudden come to life. "Take a picture and move on people!" I pushed through the crowd, got by the head of the Bull and Schweppes took a picture. See the Wall Street Bull. CHECK!

We walked a mile further to the Freedom Tower and took another picture. See the Freedom Tower. CHECK! Hungry again! We ate some Middle Eastern style chicken on a stick from a street vendor. It was fantastic! Eat street style ethnic food. CHECK! Okay, subway time. "Let's go to Chinatown." We go down and have to buy a "metro card" from an automated machine. It seemed simple, but in the end, the machine was too tricky and I got frustrated before figuring it out. Get frustrated with public transportation. CHECK! Caught the subway and ended up only going two stops away. "Oh well, we rode the subway." CHECK!

There were advertisements and movie posters in the subway tunnel posted on the walls. People had scribbled, drawn, and written their own messages all over them. It was quite entertaining to view and read. Enjoy local modern art. CHECK! We got street side again to find that it wasn't Chinatown. I asked a cop on the corner of the street "Which way to Chinatown?" He pointed and said, "Go that way and when you see a bunch of Asians, you're in Chinatown." I joked back to him, "So this whole city is Chinatown?" He laughed. Get chummy with local law enforcement. CHECK! We headed in the direction he pointed and about ten minutes later we were there.

Exotic markets and stores galore! Live fish, live frogs, live turtles, live eels, live shrimp, and assorted other oddities and vegetables for sale everywhere. "Yum." We went into a store and bought a green melon flavored soda with a crazy pop top that sprayed fizz in your face when you broke the seal. Surprisingly, it was pretty damn good. Drink an ethnic soda pop. CHECK! We ate in a little hole in the wall restaurant and surprisingly the food was not good at all. "Oh well!" CHECK!

Then, the news you've all been waiting for! What happened to my lost gold chain necklace? Well, the hiker "Rodeo," had been way behind us this entire time. She never caught up and I never managed to give her an address to mail the chain, so she just held onto it. Guess who had caught a ride from a train station back in New Jersey? Guess who was in the city the same day we were? That's right, Rodeo. Stardust knew her and kept in touch regularly, so when they realized they were both in the city, Rodeo met us in Chinatown and slapped my necklace into my hot little hands. At this point, it had been missing for nearly two months. Never in a million years did I expect to get my grandmother's gold chain back, let alone run into the person who had it in New York City – which was my grandmother's birthplace; Talk about synchronicities and serendipity! What were the odds? Nine million to one I'd wager. Experienced a miracle. CHECK!

I thanked her profusely for holding onto it for all that time before we all began walking again. She came into the city with another hiker named "Gandalf," who was actually from there. How did he get the name Gandalf? He also carried a wooden staff. Baltimore Jack, the trail guru and oracle had been right in advising me not to take that name. I would have ended up being one of many "Gandalfs" on the trail that year.

We made our way to a huge REI outfitter store, where I tried on some new shoes and fell in love with a pair of rugged Keen Newport Sandals. Just the thought of not having to worry about wet shoes anymore was too much to handle... so I bought them. Shop in New York City. CHECK! After shopping we caught the subway again. "Empire State Building here we come." We arrived to find that the base of the Empire State Building was a Walgreens. This was unexpected, but whatever. See the Empire State Building. CHECK!

After the Empire State Building visit, we got more food. I ate two lamb gyros. "I'm gonna miss those." It was beginning to get late, so we decided to start making our way back. Subway time again. Our subway navigation skills were still subpar and we only got within ten minutes of the ferry and had to walk the rest of the way. We caught the ferry as well as the sunset over the city. I enjoyed seeing New York City from a distance much better than being in it.

Caught the train on Staten Island and after a relatively smooth day of public transportation, we got off at the wrong stop. It was already after 9 pm by this point and we got off in Tottenville about 2.5 miles from where we needed to be. We began walking again. We must have looked like easy targets with our bags and hiking clothes, walking around the neighborhood at this hour. "Thank Google for Google Maps!" We made it back in a little less than an hour without being stabbed, kidnapped, murdered, or mugged. "Staten Island, you're alright!"

What a crazy day it was. I was more tired from a day in the city than I was after a thirty-mile day in the wilderness. The city just took it out of you. The whirlwind NYC experience wasn't just fun and games though. Oh no, going from months in the wilderness to the chaotic city in the span of a day put some things into perspective and taught me a few lessons.

One thing it really solidified for me was to not be so uptight; to not worry about things that really didn't matter that much anyway. Everyone in this city looked like they were trying incredibly hard to project a certain image. Everyone was so concerned and in a hurry to get where they wanted to be. You constantly caught small bits and pieces of conversation as you walked around, surrounded by people. You never heard a full conversation, just bits and pieces. Putting the pieces together, you would find that people concerned and worried themselves with superficial things that really didn't/shouldn't matter. This is just my personal opinion. I'm sure that everything that everyone was doing, saying, and worrying about was important to them, and it's not my place to judge. It's just my opinion that their energy and focus was misplaced. I used to have the same thought process, but now I felt more enlightened seeing it from a new perspective.

It was interesting being on the outside looking in; sitting in the middle of this city with nowhere to be, no schedule, no real agenda, able to observe everything going on. It was like being a part of it without actually being a part of it. Having this perspective allowed me to make observations about things that I previously wouldn't have had the cognizance to observe as closely.

Everything in the city was created by people; even the natural areas that were supposed to mimic nature were manmade. New York City was a giant terrarium full of everything that I would deem "wrong" with our society. Interesting and fun to witness, but ultimately, when I stepped back and really looked at everything and all of the people that made up this city, I didn't see happiness. I saw stress, anger, frustration, and weathered faces. I saw a giant rat race of competition and materialism. I saw people breaking their backs and giving up all of their time just so they could afford to live and work in that zoo. I would imagine that a great majority of them make only enough money to live there, go to work, eat and watch the side show that is that city. That's not my view of a fulfilling existence. Maybe it is to others, but not me.

Another personal observation is that for all the millions of people in this city, they all seem to be invisible to one another. They say the best place to hide is in plain sight because that's the last place anyone ever looks. That statement couldn't be truer. In my opinion, this was a city full of people that only talked to you when they wanted something from you, or when you wanted something from them. I would only live in this city if I wanted to be invisible, alone, and ignored. What a catch 22 this place was. For all of the people and activities that go on there, I had a better chance of meeting and having a meaningful conversation with a random person in the wilderness than I did there. New York City was an eye opening experience that only intensified my appreciation for all things tranquil and natural.

The journey back to the woods turned into quite an adventure in itself. We got up at 4:15 in the morning to find that it was raining. We walked a mile and a half to the Staten Island Train Station and missed the first train by four minutes. We caught the second one a half hour later to the Staten Island Ferry, but missed the original planned ferry by ten minutes. The second ferry was late, so we waited nearly an extra hour.

We took the ferry back into downtown Manhattan. Now we had to get fifty-five blocks up to grand central station. I put money back on my metro card, caught one subway, transferred to a second, then a third, and then transferred to a "shuttle train" that took us into Grand Central.

We got to grand Central and had to figure out which train to catch back to "Pawling." We figured out the trains and bought tickets, then waited an hour and a half for departure and then another ninety minutes of travel time before disembarking and getting onto a second train that would eventually take us to Pawling after another thirty-minute ride. We got to Pawling and caught a cab that charged $20 to take us four miles back to the trail head.

I did all of this with a dog on my shoulders. We made it back to the trail at 12:30 pm and still managed to hike seventeen miles out of New York and into Connecticut before dark. We were putting that madness as far behind us as we could. Eight hours of commuting on public transit to go less than a hundred miles. What did I learn? The woods are a far simpler place.

CHAPTER 13: CONNECTICUT

"The Home of EVEN MORE Mosquitoes and Lots of Rich Accomplished People."

Lion King near the Connecticut border.

In the grand scheme of the trail, Connecticut is only a blip on the thru-hiker radar. Like Maryland, only a little over forty miles of trail actually resides in Connecticut, but for as small as it was, it actually left quite an impression on me. Nothing was ever really said about the terrain there, as most of the rumors and information swirled around the people and towns. The reviews of both seemed mixed.

Some would say the people were rude, rich snobs, with the townspeople looking down on hikers, and some businesses going as far as putting up "Hikers not welcome" signs. Others would tell you they received the greatest hospitality of their entire journey there, citing their stays at private multi-million dollar homes residing on lakes and mountain sides where they were treated like family and permitted to jet ski and drive golf carts all around the property. I neither saw nor experienced either of those negative or positive reviews firsthand. However, my experiences in Connecticut were nothing but positive.

On the night that I crossed from New York into Connecticut, Viking, Schweppes, and I camped on an island in the middle of the Ten Mile River. Stardust slept in a shelter a few tenths of a mile away. The only thing I can say that I truly disliked about Connecticut was the ban on campfires. You were not permitted to have a campfire on the Appalachian Trail in the state of Connecticut. This was a major turn off for me because fire was the only way to keep the bugs at bay in the evenings. Without fire, I resigned myself to setting up my hammock and promptly crawling into bed. There was no point in staying up and swatting at bugs all evening while trying to hold a conversation in the dark.

The next morning, Viking and Stardust left sometime around 6 am, about two hours before Schweppes and me. We'd settled on a rendezvous point the night before, so we all knew where to meet up. I didn't know it at the time, but that first night we camped in Connecticut was the last time I would see Viking or Stardust. Try as we might to reconnect, fate seemed to have different plans.

Right off the bat, Connecticut proved challenging. Not overly challenging, but just enough to really work up a good sweat. Short but steep climbs that came one after the other was the name of the game. The rocks weren't too bad, or at least not bad enough to complain about. There were some rocky descents, but for the most part the trail was mainly dirt. The worst part about the Connecticut experience was easily the bugs.

New York had nothing on Connecticut in the biting insect department. Huge mosquitoes, black flies, yellow flies, gnats, and a half dozen other winged pests I couldn't identify. They bit through your shirt; they flew in front of your eyes, into your eyes, all around you all the time. I could feel myself breathing some of the smaller gnats in at some points. They stuck to the back of your throat, sending you into a hacking fit. It was absolute madness and there was no getting away from them. The faster you went, the more reckless and relentless the insects became to catch you.

This infestation of insects led me to an adaptation that would eventually come back to bite me in the ass. I couldn't bring myself to stop and filter water any longer, out of fear of all the bites that I would contract. The bugs had me running scared and I was too afraid to stop. As I passed a fast moving stream, I pulled out my Gatorade bottle, leaned down quickly, scooped, and took a swig. It was instant gratification as once again I felt like I was living.

After that first unfiltered scoop of water, I knew there was no going back. This was the first time I'd done it from somewhere other than a high altitude spring. This source had only been a fast moving stream that was running down a low mountain. When I finished downing that liter of water without instantly turning green or collapsing in a heap of sickly flesh and vomit, I knew that I'd never filter again. It was simply too convenient to scoop and go.

At the top of Caleb's Peak, I came across a man, his wife, and their teenage son. After a short greeting and the exchange of a few words, the man gave me a salami sandwich and a bag of chips right out of his day pack. This was the first time that a day-hiker had ever handed me a full lunch right out of their own backpack. I thanked him for his generosity, put it in my pack, and after some small talk, as well as a treacherous descent, I ate it down by a dirt road with Schweppes.

The sandwich was nothing more than a thick slice of hard Salami, sharp cheddar cheese, and some spicy mustard sandwiched between white bread. It was as simple a sandwich as you could make, and it was absolutely

DEE-LICIOUS. "Why had I never thought of this before?" That day-hiker had inadvertently transformed my hike once again. From that day forward, at every resupply, I always bought two pounds of hard salami, one pound of sharp cheddar, six everything bagels, and a small bottle of brown spicy mustard. I never got bored with them for the rest of the journey. Salami Bagel Sandwiches were my saving grace.

Even the magic of cereal had gotten old at this stage of the journey. I think my breaking point was when my pouch of powdered milk busted in my pack while it was still wet from a recent rain storm. This was not a good combination, as globs of nasty powdered milk had been all over the place and caked onto the inside of my backpack as well as all my gear. I don't recall ever buying powdered milk or cereal ever again after that.

Not long after we began to have lunch, the man and his family caught up to us at the road and offered us a ride into the town of Kent to get supplies. He even offered to hang around and drive us back. This was an exceptional offer that took the extra effort and time out of finding a return ride, so we accepted his second kind gesture for the day. He dropped us off at a local IGA grocery store and informed us that he was going to drop his family off at home, but would be back in half an hour. We finished all of our shopping in about fifteen minutes.

We were out front taking everything out of its packaging and breaking it down to its simplest form, when a man walked by and asked, "Have you seen many rattlesnakes out on the trail?" "Yes actually," I replied "In fact I've..." The man cut me off as he sharply remarked, "I photograph rattlesnakes as a hobby," before promptly walking away without another word or waiting for a response from us. "Well thank you for sharing your hobby with us," I thought to myself. Schweppes and I laughed about this for a while. Who walks up and says that to someone, then walks away before they can even reply? That guy, apparently.

When our trail angel driver returned to pick us up, we were able to talk quite a bit more on the drive back. Turns out the guy was a retired lawyer from San Diego, owned an antique shop, owned a summer home and a boat in Florida. He was also a volunteer and assistant chief at the local fire department, had rock climbed, and knew Kevin Bacon, who also had a home in Kent! "HOLY CRAP!" Connecticans, you guys are impressive!

He told us some brief history about the town and some of the celebrities that lived there, as well as pointing out buildings and giving us their backgrounds as we drove back to the trailhead. Come to find out, Seth MacFarlane, the creator of "Family Guy," was born and raised in Kent. Besides Seth MacFarlane, another funny thing about Kent was that for as small as it was, it had two high schools practically right next to each other. "This one is for the rich smart kids, and this one is for the rich dumb kids," our driver said as we passed by and pointed them out. "Ya don't say?" I thought.

After the most interesting man in the world had dropped us off, we pushed on another seven miles to where we thought our rendezvous spot was. We knocked out twenty-three miles and it was now pitch black as the bugs descended upon us thicker than ever. The slower pace required by night hiking gave the bugs their chance to really get a hold of you. We soon realized the real rendezvous point was actually a spot that was three miles further than what we originally thought it was. We'd fallen short, while Viking and Stardust remained ahead of us. We decided the bugs were too bad to suffer over the course of a three-mile night hike, so we planned on catching them the next day.

I nearly lost my mind the following morning while packing up due to the mosquito hordes. It took me twice as long to break camp because of my constant swatting of the air and myself. The bugs were really beginning to get to me psychologically.

You know when you stub your toe, trip, hit your head, or do something in general that hurts you or pisses you off when you're already in a volatile mood? Do you get that feeling that you want to damage or destroy whatever is causing your grief at that particular moment? For instance, let's say you stub your foot or trip on a rock right after stubbing your foot or tripping on a different rock perhaps seconds earlier. You reach down, pick up the rock and throw it out of spite or slam it back down on the ground. Does it make you feel better? Maybe, but not really. Why not? You don't feel better because a rock is an inanimate object and it doesn't care. You can't hurt it or exact revenge upon it. This goes for any inanimate object that you might have a vendetta against. You can't make yourself feel better by taking out your frustrations on something that doesn't care.

Mosquitoes are different. They are tiny, living, winged, demonic spawns of Satan with no other purpose than to annoy you and spread disease. I take much solace and greater satisfaction in knowing that when a mosquito bites me, my revenge will mean something when I bite back. I mean biting back in the form of turning that mosquito into mosquito dust. It makes me feel better for approximately two and a half seconds, until the next mosquito attacks. That's the only downside to killing mosquitoes. You can have all the revenge you want, but the mosquito ranks are endless. Like the Lernaean Hydra, when you killed one or two, more came to take its place. It's a battle that can't be won. You fight back when you have to, but mostly you just run. Sadly, no amount of bug spray will keep them away (trust me, everyone tries); you simply have to suffer through it.

I walked along the beautiful Housatonic River for a good portion of this stifling, bug infested morning. The Housatonic was beautiful and lined with many equally beautifully unique houses. I reached a road before long and began walking through the town of Falls Village. This little town was a gorgeous and quiet area that I couldn't help but love. The houses and the properties they sat on were perfectly manicured with quaint wooden sheds, small mother in-law houses, stone walkways, and other small structures and aesthetically pleasing decorations.

I hardly saw a soul or even a vehicle as I passed through Falls Village. Either everyone was hiding indoors from the heat, or had gone down to my neck of the woods on summer vacation. The quietness and seeming abandonment of the town wasn't eerie like you might think, it was peaceful. I came to the Housatonic Bridge towards the middle of the neighborhood I'd been walking through. The bridge itself was big enough for a vehicle, but had been blocked off by huge concrete barriers to allow only foot traffic. Painted on these barriers in traditional Lord of the Rings styled writing were the words "You Shall Not Pass." Seeing this ode to Lord of the Rings completely made my day, and I couldn't stop smiling the whole way across the bridge.

I'll admit that I couldn't help but re-enact the scene where Gandalf shouted the "You Shall Not Pass" command at the Balrog, while on the bridge to Khazad-dum. My inner nerd was shining through my barbaric appearance pretty hard on this day.

I walked through more quiet neighborhoods before the trail branched off the street and back under the cover of trees. I followed this for a short distance, all the while the Housatonic flowing steadily on my right. Then, quite unexpectedly, an enormous waterfall opened up out of the forest. I hadn't seen a waterfall this big since Tennessee, so I wasn't about to pass it up. "Great Falls" was its name and remains my favorite waterfall of the entire journey. The location of Dismal Falls back in Virginia definitely beat this one out overall, but from strictly a waterfall standpoint, Great Falls was far superior.

The falls themselves were impressive, but what I personally thought made them great was the vast open areas of pale limestone rock that surrounded the falls. There were tiers of smooth rock leading all the way up to the top. Each tier had its own pools of calm water of varying depths that were fed by the main flow of water. It was what I can only describe as a waterfall "spa" area. I popped off my shoes, ankle brace, and socks, and began to walk around.

I laid down in a couple of the pools and even made my way over to some of the quicker currents that fed them, holding myself steady in the fast current and letting the water rush over my body. Then I got a little bolder as I climbed down some rocks and hopped over some deeper pools to the main bulk of the falls. While holding onto the rocks, I was able to pass behind the main waterfall and even dunk my head into it. If I hadn't been holding onto other rocks, the force would have sent me over the edge. I kept putting different parts of my body underneath the main blast of the falls, feeling like I was getting a pressure wash. Once again I was streamlining laundry, bathing, and fun.

After the splish-splashing fun, I went back to Katana who had already laid down and begun her nap on the smooth rock. I was in the shade, but the surface of the rock was still warm from the sun. I quickly drifted into a peaceful sleep while my body and clothes dried in the warm air. Maybe it was the open exposure of bare limestone and no vegetation, but there were almost no bugs at this waterfall besides the odd house fly.

I was only awoken by Schweppes' arrival. He was as obsessed as I was with waterfalls and went through the same process of soaking in the pools and dipping under the waterfall before settling into his own nap.

"Yup, this is what it's all about," I said through a yawn with my hands folded behind my head while looking up at the sky. "Not being on a schedule and taking a nap next to an epic waterfall..." "Mhmm." Schweppes replied without even opening his eyes.

Right before we'd gotten to New York, Schweppes had converted back to ground dwelling. He'd been all about the hammock experience, but after a few cool, sleepless early mornings, he decided that he liked his tent better. All he needed was an under quilt or a nice thick pad and his "cold butt syndrome" would have been cured. I was sad to see him leave the ranks of the hangmen.

I think we killed almost four hours at that waterfall and completely forgot about catching Viking and Stardust. We finally got moving after a quick Lion King picture in front of the falls and were on our way once again. We knew our companions were stopping at a spot ten miles from the waterfall, but it was 4 pm when we finally left. We could easily make that distance by shortly after dark.

The next seven miles were filled with bugs and a beautiful sunset from the summit of Prospect Mountain. Not long after that we passed into the town of Salisbury. We never went into the actual town, but the trail itself made its way through more quiet neighborhoods on the outskirts. In the dark of night, we passed the houses without a soul knowing that we were even there. We were ghosts passing through on our way to new lands.

We were making our way through a pitch black pine grove on the edge of a neighborhood when lightning and thunder began to flash and rumble in the near distance. The wind began to pick up, bending the small pines as evidence of an approaching storm became undeniable. We could grit it out and finish the last 2.5 miles up Lion's Head to catch Viking and Stardust, or hunker down before the rains started. "What's an extra 2.5 miles tomorrow?" we reasoned. "Let's stay dry now and make up the small distance tomorrow." We pulled off the trail, faded a couple hundred feet back into the pines and made camp before the vicious rainstorm ensued.

On my last day in Connecticut, the bugs didn't make the transition smooth. We only had several miles until we reached Massachusetts from where we camped the night before. We had only to climb Lion's Head, pass along a ridge and then summit Bear Mountain, the highest point in Connecticut on the AT. Somewhere on the climb down from Bear Mountain was the Massachusetts border.

When we reached the summit of Bear, there was a giant mound of rocks where a fire tower had once been. We climbed the stack and rose above the short tree line to find an American Flag planted at the top. There was a comfortable and steady breeze as well as a gorgeous view of a vast lake in the distance. Most importantly, there were no bugs! As a rule, normally the higher in altitude you get, the less bugs there are. Ever since Pennsylvania we'd consistently been under two thousand feet, but closer to one thousand feet above sea level. That was the bug sweet spot as far as altitudes went.

We sat atop Bear Mountain for over an hour, soaking up the sun and enjoying the reprieve from insects. Relaxing on the summit of mountains was without a doubt one of my favorite past times while hiking the trail. The peace, solitude, feelings of accomplishment, and views out across the earth, reaffirmed all the reasons for climbing the mountain in the first place. With much effort, we dragged ourselves up and made our way down the pine covered mountain and onward into Massachusetts.

CHAPTER 14: MASSACHUSETTS

"HAH! More like MosquitoChusetts!"

The first thing you'll notice as you approach and cross into Massachusetts towards the base of Bear Mountain is the abundance of small to medium sized waterfalls, along with streams and creeks cascading and rushing down in all directions. It feels like you've crossed into some kind of forested mini waterfall Utopia. You walk along ledges and narrow footbridges covered in pine straw and leaves as you make your way down and across the terrain towards the slopes of Mount Race. Out of the thirteen borders that I crossed through fourteen states, I would say that the Connecticut/Massachusetts border was by far the most beautiful and dramatic.

Being total suckers for waterfalls, the CT/MA border really put a dent in our "catch Viking and Stardust" pace; as we slowed down to smell the roses once again. Since reaching New York we'd begun to see more "southbound" (SOBOs) thru-hikers. The south bounders had a much later starting season than us north bounders (NOBOs). South bounders started in Maine at Mt. Katahdin usually in early to mid-June, but sometimes later. We were seeing the first South bounders that were approximately seven hundred miles into their hike in late July and early August. Those were the fast ones that were in Connecticut and Massachusetts already, and we met four of them atop Mount Race.

They were three women and one man, all in their mid-twenties. We stopped and chatted for over an hour while they had a quick dinner and we enjoyed a few snacks. We traded information on what was ahead of each other. That was usually the favorite topic between north bounders and south bounders that crossed paths. Everyone wanted the inside scoop on the terrain they were about to approach, as well as any hot spots or good eats in upcoming towns.

There is somewhat of a friendly rivalry amongst north bounders and south bounders. I always found south bounders to have a little bit of a chip on their shoulder and rightly so. Beginning a southbound hike is much more difficult (terrain and logistic wise) than a northbound hike. South bounders know this and it boosts their confidence quite a bit. So when I have fifteen hundred miles under my feet and I cross paths with a south bounder that only has seven hundred miles under their feet, a lot of times they will speak to you like you're some kind of rookie who just got on the trail. This comes from their knowledge that they've encountered much worse terrain than the north bounder at this point. Without a doubt, this is true.

The south bounder at seven hundred miles has proven their physical capabilities. They have defeated the worst of the terrain while avoiding debilitating injury or quitting. However, what the north bounder has at this point, that the south bounder usually fails to recognize, is their proven mental endurance. By the time most north and south bounders meet, we have been on the trail for twice as long, if not longer than they have. Anyone who has ever thru-hiked will tell you that mental endurance is the major deciding factor in who completes a thru-hike and who doesn't. You can be as fit as a fiddle, but as soon as you begin missing home, get tired of walking in the rain, walking with sore feet, and eating the same foods every day, it's your level of mental endurance and fortitude that will get you to the finish line. If you have that, then you can complete a thru-hike on a broken foot, ankle, or leg... and it has been done.

After we chatted and traded information with our new southbound friends, the twilight hours had snuck up on us. We pushed down Mount Race and quickly scrambled over Mount Everett, which ended up being the steepest little climb we'd encountered in quite a while. When we arrived at Guilder Pond on the far side of Mount Everett, the light was gone and we had only made it thirteen miles that day. We smelled the roses a little too much, because our companions were still fifteen miles ahead of us.

We sat there in the early dusk and sipped from our water bottles and ate a few more snacks. "Do you wanna just go for it?" Schweppes asked. "Catch Viking and Stardust?" I inquired. "Yeah, just pull an all-nighter and catch' em," Schweppes answered. "I'm down if you're down," I replied.

It was settled, we were going to make up for our waterfall diversion that had put us further behind, by pulling an all-night hike. Our goal was to catch them at the shelter where they had planned to stop. We set out at a fast pace, but right off the bat, while on our way down Mount Bushnell, we encountered a rocky hell. We might have knocked out a little less than two miles over the course of more than an hour. I even took a hard fall when my foot slipped on some moss at the edge of a rock ledge, and slid several feet down a dirt embankment. This was not how you wanted to start an all-night hike.

The majority of the trek was lots of grassy and swampy flat lands. As the hours ticked by, the temperature dropped and the grass and vegetation became soaked in dew. Luckily wet shoes were no longer an issue for me, as my hiking sandals had been performing flawlessly. A couple of hot spots here and there, but for the most part, my new shoes were well suited for the terrain.

Schweppes was having the opposite problem. His shoes were on their last leg, with the tread all but gone and the soles peeling off, as well as the sides being ripped open. During the course of the night, I saw him slip and fall no less than seven times. The first couple times were humorous, but after that I began to feel really bad. It wasn't clumsiness that was putting him on the ground, but zero tread on wet grass.

Upon completing the swamplands, we reached June Mountain and East Mountain around 1 am. That was the home stretch, all we had to do was go up and over those rocky little demons and we'd be done. The shelter was only a little way down from the top of East Mountain. After reaching the summit and beginning our descent, we knew we were home free.

After we descended East Mountain for a while, things started to get confusing. The trail began to go up again, then went flat, then down, and then up again, until finally I had no idea where we were. We hit a bog area at the bottom of another descent and found ourselves up to our ankles in mud.

At this point it was after 3 am and we were exhausted. Both of us were fairly certain that we should've already hit the shelter. After trudging through the mud pits, we came to another climb. That was the last straw for both of us, as we agreed that we must have missed the side trail for the shelter and passed right by. We pulled off the trail, set up, and collapsed. We were confident that we would be awoken by Viking or Stardust passing us when the sun came up.

I awoke naturally at 10:30 the next morning to my first thought being, "Damn it, no wake-up call from our friends." This instantly put me in a bad mood. We had done twenty-eight miles in an attempt to catch them, fifteen of which were in the dark. After we packed up, I rolled out about ten minutes ahead of Schweppes. I hit the small climb that we'd camped in front of and quickly reached the top of it. What did I find on the other side, only a couple hundred feet from where we'd given up? You guessed it, the shelter.

There was one hiker still there, so I inquired about Viking and Stardust. He informed me that they had left around 7 am. That meant they had a three-and-a-half-hour head start on us. I could have screamed. All of that hiking and suffering through the night, only to miss them by a couple hundred feet. Oh it was maddening! This shouldn't have mattered, as we could've just matched their miles again that day since we were basically starting from the same point. This wasn't really an option though, because I was completely out of food and also had a package waiting in the nearby town of Tyringham. Schweppes also had some new shoes waiting for him there as well, making it the perfect opportunity to resupply. Viking and Stardust had resupplied in Salisbury which afforded them the food stores to hike further than what we were capable of doing, before needing food for ourselves.

After another thirteen miles of traversing short but steep rollercoaster climbs that reminded me a lot of New York, we finally arrived in Tyringham, fifteen minutes before the post office closed. A light sprinkle of rain had begun just as we half jogged down the back country road that led us into a quiet neighborhood, as well as the front door of the Post Office. We sat on the stoop under the over-hang for over an hour, as we waited out the rain and enjoyed the contents of our mail drops. I'd never seen someone so happy to get a new pair of shoes. I was secretly going to miss watching Schweppes trip every tenth step, but I was genuinely happy for him. My package contained a few snacks and an "Otterbox" for my Kindle, that my girlfriend had sent me. Since I had damaged two kindles on the trip already, I was going to take extra precautions with the third one.

As it turned out, the town of Tyringham didn't have much in the way of places to buy food. In fact, the Post Office and a fire department were pretty much the only non-residential buildings that Tyringham had. We stopped a passerby and asked where the nearest grocery store was. "Five miles down the road you're standing on, in the town of Lee," was the reply. After thirty minutes of unsuccessful hitchhiking attempts, we decided that we'd better get busy walking or get busy starving. I slung the CatFox over my shoulders as we began walking west.

Less than a mile into the road walk we passed a middle aged man and woman sitting on their front porch. "Are you carrying that dog because it's injured?" the man called out. "No sir, I just like to carry her on roads because it keeps her paws from getting cut up by the glass in the asphalt." "Good idea," he responded. "You know you guys are a little late in the season to be passing through here, right?" "That's what we keep hearing," I replied. "Where you fellas headed to?" he asked. "We're trying to get into Lee so we can buy some food," I responded. "Well come over and hop in the truck, I'll take you to the local Price Chopper," the man offered. "Thank you!" we said in unison.

During the ten-minute drive into Lee, we learned "that old home" of theirs was just a "summer home" they'd owned since 1999, and that the couple actually lived just outside of Boston. They also told us that they'd lived in New York City, as well as abroad in Milan, Italy. Florida was another main destination for their vacations as well, and they had a boat down there too. Congratulations Massachusetts! You guys are as successful and impressive as the Connecticans!

I personally found the people in New England to be extremely friendly and kind; however, many seemed very eager to tell total strangers all about their successes, possessions, and endeavors in life. I've never really encountered that very much in the South. I don't know if it's a cultural thing up there or if it was only specific to the places I walked through in New England. This was simply an observation I made; I took their kindness for what it was and tried not to look beyond that.

The "Price Chopper" proved to be a very good grocery store indeed. They met all my hard salami sandwich, oatmeal cookie, and cosmic brownie needs at competitive market prices. It was great to experience all of the different grocery stores along the Eastern Seaboard during the course of my adventure. Before the trek, I'd only been familiar with Winn Dixie, Publix, Safeway, Tom Thumb, Sam's club, and Wal-Mart for all of my grocery shopping needs. Now I was familiar with Ingles, Food Lion, Big Y, Price Chopper, IGA, Piggly Wiggly, Turkey Hill, Kroger and many other different types of convenient stores and gas stations. I couldn't help but feel like I'd broadened my grocery shopping horizons.

It had gotten dark when we left the Price Chopper to make our way over to the local McDonalds. We planned to get our twenty-piece Chicken McNuggets and look for a ride in the process. While en route, a small station wagon pulled over next to us and a little old lady jumped out. "Do you boys like Klondike bars?" she asked. Schweppes and I exchanged looks before simultaneously replying, "Yes!" The woman gave us each a Klondike bar, but as she was turning to get back in her car, she stopped again and said, "Well how fast can you eat those? You can each have another if you think you can finish the first one before the second one melts!" "Oh, we won't have a problem with that ma'am!" we exclaimed as she handed us each another Klondike. This lady was like the grandma that wanted nothing more than to spoil the little kids. Even if that spoiling meant giving them lots of sugar that was going to have them bouncing off the walls when their parents finally took over again. That's the way grandmas should be, that's a good grandma!

We hunkered down at McDonalds and set about our business as I ended up with forty chicken McNuggets. This may seem excessive to your average person, but to a thru-hiker it was only an appetizer preceding my Double Quarter Pounder burger. In fact, I asked them if they could make it a "Triple Quarter Pounder" and add another piece of meat. You know what they said? They said, "There isn't a button for that on the register, so we can't do it." Is this the country we live in now? A country where we can put the first man on the moon, but can't put an extra piece of what's probably kangaroo meat on a sandwich because there's no "button" for it on the register?

It took more than two minutes of debating and speaking to a manager before I finally convinced them to put another meat patty on the sandwich and charge me a dollar or two dollars for something else. Maybe this messed up their "inventory" or something, and that's why they were so reluctant to do it; but I felt like a place such as McDonalds should be capable of adding an extra meat patty to a sandwich without too much fuss. Maybe I was "THAT" customer, but once they said "we can't," I was determined to prove to them that "they could!"

Our attempts to catch a ride at McDonalds were met without success. As usual, hitchhiking in the dark was a lost cause. Besides, Lickdale had shown us what kind of people picked up hitchhikers at night. Manic depressive, bipolar, drug dealers, that's who; although I will add they were friendly ones.

Playing "Hey Mister" hadn't worked in McDonalds, especially without the aid of Katana. She'd been outside tethered to my backpack dealing with her own issues. I shouldn't say issues, because she was doing what she did best. She was procuring food from innocent bystanders. Some local kid with a skateboard was sitting on a table while feeding Katana pieces of his chicken nuggets. Her night didn't get any better than that.

When midnight rolled around and McDonalds began shutting down, we accepted that we'd be looking for a spot to camp somewhere in Lee. Just for kicks, we asked the skateboard kid (who I am fairly certain was high as a kite) if there were any good spots to camp nearby. "Yeah, there's some woods and a clearing behind the skate park just up the road, follow me!" he said enthusiastically. I was glad we asked, because this was turning out to be easier than I thought it would be. Finding a camp spot in the middle of a bustling town can always be a tricky situation.

We reached the skate park a few minutes later and walked through the front gate. After crossing the park, we passed through a gap in a fence at the very back and into some very thick forest and vegetation. All the vegetation was soaked with the night's dew and very soon I was too. "It's right back here somewhere," skateboard kid said. There was nothing. We kept pushing through the undergrowth and tightly packed trees with our headlamps set to their brightest setting. Finally, I took a step and was up to my ankles in mud. My tension started to rise... "Look for a tree with a purple mark on it, that's where the spot is," the kid said. I remained quiet.

After a few more minutes the kid finally exclaimed "Here it is right through here!" He said this while pointing through some thick vegetation. I caught up to him and looked to where he was pointing. It was literally a swampy pond full of cattails and reeds. "Are you kidding me?" I thought to myself. "I'm done with this. "Hey man, thanks for trying, but I think we're gonna call a cab," I said to the kid. "Oh okay, sorry, if it was daytime, we would've definitely found it." "Sure we would have," I thought sarcastically to myself. We waded out of the mud pit and skateboard kid rolled away into the night.

As luck would have it, no cabs were running this late at night and none of the hotels permitted dogs. At our fourth hotel, the lady felt bad and gave us a $20 discount while telling us that she'd turn a blind eye as we walked Katana in. I love people like this; people that are willing to bend or break rules at times when special circumstance calls, or when they don't really hurt anyone. I call it "victimless rule breaking." Of course this works best on a "case by case" basis, so as not to apply the argument, "well what if everyone decided to bend or break the rules, there'd be complete anarchy!" The night was saved, but my wallet was just a bit lighter.

Our little stop off in Tyringham, as well as our delay in Lee, had put us quite a distance behind Viking and Stardust. They both committed to finishing the trail by a certain date, and were now a good distance ahead. We could've caught them over the course of a couple days, but decided that route would take a lot of enjoyment out of the hike. Pushing yourself is fun, but killing yourself every day is senseless, so Schweppes and I were once again a two-man crew.

We'd both been in contact with DSOH and learned that he was several days behind. He'd been having some serious knee problems during and after Rocksylvania, but despite all the pain, was still making his way up behind us. Schweppes and I made the decision to slow down and let him catch up. I confided in DSOH that if and when he caught us, I would finish the trail with him no matter how slow his knee issues forced him to go. I liked the idea of finishing with people whom I'd known from the very beginning of the journey. DSOH and I had been close hiking partners from Georgia all the way into most of Virginia, and had seen each other through some tough times. It seemed fitting that all of us should summit Katahdin together.

Massachusetts really didn't stand out to me very much. Besides being crowned as the most beautiful border crossing, many of the things that I remember about Massachusetts were negative. The endless ranks of mosquito hordes, and frequent stretches of trail that became nothing but deep mud pits, will always stick out the most in my memory. The bugs were so bad; however, I won't reiterate those detailed descriptions again. They reached a level of utter lunacy throughout that section. Suffice it to say, they were the worst they'd ever been on the entire trail. While in Massachusetts, I knew of more than a few people who quit the trail in that state because they couldn't deal with them. In all actuality, if I had to pick a single factor that created the most misery and thoughts of "quitting" out on the trail, it would undoubtedly be the bugs. It truly felt like torture; the most torturous part being that you knew you couldn't escape them, and didn't know how long they would last.

The mud offered a new obstacle. I very quickly accepted that the only way to deal with it was to trudge through it. Katana however, was not that open minded and would stop at the edge of every mud pit, forcing me to double back and carry her across. This was cute the first couple of times because I understood her dainty nature and unwillingness to get dirty. I mean the dog would run ahead of me just so that she'd have enough time to clean any dirt or mud she might have accumulated on her fur, because she couldn't stand to be dirty for more than a few minutes. She could be covered up to her little armpits in mud, but then ten minutes later be immaculately clean again. She was obsessive about licking her fur clean. I don't know if it was vanity or hygiene, but I wouldn't put vanity past her for one second.

Doubling back to pick up Katana and carry her over the mud got old very quickly. On one particular day, I was doubling back for perhaps the twentieth time to get her, when I had an idea. It was time for Katana to overcome her fears. I was halfway through a mud pit, cradling her in my arms, when I stopped and began to lower her down. As soon as she realized what was happening, she stiffened up and began to grunt as if to say "Oh no! No! Please don't! No! Please! Stop!" TOUCHDOWN!

I set her down and released her. She lifted one paw out of the mud and held it up daintily while standing on her other three legs. She stood there frozen, looking all around her. "See, that's not so bad, is it?" I said to her. Upon hearing my voice, she turned her head to look up at me. Her look very clearly said, "You Mother-Effer! You DID-NOT just set me down in this mess!" "Oh yes I did Katana, you're gonna have to learn to accept the mud just like everyone else; dogs are supposed to love mud!" I said out loud.

After a couple of long bounds, she was on the other side, rolling around on the dry earth and bolting up and down the trail. We didn't have any more problems with mud after that. Whenever she would stop, I would turn around and act like I was coming back to get her while jubilantly saying, "Somebody wants a mud bath!" Upon seeing and hearing this, she would quickly bound across before I began to make my way back. We had reached what you might call...another understanding.

I would have to say that one of the only positive things I remember Massachusetts for, were the Buffalo wings I had in the small town of Dalton. After descending Tully Mountain and walking down Depot Street, which was actually a part of the Appalachian Trail, I came across "Mill House Tavern." Any place with the word "tavern" is going to have your typical American finger foods. You know - wings, pizza, cheese fries, beer, and other things of that particular nature; so we stopped in without a second thought.

I must confess that I consider myself a little bit of a wing snob. I think most people might admit to being a snob about a certain food they really like. Always comparing whatever that food may be to the establishment or person that makes it the best, in their personal opinion. For me it's wings, pizza, salsa, hot and sour soup, and fried rice. I measure the entire restaurant on the quality of one of those particular food items, depending on the theme of the eatery. Those food categories will cover just about any tavern, bar, grille, pizzeria, oriental, or Mexican restaurant, because those are the main food establishments I prefer.

I have my ONE place back home that I always go to for wings, and I compare all other wings from other establishments to my ONE place back home. Let me tell ya, I'd ordered wings at almost every town I'd stopped in, but none of them ever came close to my favorite place back home. Mill House Tavern however was a different story. Their wings blew me away, especially their garlic parmesan wings. I'd never seen garlic wings done the way they did them. Maybe I caught them on a good day, but these were fantastic beyond measure. It's very hard for me to concede defeat to my place back home, but these were damn good wings. The only thing my place back home did better was their homemade Bleu Cheese.

When you find a place such as this, you have to really soak it in. Over the course of about three hours, I ate twenty-five wings, one large pizza (that was also amazing), and a huge plate of cheese fries loaded with bacon. I was on cloud nine. "Why couldn't I eat like this during those pancake challenges?" I wondered to myself. Schweppes also ate way too much.

We were waddling by the time we left that place and there was no way we could go any further that day. We doubled back up the road and made our way into the woods a short distance off the trail. I was one fat, happy hiker, but no sooner had we gotten setup; the cries from a pack of coyotes pierced the darkness and echoed through the forest along the mountain side. Every few minutes they'd start up again from another direction, indicating they were moving along at a pretty good clip. I kept my ears open so that I could bring Katana inside if they got much closer, but they never did.

I awoke sometime around 11 pm to my bladder screaming to be depressurized. I was still way too full to even want to move, so I did what any practical hiker would do and improvised. I unzipped my canopy and rolled way over onto my side while pulling the edge of the hammock down to give myself a clear shot. "Ahhh," the technique worked perfectly. "Now this is camping!" I thought. Peeing without even having to get out of bed! There was only one problem with my master plan of laziness. About three quarters of the way through my bladder evacuation I realized that I was peeing right onto my sandals. "DAMN IT!" I hissed as I quickly adjusted my aim and finished up. I was highly annoyed with myself for several seconds, but laughed it off fairly quickly. Luckily, they were sandals, because had it been my other shoes, that pee would have been soaked in there for days, causing me to reach new levels of annoyance.

Massachusetts slowly passed by as we crossed into late summer. We continued to take the days slow and short to afford DSOH the time to catch up. Most of those days were spent in a light downfall of rain; nothing too heavy or torrential, just a light and steady rainfall that lasted all day, or on and off throughout the days. This was what the conditions were like on the day we summited Mount Greylock, the tallest mountain in Massachusetts. It was windy and cold, with light on and off rain, made worse by the constant twenty to thirty mile per hour winds that whipped the rain into our faces with a stinging ferocity.

Greylock wasn't a very big mountain or a tough climb compared to most mountains on the AT, but at three thousand five hundred feet, it was big for Massachusetts. The most notable aspect of this mountain was the top, and besides a few other particular mountains, Greylock had one of the most unique and memorable summits of the entire trail.

Atop the mountain sat an enormous observation tower made of stone that also served as a veterans' war memorial. Powerful were the words inscribed in the granite that made up this tower...they read: "ERECTED BY MASSACHUSETTS IN GRATFUL RECOGNITION OF THE LOYALTY AND SACRAFICE OF HER SONS AND DAUGHTERS IN WAR. THEY WERE FAITHFUL EVEN UNTO DEATH." Finished in 1932, it served to honor the state's dead from WWI and subsequent conflicts. The entire structure was beautiful, while the view across the Berkshires was equally breathtaking. I could have spent the entire day up there if it hadn't been for the dismal weather conditions.

We were slated to enter the municipality of Williamstown after descending Greylock and a few other mountains that made up the climb to its summit from the north side. Williamstown was where we planned to stay the night and meet DSOH the next day. As we traversed Mt. Williams and were on our way down Mt. Prospect, we decided to get our ducks in a row for our stay there before the weather got any worse.

235

One noticeable change between the northern and southern sides of the eastern United States, besides sweet tea and iced coffee, were the prices of just about everything. The cost of everything up north seemed to be exorbitant. The prices for hotels were two and three times higher than the prices of hotels in the south. What used to cost us $40 a night down south now cost $90 to $110 up there. It was quite a kick in the pants since most of us were getting poorer and poorer the further north we went. However, where there's a will, there's a way, and the system can always be played.

We took a break and sat down under a grove of pine trees to make some phone calls. We had the numbers of about half a dozen hotels for Williamstown in our guidebook and decided to do some price checking ahead of time so that we weren't wandering around in the rain when we finally got down there. The town of Lee had taught us that lesson.

Schweppes did all the talking on speaker phone in his smooth south western Virginia accent. I'm going to leave out the names of the hotels and just refer to them in the order we called them. We dialed hotel #1 and an Indian person answered the phone. "Yes hello, I'm a thru-hiker on the Appalachian Trail and I'm looking for a room tonight for me and one other person as well as a small dog, what are your rates?" "One hundid dollah per-nite," the voice replied. "Oh come on! Were on a budget, can you do any better?" "Sevendie-five dollah plus tax!" "Ok, we'll think about it and call you back."

Schweppes called hotel #2 and another Indian person answered the phone. This was a comical coincidence that had us exchanging smirks. "Yeah, I'm a hiker looking for a place tonight, what's your rate?" "Ninetee nine dollah per-nite!" "Oh come on! We just called Hotel #1 and they said they would do $75, could you do any better?" "I do Sevendie!" "Ok, we'll think about it and call you back."

Schweppes dials hotel #3 and ANOTHER Indian person answered the phone, each one having a heavier accent than the last. By this third phone call, we were trying very hard to suppress our laughter at the subsequent monopoly that Indians seemed to have on the hotel business in Williamstown. "Yes, I'm a hiker looking for a place to stay tonight, what are your rates?" "One hundid ten dollah!" "Aww man that's pretty steep, we just got off the phone with Hotel #2 in the area and they said they would do seventy." "I do Sevendie, pick you up and bring you back!" "Ok! Not a bad deal! We're on the mountain right now, but we'll call you when we get down to the road!"

We ended up calling hotel #4 simply because we were having too much fun, and once again an Indian person answered the phone. We were giggling like school girls and I'm sure they could hear it over the speaker phone. Schweppes gave the guy the spiel and waited for the response. "Ninety dollah per night!" he said emphatically. Schweppes came back with, "Wow, that's just not gonna work for us, hotel #3 just said they would do seventy." He quickly replied, "Ok, I do sixty." Schweppes then asked, "Can you pick us up too?" ...short pause... "Yah, I send someone to pick you up."

The exchange continued, "We have a dog with us, a very small dog, about 15 pounds, is that ok?" ...longer pause... "Uh, that's ok." Then our final response was, "Perfect! We'll call you when we get to the road!" He replied, "Ok, see you soon."

"BINGO!" Just a little haggling and friendly competition between local businesses and we had gotten the price down $40 from the town average. Honestly, it still felt like a rip-off due to the quality of the rooms, but that's the price you paid up there.

The next day in Williamstown was another rainy and cold one. DSOH rolled in around 3 pm and we all got to catch up after not seeing each other for over a month and a half. Laser and Coma were still several days behind, although DSOH wasn't sure if they were hiking together. We all needed a few gear replacements and set out across town in the rain to where an outfitter was supposed to be. We arrived only to find out the building had been closed for over two years. It ended up being a three mile round trip in the rain before we finally got back to our hotel room. It turned out the place we really needed to reach was less than half a mile in the opposite direction we originally went. It just wouldn't have been the same adventure without those little turnarounds.

August 14 was my 138th day on the trail, my last day in Massachusetts, and my first day in Vermont. After rounding up over a two-thousand-foot climb, then a nice flattish walk for a little over a mile, I ran smack into the border sign, as well as the sign announcing the start of the "Vermont Long Trail."

The Vermont Long Trail is older than the Appalachian Trail, and actually served as an inspiration for the creation of the Appalachian Trail. At around two hundred and seventy miles long, the "VLT" and the AT share the same trail for one hundred and five miles before the VLT branches off towards Canada, while the AT continues on towards New Hampshire. I was 1,592.8 miles into my journey as I stood at that sign.

237

CHAPTER 15: VERMONT

"HAH! HAH! More like VerMUD!"

Vermont was a tough state for me. If there was ever a place where my luck truly ran out, it was Vermont. It seemed like everything that could go wrong for me, did go wrong in this state. Around one hundred fifty miles of trail resides in Vermont, and after a record setting amount of rain that wasn't quite finished that summer, the trail had turned into a sea of mud. The mud in Vermont made Massachusetts mud look like child's play. Out of the one hundred fifty miles of trail there, I would say close to a hundred miles of it was nothing but mud when I hiked through.

Besides the mud, Vermont would also prove to be the state where we began climbing mountains again. Ever since Pennsylvania, the frequency and size of the mountains had diminished considerably. That was why all the states from Pennsylvania up until Vermont had been plagued by insects; because the elevation had been in the bug breeding zone. In Vermont, at higher altitudes, I enjoyed a bug-free wilderness once again. It was almost like magic. No sooner did we cross into Vermont, the bugs all but disappeared; but... the mud increased ten-fold.

I only went a few miles into Vermont on my first day. Schweppes, DSOH, myself, and another hiker named "Loba" stopped atop a nameless mountain and made camp near some power lines.

Loba was a female hiker from Chicago who was in her mid-twenties. The word "loba" means "female wolf" and connects to Native American folklore. She earned the name due to the fact that she used to work with wolves on a reservation prior to coming out on the trail. Loba was well-traveled, a Biology major, and also had a wealth of knowledge that pertained to all things natural. I first met her as one of the hikers at Dismal Falls. I'd seen her intermittently from then on, and continued to run into her all the way through New Hampshire, before she "flip flopped" and skipped up to Katahdin to beat the cold weather; then, she hiked back south to the Maine/New Hampshire border and completed the trail.

Power lines were always interesting structures to come across on the trail. All the trees were cleared out in a perfectly straight path so the power line towers have an uninterrupted journey to the next town. A string of large power lines will literally cut a perfectly straight path up and over a mountain, and on to wherever the next pocket of civilization may be. You can see the clear cut path they make through the forest for well over fifty miles sometimes. I often daydreamed about following the power lines just to see where they'd take me. They seemed to use the most direct route, as no matter what the terrain, they always traveled in a straight line in order to get to their final destination.

At this point in the journey, I considered myself a veteran of hammock camping. It had also become a game for me to hang my hammock in awkward and noteworthy places. Across streams, in front of waterfalls, on cliff edges, on rocks, fire towers, in shelters, you name it! I was building quite an impressive collection of cool places to hang. On my first day in Vermont, I checked "power lines" off that list. The distance between the two poles was perfect. I got my hammock strung up and immediately dubbed this new technique "Power Hanging." Not the smartest place to hang a hammock, but what's living if you're not living dangerously or foolishly every once in a while?

We enjoyed a gorgeous sunset afforded to us by the power line clearance of the forest. Had there been no power lines, then there wouldn't have been a clearing, and subsequently no view from atop this mountain. At just over three thousand feet, it was quite cold. I set up my rain fly as a blocker from some of the wind and drifted off to sleep as thousands of volts of electricity surged above me; a power-hang indeed!

The next morning was freezing, and rain drizzled down. I hadn't been expecting rain, so it was pure luck that I had put my rain fly up the night before. I was no longer prepared for this type of cold due to the fact that I'd sent all my winter clothes and gear back home while in Southern Virginia. I was going to need those back soon if I was going to survive the Northeast chill during the fall months.

DSOH and Schweppes had left about two hours ahead of me that morning. I couldn't bring myself to crawl out of my cozy warm hammock to pack up in the frigid wet air. Something about sleeping in a tent makes you get up early I suppose.

Setting out that morning, I felt as if I were in a freezing wet jungle. Everything was so green, alive, and overgrown; but every step was in mud. Normally, I'd try and hop from rock to rock or skirt the side of the mud pit by tip toeing along the edge of the vegetation, while trying to keep my feet dry and clean for as long as possible. As soon as the first misstep occurred, and a foot would sink down to ankle level in the mud, it was game over. There was no more tiptoeing around or through the mud once that happened. Once I was muddy, with nothing left to lose in the way of foot warmth and cleanliness, I simply steamrolled through it from then on. I suppose this was for the best, since I definitely moved much quicker when I wasn't worried about how muddy I got.

I was less than two miles out from the power lines while steamrolling through the Vermont wilderness, when I crashed through some vegetation to find DSOH and Schweppes standing around a modest fire. I'd previously been under the impression I was going to have to push really hard in order to catch up with the two of them.

"I figured you guys would be six miles ahead of here by now," I said to them. "We got here and found this fire was still smoking from someone else the night before, so we built it back up and haven't been able to move for the last hour and a half," DSOH replied. I huddled up next to the flames, and there we sat for the better part of the next hour. This was the coldest weather we'd encountered in months, and none of us had expected, nor prepared for it. The warmest thing any of us had were our rain jackets and that fire.

We planned to push through the muddy back country for another nine miles until we reached a road that led into the town of Bennington. The weather was only slated to get worse, so we figured we might as well get into town and purchase some warmer socks or thermals until we could get our families to mail our warm clothes back to us again.

I got ahead of DSOH and Schweppes, finding myself in quiet solitude once again. When the trail wasn't mud, it was wooden planks laid across the areas that were prone to getting dangerously deep with mud and water. If the trail wasn't wooden planks or mud, it was overgrown vegetation brushing against your body and face, getting various bugs, spider webs, and other debris caught up in your beard and hair.

Throughout the trail you constantly passed through different state parks, national parks, and mountain ranges. All of them are unique in their own way, but most places bare little difference from the previous locations you pass through. Every now and then, you will cross into a new region that is visibly different in a multitude of ways from the prior area you came from.

Vermont was the start of one of those new regions, as you could visibly tell that you were in a different place just by looking around. The climate was different, the topography was different, the trees and vegetation varied, while the abundance of water was distinctly different too. Swamps and ponds that had slowly become more commonplace on the trail up until this point were all of a sudden in great abundance-they were everywhere you looked.

Every single pond and swamp looked as if it should've had a moose wading across it. Every picture and video I'd ever seen of a moose was in a setting exactly like the ones I passed through many times a day throughout all of Vermont. This was without a doubt the start of moose country, and I wanted to see a moose ten times more than I'd wanted to see a bear. I'd seen dozens of bears in the wild and even residential neighborhoods before I came out on the trail; but never a moose. I knew they were rare to see (even for hikers), often being referred to as the "Unicorn" of the trail. Even locals who lived in these regions their entire lives confessed to never having seen a moose for the entire time they lived there. Most only admitted to seeing them on the side of the road as victims of vehicle collisions, or licking the salt that was laid down for the ice and snow.

Since the porcupine in Caledonia, I had seen virtually no wildlife besides snakes, chipmunks, and squirrels. I could count on one hand the amount of deer I saw between Pennsylvania and Vermont. The supposedly "bear-ridden" New Jersey hadn't produced a single bear for me. Not seeing much wildlife for such a long stretch had been a real drag. I was ready for all that to change. Knowing that I was finally in moose country, I wanted to see a moose with every fiber of my being. It gave me something new to look forward to when I woke up every morning.

As I began a gentle descent down Harmon Hill, I ran into a local hunter who said he was checking his trail cams to see if there were any deer nearby worth hunting that season. He confessed that out of all the trail cams he had placed in different locations, he'd only captured a few deer on them over the past couple weeks. I jokingly informed him that I hadn't seen a deer since Connecticut and his chances looked pretty slim. As we walked along and chatted about the local wildlife and places to eat in Bennington, he dropped an interesting little piece of information on me.

"You know, last week I caught a Catamount on one of my trail cams," he said. Initially, this statement meant nothing to me. "What's a Catamount?" I asked. "A panther, a mountain lion," he replied. "Really? I didn't know you guys had them all the way up here," I commented. "Oh, we have them up here, but if you do some research, everything you'll find says they don't exist this far north, but believe me, they do!" he zealously exclaimed.

This was some very intriguing information, as the thought of seeing a mountain lion out there was even better than the thought of seeing a moose. This got me wondering about how many animals I'd walked by, without even noticing them? Eighty percent of the time, the only way I ever saw an animal was if I heard it run away first, or if it was sitting in the middle or next to the trail. What about the ones that didn't run away? The ones that sat quietly in the underbrush, watching me as I walked by... For all I knew, I could've walked by a dozen Catamounts between Georgia and here without even knowing it. They could have been watching me walk by, completely oblivious to their existence, all the while contemplating whether I was worth turning into an easy meal. These were happy thoughts I pondered for a great while after talking to the hunter. "To believe or not to believe...?"

The eight hundred foot drop down to the road that led into Bennington was a treacherous one. It was nothing but huge slick rocks that were jumbled into a slippery, joint pounding staircase. The impact on the knees was considerable and the threat of falling was high. The hunter told me that he made that climb and descent twice a week to check his cameras. He was a young guy, and despite his familiarity with that area, he had a heck of a time keeping up with me on the descent. That made me feel good in a strange way because the territory was new to me, but familiar to him.

Whenever it felt like I was getting my ass kicked out there, it was nice to get some perspective on just how far I had come. It was encouraging to noticeably see how well I had adapted to the madness of the terrain, compared to the average person who lived around that particular terrain their entire life. It illuminated the huge difference between living "around" something and living "in" it. When you eat, sleep, AND breathe something every day for months at a time, it can sometimes trump someone who has maybe just ate and slept around it for their entire lives. It's that "breathing" element that sets you apart...

Once at the road, the hunter offered me a ride into Bennington, but I respectfully declined as I cited my plan to wait for my companions. I wasn't sure how long it would be until they arrived and I didn't want to keep the hunter waiting. He understood as we shook hands and bid each other farewell. Less than an hour after that, DSOH and Schweppes arrived, and we were able to catch a ride in a Jeep.

Bennington was everything I pictured a small affluent town in America to be. Almost nothing was commercialized, as hobby shops, small restaurants, Mom and Pop stores, cafés, and bakeries dotted the clean sidewalk-lined streets. Bennington had a classical old look and feel to it, but also a modern feel at the same time; it seemed perfectly balanced between the two. For this reason, it will always remain one of my favorite towns. It had that very modest small town feel, without some of the draw backs that many of the small towns along the trail suffered from - such as the lack of grocery stores or other simple commodities that most of us took for granted.

To our pleasant surprise, we were able to split a room for fifteen bucks each. This was the lowest motel price we'd encountered up north so far. The biggest plus being that it was across the street from a thrift store, where we were able to find some cheap thermals and heavier socks to get us through the cold Vermont nights.

The next morning was cold and rainy once again, but we still decided to hike out nevertheless. As we were all packed up and ready to head out the door into the rain, I looked over at the other two, and half jokingly said, "I wouldn't be against staying here another night, I mean the price was certainly right." DSOH and Schweppes were silent as they both stopped what they were doing; I knew they were thinking about it. No one wants to leave a warm, dry, cozy room when it's cold and rainy outside. DSOH finally broke the silence by saying, "Yeah, me either." We both looked at Schweppes who was still sitting on the edge of his bed in silence, staring at the floor. Then DSOH kicked off one of his boots and exclaimed, "Whoops, my boot's off! Now we have to stay!" "Yeah I agree," Schweppes quickly replied; and just like that - it was settled.

Very early on in Vermont I once again began to feel the monotony of the journey, and for the first time during the adventure, I wanted to hurry up and be done. I felt like I hadn't enjoyed myself at all since the end of New

York. The combination of bugs, mud, rain, cold, and lack of wildlife was eating away at me more than ever. I was missing my little beach community back home. I had begun living in a constant state of dispirited melancholy, and it was taking a huge toll on me psychologically. Since the latter half of New York I'd been covered in bug bites or mud almost continuously, with nothing to make the suffering feel worthwhile. I didn't see or experience once in a lifetime events or views anymore. I was simply suffering along, day after day, with no end in sight and the promise of knowing the terrain was only going to get more difficult as I crept further north. I was ready for the big payoff and the momentous feeling of accomplishment that would come with touching the sign at the top of Katahdin. Staying focused on that goal was what kept me going through all the malaise.

If there was one thing I prided myself on, up until Vermont, it was my ability to never be caught in the rain unprepared while I slept. What I mean by this, is that I always had my rain fly set up on the nights that it rained. There were plenty of nights when I put up my rain fly and it didn't rain; but there was never a night when I didn't put it up and it did rain (besides that momentary drizzle one morning back in Georgia). My luck had held out for over sixteen hundred miles. I never wanted to erect my rain fly if I didn't feel like I absolutely had to. It normally added around five minutes onto my set-up time and ten minutes onto my breakdown time. Plus, dealing with the tiny knots and aluminum stakes in freezing cold weather was just a pain in the ass that usually resulted in dirty numb fingers. I only erected my rain fly when I was almost certain I might get showered on.

On one of those nights, early on in Vermont, while camping near the summit of Glastenbury Mountain, my luck ran out. It had been a beautiful evening, and although it was very chilly, the skies seemed relatively clear and calm. I made the decision to leave my rain fly in the pack, as I fell asleep that night without giving it a second thought.

At 3 a.m. I awoke to water dripping onto my face as it soaked through my canopy. If I thought putting on wet clothes and shoes in the morning had been miserable; this was on a whole new level. The panic of waking up and realizing that my warm dry shelter wasn't so warm or dry anymore, is just the half of it. I then had to scramble out as fast as I could and began to dig in my backpack (that was also soaking wet), grab my rain fly, unpack it, and set it up in the pouring rain. All of this while knowing that every extra second it took me...hundreds of drops of water were soaking the only warm gear I had. In the right location at the wrong time, this sort of mistake could be downright fatal.

By the time I got my rain fly up, I was soaked and my sleeping bag was very damp. I crawled back in, too tired to waste any extra energy being upset with myself. "Just another obstacle to overcome, Kyle; it's all gonna make that last day on Katahdin seem that much sweeter..." I told myself. I laid there for a moment, letting my sleeping bag absorb all the new moisture off my body. My canopy was still soaked and the water was periodically dripping onto my sleeping bag and face. I pulled the hood of my bag over my head, rolled over, and went back to sleep.

The next couple of days after that rainy morning were actually quite gorgeous. Those were the most beautiful days that I could remember since probably New York or Pennsylvania. The temperature was in the seventies and the air was dry with a gentle breeze, all beneath a mackerel sky. It was unbelievably uplifting, and did wonders for my morale. Besides the good weather, magic and coincidence were also in the air.

I spent most of the day walking along with DSOH, talking about anything and everything, just like we used to do back in the early days. We embarked on a huge climb up Mount Stratton when DSOH randomly said, "Man I've been craving some real meat lately." He continued with, "Like some steak or some ground beef, you know...REAL meat!" "I know what you mean man, me too," I replied. After that short exchange, we never said another word about it.

Mount Stratton is famous for being the birth place of the Appalachian Trail. It's said that Benton MacKaye was on the summit of Mount Stratton when the plans were conceived and drawn out for the AT. This summit turned out to not only be the birth place of the AT, but also the birthplace of some impending magic. We reached the summit at four thousand feet a little after noontime, sat on some rocks near a large fire tower, and soaked up the sun.

We sat there and snacked for over thirty minutes when three day-hikers approached us from a different side trail. The man and two women chatted with us while picking our brains about thru-hiking as they expressed interest in thru-hiking the trail one day themselves. We'd been chatting for around ten minutes when the man randomly asked us, "Do you guys want some Syrian Meat Pies?" Simultaneously, DSOH and I turned to look at each other, remembering his statement from earlier while climbing the mountain. WHOA! "Yes, please! Thank you so much!" we replied.

The pies were a triangular shaped croissant type bread, that were stuffed with some type of ground meat (like ground beef). It was too weird how something like that could come to you right after talking about it, on top of a four-thousand-foot mountain no less. Like I said previously, you could "will" things to yourself out there, as DSOH had willed those Syrian Meat Pies right into our hungry little hands.

A short time later, DSOH and I descended Mount Stratton together. Since DSOH's knee trouble, he was hiking considerably slower, probably half the speed I normally liked to maintain. On that day, speed didn't matter; I was going to enjoy the weather, the good conversations, and the good company - regardless.

After descending Stratton, the terrain became mild. The miles slowly ticked by as we crossed rivers and streams, while passing beneath the pines that grew so abundantly at those elevations. Once again, as we walked along, DSOH thought out loud and said, "I could really go for a couple of ice cold beers right about now." That was all he said. Nothing further was mentioned and we didn't give it a second thought.

Several miles later we crossed a dirt road before reaching a side trail that led to a spot called "Prospect Rock." We were still in no hurry and decided to check it out. Several hundred feet down the side trail, we hit Prospect Rock, but also ran into an older couple as they sat and enjoyed the surrounding view. It was unique to most of the views that I was accustomed to seeing out there. The majority of views were at the tops of mountains or at least high enough to tower above the landscape. This one was just the opposite. It wasn't low, but it certainly wasn't the top of a mountain either. Prospect Rock seemed to be sitting in a giant bowl. When you stepped out onto the precipice, you could look around one hundred and eighty degrees while looking up and out at the surrounding mountains. It was a paradox when compared to most of the views out there. You were looking out and up, instead of down and out. We didn't want to interrupt the couple too much, so we took in the view and started to head back to the main trail.

When we got back on the AT, we hadn't gone more than a hundred feet when we heard a voice call, "Wait!" We turned around to see the older man walking after us. "Would you two like a beer?" he asked. I can't be positive, but I'm pretty sure my jaw hit the dirt, as it dropped in disbelief. "Yes please! Thank you so much!" we replied for the second time that day. "Dude, what's going on?" I said to DSOH in a low voice. "Man I don't know, this is too weird," he replied.

The man went over to his truck (which was parked on the side of the dirt road) and returned with a couple of Anchor Steam beers from a brewery out in San Francisco. To this day, that was the most refreshing beer I ever had. It quite literally quenched my thirst when all beer usually did was quench my social anxiety.

As we toasted and cheered our beers in celebration of lightning striking twice that day, we couldn't help but talk about the crazy coincidences that had taken place. "I think there might be something to this," DSOH said. "Don't abuse the power!" I cautioned him. "I'm gonna try this one more time," he replied before following up with, "I could really go for some jelly beans." Our pace quickened for the first time that day, as we were now eagerly walking faster in anticipation of our arrival at Spruce Peak Shelter.

We finished up the last two miles of our eighteen-mile day into Spruce Peak just as it was getting dark. There were five other hikers already there, including Schweppes. As we walked into the shelter area, I enquired loudly, "Does anyone have any jelly beans?" There was silence for a few seconds before one guy (we later found out was named "Sugar Glider") answered, "I have some gummy bears..." "Close enough!" DSOH exclaimed.

As I lay in my hammock that night, I realized I only had around five hundred miles left to go. It felt like the end was just around the corner. I remembered when the first five hundred miles of the journey felt like an immeasurable accomplishment. Now it felt like the end was rushing towards me faster than I would've liked. Several days before, I'd been in a low place and thoroughly worn out with the journey. The recent beautiful and magical days once again reminded me of how amazing it was to be out there. It gave the bad days their place and made the good days seem better than you could ever imagine.

I thought back to what I was doing at my first five-hundred-mile mark. Oh yeah, lying on the ground in excruciating pain with a mangled ankle, thinking my hike was over. I couldn't help but marvel in disbelief at how far I had come since then. This brought me to another interesting realization. Several weeks into the adventure, as my confidence began to grow and I'd seen countless people drop off and quit, I'd always felt like "hot shit" (for lack of a better description) for undertaking the journey and remaining on the trail. This was true for many thru-hikers. We took a lot of pride in knowing that not many people could do what we were doing, and it showed. I'm sure some of us came off as cocky or arrogant at certain times when dealing with day-hikers or townsfolk. We were simply excited with the discovery of our new-found abilities within ourselves, but hadn't quite learned how to project that confidence with grace.

As time went on, I would always reflect back to the different stages of the journey when I'd felt like a hot shot. I would intermittently remember the 200 mile Kyle, the 500 mile Kyle, the 1,000, the 1,500 mile Kyle, and then think to myself, "That Kyle was an amateur compared to what I had become now." As I sat in my hammock that night and realized that in another hundred miles, after more experiences and hard lessons learned, I'd look back on the Kyle of that night and think, "That guy was a dilettante compared to who I am now." It was with that realization that I felt myself grow as a person and gain some much needed humility. As human beings, we are always growing, as well as learning, and should never lose sight of that. Who "you" are tomorrow can be that much wiser, better, and knowledgeable than who "you" were yesterday. Never let your pride get the best of you, because you can always be better than you are, and you're always learning. Recognize it and be humble, while helping others grow as well.

A couple days later my luck ran out once again. I was camped on the side of Bromley Mountain when for the second time on the journey I was caught in the middle of the night without my rain fly. "You're a tricky devil Vermont!" I handled the situation slightly differently this time, and instead of killing myself in an attempt to get my rain fly set up properly, I simply pulled it out, draped it over my hammock and brought Katana inside. The problem was solved in about thirty seconds. It rained steadily for the rest of the night and kept right on raining all the next morning, all that afternoon, then all night again. On the second morning it still rained and I couldn't bring myself to step out into it. I lay in my hammock till nearly noon before it finally slowed down.

After two continuous days of rain, the muddiness of Vermont had been taken to a whole other level. Water was bursting forth from everywhere. I couldn't tell if I was on the trail, walking up creeks, or slogging through swamps; the white blazes were the only beacons that kept me on track. It got so slippery at times, that unless there were rocks on the ground, I almost couldn't make my way up some of the steeper inclines due to the slickness of the mud. It was so ridiculously bad, that it surpassed anything you could even get frustrated about. It was so bad that it was comical. I couldn't help but laugh at how absolutely extreme the mud situation had become. I felt like a mad man out there, as I navigated that insanity.

Of all the good and bad things that Vermont had been so far, I felt like this was the state where I truly lost myself on the trail. I went slightly mad and "went native" so to speak, as I finally began loving every last bit of the experience; the good, the bad, and the ugly. The indifference, acceptance, disdain, and hate for all the obstacles and challenges I encountered out there had all but vanished. Now, all that was left was this crazy maniacal love for all of it... the mud, the rocks, the cold, and the terrible weather. I was done trying to ignore or curse them, and instead embraced all of it. I finally realized that it was an attitude such as this that set thru-hikers apart from every other person that couldn't or wouldn't complete this adventure. Aristotle said, "Suffering becomes beautiful when anyone bears calamities with cheerfulness, not through insensibility, but through greatness of mind." That quote pretty much sums up the state of mind that you have to adopt in order to overcome the challenges of the Appalachian Trail. You'll look like a crazy person, as well as a glutton for punishment in the eyes of most, but this is the state of mind required to complete such an endeavor without quitting or having a terrible time.

There are some things that money can't buy, and greatness of mind is one of them. You can have all the money in the world, to do whatever and go wherever you want, but it won't help you walk every step of the 2,185 miles that make up the Appalachian Trail. You can have all the money and fancy gear, but when the shit hits the fan, the temperatures drop, the sky falls out, and you're up to your shins and eyeballs in mud and bugs, money isn't going to be the deciding factor in whether you go home or keep going. In order to do this, you have to have the strength, will, and determination within you. That's something you can't buy, because you're either born with it, or life molds it into you. This is the appeal of undertaking endeavors such as this. You gain something that nobody can ever take away from you; something that not everyone has; something that even the people who seem to have it all... can sometimes lack.

August 23rd was the day before my 25th birthday. I'm not really that big on birthdays, and the thought of spending it out in the woods, while not hearing from anyone felt like as good a birthday as any. I simply wasn't in a hurry to get anywhere or do anything in celebration of the day I was born.

Most of the forest I walked through at that time was pine grove and paper birch that was frequently bisected by overflowing streams and creeks, from all the rain we'd been having. In the middle of one particularly beautiful pine grove, I came across what I can only describe as a rock garden. The rocks were stacked in every which way; bridged, piled, leaning, balancing, sitting on branches, and wedged into nooks. There wasn't a loose rock on the ground, as every single one of them had been collected and put towards this modern art spectacle in the middle of the woods. It was almost creepy to look at; there seemed to be no rhyme nor reason for any of it, whatsoever. It was like the twilight zone, as if these rocks had all levitated off the ground, then settled in bizarre amalgamations, leaving not a single one of them in a natural spot. The pine needle strewn floor was clean, clear, and smooth of all rocks. I took some pictures and moved on.

I caught up to DSOH a little while later as we hiked together for the rest of the afternoon. Not long after meeting up, we reached a cliffy overlook with a view of a remote airfield in the distance. We sat down and relaxed while Katana milled around and explored the area, as she usually did when we stopped for short breaks. About five minutes after we stopped, I heard a tumbling crash and a thud to the right of the cliff. I looked around, but didn't see Katana anywhere in sight. "KATANA!" I yelled. I still didn't see her, but heard something rustling over the edge. I quickly bounded over to the ledge and looked down. Twenty feet below was Katana standing on another ledge looking back up at me.

The ledge where she stood was covered in shrubs, and was about six feet across by three feet wide, jutting out from the cliff face. There was a forty-foot drop on all sides of the ledge; she was incredibly lucky to have fallen onto the little outcropping. If she had fallen anywhere else, I have no idea if she would have survived, or if I would've even been able to get to her.

For the life of me, I couldn't figure out how she managed to fall down there. The rock face going down was covered in shrubs and bushes, so I assumed that had slowed her fall on the way down and cushioned her landing. She was frantically trying to climb back up, but kept tipping backwards onto her back, perilously close to the ledge. "STOP!" I loudly instructed. I looked to see where I could make my way down, but there was no safe path. The worst thing I could do was nothing, so I began to climb down while I held onto whatever rocks I could grab, and also gripped the bases of some of the larger shrubs growing out of the side of the cliff.

I made it down and picked her up. "Now what?" I thought to myself as I looked back up at DSOH. I tucked her under my arm and began to slowly claw my way back up. It was treacherous and more than once I thought I wasn't going to be able to climb any higher while utilizing only one hand. Finally, I was able to get high enough to reach up and pass her off to DSOH before pulling myself the rest of the way up with both hands. Yet another life or death crisis had been averted.

We reached a road several miles later, and DSOH bought me an early birthday dinner at a little joint that was situated a half mile down the road called "The Whistle Stop." We had no plans of going into town, but a nice elderly couple in a Subaru randomly offered to take us into the city of Rutland. One rule of the trail is that you never passed up an offer on something that you'd normally have to work for, so we accepted. We stayed at a free hostel called "The Yellow Deli," where the atmosphere was friendly, laid back, and a nice reprieve from all the mud on the day before my birthday.

August 24th arrived as I turned a quarter of a century old. Where had the time gone? Who knows, but I should've spent more of it doing things like hiking the Appalachian Trail. In celebration of the quarter century milestone, I decided to attempt a 24-hour hike. Since I missed the four-state-challenge back at the end of Virginia, I was going to make up for it by hiking as far as I could over the course of 24 hours. My goal was to try and do sixty miles and end up in Hanover, New Hampshire. Looking at the elevation profile, I knew this was a long shot with a high chance of failure.

Over those sixty miles, I literally had no flat ground. The map showed climb after climb, many of them a thousand feet or more, including a brutal three thousand foot climb up Mount Killington. It was pretty obvious that was probably the worst place to attempt sixty miles in 24 hours, but since it was my milestone birthday spot, that was where I was going to attempt it. To add to the idiocy of it all, we had trouble getting a ride out of town and didn't end up getting back to the trail until almost noon. That meant I would start the 24-hour hike at noon. That was genius!

As I stood there at the base of Beacon Hill with DSOH and set the timer on my watch to "zero," he handed me a Mars candy bar. "Don't eat it until you reach Hanover," he instructed, then added "You can do this Mayor!" I felt quite jittery at that moment, as this really excited me for some reason. It was nothing I hadn't done before; hiking all day and all night that is, but this felt different. I had a time limit and a seemingly impossible distance to cover, with the largest mountain in Vermont right at the beginning. "We'll see," I replied. I took off at 11:55 am. "I'll see you in a few days!" DSOH called after me.

I kept up a blistering pace as I started down the trail. It was ten miles from my starting point to the summit of Mount Killington. I roared through the pine groves, over small streams, and across a river. Katana felt my urgency, as well as excitement, and was feeding off of it. I felt unstoppable, as nothing seemed unattainable to me as I first set out.

As luck would have it, there was a reroute of the trail from Hurricane Sandy and I missed a sign. I traveled three miles over trail that was supposed to be closed off, and when I finally crossed a half constructed bridge over a river, I completely lost the blazes and the trail. The bridge crossed over onto a crude dirt road that wasn't marked in any way. For half an hour I searched around the road and surrounding forest for a blaze, but couldn't find one. Finally, I gave in and followed the road. Several hundred yards down, I ran into a sign that had a laminated map nailed to it explaining the reroute. That's where I learned that I should have turned down a different trail three miles back and come down this road from the north instead of the south. Either way, the trail picked back up into the woods right at the sign and I was on my way once again.

Soon I was going up, up, up towards the summit of Killington while picking my way over the exposed tree roots that were ridiculously abundant on this mountain. The climb felt as if it went on forever, even though I was pushing myself as fast as I could the entire way up. I finally reached the summit and sat down for a quick water break and a snack. I checked my watch to find that it took me four hours and five minutes to go ten miles and climb Vermont's tallest mountain. That time should have been thirty minutes faster, but such is life.

After a ten-minute break I was off again. The descent down the north side of Killington was much more forgiving than the south side. It was more gradual and at certain points I would run and race Katana down the trail. At 6:30 pm I stopped to have a quick dinner as the sun began to sink low in the sky. It was going to be a long night and I needed to fuel up as much as I could now. I ate three hard salami bagel sandwiches in about twenty minutes before hitting the trail again.

As twilight faded and darkness fell upon me, the trail began to roller coaster, then slowly ascend. I pulled out my headlamp and pressed on. In the now slightly oxidized illumination of my lamp, it became very difficult to discern the mud from the water, from the half-covered rocks and roots. After a couple of slides and stumbles, my pace began to slow way down as the state of the trail worsened.

Sometime around 9 pm I began descending sharply over roots, rocks, and mud. Katana became stubborn and refused to walk, so I picked her up, slung her on my shoulders and continued on. As I was stepping down from some rocks, my back foot slipped off, causing me to land feet first on the muddy slope. When my feet hit, they kept right on sliding. My body went with them, until they got too far ahead and shot out from under me. I landed hard on my tail bone as I felt a stab in my hand, and the frame of my pack jammed and raked across my lower back.

I was covered in mud, but Katana was fine. I'd grabbed hold of her as I was slipping and used myself as a cushion for her when I fell. Truth be told, I probably wouldn't have fallen if both my hands had been free, but when I'd begun to fall, all my focus was on Katana's safety. When I normally would've put my hands out to catch myself or balance, they instead went to protecting her and letting my body fall where it may. I think she realized she was probably better off walking after that, and seemed very happy to do so. As a consequence of the fall, my right hand had a short but deep gash on the heel of my palm that was now oozing blood. As we often said there, "No pain, no Maine." I shook off the fall and kept going. It was shaping up to be a long night.

Not more than ten minutes later we encountered another short, but steep, smooth rock face. As I attempted to shuffle my way down, I felt my feet begin to slip. I should have crouched and slid the rest of the way down on my ass, but instead went with the sliding of my feet, and let my momentum carry me faster down the rock face. I hit the bottom fast as I felt my feet slide out from under me once again. Then...darkness.

When I saw light again, it was the tops of the trees illuminated by my headlamp as I lay flat on my back. My head throbbed and I quickly reached back, probing through my hair before pulling my hands back into the light. No blood, however the back of my head and my backpack were covered in mud. I'm not entirely sure what happened, but I can only assume that I slipped backwards hard enough and far enough to smack my head on the muddy earth with enough force to momentarily knock myself unconscious.

This shook me up a little bit. "What if I had hit my head on the rock I just slid down?" I thought to myself. I might have been unconscious up there bleeding out all night and exposed to the elements before anyone found me. Katana probably would have tried to eat me before she went in search of help! It was a scary thought, but I picked myself up and continued on.

My lower back felt like it was on fire. The force of my pack's frame scraping against me during the two falls had peeled the uppermost layer of skin from my lower back. Sweat and mud poured into my raw skin causing it to burn like hell. At this point I was beginning to second guess my Vermont night hiking decision. The terrain and conditions were just plain dangerous, but I didn't want to give up.

I kept moving at a snail's pace as my head throbbed, my hand throbbed, and my back burned. I made it down the rest of the climb and continued on through some private campground, across a road, past a pond, and into a pine grove where I stopped to assess my situation. It was after 10 pm as I calculated that I'd gone approximately twenty-five miles. I looked at the next thirty-five miles ahead of me, and they didn't look good. I had a fifteen hundred foot, nearly vertical climb ahead of me, then over a dozen nasty steep roller coaster climbs after that. I needed to make a decision before I went any further.

I had accepted there was no way that I was going to make it sixty miles in twenty-four hours over the current terrain. I was faced with a conundrum. "Do I continue on to see how far I can get in 24 hours, or do I hang up my shoes right here?" In the end, the pain of my lower back got the best of me. I didn't want to make it any worse than it already was by continuing on and letting the constant shift of my pack exacerbate my injury further. With my dignity hurting more than my injuries, I picked two pine trees and called it a night. "Happy Birthday to me..." I recall thinking.

That next morning my body felt as if it had been put through a ringer. My head was still tender and crusted with mud, while my hand was stiff and swollen to the point that I couldn't even wrap my fingers around my walking staff. The gash was packed full of mud and coagulated blood, but I had nothing to clean it out. I figured having the mud packed in there was probably a good thing, as it was keeping other germs from getting in. It brought on a whole new meaning to the phrase "just rub some dirt in it."

Something new that I hadn't noticed the night before, was that my right heel was also cracked. There was a deep split in the dried out skin on the back left side of my right heel, that was giving me a sharp stinging pain with every step. Regardless of my heel discomfort, out of all my little aches and pains, nothing hurt as badly as my back. My entire lower back felt as if multiple layers of flesh were peeled off. I felt it when I first got up, but didn't

251

think too much of it initially. Once packed and ready to go, I put on my sweat soaked shirt from the night before and threw my backpack over top of it. As I did this, the sweaty shirt was pressed into the raw area of my lower back and the resulting sensation was that of thousands of vinegar-soaked razors dragging across my skin. I winced in pain as I stood frozen, trying not to move. The pain slowly faded and I attempted to walk again... the razors came back after the first step. "Damn, this is going to be one long day," I thought.

The burning back pain persisted for most of the morning. I don't know if my body got used to it, or turned off my pain receptors, because the burning eventually faded into a warm dull feeling. The going had been incredibly slow up until that point. I passed Thundering Falls early that morning, another huge cascading waterfall that reminded me a lot of the first waterfall I'd seen on the trail back in Amicalola. The waterfall proved to be nothing more than a pleasant distraction before the hellacious climb up Quimby Mountain that probably felt tenfold worse, due to my aches and pains.

During the ascent of Quimby, I was intensely focused on the task at hand as I dug into the climb with my head down. I was perhaps three quarters of the way up when I unexpectedly smacked the top of my skull into a thick, low hanging branch. I'd hit my head on many a branch during the course of the journey, but this one felt like a slap in the face when compounded with all of my other painful distractions. To add to that, on the way down from Quimby, I slipped on another rock and fell on my ass again. It was really beginning to feel like a comedy of errors.

I didn't see another soul for most of that day, besides a one-day hiker near the falls. I was also fairly sure that Schweppes was ahead of me, as I hadn't seen him for several days when I lost him during the two -day downpour. This day and the day before had been gorgeous with perfect temperatures and clear skies. I hadn't been too fond of Vermont up until this point, but with the presence of such beautiful weather, what wasn't there to like?

When I finally finished Quimby Mountain, the mud had all but disappeared. There seemed to be a subtle change in the terrain as well. I couldn't put my finger on it, and perhaps it was only the lack of mud that I noticed, but I felt like there was something else. I couldn't pin point it exactly, but all I can say is something felt different.

Somewhere around ten miles into the day, during the early afternoon as I was steadily making my way up an extremely steep six-hundred-foot climb, covered in small pines, I noticed something I'd never seen before. It was a huge pile of crap. Not just any crap though; this was crap the likes of which I'd never encountered before. It looked like gigantic oblong bunny turds. It was much smaller than horse dung, but much, much larger than anything that could come out of a rabbit. That is unless we're talking about the rabbits from the horror movie "Night of the Lepus," but that's a different story...

As I stood there on the side of the mountain, trying to figure out what could've possibly expelled this poop; my mind settled upon the only animal I hadn't seen yet... a moose. I wasn't completely sure of that deduction, as the climb seemed way too steep to accommodate a creature as large as a moose, but I couldn't think of what else it could be. That temporarily got my mind wandering back to "Night of the Lepus," but in the end I settled on moose instead of mutant rabbits.

Keeping my eyes peeled even more than I had before, I continued on through the backcountry. I came across a crystal clear creek that ran down from some large rocks that formed a perfect bathtub. It was too good to pass up, so I gave Katana a quick soak and wash before I gave myself a turn in the natural tub. As I bathed, Katana ran up and down the trail grunting and rolling around in the dirt; making herself filthy again. It didn't make any sense. She was such a cleanly animal, but she only liked to be clean on her terms. She wanted no part in whatever cleanliness I had in mind for her, as she always preferred to lick herself clean, much like a cat. I really think she did it out of spite. If I wanted her to be dirty, then she wanted to be clean. If I wanted her to be clean, then she wanted to be dirty. She's a contrary little animal.

That little soak was exactly what I needed all day. Only a few miles after that, I came to a side trail that was marked "Lookout Tower" on my map. It was only 3 pm, but I decided I could have an early dinner at the tower, then continue walking until dark. I followed the trail for a couple hundred yards before it ended at a small cabin-like structure that had a ladder leading up to a lookout platform on the top. The cabin door was open, revealing that the inside was an empty, but open room with a loft. It had windows, a fire place, and four walls. It was basically an upscale version of a shelter, except that it wasn't labeled as such in my guide.

I ate a couple hard salami sandwiches before climbing the ladder to the observation deck. The view I encountered completely took my breath away. I had a three-hundred-degree view of rolling hills and mountain peaks for as far as the eye could see. This was without a doubt, the most dramatic and favorite view of mine in all of Vermont. It was in that moment while standing up in the tower that I decided Vermont wasn't half bad. I also realized there was no way I could hike any further that day. This was the most beautiful spot I'd found thus far in all of the one hundred fifty miles of this state, so I wasn't about to pass up the opportunity to sleep there. Plus, I wanted to get pictures of the sunset when that magical hour finally arrived.

I sat down on the porch of the seemingly abandoned cabin and began reading my book "The Temporal Void." When the sun finally did set, I was treated to one of the finest panoramic sunsets I'd ever seen. Little did I know, those particular sunsets were about to become commonplace as I inched further and further north towards New Hampshire and Maine.

The next morning the crack on my heel felt worse, my hand felt almost normal, my head felt fine, and my back had dried out even more. As long as I didn't exert myself too much, my back wouldn't be rubbed raw again when the pack shifted against my skin. The crack on my heel was now my biggest issue. I don't know what it is with every injury feeling like razor blades out there, but every step felt like someone was nicking my heel with a box cutter. To combat the pain, I began walking on the front balls of my feet to avoid setting my heels down. This worked wonderfully for my heel, but my calves were subsequently set ablaze with lactic acid. I will say the lactic acid was infinitely more tolerable than the heel pain.

Around lunch time, I descended a vast field strewn with round hay bales before ending up at a road that had a small farmer's market several tenths of a mile to the west. I wasn't about to pass up some good country food after the suffering I'd been through the previous days, so I decided to stop in. I ended up eating a pound of smoked Gouda cheese, a pound of smoked chicken breast, a blueberry pie, an apple pastry, and three Gatorades. You could have stuck a fork in me after that, because I was done.

It was another fantastically beautiful day, if not slightly too hot. The erratic temperatures were really throwing me for a loop, but I welcomed anything that wasn't freezing. I sat down on a bench in front of the small farmer's market where I fell into a peaceful sleep. I awoke some indeterminable amount of time later to Schweppes' face standing over me, smiling while holding Katana like a baby.

"Damn dude, I thought you were ahead of me," I said. "I thought I was ahead of you too," he replied. I told him about my failed sixty-mile 24-hour hiking attempt. "You know Mayor, this really isn't the best terrain to attempt something like that," was his response. "Yeah, I figured that, but it was my birthday, so I had to do something memorable." "Why didn't you go into town and get shit hammered on beer like a normal person?" "Because we're not normal people Schweppes, that's why we're out here torturing ourselves in the first place." "Good point," he replied.

We ended up figuring out that I'd passed him sometime in the dark after Mount Killington when he'd gone into town for a quick resupply at another small road. After Schweppes had his fill of cheese, chicken, and pie, we set out together into the hot Vermont afternoon.

The next six miles were brutal, with a seemingly endless rollercoaster of short but steep climbs. Most of them were smooth without rocks, making it exceptionally painful on the calves. That was the difference between a steep rocky climb, and a steep smooth climb. On the rocks, you were forced to take huge stair-stepping steps that burned your quads and strained your knees. Smooth climbs forced you to lean into the ascent and dig in with the front pads of your feet. That was my technique for most of the day, but not on anything that steep. The burning of lactic acid was once again elevated to new heights.

As we traversed the rollercoaster, we got a glimpse into the acquisition of maple syrup. We walked through huge groves of maple trees that were all being tapped for their bounty of sap. Networks of clear tubes surrounded and connected the trees like the cordoned off area for the long lines of some theme park ride. We intermittently saw the tube networks strung throughout the maple groves as we slowly chugged along.

Unexpectedly, we heard a loud crack behind us at one point and turned around just in time to see a huge oak branch come crashing down onto the trail only a couple hundred feet behind us. This was slightly unnerving. After being in the woods for so long, I'd been present for plenty of large branches randomly snapping off and falling within my vicinity; even witnessing one tree snap completely in half and fall down for apparently no reason in North Carolina. That doesn't include the branches and trees that I saw snap during horrendous storms.

What made this one unique was that this branch had fallen directly onto a spot that we'd just walked over. Sure, it missed us by a mile, but what were the chances that this exact branch would snap at the exact moment we were walking by, within easy earshot and fall right onto a spot where we'd just been? The chances couldn't have been much greater than if it had snapped seconds earlier and possibly injured or killed us...or maybe just given us a greater scare. It was one of those random occurrences that gave you something new to ponder, as you ran out of things to think about after five months of hiking through the woods.

That night we camped on Thistle Hill and built a modest fire. I roasted some hard salami over the flames and found it was even tastier than roasted summer sausage. The resemblance to the flavor of bacon or a nice steak was uncanny. All in all, it was another tough day made better by the surprise of a familiar face and a warm fire on that Vermont summer night. It was to be the last Vermont night of my Appalachian adventure.

My heel was once again in a more painful state the next morning as the crack continued to get longer and deeper. When I examined the wound, it reminded me of a crevice containing lava at the bottom. The skin was dry and dirty around the initial crack, but several millimeters down was bright red blood and gore. Unfortunately, my mind was focused on the pain in my heel for a good portion of the fifteen miles that day.

Nine miles out from New Hampshire, we passed into the town of West Hartford. We crossed a rather large bridge that spanned the White River, and when we reached the other side, a woman popped out of her house and beckoned us over. She cooked us breakfast in the form of omelets and sausage, then told us that over the years she had cooked breakfast for over a thousand hikers. That was generosity on an epic scale, as she asked for nothing in return. It made her feel good to do a kind deed for the strangers that passed through.

Besides feeding us, she also informed us that the bridge we just crossed was a hot spot for jumping into the White River. When someone tells me that I can jump off a bridge... I go jump off that bridge. It was maybe a little more than a thirty-foot drop, not as high as peace rock, but the difference here was that the water was clear enough to see the bottom.

The water clarity was deceptively nerve racking because it made the river look dangerously shallow. On top of that, the current was actually

255

moving at a fairly good clip. Since the jump spot was situated almost directly in the center of the river, it meant that you had over a hundred feet worth of sideways swimming through the current before you could reach the shore. "Let the streamlining begin!" Once again, I combined fun with laundry and hygiene. Four jumps later we were on our way again.

The rest of the day was full of beautiful young pine groves and a collection of slightly steep and longish climbs. It seemed that whenever you had something to look forward to at the end of the day, that day always dragged on no matter how many miles were planned.

We came across two south bounders in a pine grove that informed us they had seen a mountain lion no more than thirty minutes prior to our meeting. Both said they startled it while passing through a different pine grove before it ran off. They seemed genuine enough, but whether they really did see one or not, I'll never know. You never can trust those south bounders...

By this point, we crossed paths with dozens and dozens of our southbound counterparts. When it used to be commonplace to exchange useful information, it had now also been common to include a few false pieces of information as well.

More than once, a south bounder would inform me that there were drink machines atop an upcoming mountain. I would then kill myself racing to the top, only to find a normal mountain top strewn with trees and rocks... and no drink machines. "Those jokesters!" All they did was ruin it for the south bounders behind them. I couldn't return the favor to the original pranksters, but I could return it to the unsuspecting hikers that followed in their footsteps. It was a classic case of "not punishing" the individual who broke the rule, but punishing their peers that would now hate them for incurring the undeserved, cruel joke upon them. It was all in good fun, but I will admit that I told a couple of white lies about drink machines, snack bars, as well as a few other things that may or may not have existed on future mountain tops that the south bounders had yet to conquer.

Schweppes and I had developed a friendly rivalry as well. We'd been hiking with each other almost constantly since Damascus, Virginia and had forged an almost brotherly bond. Other hikers we ran into constantly reminded us that we acted like brothers when we were around each other. Like brothers sometimes do, we tended to bicker a lot.

When you voluntarily spend copious amounts of time around someone, a strong bond is naturally formed. What also happens when you spend copious amounts of time around a particular individual is that you also tend to get on each other's nerves quite a bit. I couldn't tell you how many hours Schweppes and I spent arguing about stupid things, trading insults, and genuinely trying to annoy each other. It became a game to pick subjects that the other was sensitive or passionate about, then make light, or make fun of them until one of us was seeing red. It was always in good fun, but I know both of us probably didn't have enough fingers and toes between us to count how many times we probably wanted to hike away and never see one another again. Of course no matter how bad the ribbing got on either of our behalf's, we were always happy and relieved to see each other at the end of the day.

If you spent enough time around Schweppes, the one thing you would find undeniably apparent was that he loved statistics. To be more specific, he loved sports statistics and knew crazy little details about almost any sports team or athlete you could think of. He was like a giant, red headed, walking sports almanac. The amount of information he knew about different sports and athletes boggled my mind. Naturally, this was the subject that I always used as a direct line to piss him off. I would casually bring up a sports subject that I knew he was passionate and well informed about. Then I would act like I knew more about it and discount anything he said while making up my own facts and telling him he was wrong. Even though he knew I was full of shit, it almost always got to him, because I wouldn't drop the charade until I knew he was positively irate.

When he didn't have sports statistics to talk about, his next favorite subject was hiking statistics. This was one way he annoyed me without even trying to. It was simply something he genuinely loved to talk about, and I'm almost positive he knew it got on my nerves. His hobby was to scour the shelter logs for familiar names of people, then look at the date for when they were last at the shelter. He would then compare how many days ahead of us they were, based on where we were on that same date, as well as the last time he saw them before that. After figuring that out, he would then begin making estimations on where they could possibly be now. Next, he would calculate how many miles per day we'd need to do in order to catch up to them at the current pace he estimated them to be going. We never had any intentions of actually catching up to those people, but he loved to crunch the numbers anyway. You could bring up a random hiker's trail name and he could tell you everything about how fast they were hiking, what their average miles per day were, when they started the trail and when he predicted they would finish the trail. He could even tell you about their gear and their base pack weight, as well as their total pack weight. The guy just kept all this information filed away inside his head. He was like some kind of Matt Damon, Good Will Hunting, statistics genius.

Since I didn't care about anyone else's hiking style besides my own and the people I hiked with, none of this information really mattered to me. That didn't stop him from droning on about it for hours at a time though. I knew he honestly enjoyed the subject, so I would usually listen in silence, giving input whenever I saw fit.

On the flipside, he also had angles that he would intentionally play against me in an attempt to annoy. His tactic was to ambiguously over-compliment me to a level of complete ridiculousness. He would do it when it was just the two of us, or even in the presence of company, it didn't matter. He would start spouting off one ridiculous compliment after another to me, and wouldn't stop until he was sure I was mad. "Mayor you're the best there ever was," or… "Mayor's arms are really big," or… "Mayors the best looking guy on the trail," or… "Mayor you're probably the best hiker out here…" and countless other ridiculous, unfounded compliments that were so skewed that I can actually feel myself getting frustrated while writing this.

Once he got started, there was no stopping him. He would start shooting off these crazy random compliments that we both knew were either completely untrue or grossly exaggerated. He knew it drove me insane, but he wouldn't stop until he'd worn me down and won. He knew he won when I became silent. I would try to sarcastically accept his compliments or even embellish their already over embellished nature in an attempt to thwart his verbal attacks. I almost never won and would always end up in brooding silence as he pelted me with several more embellished compliments for good measure. It really was ingenious, and a testament to how "killing someone with kindness" really does work, even if that kindness is less than genuine.

The trail passed into the town of Norwich as we walked along the quiet shady streets for a couple miles before emerging onto a busy expressway. New Hampshire was getting close. We walked along the sidewalk next to the busy road for over a mile, while the curious eyes of strangers passed by. They quickly surveyed the homeless looking duo that walked with a fox.

We reached the Connecticut River Bridge where the state border lay half-way across. The excitement and adrenaline rose within me at being so close to the next stage of the journey. As we approached the pillar that marked the state line, I broke into a run and threw all my pain and caution to the wind as I leapt across the state line into New Hampshire…

CHAPTER 16: NEW HAMPSHIRE

"...And I Thought Everything I Went Through Before Was Tough!"

New Hampshire was a fabled land shrouded in mystery and danger to us northbound thru-hikers. Ever since the beginning of the journey, anytime you ever complained or voiced your concerns over the difficulty of the trail to someone who had done it before, they always had the same response: "Just wait until you get to New Hampshire!" Then, when you asked, "What's in New Hampshire?" They always replied, "The White Mountains." "What's so bad about them?" you would inquire further. "You'll just have to find out if you make it that far..." was the final answer.

I didn't know exactly what to expect from New Hampshire, but I knew the White Mountains were billed as the most challenging section of the entire trail. Insanely challenging! Maybe even life threateningly challenging! New Hampshire had been built up so much over the last 1,740 miles that I didn't know what to expect or believe. I had nightmarish visions of climbing vertically hand over hand for miles on end, where one slip would mean my death! Visions of snow drifts over my head with frost bite and the threat of freezing to death looming around every corner!

Yes, I would be lying if I said I wasn't just a little bit nervous about what New Hampshire might have in store for me. It was an excited nervousness though. Besides the purported difficulty of the next region, it was also said that from New Hampshire to Katahdin was the wildest and most remote section of the entire trail. This awakened a new sense of wonder in me that I hadn't felt since my first weeks out there. I remember thinking eagerly to myself, "I'm crossing into an even wilder unknown!" Despite my anxieties, I'd become one with the trail, ready to take whatever else it threw at me... with a smile.

The first obstacle of New Hampshire wasn't a mountain. Funny enough it was the town of Hanover, but for the sake of accuracy, you couldn't really call it a real town. Yes, people lived there, and there were businesses and super markets, but to be more precise, Hanover was nothing more than one big college campus. The Ivy League college of Dartmouth consumed the entire town, as everything there seemed to only exist to serve the students. Everywhere you turned, you saw Dartmouth related buildings or athletic fields, while the options for places to eat were endless. Hanover was certainly the most modern and bustling town I passed through on the entire journey. The trail snaked its way through the grid of streets for about a mile before it skirted by a soccer field and disappeared back into the woods.

The obstacle for me wasn't only to avoid getting stuck in this town that seemed to have an endless choice of restaurants and cafes to sample, as well as places to relax. The main problem was I couldn't hike any further than Hanover without having my cold weather gear. I had contacted my family several days before and asked them to send my warm clothes and accessories to the Hanover Post Office. It was closed when we got there, so I was stuck until at least mid-morning the next day. This wasn't a problem, because after the rough stretch of trail and all the pain I'd endured, I was ready to take a day or two to recover. Schweppes and I made camp at the trailhead, just beyond the soccer field, behind the tree line and called it a New Hampshire day.

The next morning, I picked up my package, but was disappointed to find that my second package hadn't arrived yet. That meant I would be there until the post office opened the next day. Once again, I didn't complain about being forced to wait another day. The late package was nothing but a blessing in disguise. DSOH hiked in that afternoon and the three of us had dinner at a local burrito joint.

That evening, while walking Katana, I was stopped by a middle aged woman, her husband and their teenage son who thought she looked like a fox. "Actually she is a fox ma'am." "WHAT!?" the woman exclaimed. "Yeah, I caught her way back in Tennessee when she was clawing into my food bag." "No fucking way!" the lady half screamed in excitement and bewilderment. "Oh yeah, she was pretty feisty! She bit me multiple times, but eventually I beat the wild out of her and now she's tame as a house cat." "You're fucking kidding me!" She repeated. "Nope!" I declared with assurance.

The look on this woman's face, combined with her vulgar and surprised reaction, was too much. I couldn't keep my poker face, nor suppress my shit eating grin any longer. "He's fucking with you Mom," her teenage son finally said with a chuckle. "Yeah, he's fucking with you hunny," her husband chimed in. "What, no? Are you fucking with me?" she said with surprise, still wanting to believe the whopper I'd just told her. "Yeah, ya got me, she's a Shiba Inu," I managed to say through my laughter. "I'm sure you get asked that all the time and I'm sure you're sick of it," she added. "You have no idea!" I replied. This mild looking foul mouthed family had made my day.

DSOH and Schweppes hiked out the next morning as I walked back into town to get my late package. With all of my cold weather gear and snacks my family had sent, I could hardly get everything into my pack. I spent over an hour packing, unpacking, and moving things around in an attempt to make it all fit. When I finally did, my pack weighed close to sixty pounds. That little radio backpack wasn't built for that kind of stress and I knew its days were numbered.

The pack was so uncomfortable and already in a rough state of disrepair after being dragged over seventeen hundred miles, that I feared it might not complete the journey. It had tremendous sentimental value to me after everything I'd been through, so I really wanted to see it go all the way.

That's another funny thing about hiking the trail. I don't know if it's just me, or if it's other people too, but the silliest things gain a crazy amount of sentimental value out there. I started with a two liter Gatorade bottle at the beginning of the journey, before finally losing it somewhere in New York. After taking a break, I'd forgotten to pick it back up when I moved on. I thought I might cry when I eventually realized it was gone. It had come so far with me, only to be lost all alone in the wilderness.

Many people had new shirts or shorts sent to them as their current ones wore out or got too dirty and sweat soaked to even wash anymore. Not me, I was taking all of my original clothes all the way to Katahdin. I had the same two pairs of socks, underwear, t-shirts, and shorts since the very beginning. Every single one of them had holes, tears, and pieces of fabric stringing off, but I'll be damned if I was going to cast them aside and not let them make the entire journey.

Another terrible loss was my Sealine Dry Bag that finally split open later on in Maine. It was a sad day having to leave it in a dumpster and replace it with a new dry bag. Every time something got lost or broken, I felt like I was losing a teammate. Call it pathetic if you will, but one becomes attached to the few possessions that help form the thin barriers between comfort and misery or life and death; little things that made life more bearable and possible while out there.

My wooden walking staff was another piece of memorabilia that I was very attached to. There were many times that I'd forgotten or left it places, but I'd always doubled back to get it. Although there were plenty of better alternatives to that staff, I couldn't bring myself to part with it. I'd made it myself, and as you might expect, it had literally been with me through every single step of the journey. It was my little piece of Florida that I always kept with me, and I had a spot on my wall picked out for it when the adventure was over.

Out of all the little items that did or did not go all the way with me, there was one single item that I was most attached to. That item was my little white Bic Lighter. I bought it a couple weeks before setting out, and that little lighter had been there at every meal I cooked, as well as every fire I'd started for the entire journey. Lighters are one of those things that people lose and replace on a regular basis and don't give a second thought to. Not this lighter, this one was special. Somehow, through the strange powers of the universe, this little miscellaneous item made it the entire way without being lost, broken, emptied, or unreturned when someone asked to borrow it. I am proud to say that I still have that lighter to this day; in fact, it sits on my desk in plain sight as I write these words. I'll probably get it a small frame or its own little shadow box one day. It still has a tiny bit of fluid left in it, but that little guy is retired!

It was nearly noon when I received a message from Laser that he'd be hiking into Hanover the next day and was wondering where I was. I informed him that I was on my third day in Hanover and I didn't mind spending a fourth if he actually planned to arrive the next day. I hadn't seen Laser in months, and felt I couldn't leave when he was so close to catching up with me. I made the executive decision to take another zero day in Hanover, but once again I didn't complain. This was the kind of rest my poor feet and body needed before I took on the slopes of the White Mountains.

Day four in Hanover felt like a hiker reunion when Laser, Coma, Powerhouse, Space Ranger, Lobster, Baguette, Grizelle, Dancing Feather, Bangarang, Loba, Caboose, Lorax, Patches, Yellow Beard, Cherry Blossom, and quite a few others all hiked in throughout the next day. The little bubble of hikers that had been behind me for weeks, had finally caught up. It was nice seeing the familiar faces, although hairier, thinner, and more weathered, after months of not quite knowing what happened to some of them.

I was relieved to see that some people were still on the trail and saddened to hear the news of others who had gotten off for various reasons. The decision to stay, spend time and catch up with all of them, was a no brainer. Nevertheless, I also made the decision I would hike out the next morning whether they were going or not. I knew there was a good chance they would want to take a day to rest after the harsh exit from Vermont; however, Powerhouse and Lobster agreed to join me.

Powerhouse was from Maryland, in her mid-thirties, and used to say that she would hike any amount of miles if it meant a cigarette when she got there. She had a hilarious sense of humor and could give it back to the guys even worse than we gave it to each other. She got her name for being a powerhouse. Like many people, she was a little bit heavier when she started the trail. If you looked at Powerhouse at the beginning of the journey, you wouldn't have guessed that she could knock out a twenty-mile day that early on in the thru-hiking game. She surprised you though, because she could do a twenty-mile day even at the beginning of the adventure. This earned her the name "Powerhouse" early on, because she could power through a huge day when most people who looked more capable could not.

Lobster was another guy that I'd known for as long as Viking. Lobster had been part of Viking's original group before it broke apart as people dropped off or started going at different paces. Lobster was from New Jersey and of Italian heritage. He was "Jersey proud" as I liked to say. He wouldn't hesitate to speak his mind or let the New Jersey attitude that so famously resembled the New Yorker attitude shine through. It was quite entertaining, as I always loved to hear his take on situations, as well as people he encountered. He liked to use the words "Puhtz" and "Potato Head" quite often, and after hiking with him for an extended period, those words began to rub off on me. Lobster had gotten his name when he received a bad sunburn his first few days on the trail. They said he looked like a boiled lobster. This was another trail name earned in the righteous and traditional fashion. One other thing I will always remember him for was an expression he used on a regular basis. Whenever we got into difficult terrain, he would always say, "I hope you drank your glass of Tuffin this morning." This statement was usually followed by a short pause before he exclaimed, "Toughen the fuck up!"

That next day we hiked out together, but were quickly spaced out by our own unique paces. Right off the bat, New Hampshire was a gut check. Some of the spots coming out of Hanover were hand over hand steep with giant rocky steps and huge, smooth rock faces. The first mile was enough to make you think, "Wow, New Hampshire is gonna be the real deal!" Despite its harsh introduction, after a few initial steep climbs, it leveled out, turning into a leisurely walk for the rest of the way to Moose Mountain.

One great thing about New Hampshire was the reemergence of wildlife. It wasn't crazy overdoses of wildlife, like in Shenandoah, but nice moderate New Hampshire doses of wildlife. One of the first things I saw on my first day hiking in this state was a wasp. I was gathering some water when I heard the sounds of insect wings vibrating and rustling in the air nearby. I turned just in time to see what looked like a large insect fall out of the air and onto the ground. Out of curiosity I walked over to investigate.

It turned out to be a wasp that had caught an enormous black fly in mid-flight and wrestled it to the ground. The black fly was probably three times the size of the wasp, but the wasp was now clinging to it while repeatedly jabbing it with its stinger and using its enormous mandibles to work its way through the fly's neck and decapitate it. It was a unique and crazy thing to witness. The wasp was doing wholesale slaughter on the fly. If there was one dimension of the food chain I wouldn't want to be a part of, it would be the insect world's food chain.

An insect's abilities, strength, appearance, as well as plethora of other things are absolutely terrifying to think about. Imagine if they were scaled up to our size or even half our size. It would be no contest, because in a size to strength ratio, insects rate in their own bad ass category on this planet. Any person with the strength or abilities of something like an ant or a wasp would basically be a living superman. What I'm trying to say is that insects are pretty amazing, and if you took the time to sit down and think about what they would be capable of doing to you if they were just a bit bigger, it would probably freak you out.

I pondered these thoughts for a while, as I envisioned ants the size of dogs invading our cities and tactically eradicating humans. I also imagined wasps the size of humans conducting air raids across the world at lightning speed with the strength to lift cars if they pleased and dismember just about anything with a snap of their huge mandibles. These thoughts entertained me through the last several miles as rain began to drizzle, and then pour down as I made camp atop Moose Mountain.

My second day hiking in New Hampshire was another day of wildlife and gut checks. Do you remember earlier on when I described what "switchbacks" were and their purpose? Well, if there was ever a place that needed switchbacks, it was New Hampshire. Unfortunately, switchbacks had completely disappeared; I was now in the land of straight lines. When they built the trail through New Hampshire, they stuck to the age old rule of the "quickest way between two points." No matter how steep or tall the mountain or climb was, the trail went straight up. It didn't mess around by skirting the side of the mountain, wrapping around the mountain, or switch backing up the mountain. No way, that would be too easy for the hikers and too time consuming for the trail blazers. They simply cut the path straight up over boulders, cliff faces, and anything else that was in their way. If the path was too steep to walk on, too smooth to hold onto anything, or too tall to reach; they sunk rebar into the rock for you to step or grasp onto. Half the time you found rebar in spots where you wouldn't really need it, but absent in the places that seemed determined to end your hike.

I came up and over Holt's Ledge, and even though it was only a thousand-foot climb, it kicked my ass! When I got to the bottom, I collapsed in a grassy field near a pond, ate some snacks, and relaxed. While sitting down with my feet pulled in and my forearms propped up on my knees, eating a cosmic brownie, I noticed something coming across the small grassy field towards me. It was flying about six feet off the ground, and even from eighty feet away I could tell that it didn't look natural, so I focused my full attention on it.

"What the hell is that?" I said out loud, but quietly to myself, as it drew closer and closer and I was still unable to identify it. "Another fairy?" I wondered. The creature flew right by me, four feet from where I was sitting. Only once it was parallel to my head did I realize exactly what it was. "Holy Corn Nuts! It's another wasp!" Not just any wasp, but a wasp carrying a huge grasshopper that must have been five times or more its own size! I'd never seen nor heard of anything like it. I tried to imagine for what purpose this wasp was carrying such a large grasshopper, and to where? Was it just showing off? I had no idea they were THAT strong. I don't know how rare it was to see something like that, but I felt privileged. New Hampshire had some very scary and overly ambitious wasps.

After the insect shenanigans, I began tackling Smarts Mountain. This nearly two thousand five-hundred-foot climb proved to be a combination of the longest, steepest, and most challenging climb I could ever remember doing...ever. They should have named this mountain "Moose Mountain," because Moose crap was all over the place. This once again puzzled the hell out of me, because the terrain there seemed like an even less likely place for a moose to be traipsing about than the last mountain I'd seen moose poop on.

After more than two hours of sweating and slipping my way up the mountain, I reached the bumpy levelness of the top. There was an old, decrepit fire tower from a bygone decade still standing upon the summit, as well as an equally old Fire Warden's Cabin a short distance from that. I had options on where I could hang for the night; simply having to choose the more appealing spot. I could hang on the metal frame of the rickety old fire tower, or the rafters and beams of the haunted ghost cabin. In the end, I settled for a grassy vista surrounded by small pines that overlooked the vast New Hampshire wilderness of rolling hills and pointy mountain tops; all of which served as the foreground of a blood red sunset.

It was times like those that I wished I had a professional grade camera, some professional grade camera skills, or the words of Fitzgerald to paint a better mental picture of the things I saw from New Hampshire to Maine.

That night I lay in my hammock and thought about the challenges I faced that day. "Today was going to be small potatoes compared to the Whites," I thought to myself. I was really building it up inside my head, and much like Pennsylvania, I was trying to put an idea together in my mind of what it would be like in the Whites. Based on what I'd heard and already experienced, I tried to imagine all of it on a larger, more difficult scale. As always, your imagination never seemed to prepare you for the reality of it.

Smarts Mountain was the last time I ever saw Coma on this adventure. Due to time and money constraints, he turned on the after burners and made a blitz for Katahdin after reaching New Hampshire. He was successful in achieving his Appalachian dream.

The next day I planned to do a big day into the town of Glencliff. This town was the gateway into the White Mountains via the Appalachian Trail, and with a population of only two hundred people; you might say it's the very definition of small town America. The trail didn't pass through the town per se, but briefly crossed a small road on the edge of a residential neighborhood. At that crossing you had the option to go left or right ... to nowhere really. There were only houses and nothing else besides a hiker hostel about half a mile down the road to the east. I aimed for that hostel.

My last day before the Whites was a long and painful one. I had a long four-mile descent down Smarts Mountain that wasn't nearly as steep as the climb up the south side, but a monotonous descent nonetheless. As Katana and I were quickly making our way down the slopes, a rather large garter snake shot out in front of us. Katana pounced, pinning it with one paw, holding it there as it whipped around trying to escape. She stood there watching its futile efforts to attain freedom for probably ten seconds before she lifted her paw and watched it slither off without even flinching. When it finally disappeared from sight, she continued down the trail. This was amusing, because I interpreted this as her imitating me catching snakes and then letting them go.

At the bottom of Smarts, the trail immediately went up the next mound of rocks that just so happened to be a fifteen-hundred-foot climb called Cube Mountain. I assume they named it "Cube," for all the cube shaped rocks that were stacked from the bottom to the top of this death trap. In the early morning, rocks can be "sweaty" due to the humidity, fog, or dew from the previous night. The term "sweaty" refers to the beads of water that resemble beads of sweat clinging to the rocks. It can create a very slippery and dangerous surface, depending on the smoothness of the rock.

While making my way over a huge, slanted chunk of granite, my feet slid sideways out from under me as I landed hard against the rock, directly on my hip. "Ooooooooh!" I groaned. While trying to catch myself, I also smashed the top of the base of my thumb. The bone felt cracked, but I was sure it was nothing more than badly bruised. I hated falling, especially on those types of rocks. It always felt like it was happening in slow motion, giving you enough time to think as you're going down, "Is this the fall that's going to break something and do me in?" It's always uncertain on rocks such as those. Too many jagged corners and edges waiting to give you a permanent injury.

After the craziness that was Cube Mountain, I tackled another thousand-foot climb over Ore Hill, then a series of smaller climbs before Mount Mist. Mist was the last small mountain of my twenty-mile day that would spit me onto the road that eventually led me to the hostel. I found DSOH at the hostel when I arrived, as well as Laser who arrived twenty minutes ahead of me, and Lobster who arrived about thirty minutes ahead of him. Oh the advantages of early risers! Powerhouse arrived an hour later as I learned that DSOH had gotten there the day before, while Schweppes had already passed into the Whites and tackled the first mountain before continuing on.

The level of giddy excitement inside of me was palpable. The first mountain you had to conquer in order to gain entrance to the Whites from the south was Mount Moosilauke. There is some debate over the pronunciation amongst hikers, as some pronounced it "Moose-uh-lock," while others pronounced it "Moose-uh-lock-ee." Whichever way you pronounced it - you couldn't help but say it in a deep, foreboding voice when you did speak it aloud. I pronounce it the first way, but that's neither here nor there.

Regardless of how you say Moosilauke, the fact of the matter is that this is one badass BFM (Big Fucking Mountain). This megalith is five thousand jaw dropping feet tall, with four thousand of those feet having to be climbed with your own feet...and hands. This made it the single largest continuous climb on the entire trail up until this point going north. Those were the types of mountains that everything prior to this had been leading up to. I genuinely had the nervous excitement that I hadn't felt since the first day... and I loved it.

There was much more to the White Mountains than just their steep climbs and inhospitable terrain. This entire range was billed as having the most extreme and unpredictable weather in all of the United States. Exposed rocky ridgelines, freezing temperatures, and hurricane force winds were unpredictable and commonplace all year round in the White Mountains. The strongest gust of wind ever recorded in history for over sixty years was measured on top of Mount Washington in the Whites, at 231 miles per hour. This record was beaten only by a Typhoon in Australia in 1996, with the measurement of a 253 mile per hour wind gust. More than a hundred people had died from falls, exposure, and other accidents over the decades in these mountains. Little did I know, those mountains would add one more name to their list during my time spent in them.

The White Mountains National Forest came with some rules. The main rule was: "No stealth camping." Just like the Smokies and Shenandoah, this meant you weren't allowed to camp in undesignated camping spots. The only difference here was that all of the designated camping spots cost money.

The other option was the "Huts." Huts were lavish lodges that housed anywhere from forty to ninety people depending on their size. The huts had crews of three to five caretakers that lived in them for months at a time while cooking for the guests and taking care of them during their stay at the hut. Every hut was placed in a remote yet ideal location that was only accessible on foot or by helicopter, as all the supplies at these lavish cabins were either packed in on foot by the caretakers or air dropped by helicopters.

Staying at huts was referred to as "rich man camping" amongst us thru-hikers. At around $140 per night, you could enjoy your nice bunk, baked goods, hot drinks, and hot meals provided by the caretakers, while you spent the day hiking the surrounding trails and admiring the beauty of the region.

After eighteen hundred miles of camping wherever we wanted, the vast majority of thru-hikers were not about to pay money to camp in the wilderness, or the exorbitant prices to stay in something that had less amenities than a hostel that cost $10 per night. So you had three options to choose from.

Option one was to follow all the rules and pay the prices of whatever sanctioned area you decided to lay your head. This was the expensive, honorable, but ultimately least chosen option by thru-hikers. We north bounders were all going broke by the time we reached New Hampshire anyway, so following the rules simply wasn't economical or affordable for many of us.

Option two was to avoid the sanctioned areas and stealth camp off the trail wherever you could find a good spot. This was the most preferred option by thru-hikers and even though the "No Stealth Camping" rule was in place; it was very difficult to enforce. The terrain was harsh and the temperatures cold, so there wasn't a squadron of National Forest Police running around the mountains every night, searching high and low for people camping in undesignated areas. The trail itself was challenging enough, and no one was going to stray very far from it, least of all the officials. I never heard of a single person getting busted for stealth camping before, during, or after the Whites.

Option three was "work for stay" at a Hut. Work for stay referred to doing chores for the caretakers (i.e. washing dishes, sweeping, cleaning bathrooms, etc.) in return for a place to stay that was warm and dry, as well as receive some food. They didn't give you a bunk or a bed, but instead let you sleep on the floor in the dining room. This was perfectly fine because that's basically what we had been doing for all these months anyway. The food they gave you in exchange for the work was left over from whatever the "Hut guests" didn't finish. Leftover "hut food" beat the hell out of backpack food any day of the year, so no one complained.

The only downside was that work for stay was not always available and you couldn't predict when it was. Depending on the caretaker's philosophy of not wanting to give any unused floor space or uneaten food away for free (even at the expense of your safety), you could sometimes find yourself on the bitter end of an exchange that found you stuck more than four to five thousand feet up a mountain at night during inclement weather.

Those were the options in the Whites. They were options made even more critical by the topographical layout of the Whites themselves. There were hardly any roads and barely any towns throughout the one-hundred-mile stretch of the White Mountain range. Resupply options were usually very slim and depending on how fast you made your way over the harsh terrain, you might find yourself resupplying with the over-priced snacks and baked goods from the Huts.

Many areas through this section were so high up that they were above the tree line. This meant there were no trees or vegetation to shelter you from the high winds and extreme weather. All you had was bare exposed rock. Those exposed ridges that resided above the tree line could go on for miles and miles before dipping back below tree level. In the event of an emergency weather situation, you could find yourself stuck on one of those ridgelines in life threatening conditions with only several options. Those options included: Grit it out, hide amongst the rocks, run down the mountainside to the tree line (not usually an option), or seek shelter in a Hut that's normally strategically placed on some of the above tree line sections.

When you've never been to this region before and have relatively no idea what to expect, things can get difficult. Even when you know where everything is, it's almost impossible to know how long it will take you to traverse certain distances. That made it very hard to plan your miles, stopping points, and safety areas along the way. No matter how fit you are, or how fit you think you are, the Whites are unlike anything encountered previously to the south. Of course there are exceptions to every rule, but most will find that their progress slows dramatically upon reaching the Whites. I ended up not being able to reach certain distances that I would normally have no problem reaching. This could unexpectedly leave someone in dangerous locations or situations at the wrong time. A good rule to follow and remember in the White Mountains is that for every mile you hike there, it will feel like two miles. A ten-mile day will take the effort and sometimes the duration of a twenty-mile day anywhere else. I learned this the hard way more than once during my stint in the White Mountains.

September 3rd was my 158th day on the trail, and a day that I had dreamed of and dreaded since the start of my journey. I set out that morning thoroughly not knowing what to expect from Moosilauke, besides a great deal of sweat and burning muscles.

The climb started off gradual and soon became a monotonous never ending ascent over large rocky steps. No real scrambles, but giant rocky step after giant rocky step, on and on, up and up. In all actuality, it wasn't that bad or even difficult. I even saw a seventy-year-old woman coming down as I was going up. The climb up the south side was nowhere near as bad as I'd psyched myself up for it to be. It was simply long, monotonous, and moderately steep.

Another observation I made, was this mountain leaked water from just about everywhere. There were springs and trickles of water coming out of every rock and crevice that seemed to turn the trail itself into a shallow creek at times. I filled my bottle directly from a spring and took a swig. "DAMN!" Moosilauke water was the coldest and tastiest water I can remember drinking on the entire trail. I imagined myself absorbing the mountains strength by drinking its water as it came straight out of the rock. Silly, I know, but I felt seriously pumped after a couple liters of Moosilauke water.

When I finally reached the summit of Moosilauke, far above the tree line, at nearly five thousand feet, I was rewarded with the most spectacular view I'd seen in months. It was a semi overcast day, as the summit of Moosilauke had me standing just below a ceiling of clouds. It was surreal, as I looked out across the earth for over a hundred miles while a flat ceiling of clouds stretched equally far, seemingly within arm's reach above me. It gave me the sensation that I was looking at two earths. The green and brown textured one that was far below me, and the flat, smooth, light gray one that was just above my head and almost level with my eyes.

The winds were sustaining close to thirty miles per hour on the exposed summit, but I was able to find some protection on a grassy knoll behind some rocks near the top. I ate lunch as I soaked in the view of all the other mountains that I'd eventually have to climb throughout the next hundred miles or so. Being able to see everything that was ahead of me was both a blessing and a curse. It was a blessing to those who lived in the moment and took the journey one step and mountain at a time; while it was a curse to those who sought to psyche themselves out by worrying about what was in store for them.

The north facing side of Moosilauke was completely different from its south facing brethren. This descent on the far side of the mountain was exactly what my nightmares had been made of; but what those nightmares didn't reveal...was the sheer beauty of it all.

Despite a descent full of treacherous scrambles and huge rocky step downs, there was a narrow, but swiftly cascading waterfall that went on for thousands of feet paralleling the trail. It was one of the most beautiful sites I'd seen up to this point.

The Whites had mesmerized me…and it was only the first day. I think Laser, Lobster, and I only made it halfway down the backside of Moosilauke before we made the decision to camp. To my proud surprise, Laser had switched over to a hammock since the last time I'd seen him way back in Virginia. This gave him a lot more flexibility when it came to choosing camping locations, as anywhere with trees was more or less fair game.

We pushed through a thin layer of pines to get to the waterfall, which resided on a smooth, granite rock face, with the water cascading down the steep slope in tranquil grace. The stream of flowing water was narrow enough that I could hang across it if I found the right trees. After ten minutes of determined searching and eyeballing of suitable trees, I was finally forced to settle on two trees that were much smaller than I would've preferred. They would only hold me a little less than a foot above the fast moving water. Laser found a spot perpendicular to me and parallel to the waterfall, while Lobster was able to clear out an area for his tent on a small outcropping of rock. I brought Katana into the hammock with me.

That first night I slept above a gorgeous cascading waterfall, atop the great Moosilauke, amidst the fabled White Mountains. Once again I was living in a dream that I didn't want to awaken from. In the fading twilight, I attempted to read my book, however the gentle, hypnotizing sounds of water had other plans for me. I don't think I made it past the first page before I was waking up to the morning sun and the early calls of songbirds.

My second day in the White Mountains was not nearly as forgiving as the first, but no less enchanting. The rest of the climb down Moosilauke was fairly treacherous and required a great deal of scaling jagged rocks and smooth faces. Once at the base, the next order of business was Wolf Mountain. The first initial eight hundred feet were nearly straight up over manageable stair stepper rocks. The next eight hundred feet were done in ascending tiers that were more or less gradual, but made challenging by climbs over large boulders and short but steep rock faces. We were also forced to navigate our way through vast expanses of exposed tree roots and long stretches of slick mud.

It was while climbing all over Wolf Mountain that I saw my first actual moose track. I couldn't believe what I was looking at when I first saw it. Imprinted perfectly in a stretch of hard packed mud, it looked more or less like a deer track, the only difference being the size. This foot print put a horse hoof to shame. Hell, it even put my size fourteen shoe to shame when I stood next to it. "How is a creature this large eluding me out here?" I wondered. The tracks continued on down the trail for several hundred feet before disappearing off the side and into the forest without so much as another trace.

The three of us caught up to DSOH and Powerhouse at the bottom of Wolf and the base of Mount Kinsman. Kinsman will hold a special place in my heart for being the "first" most "physically demanding" mountain I've ever climbed. As I said before, the first cut is the deepest, and Kinsman will always stick out in my memory for being one of the most challenging mountains of the entire journey. Even though there were much harder climbs than this one, I couldn't imagine them at the time, and my mind will always wander back to Kinsman when I think of the most difficult climbs of the AT.

On paper, there appeared to be nothing special about the two-thousand-foot climb that was Kinsman. Once boots were on the ground, it was an entirely different story. The base and initial climb of Kinsman was gorgeous, with small waterfalls, trickling streams, and many areas to soak or take a dip. However, beyond those elements of beauty was a mountainous hell. Stacked rocks, jagged rocks, huge smooth boulders, smooth rock faces that were slick as a water slide, mossy rocks, roots, trees, shrubs, you name it. There wasn't a level spot to put your foot on; in fact, there was almost nowhere to even stand up. You were constantly leaning and clinging onto rocks almost the entire time. The last half of Kinsman was more or less rock climbing, no hiking, just hand over hand. We kept calling back and forth jokingly to each other, "I thought this was supposed to be a FOOT path," or "Isn't this a HIKING trail, not a CLIMBING trail?"

I am proud to say that Katana was destroying it. She was bred for this type of terrain; she was eating it up and asking for more. I'd never seen her so enthusiastic about going uphill, as she left me in the dust. Areas that would take me serious time and consideration to navigate were taking her mere seconds. She was literally doing pull ups to get herself up and over some of the rocks. When we encountered a sheer rock face that was taller than me, her plan of attack was to charge it and scramble up as fast as she could. As she lost her momentum near the top, she would dig her front paws in and literally do a pull up to get up and over the top edge of the climb while dragging her back feet behind her (because they had lost traction). It was incredible and I really can't brag enough about her. I had previously worried about how she was going to handle and survive the Whites, but now I had my answer. She was going to THRIVE!

After hours of pulling ourselves up and over rocks, we were finally able to enjoy the payoff. The summit of Kinsman was a series of huge, flat, rocky slabs that were ideal to sit or lay on. Not to mention the view was staggering. We arrived at the top just as the sun was getting low and the world was awash in golden light. We had views back to Moosilauke as well as ahead to Mt. Lafayette and Mt. Washington; two other behemoths that were famous in the Whites. I could have lain up there all day, but unfortunately there wasn't much "day" left, and the descent from Kinsman was over three thousand feet and six miles long.

The north side of Kinsman was just as treacherous, if not more so, than the south side. It was made harder by the fading light and the fact that you were now lowering yourself down those treacherous rocks instead of pulling yourself up. As a rule, the level of danger while going down is significantly greater than going up. The first thousand feet or so of the descent felt dangerously life threatening. I spent a great deal of those thousand feet on my ass, trying to safely slide down over rocks to eliminate the threat of falling or tearing up my knees.

It was almost completely dark, except for the slivers of light that made their way down through the trees, when the trail finally softened into a descent that you could actually walk on. The five of us had fallen into a line, with Katana periodically making her way up and down that line, taking turns walking between each of us.

Quite abruptly, and without warning, Katana shot off the trail to the right, crashing through the forest chasing after something. We all looked simultaneously… "SKUNK!" All five of us began yelling at the same time. "KATANA!" "STOP!" "SKUNK!" "NO!" "COME!" "KATANA!" "COME HERE!" "STOP IT!" "HOLY SHIT!" "SKUNK!" It was a rapid fire cacophony of commands and curse words from all of us at the top of our lungs, and I think Katana's little brain was overloaded by the barrage of words and commands.

She ran that skunk down so fast that I could hardly believe it. She was less than two feet behind the skunk as it was climbing over a fallen log when she finally froze from our screams. She stood locked in place, looking at us, then back at the fleeing skunk, with what I can only describe as a smile on her face. After twenty long seconds, she pranced back over to us and continued down the trail. Yes indeed, it was yet another crisis averted!

Almost everyone I met on the trail, as well as every single one of my friends out there, loved spending time with Katana, petting and cuddling her at the end of each day. She made you feel good, because you didn't have any other outlet for your affection out there. She was a little creature that let you hug and love on it, and in return loved you back. You couldn't get that anywhere else on the trail. We were a bunch of sweaty, smelly, hiker dudes and chicks, that weren't about to start hugging and cuddling each other in an attempt to fill some void, or make up for the hugs and cuddles we were missing from our girlfriends and other loved ones back home. Katana would've been ineffective as a cute and cuddly little dog if she had all of a sudden began smelling like the butthole of a skunk. I probably would've lost all my hiking friends too.

It was on this night while walking through the darkness that we came across our first Hut in the White Mountains. We came upon it quite suddenly and unexpectedly, and as we did, Katana bolted around the back to investigate. Anytime we encountered any kind of man made structure out in the woods, Katana would run ahead to check it out first. It was cute, but it got old, because sometimes these structures were a good distance off the path and I never had any desire to visit most of them. There was almost never a way to call her back either, because once she was on her way to explore, there was virtually no stopping her unless you really wanted to overreact (like with the skunk). I always ended up having to physically retrieve her.

We never had any intentions of visiting the Hut or trying to stay there, but now that Katana had run around the side of the building, my presence was going to be known one way or another. I turned to everyone with an exasperated look on my face. "Maybe something good will come of this," I said to them as I began to make my way around the building. I had long since accepted that curses were sometimes blessings in disguise out there.

On the far side of the building I found two of the Hut caretakers already petting her. No surprise there. I fielded some typical Katana questions before they asked me if I wanted to wash dishes in exchange for left-over food and a spot on the dining room floor. Out of their entire offer, the food sounded the most appealing. I preferred my hammock outside to almost any floor indoors, but I would suffer the floor if it meant hot food. I consulted with my companions, and in the end Laser and Lobster agreed to stay. DSOH and Powerhouse decided to push on through the night in an attempt to get closer to a small road that lead into the town of Lincoln.

The caretakers fed us a hearty meal of bowtie pasta, bread, and veggies before having us wash and dry a plethora of dishes by hand. While making our beds on the wooden floor of the dining room, I made up my mind that the food was definitely worth the work and sleeping arrangements. I decided that I would try and score a "work for stay" at every Hut I encountered near the end of the day from then on.

Everything in New Hampshire had been different, as well as more difficult than anything else I'd encountered along the trail. It was the same for most thru-hikers, and you could see it in their faces. Since arriving in New Hampshire and meeting the new obstacles and terrain, I'd seen more than a couple other hikers break down in tears of frustration and pain. Quitting or talk of quitting had become more commonplace since reaching the "Live Free or Die" State.

As I mentioned before, everyone handled challenges and extreme situations differently. Everybody that was still out on the trail at this point, had been so for months. We were all beaten down, tired, and hurting. Stripped to the bare essentials for months on end, some people were barely hanging on. Injuries, aches, and pains that had been dealt with and suffered through for hundreds of miles were all of a sudden being exploited, as well as exacerbated by the brutal terrain. People were coming face to face with their own mortality. Some of them realized that their bodies may no longer have what it took to wake up every morning and traverse those insanely challenging mountains for another four hundred miles into the better part of Maine. This realization made a lot of people emotional.

I dealt with it by making light of it. I played games in my head, tried not to be too serious, embraced every situation and tried to keep my sense of humor no matter what. Most importantly, I kept myself focused on the end goal. That was my master plan to carry me through to the finish line. DSOH would always say, "It's important to remember that the mind always quits before the body." When your brain is telling you stop, your body almost always has much more to give.

Day three in the Whites was a day that made me wonder how so many amazing things could fit into a span of 24 hours. I hadn't seen it in the dark, but just a stone's throw away from the Hut was a small, serene body of water called Lonesome Lake. As I sat there on the back deck of the Hut and packed my bag, the wail of a loon that was out on the lake, rose and fell through the mountain air.

Few things in nature can compare to the long, mournful wail of a loon echoing across water and through the forest. It's an evocative sound that will stick with you for the rest of your life and make you nostalgic for things that never even happened to you. Eerie, yet beautiful, the sound will conjure up images of solitude near mountain lakes and ponds, shrouded in fog during the early morning or late dusk, surrounded by the silhouettes of pine trees. It's a sound that relaxes and submerges you into the tranquility of nature. I don't think there is another sound in the world that reminds me of the wilderness more so than the wail of a loon.

On many evenings, nights, and mornings throughout this final stretch of the journey, I would lie awake in my hammock, or be walking along a glacial lake or pond and hear their calls echo through the wilderness. It gave me goose bumps and a tingle up my spine that I couldn't get enough of. Loons became a constant presence through this part of the trail, and my entire journey was made richer because of them. If you've never heard one, then I urge you to seek one out or look up their multitude of calls online, especially their haunting and mournful wail.

We set out together that morning, skirting the side of the lake as the early golden sunlight sparkled off the water. The three of us walked in a long line as we made our way down the trail, with a tight wall of pine trees on either side of us. Laser was first, only a hundred feet or so in front of Lobster, who was less than a hundred feet ahead of me, with Katana trotting along between us.

We were coming across a flat, straight section when I heard Laser from up ahead exclaim, "Holy shit!" Then Lobster spun around and relayed to me in a hushed yell, "There's a moose! Grab Katana!" I looked up to see an enormous bull moose emerge from the woods on the left side of the trail, maybe ten feet in front of Laser. I lunged forward to grab Katana, but she was too quick. "Grab her!" I whisper-yelled up to Lobster. He managed to snag her by her harness just as she tried to scoot by. I ran up, dropped my pack and latched Katana to it as I pulled out my phone. I looked up again to see the moose nonchalantly trudging down the trail with Laser following close behind.

I was filled with a mixture of fear and excitement as we took off following it, snapping pictures and video the whole way. The enormous beast didn't seem to mind us in the slightest, and every now and then it would turn its head to look back at us before continuing on. It had an astoundingly large antler rack with velvet draping off like dead skin. If I had to guess, I would say the head of this moose was situated a comfortable eight to nine feet off the ground. I knew these animals were big, but I had no idea they were THAT BIG!

My adrenaline was surging as the moose turned off the trail and back into the woods. We attempted to follow it, but the gigantic creature moved over the rocks and fallen trees with a deceiving grace that I never knew a creature that large and gangly could possess. It bobbed and weaved and turned its head to maneuver its antlers through the thick trees with finesse, while bowling over the smaller ones without a second thought. It was soon moving over the terrain faster than any of us could keep up, and as suddenly as it had appeared, it was gone.

All of my questions had been answered during that short encounter. That moose made us look like amateurs as it navigated the terrain, but I suppose if my legs were six feet long, then I could make short work of it too. After leaving the trail, it was gone in less than a minute, leaving us with only our photographs and memories.

For the next several miles, the moose was all we could talk about. We were riding high on our first Moose encounter, as it had been better than any of us ever hoped for. I think the sheer size of the animal was the most surprising aspect of the encounter. After that, the temperament it exhibited and the grace with which it moved through the thick forest was also unanticipated.

We caught up to DSOH and Powerhouse at the base of the climb up Mount Lafayette. The majority of the climb to the summit of this mountain was not only made up of the enormous Lafayette; there was one giant initial climb that brought you up to altitude on the ridge, then a series of ascending rollercoaster climbs over the peaks of smaller mountains. Those smaller mountains slowly built up higher and higher before finally climaxing at the summit of Mount Lafayette, nearly five thousand three hundred feet above the earth.

The first big climb was nearly three thousand feet and very similar to the climb up Moosilauke. There wasn't much scrambling, but plentiful steep rocky steps that seemed to continue on for eternity. We stopped on the summit of the first mountain in the series of mountains that we'd have to pass over in order to reach Lafayette. That first mountain's name was Liberty Mountain, and it holds a special place in my memory and heart.

The summit of Liberty topped out at four thousand three hundred feet, just above the tree line, giving you an unobstructed 360-degree view of the entire White Mountain range. We were approaching the halfway point for the Whites, and in doing so, our views of the entire mountain range were becoming clearer and clearer. Each mountain I summited in the Whites seemed to outdo the last in terms of altitude and how far you could see. Regardless of all other mountains I ever climbed on the AT, when it came to timing, solitude, and the dramatic appearance of everything surrounding us during the sinking of the sun, Liberty Mountain took the cake, hands down.

From atop the summit, I witnessed probably the most fantastic, moving sunset I have ever seen in my entire life. I had seen plenty of phenomenal sunsets and sunrises throughout this adventure, but nothing ever came close to the one I saw on top of Liberty Mountain. The very summit of Liberty came to a rocky pinnacle that you could stand atop, and never in my life had I experienced such a feeling of liberation and freedom. The entire moment and location stirred something inside of me that reinforced "why" I was out there. Almost without even realizing it, I let forth a shout that came from the core of my very being. A shout I could feel inside my bones that sent tingles all over my body. I don't know why, but it felt natural and cathartic to scream with reckless abandon and feel like the whole world could hear it. No one else in the world was seeing what we were seeing in that moment. It belonged to us and only us, and the feelings it kindled can only be remembered by the photographs we took that day. Photographs that could never do justice to the bigger picture that our experience on Liberty provided.

We couldn't bring ourselves to leave the summit, even as the sun disappeared behind the distant mountains. We wanted to hang onto the feeling that had been stirred inside of us, and we felt that remaining on the summit was the only way to sustain it. We made the emotionally driven and somewhat unwise decision to camp on the top of Liberty amongst the rocks that night.

Among other things, I will always remember Liberty Mountain as being the last mountain that we considered "cool" to camp atop. During the heat of the late spring and summer days, I always wanted to camp as high in altitude as I possibly could, in order to save myself from the sweltering heat that persisted, even through the night. In the Whites, camping on the tops of mountains was a big NO, NO, that could get you in serious trouble or even killed during any time of year. I don't recall camping at the top of a mountain ever again after Liberty.

The master plan to wake up with the sun and see an equally dramatic sunrise was squashed by the fact that Liberty's summit was sitting in a cloud the next morning; a freezing cloud full of high winds no less. It suddenly became very important to get off Liberty as quickly as possible. I hiked out before everyone else to begin the rollercoaster ascent over two more peaks while on my way to the summit of Lafayette.

When leaving Liberty, I dipped back down into the tree line for a couple of miles before reemerging almost another thousand feet higher on the summit of Little Haystack Mountain. I stopped to have some of the breakfast I skipped out on while I rushed to get off Liberty.

As I sat there and ate, the view that lay before me was unique to anything I'd seen previously. The rest of the trail heading north was all above tree line, as I could see every climb, dip, and turn the trail made all the way up to Mt. Lincoln, Franconia Ridge, and then Lafayette. My love for walking across open ridges, as well as wide open areas in general was about to be realized in epic fashion.

Looking down from Haystack, the clouds were scattered all over at different altitudes. Wispy smudges of cloud were above me, below me, and level with me, giving the landscape and the clouds themselves a fantastic 3D effect. I sat on a rock and ate my Mega Stuff Oreos while I watched the clouds below me smash into the side of the mountain before rushing up the rocky slopes as they cooled me down in a spray of cloudy mist. I remember wishing that I could have this sort of cloud smashing/misting service on a hot day in Florida.

Before I could finish my Oreo breakfast, Laser and DSOH caught up with me. It took us over two hours to go two miles over Mt. Lincoln and Franconia Ridge. This was not because it was difficult you see, but because it was beautiful and unique to anything else we'd come across so far on the journey. It felt like we'd left planet earth and were now explorers trekking across the surface of some unnamed planet. We had a 360-degree view for as far as the eye could see as we traversed Franconia Ridge, on the way up to Lafayette.

Once atop the mighty Lafayette we were rewarded with a rather spectacular view of Mount Washington. Sadly, the cloud cover had grown heavier and many sights further out were becoming invisible to us as they faded into the thick haze. The winds were fairly high, forcing us to take cover behind some rocks where we enjoyed a nice lunch. More than another hour passed before it soon became evident that we overstayed our welcome and had lingered too long. While hunkered down behind the rocks, we failed to notice the storm clouds the gusty winds had been pushing our way. We were only alerted to the storm in the form of small droplets of water whipping over our entrenched position, making it obvious that it was time to go.

A fierce thunderstorm was upon us before we had even put our food away and got our packs on. The wind was sustaining close to forty miles per hour, and with no trees to soften its punch, the rain was stinging our skin. The lightning and thunder crashed as the wind whipped and pushed us along over the now slick rocks as we made our way as fast as we could towards the safety of the tree line below. We had more than a mile to go in order to reach the cover of the trees, and even once we got there, we wouldn't be able to stop. The trees at the top of a tree line are normally very small and not much taller than a person, so they don't provide much cover, if any at all. You are forced to continue down until you reach the larger trees that will almost always be pines at those altitudes.

We were in the exact situation we absolutely wanted to avoid; caught in the open, on an unprotected ridgeline in the middle of a severe storm. Besides the stinging of the rain and the fear of things possibly getting worse, the sprint to the trees was made in relative safety. I had one close call as I tried to navigate my way down a slick rock face. I lost my traction and spun 540 degrees over the course of a thirty-foot slide down the rock before planting my hands on the ground and putting myself into a controlled fall that stopped my descent.

When we finally reached the trees, the sounds of the wind whipping over top of them was even more deafening than the thunder. We went several hundred yards past the first line of trees before they were big enough to actually take cover in. As we sprinted off the path we made our way into the thick of the forest and began staking our claims to camping spots.

When I was finally able to get a good look around at the spot we'd chosen to hunker down, chills ran up my spine. We'd stopped in the middle of what I can only describe as a forest that looked as if it were straight out of a fairy tale, a wicked one... The ground was nothing but moss, a blanketed sea of it that covered everything in its path. The rocks, logs, and fallen branches were completely covered in swaths of deep green moss. The stuff even crept up the bases of the trees that still stood. The trees themselves were not large, no more than fifteen to twenty feet tall at the most, but the most eerie aspect was how twisted they were. None of them grew straight or even straight up. They grew in every which direction with knots, twists, and evil looking splinters from being pushed and pulled around by the wind over the course of their existence. It was positively evil looking, yet at the same time indescribably stunning, in a creepy way. The rain and thunder raged into the late night and early morning as I fell asleep with Katana nestled in the crook of my arm.

Day four in the Whites was relatively uneventful compared to the first three days. That night of the storm, temperatures dropped as it became incredibly cold and perhaps below freezing. I'd awoken around 3 am to put on every layer of clothing I owned, including my sleeping bag liner. Despite the freezing cold temperatures, the morning was gorgeous and clear with uninterrupted blue skies and virtually no wind. The absence of wind made the cold temperatures very pleasant to hike in with only a t-shirt.

The terrain coming down the rest of Lafayette was full of rock scrambles beneath the trees; made all the more treacherous by the slippery water from the night before. It made little difference to the CatFox as she practically ran down every scramble of rocks.

After descending Lafayette, the narrow one-thousand-foot spike that was Mount Garfield, came immediately after. I found Laser, Lobster, and Powerhouse at the top with all their wet gear laid out on the rocks to dry. I joined them and tethered Katana to my pack some distance away to keep her from falling off any more cliffs.

It was a Sunday, and being such, the mountains of this national forest had quite a few more day-hikers than usual. Besides the AT, there was another side trail that leads to the summit of Garfield. I don't know how long that trail was, where it came from, or the level of difficulty it posed, but there was a steady flow of people, including families with children that kept periodically emerging from it while taking in the views from the top. The extra foot traffic slightly ruined the magic of what would've been an amazing summit.

CatFox was getting her usual attention from random day-hikers as she sat calmly tethered to my pack about fifteen yards away. No one could really tell who she belonged to at that distance, so I was free from the barrage of questions she usually garnered. I left the tourists to fawn over her as I ignored their comments and inquiries (which I overheard in the background during conversations with my companions).

Then I heard something I couldn't ignore. I heard a child's voice say, "This dog shouldn't be up here." Curiously, I turned around to see a boy of about seven years old and his parents standing around Katana. The boy then followed his first statement with, "It's just way too small to be hiking in these mountains and it doesn't belong up here." "What the hell?" I said under my breath but loud enough for my friends to hear. They were all grinning at my sudden interest and reaction to the new observations about my little dog.

Never have I heard a child that young make such an astute observation about something that a child would normally not give a second thought about. I don't think I could have even formed that kind of opinion about a dog's "mountain worthiness" when I was that age. Aren't we all taught from our earliest years that great things come in small packages? Katana was small, but one look at her and you could tell that she was far from incapable. I was impressed by the boy's ability to form such a strong opinion for about half a second before feeling insulted. I wasn't insulted personally, but insulted on Katana's behalf. She hadn't walked this far to have some little precocious "child know-it-all" belittle her and not be able to defend herself. The worst part was that the child's parents agreed with him, saying "Yeah you're right; it does look a little too small to be up here hiking."

Spurred on by my companion's playful comments of, "Are you gonna let a kid talk about your dog like that?" I made the heat of the moment decision to correct this family and defend my pup's honor in the process. I stood up and began walking over to them, as my companions snickered behind me. "Ahem, excuse me young man," I said. "Do you know how far this little dog has walked in the last five months?" "No." the child replied. "She's walked nearly one thousand nine hundred miles with me continuously, every day on the Appalachian Trail from Georgia up until this point right here, and we still have over three hundred miles to go before we're finished." This was a two-hundred-mile exaggeration on Katana's behalf, because she'd joined me in North Carolina of course, but for the sake of making my point, I kept it simple. The little boy was silent. I continued on in my sweet "talking-to-a-child-voice" with… "That's further than you've ever walked in your entire life young man and maybe your parents too; I only want you to realize that her size has little to do with her abilities, and she is more than capable of handling this terrain." The little boy looked embarrassed and his parents chuckled nervously not really knowing how to respond to my comments. I left them standing there awkwardly as I went back and sat down. I felt like Katana's honor had been righteously defended and minds had been expanded.

Maybe it was harsh and blunt of me to say that to a child in front of his parents, but it just hit a nerve with me. THEIR child was being presumptuous about MY child, and my child didn't speak human, so I felt compelled to speak up for the one who had no voice. Perhaps the boy learned a valuable lesson about jumping to conclusions or maybe he'll develop a strong, subconscious dislike for anyone with a beard from now on. Either way, I didn't dwell on it, as life would go on for all of us.

The descent from Garfield was treacherous, and I remember running into a day-hiker that had gotten confused and gone down the Appalachian Trail instead of the side trail she'd originally hiked up on. "You don't wanna go this way, this trail sucks!" she said emphatically as we passed by. "We know, but that's the way we have to go," I replied laughing. "I feel sorry for you," was the last thing the woman said.

While still descending Garfield, we climbed down what could generously be called a small cascading waterfall. The trail and the waterfall converged as one for perhaps a hundred feet or so. My knees were aching beneath their caps, and I can only describe the feeling as a throbbing headache, but felt deep inside the knee joint. This was another ache and pain that I hadn't felt since my early days on the trail.

The going was slow all day, and after another fifteen-hundred-foot climb straight up a mountain by the name of South Twin (I renamed it Evil Twin), we called it a day on the side of the trail in another semi- enchanted looking alpine grove. I must admit that stopping was one of the best parts of every day. That moment when you knew you were setting your pack down for the last time was one of the greatest feelings you could have during the day. We never made any fires while in the brunt of the Whites, mainly because we were in "stealth mode," but to be honest, I never had the energy at the end of the day to sit around and keep a fire going. I only wanted to hop in my hammock and go comatose.

It was about this time in the Whites that I started to run out of food and didn't have a resupply point for over fifty miles. Things were getting desperate as my body was working two to three times harder than it was used to working, requiring me to supply it with a constant stream of food all day long. I remember very vividly craving Buffalo Wings with an almost dangerous desire throughout that particular section. I wanted them so bad, that I would actually become sad, then angry if I thought about them too much.

You've never known what it's like to truly want or crave something, until you've had to walk fifty, seventy, or even a hundred miles in order to obtain it. To be stuck in ninety-degree heat and want nothing more than something as simple as an iced tea, only to realize that seventy-five miles and multiple days' worth of hiking stand between you and that glass, can really put some things in perspective. It truly is life changing. It sounds crazy, but having to work so hard for some of the simplest pleasures in life can change you forever...

On the fifth day I was forced to stop at a Hut that was situated near a gorgeous waterfall called Zealand Falls. They didn't have anything that would be considered "Hiker food," but for a ridiculously exorbitant price, I was able to purchase ten slices of chocolate pumpkin bread, as well as ten jumbo snicker bars. This was about all I could find at the Huts until I could get into a real town and buy some real food. When I say "real food," I mean the ingredients for my salami bagel sandwiches.

The fifth day was physically the easiest day of my entire peregrination through the White Mountains. The trail ran along an old railroad bed for seven miles before gently dropping down two thousand feet into a spot called Crawford Notch. "Notch" is an alternative for the word "Gap," as they are nothing more than the short space between two mountains or climbs. The Railroad bed was as flat as a table and could be described as a mall walk compared to anything else in the Whites. It was a seven-mile vacation for my joints; I had sad, watery eyes when the uneven ground and rocks had phased back into existence. We camped that night in Crawford Notch, saving the crown jewel of the Whites for the next day.

Between Crawford Notch in the south and Pinkham Notch in the north, there is a twenty-six-mile stretch of trail called the Presidential Mountain Range. It's a collection of mountains that are all named after past presidents. When going north, you encounter them in the following ascending order: Webster, Jackson, Clinton, Eisenhower, Franklin, Monroe and then the climax and crown jewel of the entire White Mountain Range; Mount Washington. Washington is the tallest mountain in the Northeast, as well as the second tallest mountain on the trail at 6,288 feet. After Washington you encounter more mountains in the descending order of: Jefferson, Adams and Madison; before a suicidal descent into Osgood Cutoff and onward to Pinkham Notch.

The Presidential Mountain Range was without a doubt the most memorable stretch of the Whites for both good and bad reasons. The vast majority of the twenty-six miles was spent above the tree line on a bare rocky ridge that afforded zero protection from the wind and other elements. It was incredibly dangerous, as this section had claimed the lives of many a hiker. The trail through there was deceptively challenging, and without the proper gear or planning, you could find yourself stuck somewhere on this ridge with miles and miles between you and any kind of salvation.

Day six kicked off with a bang in the form of Mt. Webster repeatedly punching you in the gut. As with most mountain ranges here in the Whites, they started off with one huge initial climb that got you up to altitude before continuing on with a series of roller coaster climbs and descents of various heights. Those roller coasters always ascended, slowly but surely, towards whatever high point was in the middle of the grouping of mountains. Mount Webster was a three-thousand-foot climb filled with more false summits than I could count. Despite its trickery, I give this mountain credit for having a little bit of everything. There were scrambles, steps, sharp climbs of dirt, cliffs, boulders, smooth rock faces, mud pits, root tangles, and rocky outlooks. None of it seemed to ever end, and more than once I found myself in precarious, short rock climbing situations that could have sent me to the hospital or an untimely death with just one wrong grab or unlucky tumble.

There was one very interesting species of bird that seemed to only be on Webster. A bird called the "Grey Jay." This bold little avian would land on you, if offered food. I'd already eaten all of my pumpkin bread and try as I might, they didn't seem to want any of my Snickers. Although they came very close to investigate, to my very immense disappointment they never landed on me. Laser was able to get one to land on his hand for what I think was a slice of pepperoni. I was super jealous of his bird appeal.

Laser, Lobster, Powerhouse, and I had no intentions of going all the way to the top of Washington that day. We were aiming for a Hut that sat about twelve hundred feet below the summit of Washington near a small body of water called The Lake of the Clouds. Chugging along, Lobster and I pulled ahead of Laser and Powerhouse to continue on together. Upon summiting Clinton, we rose above the tree line at four thousand three hundred feet and would stay above it for what would be the rest of the Presidential Mountain Range.

Once again, I would liken it to walking on another planet, and I never wanted it to end. The openness, feeling of freedom, and your own smallness was indescribable. It was a gorgeous day with transparent smears of clouds so high, that you couldn't even perceive them to be moving. Small vegetation resembling broccoli grew everywhere close to the ground. If you didn't look closely, it appeared to be nothing but more rocks.

Up and down, over and across, we slowly made our way higher and higher. It was the first time I'd really solo hiked with Lobster, and we were able to share a lot of our philosophies and ideas about life, as well as the things we were taking away from the journey. We were both surprised to find that we were along the same lines of thought on many subjects, strengthening our friendship.

We arrived at the Hut sometime after 5 pm completely exhausted. We'd only done a little over eleven miles, but it felt like more than thirty. We found DSOH and several other hikers already there and vying for work for stay. This Hut was the first Hut that presented a really unpleasant experience. The caretakers were all college aged kids with zero people skills and so many chips on their shoulders, they couldn't possibly eat them all.

As we went inside to escape the unrelenting wind, one of the kids came up to us immediately and said, "I'm sorry, but we don't have any more work for stays, you're going to have to keep going." "Keep going where? It's almost dark," I replied. "Keep going over Washington," the lanky kid said. "I understand, but over Washington to where?" "To the next Hut," he said nonchalantly. "That's almost eight miles from here over multiple mountains that are above tree line and it's almost dark," I said. "That's not my problem," he replied. I looked at DSOH who was standing nearby listening. He made a face at me and said, "They're trying to kick me out too." I looked back at the kid trying to keep my expression neutral and my voice calm. "You can't kick people out onto this ridge at night, there's high wind, no cover, and the temperatures will drop below freezing. You're obligated to give people shelter regardless of their financial standing or social status without discrimination; the sign on the front of your building says so (this is a fact by the way). You don't have to give us a bed, but we'll be sleeping on your dining room floor tonight and we'll do whatever chores you can find for us."

The kid knew he was stuck. He'd tried to hold his ground and bluff us into leaving, but I wasn't buying it. He couldn't say another thing to me and he knew that he couldn't physically remove us without some serious repercussions from whoever his boss was, and myself for that matter. However, the kid wasn't done; "I don't have any chores for you, but for $20 I'll give you leftovers and you can sleep on the floor." I wasn't going to argue with him anymore, and $20 wasn't completely unreasonable for a hot meal and some shelter from the harsh winds and temperatures outside. I knew what game he was playing; he was going to pocket the twenty bucks. I gave him my debit card instead so that he was forced to manually scan it with an old school ink slider and fill out my receipt by hand so that it wouldn't be possible for him to pocket anything. He told me he would prefer cash when I handed him my debit card, but I told him I was completely out due to buying pumpkin bread at $3 a slice from the other Hut.

I'll never understand why it was such a big deal to allow people to take shelter at that Hut to avoid the dangerous ridge that night. The kid was so determined not to let us stay there, that it made one wonder what his reasoning could possibly have been. I could understand if we'd gotten there in the middle of the day, with plenty of time and daylight to make it to the next sheltered area, however that wasn't the case. The days were getting shorter and night wasn't far off. This terrain was suicidal to navigate in the daylight, not to mention the dark, and if anything was to happen, you'd be helpless.

That night we enjoyed an endless supply of Goulash soup and boiled chicken. It was completely worth the $20 and not letting that kid push us around. Powerhouse showed up over an hour later, but there was no sign of Laser. Powerhouse informed us that he'd complained about his foot hurting, and as a consequence had slowed way down. I was worried about him and wasn't able to reach him on his cell. That ridge was deadly at night, as well as devoid of trees and he only had a hammock. He never showed up that evening...

The next morning, I got up early with DSOH, Lobster, and Powerhouse to pack up. We waited a while to see if Laser would arrive and to our immense relief, he did, although with a little hitch in his step. As it got late, Laser realized he wasn't going to make it to the Hut before dark. He went off the trail and descended the side of the ridge where he'd seen some trees not too far down. They were very small, but he managed to get his hammock strung up and stay warm throughout the night. He was also lucky enough that the side of the ridge he camped on stayed out of the wind for most of the night. We were all glad to hear that his night hadn't been too bad and that his foot problems were stemming from the fact that his last pair of socks had completely worn through, causing some nasty blisters to develop. It would be an easy fix once he got into town and bought a new pair.

That seventh day was mentally and physically one of the most challenging days I remembered having out on the trail. The combination of pain, frustration, and helplessness was nearly overwhelming while attempting to maintain a positive outlook. The plan was to finish the rest of the Presidential Mountain Range and knock out the last fifteen miles to Pinkham Notch, then hitch into the town of Gorham.

That morning began easily enough with a rocky mile and a half climb over the last twelve hundred feet to the summit of Washington that ended up being relatively unchallenging. In fact, it was pleasantly easy. The climb was nothing more than a series of moderately high rocky steps that never got too terribly steep.

Upon reaching the summit of Washington, I was disappointed, but not even slightly surprised, to find that it was a tourist trap. Leave it to commercialism to take the highest mountain peak in the northeast and turn it into a tourist attraction. They'd done the same for the tallest peak in the southeast at Clingmans Dome as well. I won't be surprised on the day they decide to build a road to the top of Mt. Everest and put a snack bar and souvenir shop that sells "I just climbed Everest" t-shirts to the people climbing out of their cars. That was what the top of Washington was like. You couldn't see any of it when approaching the summit from the south side, but there was a road, a big parking lot, a souvenir shop with a snack bar, a post office of all things, and a railroad that gave you a one-hour train ride up the mountain from some other parking lot far below for the modest price of $40.

The only thing I didn't complain about was the snack bar. It would be hypocritical of me to say that I didn't support the snack bar, because I did purchase snacks while up there. The commercial display of things looked ugly, but the snack bar was a welcomed sight. Anything that had food was always a welcomed sight out there, no matter where it happened to be.

We stayed on the summit of Washington until noon, eating snacks and enjoying the view of the world from those dizzying heights. With more than thirteen miles and three more mountains ahead of us before we could reach some kind of cover, DSOH and Powerhouse opted to take the train down. They cited the reason for their decision was that they didn't think they could make the distance required before dark. They planned to come back up early the next day in order to complete it with a sufficient amount of time. It was shortly after their decision to do this, that I realized they had the right idea.

Lobster, Laser (with his new socks from the souvenir shop), and I set out. The two of them left a short time ahead of me because I was still talking to DSOH. My troubles started almost immediately as I began descending Washington. There was no trail and the rocks were different there from anywhere else I'd been. They'd developed a very coarse and jaggedly rough surface that was worse than one hundred grit sandpaper. Katana couldn't do it, due to the coarse rock surface hurting her feet. I had to carry her... and carry her... and carry her. With all of my winter gear plus her on my shoulders, I was pushing close to seventy pounds on my back. Fortunately, I was practically out of food, or it would have been much heavier.

The going was painfully slow, and painfully painful. Up and down, up and down, up and down we went. I'd never carried her for this long before; my neck and shoulders cramped while my joints screamed. After what felt like hours, I checked my map only to realize that I'd gone only a few miles. The trail was nothing but rocks and my feet were getting pulverized. To be honest, there wasn't even a trail to really follow. The area was so open and rocky that they couldn't even paint blazes on the rocks in hopes that you would spot them. Instead you had to follow "Cairns."

Cairns were small stacks of rocks anywhere from one foot to five or six feet tall. They were interesting little works of art in their own right and very unnatural looking. Their unnatural appearance made them easy to recognize on the rocky terrain so that you could follow one Cairn to the next.

As the hours ticked by and the miles ticked by even slower, my level of discomfort rose to unbearable heights. The combination of hurting feet, carrying a dog that was throwing me off balance, my cramping neck and shoulders, slow pace, high winds, cold temperatures, and the knowledge that I wasn't going to able to stop until I reached some kind of cover, was incredibly disheartening. In a situation like this, I would normally call it a day and stop wherever I was, but on that day I didn't have the option. As with all situations out on the trail, I accepted and embraced it. I knew I was committed to playing the game that I'd signed up for until it was over.

Once again, I can't even describe to you what this terrain looked like. Just imagine rocky jetties, only sharper and smaller. Now imagine mountains and valleys of them with no trees, almost no flat spots, and no dirt. You're simply rock hopping and stepping over rocks for mile after mile after mile with no real sense of distance and no end in sight.

While trudging along and staring at my feet, watching every step, I noticed a splash of blood on the rocks. It looked fresh and as I continued on, I began to see more and more splashes of blood that continued looking more and more fresh. They were dry on the sides but still wet in the middle.

I came upon two day hikers and asked if either of them was injured. They replied with a puzzled "No, why?" that equally puzzled me. "You haven't seen all the blood on the ground?" I asked. "No, we haven't seen anything," they replied. How people could be so unaware of their surroundings completely baffled me. I couldn't understand how they could miss it while going in the same direction as me. "Keep an eye on the ground and you'll see it," I commented as I passed them. I was thoroughly surprised that I was actually moving quicker than others through that area, because it felt as if I was crawling.

I finally reached the next Hut at almost 5 pm to find Lobster. I asked him if he'd seen the blood almost as soon as I walked up. He told me that not only had he seen it, but also found the source. A woman had brought an eighty-pound white lab up the mountain with her, and as a consequence, its paws had been cut to pieces and bleeding all over the rocks. She hadn't been strong enough to carry it and was forced to go back down another trail with the poor dog faithfully following behind her.

This story made me very annoyed and sad at the same time. I didn't know how much blame to put on the owner, but I felt like one good look at those rocks was a no brainer for not bringing a dog up there. That goes especially for a dog that you couldn't physically carry yourself. The splashes of blood had gone on for miles and I couldn't imagine the pain and discomfort that poor animal must have been in. If I thought I'd been having a bad day, that poor lab was having it a hundred times worse. My predicament didn't seem so bad anymore.

Everything is perspective out there. No matter how bad it was, or how bad you thought things were, it could always be worse; there is always somebody out there having a harder time than you are. The question is…are they complaining or feeling sorry for themselves?

We still had almost eight miles to go over one last mountain and one last huge descent in order to reach Pinkham Notch. Lobster got a big head start on me while I rested and aired out my feet at the Hut. Mount Madison was what I thought would be my final obstacle of the day, but I couldn't have been more wrong.

Madison was only maybe a six or seven-hundred-foot climb, but it was straight up. It was quite literally a stack of boulders that came to a sharp point and nothing else. You could look up and see the point of the summit far above you with no path and virtually no Cairns. All you could do was get on the rocks and start climbing towards the top. Once again Katana was riding shotgun on my shoulders, and when I hit the top of Madison, my jaw dropped.

Spread out before me was a striking view of the entire mountain ridge that I'd just traversed; I could see it wrapping all the way around and back up to the summit of Washington. In front and below me I could see for over three miles of the rocky ridge that I stood on, as it plummeted in tiered sections for more than three thousand feet down. There was hardly a tree in sight. This entire three-mile, three-thousand-foot descent that consisted completely of jumbled up jagged rocks and boulders was the most incredible thing I'd seen so far. When I say incredible, I mean incredibly ridiculous! It was gorgeous, but it was another one of those moments where you thought to yourself, "You have got to be kidding me!" It was so dangerous and difficult looking that I couldn't help but laugh and be excited for the challenge, despite all my pain, exhaustion, and discomfort.

As I admired what lay before me, I noticed a little red speck over a mile away and a thousand feet down, hopping along the rocks. I guessed it was Laser, his bright red shirt giving him away. "KAAAA--KAAAAW!" I called at the top of my lungs from the pin point summit of Madison. A few seconds passed as I heard the call echo over and over again through the mountains and valleys. I saw the red speck pause after several seconds as I guessed he was trying to find the source of the call. I waved my walking staff over my head and called, "RIDERS OF ROHAN, WHAT NEWS FROM THE MARK!" This was a quote straight from The Lord of the Rings (LOTR) that felt just a little too perfect in that Middle Earth landscape. I heard a reply several seconds later. "GANDALF WE MUST TURN BACK!" This was another direct LOTR quote, although from a different scene. The LOTR quotes were shouted back and forth over the great expanse for some time before we got back to the job at hand. Lobster even chimed in with a, "LEGOLAS, WHAT DO YOUR ELF EYES SEE?" from somewhere in-between us, although I wasn't able to spot him amongst the rocks.

After the LOTR quote-a-thon, my spirits soared once again. That little distraction and bit of fun was all it took to turn my terrible day completely around. It truly is the simple things in life that matter. Like listening to the echoes of your epic Lord of the Rings quotes bounce off the mountainside. I once again threw caution and pain to the wind as I began rock hopping back towards earth with the prowess of a mountain goat. My knees had long since gone numb and the only pain I could feel was that of my smashed up feet. That three miles of rocky ridge was the longest and most treacherous descent I ever encountered on the entire trail, except for one more that I hadn't reached yet and wouldn't even lump in the same category as that one. Katana rode on my shoulders like some kind of CatFox cowboy the entire way down.

At the bottom of Madison, I caught up to Laser and Lobster as they were getting water from a stream. For the last five miles, we were back in the trees, as well as the dark. We donned our headlamps and began some New Hampshire night hiking. Finally, out of the rocks, Katana was able to hike on her own and gave me my first break from carrying her in almost ten miles. The three of us passed the time as well as the miles while talking about what we would do after the trail and how this crazy journey had changed our lives forever.

When we finally reached Pinkham, it was nearly 10 pm. We all agreed that day was easily the most physically challenging day we could remember. Kinsman still stuck out to me, but this had honestly been much worse from a distance and pain perspective. Kinsman had only been a warm up to that stretch. The Presidential range had kicked my ass, and although beautiful, I was glad to put it behind me.

In Pinkham, we managed to catch a ride with a guy that was a member of a local search and rescue team. We'd received word from DSOH that he'd gotten a hotel room in Gorham and awaited our arrival. Not only were DSOH and Powerhouse there, but Schweppes was there too. Schweppes was actually twenty-three miles ahead of Pinkham Notch, but had come into Gorham by a different road. I hadn't seen him since Hanover, more than ten days prior, and it was going to be a little while longer before we closed the gap between us on the trail.

We all planned to start back at our respective trailheads whenever we left Gorham. That twenty-three-mile gap between Schweppes and I was all that was left in the Whites, and I hadn't taken a day off since Hanover. Since then, New Hampshire had kicked my ass six ways to Sunday. The descent down Madison had split my heel open again, as well as the other one too. I was now working with two severely cracked heels and there was no question I was taking the next day off.

That next day proved to be cold, windy, and rainy, all the more reinforcing our decision to stay and rest. Everyone was in the same frame of mind, even Schweppes. Gorham was a medium large town with pretty much everything you could ever want or need, such as restaurants, cafes, bars, shops, hotels, fast food, and Wal-Mart. Among a few other things, Gorham will always be remembered by me as the last town on the trail that had a Wal-Mart.

Wal-Mart was like a thru-hiker beacon out on the trail. You could always look forward to a pleasant one-stop shopping experience with reasonably cheap prices. Resupplying at convenience stores and gas stations was expensive; it made you want to weep when the barely three days-worth of gas station food and snacks rang up to more than $60. Although you encountered plenty of legitimate grocery stores along the trail, you still ran into quite a few small towns that didn't have much more than a gas station. If you were lucky, there might be a Dollar General.

We strategized the next leg of our journey, as DSOH and Powerhouse were determined to go back and finish the stretch from Washington to Pinkham. The plan was to wait for DSOH and Powerhouse, then hike out the next day. Schweppes, Lobster, Laser, and myself were afforded a second zero day to sleep in and do nothing besides eat "Poutine Fries."

Poutine Fries were something of a new experience to me. It was a Canadian dish of French fries with a light brown gravy and cheese poured over top of them. I hate to say it, but it beat the hell out of chili cheese fries any day. I concede that Canada won the war on cheese fries.

When DSOH and Powerhouse arrived at the end of the day, they were in rough shape. DSOH's knees were in a very bad way, and he was in a lot of pain. At Schweppes's behest and encouragement, it was decided that DSOH would forgo the twenty-three-mile stretch between the two roads into Gorham. According to Schweppes, that twenty-three-mile stretch was the steepest and most dangerous section that he'd seen in the entire Whites. DSOH was to start with Schweppes at the northern boundary of the Whites, while Lobster, Laser, Powerhouse, and myself were to finish up the grand finale.

It was an extremely cold, windy, and overcast day when we picked the trail back up at Pinkham Notch. We were getting a fairly late start at around noon, due to not finding a ride out of town. The first climb was a two-thousand-foot bruiser named "Wild Cat Mountain." This son of a gun went straight up the entire two thousand feet in just a little over a mile. This marked the steepest climb that the Whites had to offer. Nothing could really get any steeper than Wild Cat without turning into a legitimate rock climb. The only differences that you could distinguish when trying to compare or gauge the difficulty of different climbs, was the length and frequency of scramble-like obstacles. Wildcat had enough to easily place as the top contender for "steepest climb." The top of Wildcat was a series of shorter rollercoaster climbs that took you past a ski lift that wouldn't be in operation until snow fell. It wasn't far from this ski lift that Lobster, Laser, and I took a snack break and made a chilling discovery.

While sitting around on the summit of Wildcat, eating a few snacks, Laser repositioned a medium sized rock so that he could sit on it more comfortably. Under this rock was a perfectly folded piece of notebook paper. Out of curiosity, we opened it and found it to be dated for January 2013, over a year and a half earlier. It was amazing to see that the paper had been preserved so well just by sitting beneath the rock.

The contents of the letter were of a very personal and sad nature. It was obvious that it was not meant to be read by anyone else, except who it was written for. Full of feelings, memories, confessions, and reminiscing, the letter was written to someone that had died. It contained their name, but no cause of death or location of their death. I could only assume that the person's demise had something to do with Wildcat Mountain, and I was suddenly very intrigued to learn more about what happened to the individual that had prompted such a heartfelt and beautiful letter. We carefully folded the letter up and placed it back where we found it before continuing on.

I would later do some research into recent deaths on Wildcat Mountain and found that an eighteen-year-old boy had died there in December of 2012. I will leave out his name, but the individual in question and two of his friends had climbed the closed ski slopes of Wildcat Mountain around midnight in late December. They had snow sleds with them, and planned to sled back down the steep ski slopes of the mountain and back to a parking lot. Upon reaching the bottom, the two friends of the individual realized that he was nowhere to be found. After searching in vain, they finally called authorities around 3 am.

Ski Patrol and Conservation Officers scoured the mountain for hours with no luck or sign of him. It was only shortly before 8 a.m. that a member of the ski patrols located his sled in the woods about a half a mile down from the summit. From there it was only a short time before other rescuers located his body not far from the sled. He was found to have died largely in part by the injuries he sustained during the sled crash, while the harsh cold and snow had done the rest.

This was a tragic story that conjured up many feelings and even more questions. Situations in which an individual could have possibly been saved always got me thinking. What injuries did he sustain? How long was he alive after sustaining them? Could he have possibly been saved if he'd been found sooner? Where did people look first and did they possibly miss him in the dark? If one little thing had been done differently, would the outcome have changed? What would that little thing have been? All of these questions swirled around my head. It was like little Ottie Cline from Virginia all over again. I still had no clue that another casualty was looming just around the corner.

While crossing the multiple peaks of Wildcat, a freezing rain began to fall. As we descended the maniacal twelve-hundred-foot vertical slope into Carter Notch, the rain began to sleet. It was so miserably cold that I wanted nothing more than to get out of it. When we got into Carter Notch, we were greeted with another beautiful sight that had been molded by the dangerous conditions we were in. We couldn't help but notice that we were standing in a bowl.

The nearly vertical twelve-hundred-foot climb back up Wild Cat was on one side, while an even more vertical fifteen hundred foot climb up Carter

Dome Mountain was on the other. You could quite literally see straight up to the tops of both mountain peaks from the bottom of the notch. Situated in the middle of the notch was a gorgeous, small lake, full of aquatic plants and boulders rising out of the water and lining its sandy shores. As we admired and walked around the rim of the lake, a fog began to roll down the slopes of Carter Dome and towards the water. The creeping fog combined with the ripples of rain on the surface of the lake created a beautiful sight. On a nicer day, I might have stayed a while and swam, however the conditions were rapidly deteriorating as the wind and rain picked up. The choice not to climb Carter Dome and instead stay as low as possible was made fairly quickly.

We came across the last Hut of the White Mountains tucked away in Carter Notch. When we entered the nearly empty lodge, the caretakers almost immediately asked us to leave. I couldn't help but notice that the caretakers were once again college aged kids. Now remember that the biggest rule in the Whites is that you're not allowed to stealth camp. You have to camp in designated areas that cost money and under no circumstance are you allowed to camp near a Hut. Stealth camping was out of the question, but to stealth camp near a Hut was an even bigger breach of the rules. The nearest campground was over Carter Dome and almost ten miles away. In that terrain, it would take close to an entire day to go that distance, as it had taken us five long hours to go the six miles to reach Carter Notch.

We found ourselves facing off with the Hut crew. I casually responded once again with, "Where are we supposed to go? Your park rules forbid us from stealth camping, it's getting late, there's a freezing storm and the next designated campground is ten miles away." The kid countered, "I understand, but you can't stay here, we don't have room for you." I quickly replied, "You're lying to me right now; you have a dining room with plenty of floor space and there aren't any other thru-hikers here." He then countered, "We have a full roster of guests and we can't let you stay here." "Yes, but how does that affect our sleeping on the floor and taking shelter from the storm?" I argued. He didn't have a response for that, but instead replied with, "You're not staying." "Well where do we go then, since we're not allowed to camp?" I asked, trying to play their rules against them. "You can stealth camp, but not near the Hut. You can go up Wildcat and there are some stealth spots up there." I could have grabbed this kid by his shirt and shook him when he said this. "Are you telling us to camp on top of a mountain in the middle of a freezing storm? Does whoever is in charge of you know that you're giving out deadly advice to people and turning them away in dangerous conditions?"

I was fuming mad at this point and Lobster's New Jersey accent was starting to get heavier and heavier as he chimed in. I knew he was at the point of exploding. I was so ticked off with the irrational stupidity of that kid that I didn't want to be anywhere near him, even if they did let us stay. Too much had already been said and tensions were too high. In the end they wouldn't even allow us to at least take shelter for a short while and let the storm die down. I was thoroughly appalled that people could treat their fellow man this way. I couldn't help but wonder how many people on the list of "Casualties of the White Mountains" had been turned away from Huts and forced out in dangerous conditions such as those.

Instead of hiking back out of the notch, we went a few yards into the woods behind the Hut and set up camp. No one was going to come outside in the deplorable, freezing conditions to find us anyway. The rain, wind, and thunder lasted all night as it got colder than I can ever remember it getting on the trail. It was without a doubt the coldest night I ever experienced out there. For the first time on the entire journey, I had to fashion my rain fly into a cocoon that enveloped my entire hammock instead of using it as only a roof. The cocoon helped to block out some of the wind and rain, as well as insulate me that much more. With all my layers on and Katana tucked into my sleeping bag with me, I was still cold. Even Katana was shaking while she was nestled in the bag. Just as we predicted, no one ever came outside and discovered our fairly obvious camping spot.

It was freezing and windy as hell the next morning, and even with gloves on, my hands went numb as I packed up. It was at that time I began to wonder if all the people that had said "You're late," had been right. The cold had finally caught up with me, and now I was second guessing all of the roses that I'd stopped to smell along the way. If it was to be as cold as this for the next three hundred miles, it was going to be a miserable home stretch.

The short fifteen hundred foot climb up Carter Dome kicked my ass for some reason, taking me well over an hour to complete. My feet and heels were killing me, as all day long it was up and down rock scrambles, mud pits, and unprotected ridges while getting hammered by freezing winds. There was ice in the trees and on the ground throughout most of the day, never melting in the afternoon sun. I didn't take many breaks, because as long as I moved then I wasn't freezing. I took several sliding falls that weren't too bad, but it was a grueling day with miles that dragged by.

The highlight came atop Middle Carter Mountain in the early afternoon. It was as I looked back towards Washington and the other Presidentials across a vast landscape of rolling hills and smaller mountain peaks that I was greeted by a beautifully unique sight. A thick blanket of clouds washed over dozens of other mountains and hills, spurred on by the fierce winds. The surface of the sea of clouds was completely smooth as it rushed over the mountains, surging down, and then rushing back up as it engulfed one mountain after another. The most amazing aspect was watching it play out below me as it quickly came my way. I would have sat up there and watched it longer if the winds hadn't been so strong. I got some amazing pictures, but didn't think to take a video. As they say, hindsight is 20/20.

I met Lobster and Laser near a pleasant little stream later that evening. We were only four miles from the road, but decided to camp instead of pushing on and being tempted with going back into town. The spot was just as good as any, and for the first time since entering the Whites, we made a fire. There was a second dry creek bed paralleling the stream that was full of river rocks. We used them to build a beautiful fire ring and luckily none of them cracked or exploded on us from trapped moisture. Although still in the Whites, we were only four miles from the northern border of the park, and it was cold enough to justify risking a fire. We waited for Powerhouse, but she never arrived that night.

The White Mountains had enchanted me. Despite their extreme terrain and dangerous conditions, these mountains had left their mark on my very being. The rewarding feeling at the end of each day that came from pushing myself to the absolute limits on a daily basis was intoxicating. The views and revelations that you experienced atop these mountains were unforgettable as well as life altering. The pain and suffering that surrounded it served to make it more real, more visceral. Perhaps this entire journey was akin to the Australian Aborigine's Walkabout; I felt as if I was coming into my own. I was becoming something I never could have become without the solitude and help the mountains, rocks, rain, wind, and pain were shaping within me. I truly didn't want it to end...

The next morning, a hiker that we were familiar with named Rizzah, joined us around our morning fire as we awaited Powerhouse. He told us he passed her that morning and that she'd injured herself in a fall. He said she thought one of her ribs might be broken, causing her to move very slowly. On top of that, he told us the story of a death he'd personally witnessed while in the White Mountains only days before.

Rizzah had been coming down the Great Moosilauke with another hiker we were familiar with named K-Bar, who was a former marine (excuse me... Marine. There is no such thing as a former Marine). A day-hiker/trail runner in his late thirties had slowed down to talk to them as they made their descent. How anyone was "trail running" the north side of Moosilauke, I will never know, but somehow that guy was managing it. Rizzah recounted that after the runner had slowed down and begun talking to them, after only several seconds, the man froze up and fell backwards onto the ground. No breathing, no twitching. He collapsed wide eyed onto the rock and that was it.

Rizzah began to descend the mountain as fast as he could in an attempt to call and meet whatever rescue team would respond. K-bar stayed on Moosilauke with the man and performed CPR for well over an hour with no luck. The man was dead when the rescue team arrived and all they could do was carry the body off the mountain.

This was a terrible thing to have happen to someone while out for a run and an equally terrible thing to have to witness. Rizzah confided that he'd been having nightmares about it ever since, and K-bar had been affected by it as well.

I never discovered what the prognosis was for the man's death, but having been in the fitness and health industry for a few years, I had a slight idea. The man had been in good condition and exercised frequently, but there was no denying that he'd suffered from a massive heart attack. The question was, why? My opinion/answer could be a fairly reasonable explanation. Disregarding any family health history and his proneness to a heart attack, there is something that is known in the fitness industry that can be dangerous, if not deadly, when exercising. That condition is called "sudden stop to exercise." This is why you're always told to have a cool down period after an intense run or bout of exercise instead of abruptly stopping. For example, when you finish a long or fast run, you are supposed to walk for several minutes, allowing your heart to recover and slow back down to a normal rhythm. It is very rare, but I have read several cases of people dying after suddenly concluding an intense bout of exercise without a cool down. One case was when a man had been running up and down a stair case at his gym as a form of "stadium exercise." At the top of one of his stair climbs, he stopped and stood up straight to catch his breath. Moments after stopping, he collapsed stone dead on the floor at the top of the stairs.

It's very rare, but I believe something similar happened to this trail runner. He had suddenly stopped to talk with the hikers near a particularly rough patch of rocks and the quick stop without proper breathing and cool down may have triggered a heart attack. Extremely rare, but all of the conditions must have been just right for everything to go completely wrong inside of his body. As a result of this incident, the list of casualties in the White Mountains added one more name in September of 2014.

Late in the morning, Powerhouse finally reached our position and hobbled over to our fire. She was looking very dispirited and in pain. We walked to the road together as we said goodbye to the White Mountains. At this particular road, we were only sixteen miles from reaching Maine. We had originally planned to hike as far as we could that day, however with Powerhouse's injury, she wanted to go back into town and rest. Not wanting to leave her behind, we all went with her as we hitched a ride back to Gorham with an elderly couple in the back of their pick up.

It turned out that Powerhouse didn't have broken ribs, but they were severely bruised. She opted to stay in Gorham to rest, as Laser, Lobster, and I decided to stay with her. We could tell she was in a lot of pain, as well as in a low place all around. We all wanted to be there for her encouragement, but also to make sure she didn't make any emotionally charged, pain fueled decisions to go home.

The day that followed this first "Nearo" day (a day when you hike nearly zero miles) was perhaps one of the most random days I ever had on the trail. I would normally neither boast nor even recount an event such as the one I'm about to divulge, but the randomness, craziness, and I suppose kindness of it was too much not to share.

I woke up the next morning with every intention of hiking out, despite my severe foot pain and Powerhouse being on the fence about taking another day to heal. I left the room early to walk down to the local Dunkin Doughnuts to have breakfast, but never made it that far. Right next door to our hotel was a Bar/Restaurant which will remain nameless. As I walked by, I heard a voice call, "Hey!" I stopped and looked over to see a guy poke his head out of the emergency exit door of the bar while he motioned me over. I looked around to make sure I was the person being beckoned in. I was the only one in the vicinity, so he must have been talking to me. "Ok, I'll check it out and see what this guy wants," I thought to myself.

I walked over as he further motioned me into the bar. That early in the morning, the entire place was dark and closed down, but upon entering the main bar room, I recognized the hiker I knew as K-Bar. This was the guy that had performed CPR on the trail runner that died on Moosilauke. I hadn't seen him since Tennessee, so I was glad to see him well and still on the trail. The guy who motioned me in was a bartender that happened to be related to the owners of the bar in some way. They were both pretty drunk and I suspected they had been up all night; either that or they just recently awoke from sleeping in the pub. K-bar had recognized me through the front window as I walked by and then asked the bartender to invite me in.

They were drinking Budweiser, and as I pulled up a stool, the bartender offered me a bottle on the house. "I can't turn down free beer," I thought to myself as I decided to partake. After a few more free beers and chewing the fat, the bartender pulled out an unopened bottle of Tullamore Dew, Irish whiskey and poured three shots. Hard liquor was usually not my style and definitely NOT that early in the morning.

When the whiskey came out, it forced me to think about the entire situation for a good minute. "How often does something like this happen to you?" I thought to myself..."especially on a once in a lifetime journey such as this." I quickly reasoned that this was one of those moments you didn't pass up. Plus, it's free alcohol at a closed bar that you have all to yourself. I made yet another executive decision that I was going to ride this gravy train all the way down. As DSOH always said, "Never pass up a good thing."

Toast after toast, shot after shot, this was some of the smoothest whiskey I'd ever had (which isn't saying much). The burn was probably softened by the beer I'd consumed just minutes before, but we polished off the whole bottle in just over half an hour. My blood felt like gasoline, and after a bit more conversation, I bowed out back to my room, which was only maybe two hundred feet away. I never got to have my Dunkin Doughnuts that morning, as I had beer and whiskey for breakfast instead. I walked out of that bar, as if emerging from my chrysalis of whiskey breakfast, transformed into a true blue, whiskey drinkin, snake eatin, hard fartin, mountain man. Not really... but it was funny to think about.

I arrived back at the room and announced that I would be staying in town another day. Laser and Lobster were amazed to see me hammered so early in the morning, supposedly after going to Dunkin Doughnuts for a breakfast toaster. They were even more amazed by the story of how it happened. They nearly died laughing while they complained that nothing like that ever happened to them; however, they both agreed that it was an opportunity that wasn't to be passed. Lobster decided to hike out while Laser and I stayed with Powerhouse for one more day and night in the room. I spent that day mostly hung over and eating Poutine Fries at a local joint down the road. I knew that I couldn't let anything interfere with hiking out the next day.

It was Maine or bust on September 17th, my 172nd day on the trail. Powerhouse was still in a great deal of pain and decided to hang back. Laser and I couldn't take any more time off, but we made her promise to stay on the trail before we set out. DSOH, Schweppes, and Lobster were already way ahead of us and we were determined to catch up. It was going to be only Laser and me for the next several days as we sprinted to make up the lost ground.

With over sixteen miles to the border of Maine, we committed to the plan of getting there that day no matter what. The only thing that stuck a wrench in our plan was getting back to the trail. We had such a hard time finding a ride that it was after 11 am by the time we finally made it to the trailhead. With such a late start, we knew it would be a grueling day if we were going stick to our goal of reaching Maine.

That day was the most painful day for my feet in recent memory; due to the fact that they were quite literally falling apart. I now had three deep cracks on my left heel and four deep cracks on my right heel. My knees were constantly throbbing and my bad ankle was almost constantly twice the size of the other one, rolling on a semi daily basis, even with the brace on. Every time my ankle rolled, it brought me to the ground for at least two to five minutes as I allowed the worst of the pain to subside before pushing on.

I completely rolled my ankle close to a hundred times between the Grayson Highlands accident and finishing the journey. Some were worse than others, but all of them hurt nonetheless. It got to the point where my ligaments and tendons were so torn and loose, that the slightest slants, missteps, roots, small rocks, or uneven ground sent my ankle rolling without warning; even with the extra support of the heavy brace. The shock of pain that shot through my entire body and into my brain with each new roll was enough to haunt my dreams even when I wasn't on the trail. I didn't dare walk around towns on the flat roads without my brace. The irony of the ankle rolling situation was that it almost never happened on the more severe terrain, or while I was really exerting myself. It always happened on moderate terrain when I experienced lapses in concentration due to not having to focus so much on where I was putting my feet. This made the rolls that much more unexpected, and that much more painful, because my body was usually relaxed when it happened.

Right off the bat after leaving Gorham we had a two-thousand-foot climb. We didn't break, we didn't stop. One thousand feet down, eight hundred feet up, five hundred down, one thousand up, two hundred down, three hundred up, three hundred down, three hundred up, finally flat, then one thousand feet up again. We were relentless and only paused to break three times throughout the entire afternoon. The terrain itself was insane, as New Hampshire wasn't letting us go without a fight. Despite everything that old Hampshire was throwing at us, we remained resolved to be done with her that night.

There were steep rock scrambles and countless smooth rock faces that were so steep you had to crawl up and slide down them. My feet hurt beyond words as the feeling of razors stuck in my heels wouldn't subside. Each and every step was filled with a sharp and stinging pain that I never got used to, as each step hurt just as much as the one before. On top of that, I could feel another crack beginning to open on the front left side of my left foot. My feet were on the edge of what they could endure.

By the time we reached the top of the last one-thousand-foot climb, it was after 7 pm and almost dark. In fact, beneath the canopy of the trees, it was dark. At this time, we calculated that we still had a mile and a half to the border. New Hampshire was giving up the ghost that night no matter what!

The trail was rocks, scrambles, rocks, scrambles, and more rocks as our progress was painfully slow and it took us over an hour in the dark to complete the last mile and a half. It was towards the end of that very last half mile that I experienced one of my scariest moments on the trail yet.

We came to yet another smooth rock face descent, the biggest one I'd ever seen on the trail. Looking down with my headlamp, I couldn't see where the rock ended. It continued down into the dark and beyond the illumination of my light. I first tried baby stepping my way down, but quickly found it was too slick. I chose a different tactic and began to crouch and lower my ass onto the rock, so as to shimmy my way down. As I was approaching a full crouch, my feet slipped out from under me, my ass hit the rock and I was gone!

Sliding down faster and faster, I was terror stricken! I had no idea how far it went or if there was a turn with a ledge. I hit a rift and jammed my staff into it, attempting to slow or stop myself. I was going too fast and my momentum wrenched the staff out of my hand as it clattered against the rocks. In a ditch effort, I jammed my foot into the rift as well, but all it did was jackknife my body sideways over the raised crevice to continue my plummet down.

I was certain I was a dead man or at least in for a world of hurt. Laser was yelling above me as I continued sliding, and by that point I was desperate. I rolled over and pressed my hands to the rock in a fevered attempt to slow my wild descent. It was no good as my hands were immediately burned up. I looked back down just in time to see an object rushing up towards me in the middle of the rock face. I couldn't tell if it was a rock or a log, but hoped it wasn't a splintered log as I jammed my leg at it in desperation. I stopped abruptly with a shooting pain in my leg as I realized that it was indeed a rock. Katana came skidding into me two seconds later.

"MAYOR, ARE YOU OK!?" Laser was frantically yelling somewhere above me. "I'M OK," I called up to put his mind at ease. The reality was that my feet were throbbing, my leg was throbbing, and my palms and finger tips were burning with that icy numb feeling like someone had just taken sandpaper to them. I didn't even care, because I was happy to still be alive!

My next realization was that Katana had charged down after me. Whether she was just following or had been genuinely concerned, I'll never

296

know. I know that she must have felt the panic of the situation from Laser and me, so I'd like to believe that she charged after me out of loyalty and concern, or maybe even trying to save me. Either way it warmed my heart and strengthened our bond that much more.

We ended up having to skirt the edge of the rock and lower ourselves down while holding onto tree branches and vegetation. It turned out that if I hadn't stopped myself on that rock, then I would've continued down right into... a mud pit. Hardly deadly or dangerous, but it could've been a lot worse on my hands and the rest of me if I started tumbling or rolling. I couldn't believe how much speed I'd picked up while sliding down that rock. That was one of the incidents which contributed to the destruction of my Sealine Bag, as well as further damage to my poor radio backpack.

After another quarter mile, a small wooden sign that was staked to the ground materialized out of the darkness. "NEW HAMPSHIRE-MAINE STATE LINE" was engraved and painted black on the white wooden sign.

Maine, the final state! The home stretch! A place that at the beginning of the journey, I never thought in my wildest dreams I would reach! This was the beginning of the end; the end of the beginning; or the beginning of the beginning... depending on how you wanted to look at it. Maine had started off as a seemingly unattainable dream for each of those long months ago. All of the excruciating pain in those first weeks, that made time seem as if it were standing still, had made Maine seem like an impossible destination. Upon seeing that sign, I couldn't help but scream in my head, "This place exists! It's real! After all of these months, I'm finally here!"

The adventure was almost over. Every hardship and trial of this journey had been culminating and building up to this final stretch. On that day, the joyful realization of - "I am a thru-hiker," finally set in. I had started in Georgia and hiked "thru" to Maine. Only two hundred and eighty-two more miles of Maine wilderness and it would all be over. I would finally be able to bask in the momentous feeling of accomplishment that completing this journey would surely bring...

CHAPTER 17: MAINE

"The Beginning of the End... I Never Wanted to End."

Maine was said to be a lot of things. It was said to have the most beautiful views, the wildest wildernesses, the most rivers, lakes and ponds, the most mud, and in some people's opinions, the hardest terrain of the entire trail. What was also said was that you would love every minute of it. I found that all of those statements couldn't have been truer.

Anything beautiful that any of the other states featured, Maine also had tenfold. The abundant rivers, streams, creeks, and waterfalls that surrounded the landscape of Maine were just as beautiful, if not more beautiful and abundant, than anywhere else on the trail. The mountains, forests, boulders, and views were unrivaled. The feeling of isolation and truly being in the middle of nowhere was never greater than when I was in Maine. When you thought the views couldn't get any better than they were in New Hampshire, Maine proved that they could. Not because you were up higher and could see further than you could in New Hampshire (which you weren't), but because of the lakes, ponds, and bogs. Anytime you were atop a mountain in Maine, the surrounding landscape and swaths of trees were broken up and dotted by countless ponds and lakes of varying sizes and shapes that reflected a golden sunlight of different hues throughout the day.

The call of Loons that penetrated the forest was an almost daily occurrence, while moose tracks and their droppings were everywhere; a constant reminder that those large creatures roamed the forests in great abundance. Maine was definitely unique to any other state I'd been through on this journey, and I couldn't think of a better place to conclude my adventure.

We were so beat up and tired the night we reached the state line that we hadn't gone any further than the sign. Since we both had hammocks, we were able to find suitable trees not far behind the wooden marker and called it a night. I remember being so excited to be in Maine that I hardly slept.

What can I say about my first day in Maine? New Hampshire kicked you in the ass on the way out, while Maine slapped you in the face on the way in. It was quite overcast, foggy, and windy on that first day in Maine, and the going was very rough. Southern Maine was rumored to be harder than the Whites, and depending on your personal opinion of what you considered "difficult and grueling," it might very well have been.

The entire trail was nothing but mud, jagged rock faces, smooth rock faces, tangled roots, and moss. That's about the best way I can describe the majority of southern Maine. If towering endless climbs, and equally endless scrambles that felt as if they went on forever are your bane, then you would probably consider the Whites to be harder. If never ending fields of mud, rocks, tangled patches of raised and washed out tree roots, bogs, small scrambles (that never give you a chance to maintain any kind of pace), and no short supply of large rocky climbs are your idea of torture... then southern Maine would probably seem harder to you.

Personally, I found southern Maine to be more challenging than the White Mountains as far as keeping up a steady pace and the mentally grueling aspects. This could also be attributed to the fact that my body was falling apart at this point and everything I did felt as if it was about to kill me. That being said, Pennsylvania still remains in a category and league all of its own. Nothing will ever seem worse than Pennsylvania... EVER.

Besides being our first day in Maine, it would be a special day for another reason. It was the day that we finally reached Mahoosuc Notch. Mahoosuc Notch was dubbed, "the hardest or most fun mile on the entire trail." Whether it was the hardest or most fun mile of the trail was completely dependent on you and your frame of mind. I personally had the time of my life in that death trap of a notch.

My father had an expression he would sometimes repeat to me as an adolescent. Being an Electronics Engineer, he told me it was an engineer's saying, and it went like this: "You can view the glass as being half full or half empty, but the engineer views the glass as being twice as big as it needs to be." This of course was meant to be a humorous contrast in perspectives, from an engineer's point of view; but, it also had a deeper meaning...The glass is always full.

Mahoosuc Notch is basically a narrow ravine between two mountains that carries on for just over a mile. That ravine was nothing but a giant jumble of boulders. Now, I've used the word "boulders" before while describing other areas of the trail I traversed, but on this day "boulders" took on a different meaning.

This mile-long boulder pit was filled with boulders the size of small cars; boulders the size of large cars; boulders the size of trucks; boulders the size of busses; boulders the size of semi-trucks and boulders the size of small houses. Then, there were boulders that were jumbled together to create caverns and caves; boulders jumbled together to create tight squeezes that you were forced to take your pack off to navigate; boulders jumbled together to create tunnels that you could walk through and tunnels you had to crawl through; boulders jumbled together to create abysses that appeared bottomless. Moreover, there were boulders you could climb, boulders you could slide down, boulders you could hang off, boulders you could make giant leaps off of - onto other boulders. There were smooth boulders, jagged boulders, round boulders, and flat boulders. Of course, there were also fat boulders, thin boulders, vertical boulders, horizontal boulders and every angle in between boulders.

What I'm trying to say here, is this was a one-mile-long adult jungle gym of death, made up of...boulders. Once again, no written description would ever come close to describing what this place was like in person. No photograph could capture it well enough to give you the full picture of what it was actually like when you stood amidst it. This notch was nothing like I'd imagined, but everything I could've hoped for. The fact that it was slow going was of no consequence, because we had already averaged only one mile per hour over the terrain preceding the Mahoosuc anyway. That pace was further reduced to one mile per two and a half hours once we entered the notch.

It was so unique to anything I'd encountered on the trail thus far, that I couldn't help but love it. Don't get me wrong, the Mahoosuc Notch was no joke and nothing to play around with. It was dangerous as hell, and downright deadly if you weren't careful. This mile was a prime example of the statement "life is what you make of it." To some, this was the best time you could ever hope to have, while to others, it was absolute misery.

There were two ways you could tackle the Mahoosuc. You could stay low and thread your way under, over, and around the madness of rocks while staying relatively safe; or you could go high and try to cross over the top of all of it by jumping, striding, stepping, climbing, and anything else you could manage in order to get across. Laser and I chose high, although in hindsight, it seemed like high and low were the same path at many points throughout the notch.

Dozens of times I was forced to carry Katana. I found myself feeling very bad for anyone that did this section with a large dog. They undoubtedly would've had to go low, and even then, they still would've encountered many problems.

At one point we came to a drop-off that had only one way down. Technically, we could have doubled back a short distance and simply passed low, but going back is for quitters and people who lose things, so we decided to make the most of it. The area to climb down was tight and required some agile mobility that was best achieved without a pack or a dog. I took off my backpack and carefully climbed down first. Then we used some 550 paracord to lower both mine and Laser's packs, before lowering Katana down by her padded harness. Katana's adventure reached a whole new level that day... rappelling.

Throughout the notch, there were countless areas when I needed both my hands free. Since I couldn't fold up my staff and put it in my pack (like most people could do with their trekking poles), I was presented with a new challenge. I had to either carry it or throw it ahead of me to whatever spot I was trying to reach. In the harsh terrain of the Whites, I had engineered a new staff of the same length and then shaved it down to approximately the same weight as my original. This was done to give me twice the pushing power of only one staff. It had worked out amazingly thus far, and I was quickly becoming sentimentally attached to the new one.

On one occasion in the notch, I was forced to climb down and across some big boulders. I realized I was going to need both my hands, so I looked for a level area to throw my staffs. I picked a good spot, then "javelined" my newest staff. "Bullseye!" It landed safe and sound right where I wanted. Now it was time for my original staff to make the flight. I javelined it towards the same spot, but to my absolute horror, it slipped straight down one of the abyss holes! When I finally reached the spot, I could barely see it at the bottom through the darkness. At the time of the incident, I was adhering to a strict "NO staff left behind" policy and knew I couldn't continue without it. I maybe could've suffered losing the new staff, but not the original, not old faithful who had been with me for over nineteen hundred miles.

With Laser and Katana watching above, I climbed down into the abyss, swallowed up by the inky darkness. It was maybe twelve feet to the bottom of the hole and a moderately challenging climb. I won't deny that it was scary as hell. I half imagined that I'd find some hiker skeleton lying next to another staff that had been lost down the abyss at some previous time. Upon reaching the bottom, it was nothing more than an empty, dark, and wet cavern. I grabbed the staff and threw it up to Laser before climbing out.

All in all, after pictures, snacks, dog handling, rock climbing, and a short lunch in the middle of the notch, it took us around two and a half hours to finally complete. I had a fantastically good time and remember wishing there were more stretches like the Mahoosuc Notch on the trail. I would personally equate the notch to being like work, disguised as fun. I worked my ass off, but I didn't notice due to the good time I was having.

Directly after the notch we encountered a steep, ball breaking climb up the nearly two thousand foot Mahoosuc Arm Mountain. Once at the summit, we descended a couple hundred feet into a crater that held a body of water named Speck Pond. We made camp on the edge of this pond and

301

hunkered down for a freezing night. On our first day in Maine, we had only managed to hike barely ten miles in eleven hours. They were easily some of the hardest earned ten miles of the entire trek.

The temperature dropped below freezing that night, and even wearing everything I owned, I was still cold. Not deathly cold, but a very uncomfortable cold. I would awake intermittently throughout the night as my sleeping pad shifted beneath me, causing cold spots to develop.

Our plan for the upcoming day was to make it fifteen miles to the next road and get into our first town in Maine called Andover. We needed to resupply again, as the towns in Maine were on average further apart than the towns anywhere else. We'd have to hit almost every single one of them in order to keep our supplies up and our tummies full.

Not only did we need to resupply, but I also needed to pick up a new backpack that I had ordered online. My little radio backpack finally had all it could handle and was at the end of its proverbial rope. The bottom was ripping open, while some of the straps were tearing off the fabric. I originally hoped that my pack would make it all the way, but I couldn't risk it tearing completely open and forcing me to carry all of my things by hand. I guess I could have sewn it like a true outdoorsman, but I had zero sewing skills and really didn't feel like taking the time or risk of doing it myself.

There was ice everywhere that next morning when we awoke next to Speck Pond. It was on the ground, the rocks, the streams, and the mud as we climbed out of the Mahoosuc Arm Crater. The trees had icicles dangling from them and my hands were so frozen that I couldn't warm them up with my gloves. My battered feet were still killing me too; each day the cracks got a little bit bigger, a little bit deeper, and just a little bit more painful.

Maine showed us some more enchantment as I discovered my favorite climb of the entire trail that went by the name of Baldpate Mountain. I never thought I'd fall in love with a mountain on this journey, but Baldpate stole my heart. The majority of the trail up the entire mountain was barren, exposed, white rock that I assume was granite. It provided excellent traction, and despite the steepness, I could walk upright for the entire climb, with the exception of several areas where I was forced to do a bit of scrambling. I had to be careful looking up towards the top because of the dizzying uniformity of everything I saw. The unbroken color and texture of the rock, illuminated by the sun, almost gave me vertigo if I tilted my head back too far to look up. The views throughout the entire climb were incredible. Katana was zipping around over the vast expanses of rock, having the time of her life. Once at the top I had an amazing 360-degree view of... nothing. Only wilderness for as far as the eye could see, with nothing else around.

When we finally reached the road that evening, we were slightly dismayed (but not even a little bit surprised) to find how remote it was. Over the course of an hour, only three cars passed by and not one of them stopped. It was a long hitch into Andover, so I didn't blame people for not wanting to pick up a couple of strangers in the early evening and take them over ten miles into town. After nearly another twenty minutes of walking up and down the road in an attempt to find reception, I was finally able to call a shuttle service that was listed in my guide. Forty minutes, and the pitch black of night later, the shuttle arrived to take us into town.

Andover seemed to have about five stores. There was a gas station, a market, a little café with unusual operating hours, a post office, and an automotive repair shop. We ended up camping near an open field, a short distance into the trees. When we got set up and super cozy, after a long day, I nearly had a heart attack when, "BONG! BONG! BONG!" sounded ten times, seemingly from directly above my hammock. I peeked back out and took a proper look at our location. I discovered we were hanging among a thin strip of trees between an open field and a large church that had a huge tower with a bell and clock. It was 10 o'clock...

"You have to be kidding me!" I said out loud to Laser. "This church clock is going to ring all night long in this little town?" The value of the homes next to that church must have been zero. I was awoken abruptly for the next two hours by eleven and twelve "BONGS" as flashbacks of sleeping under the train bridge in Maryland bounced around my head. After twelve "BONGS," I was finally able to tune the rest out when they started back over at one.

Surprisingly, I slept very well that night and don't even remember hearing a "BONG" after midnight, until I awoke the next morning at 7 am. I learned that day that seven "BONGS" was my church bell threshold for sleeping. You learned so many cool things about yourself while out on the trail.

After packing up, I ran down to the Andover Post Office where I received three packages. One box had my fancy new backpack; one had a Tupperware full of blueberry, banana nut muffins from home; while the third box was from my older sister, Carly, who had sent me a plethora of snacks.

I ate several of the muffins before offering them to the lady working behind the desk. "These are fresh baked from Florida," I informed her. She smiled and took the Tupperware from me. "You guys export Lobster and I import muffins," I added as she placed them on a table in the back.

The care package from my sister was interesting to say the least. Snickers, protein bars, peanuts, sunflower seeds, ice tea packets, and ice tea flavoring for water. Those weren't even the interesting items. Along with those, she'd sent a variety of candies and other products from an Asian Market. I couldn't even tell you what they said on the packages or what they contained. All I knew was everything tasted delicious, even the dried fish carcasses that still had the bones in them. In fact, those were my favorite. They tasted like a mixture of the ocean and teriyaki with a little bit of chili pepper thrown in. That was a prime example that hunger truly is the best sauce. I was looking forward to sampling everything over the next several days, as it certainly shook my little backpack menu up quite a bit.

There was no way I was going to throw my old pack away, so I boxed it up and sent it home to Florida. I quickly shoved all of my stuff into the new pack and made my way to the market where Laser was having breakfast. I ate a quick meal before setting to work on the challenge of getting everything organized in the new pack.

It was completely different from my old pack and after nearly six months of routine and putting things in the same places, this new one presented quite a challenge. I'd spent weeks figuring out how to put everything in my first backpack just the right way; now I had to figure it out all over again, but only had about an hour to do so. It ended up taking me nearly two hours of packing and unpacking before my OCD finally got everything to fit perfectly the way it should.

Sadly, Andover would be the last place I ever used a Tupperware in my pack. I simply couldn't get it to fit the way I wanted it, and as a consequence I resigned to leaving it behind. It was back to smooshed brownies and dented cheese for the remainder of the trek.

The new backpack was amazing, as the designer had literally thought of everything. The difference between an actual long distance hiking backpack and a little military day pack was night and day. I couldn't believe that I'd allowed myself to suffer for almost six months. I suppose I didn't know any different, because the first backpack had been the only thing I'd known and seemed sufficient at that time. I never realized until the new version, that I'd been missing out on an infinitely better alternative.

I suddenly felt like anybody who ever complained about their backpack had no room to complain anymore. I'd always assumed they were feeling the same discomforts and backpack pains I was. I had no idea that I was suffering to a degree that was significantly worse than the suffering these actual hiking backpacks put you through. Besides Muzzle, I never saw anyone else on the trail with a military style pack such as mine. Everyone else had packs with a similar design to my new one; and it felt like heaven floating on a cloud. Everything in my new pack felt half as heavy as it had in my original pack. The padding, suspension, and load distribution was head and shoulders above the old one.

We caught a ride back to the trail with a Native American looking man, although I'm pretty sure he was Latin American. Whatever his ethnicity, he was trying very hard to project a Native American persona. His name was Santiago and he proved to be a very interesting individual indeed.

Santiago told us he had a hobby of collecting moose droppings, putting lacquer on them to preserve them indefinitely, and then creating jewelry and other trinkets out of them. He said, "It's a long winter up here and folks have to find some way to keep busy!" Aside from "telling all" about his moose poo lacquering hobby, he also had some other fun facts for us. He enlightened us further saying, "Moose shit is the cleanest shit in all of the animal kingdom; you could sleep in a pile of it and you'd wake up smelling better than when you went to bed." He also went on to say that the only things moose ate were twigs and aquatic plants; and the word "moose" means "twig eater" in the Native American language.

Due to our late start that day, Laser and I only made it about eight miles over a large Mountain named Wyman, where we built a roaring fire next to Sawyer Brook at the base of Moody Mountain. Moody would be a fifteen-hundred-foot vertical climb that we'd tackle the next morning. We also planned on catching up to Lobster the next day, despite the seemingly limited miles we hiked since our arrival into Maine. The miles we'd been putting up since Gorham would actually be considered huge days over that particular terrain. Laser and I had been killing ourselves in an attempt to catch up with our companions who had a significant head start on us, which translated into multiple days' worth.

The next day, we were killing it once again. We went up and over Moody Mountain without a pause, then scooped up Lobster at the base of the next huge mountain called "Old Blue" and kept right on going. Bunny hills, roots, rocks, and mud; I couldn't tell you how many times I slipped and fell. It didn't matter as I picked myself up and continued on as fast as my legs could carry me. My mind kept drifting back to the pain in my cracked feet. If we kept up the pace we had going that day, we'd make it to the last "real" town by the end of the next day.

The next town's name was Rangeley, and what made it a "real" town in our eyes, was the fact that it was the last town on the trail with an actual grocery store. Everything after Rangeley would be convenience stores and glorified gas stations. I planned to do something for my cracked heels when I got there because I wasn't sure if I could go any further if they got much worse.

After one last fifteen-hundred-foot descent down Bemis Mountain, we called it a day near a large stream. Fog was heavy in the air and the threat of rain was high, but that didn't stop us from building a large fire between our shelters. As we huddled around our newly blazing fire and ate our dinner, it began to drizzle. We were undeterred as the fire's warmth trumped the cold prickle of the tiny rain drops. Huddling closer to the fire, we sat there in the drizzling rain for more than half an hour. We knew that our carefree days of sitting around fires out on the trail were numbered, so we were determined to take full advantage of the days we still had left. It rained hard that entire night and was still foggy in the morning.

The day's hike began like any other, but yet…it was different from any other day on the trail up until then. On that day, there was a treat in store for those of us that still remained in the mountains. The majority of the year's thru-hikers had finished in August and early to mid-September, with plenty of others finishing earlier in July and even June. As far as I was concerned, that day was proof that they had all missed out.

At the top of my first big climb that morning, I was rendered speechless, as my breath was taken away. Autumn had come overnight. Everything that had been alive and green the day before had turned orange, red, and yellow, as well as every shade in between. The entire forest had undergone a color transformation, except for the pines. I'd never seen anything like it in all my life; we didn't get those dramatic color changes down in Florida. This was on a scale I'd never before experienced nor witnessed, and I found myself suddenly glad to still be out there. I made up my mind that all the cold I'd been through, as well as the cold that was yet to come, was well worth the opportunity to witness the forest go through its autumn transition.

As I walked on, I thought about the different transformations I'd seen throughout the journey. When I first embarked on the trail all those days and months ago, almost everything had been dead, barren, and lifeless, besides the evergreens that stayed alive year round. As the days passed by and I crept further and further along, I witnessed a rebirth of nature and a gradual growth that transcended into a full bloom. As I continued my trek, with time marching on, I was now getting to see everything wither and die again. I had been out there long enough to observe the cycle of three seasons - spring, summer, and fall. It was so much more apparent and awe inspiring to behold when one was out there immersed in it every day. I became so much more in tune with everything, and as soon as something began to change, I noticed it. Whether it be minor changes in temperature, moisture in the air, bugs, rocks, dirt consistency, or the lack/presence of certain flora/fauna.

All that day it was overcast and misty, although it never actually rained while I hiked. Ever since Vermont, I'd given the CatFox quite a few more liberties. Due to the steepness and intensity of many of the climbs throughout those sections, Katana was able to sprint to the top of them with little effort, where she would then wait for my arrival. This was tough to get used to at first, as I would sometimes go fifteen or twenty minutes without seeing her, but soon discovered she would always be waiting at the top. Eventually I got used to it, and I was finally able to allow her to run ahead of me and out of sight on just about any type of terrain.

Katana also had a habit of tracking down familiar hikers that were in front of us. As soon as she would catch their scent on the trail, she'd run ahead until she caught them, and I usually wouldn't find her until the hiker in question took a break, or I caught up to them. It would always be someone we already knew, as she never did it for strangers.

It was on this overcast and misty day that I had one of my most nerve racking experiences with Katana running ahead. Lobster and Laser were somewhere far in front of me, and Katana had disappeared sometime before. I didn't think much of it, because I knew she was in good hands once she reached one of our companions. Nearly an hour went by, and still I didn't catch up to anyone or see the CatFox. I quickened my pace in an attempt to overtake one of them and put my mind at ease about Katana. I knew she was probably fine, but whenever a prolonged period went by without putting her in my sight, it always got me worried. I quick-stepped it down the trail when all of a sudden a little yellowish, red blur shot past me from behind.

Startled, I quickly realized it was Katana. "Where have you been?" I asked her. Obviously there was no reply as she looked at me with her tongue hanging out. This episode troubled me greatly for a while after it happened. What it meant, was that Katana had gone way off the trail at some point, causing me to pass her without even knowing. Whenever she picked the trail back up, she managed to follow my scent in the right direction and find me again. This greatly boosted my confidence in Katana and her abilities to find me and become "un-lost," but it also scared me. "What if she didn't find the trail again?" "What if she went the wrong way?" Those were the questions that were reawakened in my mind after that incident. While I still allowed her to keep quite a bit ahead of me and out of sight after this, I always called her back after a few minutes without seeing her. I didn't worry about it on the steep climbs, but only on the flatter areas, as well as the longer more moderate climbs.

We were all able to make the fifteen miles and reach the road into Rangeley with a couple hours of daylight to spare. All of us had been busting ass all day long, but not fifteen minutes after reaching the road and sticking out our frozen thumbs, it began to sleet rain as the wind picked up over twenty miles per hour.

Car after car drove by and nobody stopped. It was frustrating because the conditions were deteriorating and the misery on our faces were easy to read. "Why isn't anyone stopping?" Then, we saw a pick-up truck approaching. Sometimes I thought there must've been a "pick-up hitchhikers" clause in the paperwork for buying a pick-up truck, because it always seemed like every time one would come along, they stopped to give us a ride. We stuck our thumbs out again and put friendly smiles on our faces. "WHOOOSH!" The truck shot past without even slowing down and we soon realized why.

The truck towed an open bed trailer with an enormous dead Moose strapped firmly to the floor of the bed. Moose season was on! It was a cool sight, but would've been even better if they'd pulled over and let us ride on the trailer with the moose. That would have trumped every hitchhiking story I'd ever heard on the trail. "Riding a dead moose into town" certainly would've won some kind of unofficial award.

Instead, twenty minutes of freezing rain later, another pick-up pulled over that was being driven by two older men in their fifties. The driver was wearing a funky looking "purple pimp's hat" with a zebra striped band around it. To each their own I suppose. We tossed our packs into the bed of the pick-up before piling into the back seat.

After letting them know of our grocery store destination, as well as a few minutes of small talk, and realizing that our drivers were pretty laid back, Laser finally said, "I gotta ask man, what's up with the hat?" The driver was silent for a moment before replying in a thick northern accent, "I dunno, I woke up this morning and realized that I could wear whatever fucking hat I wanted I guess." This had us all laughing hysterically until the man in the passenger seat replied, "This is actually my truck. We drove down to visit my mother in the nursing home today and this guy was supposed to be my designated driver; but right now he's drunker than I am." I imagine the three of us all murmured, "shit!" under our breaths at the same time. Leave it up to us to hitch a ride with two drunken older men. I guess it made sense in a sort of twisted way, because you'd have to be drunk to pick up three dirty, wet, smelly hikers on the side of the road during a rain storm in the first place.

Luckily we made it to the grocery store in one piece, and upon arrival, the two men gave us twenty bucks and asked that we buy a bottle of Bacardi for them while inside. They said if we did them that favor, then they'd drop us off at a local sports pub down the road. That seemed reasonable enough to us. Maybe we shouldn't have gotten back in the truck with them, but the sports pub was only a half mile down the road and they had already gotten us as far as the grocery store. Besides, it was still windy and rainy outside and none of us felt like walking in it.

Since we were in our last "real" town, I decided to spoil myself. I ordered a dozen wings, a plate of cheese fries, a large pizza, and a massive burger. I ate every last bit of it before we put ourselves up in a local hostel. I filled the cracks in my feet with superglue and surprisingly they felt substantially better almost immediately. Make sure you remember this piece of information: cracked heels, cuts, or blisters can be remedied with super glue. I'm not an authority, but I learned that cuts and wounds were the original reason for why super glue was invented, so I wasn't worried. I only wish I would've thought of it back in Vermont.

Besides food and super glue, I was finally in need of new socks. The two pairs that lasted over nineteen hundred miles had finally reached the end of their lifespan. They had holes all over, as well as a smell and crustiness that wouldn't wash out no matter how much fabric softener I poured into the washing machines. It was time to bury them...in the garbage.

I went to a local outfitter in search of new ones and purchased a replacement pair that brought my hiking fashion to new heights never before reached. I bought red, white, and blue, knee high, American flag socks that came complete with stars and stripes to match my flag shorts. Outfitted in sandals, knee high American flag socks, American flag shorts, a new backpack, and my pink beanie, I looked like a professional hiker. Someone could have paid me to be out there, because once again I looked like pure money. Not really, I looked like a first rate weirdo that had an unhealthy obsession with America. I had definitely been out there for way too long.

As we put Rangeley in our rear view mirrors, Saddleback Mountain loomed ahead of us. Once again, the trail was outdoing itself in every conceivable way as Saddleback Mountain was the cat's meow when it came to false summits. Although an enjoyable, yet challenging hike up, this mountain didn't seem to want to end. You could have bet money up until the last step that you were about to be at the top; but, when that last step came and you thought you were done with the climb, an entire mountain of dirt and rocks would come into view just beyond. It was a very deceiving illusion, and I'd never been fooled so many times when I was positive I was approaching the top of a mountain.

I was pleased to find the fall colors had only deepened since the day before. While in town, a local man had informed me that the seemingly overnight change was a result of the cold snap and extra moisture from the rain. That seemed to make enough sense, so I believed it.

Throughout all of the climbs over Saddleback, The Horn, and Saddleback Junior, the views were nothing like anything I'd seen before. It was a vast collage of reds, oranges, greens, and yellows all surrounding countless lakes and ponds for as far as the eye could see. The sky was crowded with heavy patches of fast moving clouds that hung wistfully over the landscape. Beams of sunlight shone through their ranks to strike the land, illuminating and contrasting the autumn colors, causing them to glisten that much brighter than the ones shrouded in cloud shadow.

It looked like something out of a fantasy book, as everything had such amazing and unreal depth to it. This might not make sense... but it looked so real that it looked fake. Nothing could be that absolutely gorgeous and perfect by happenstance. It had to be some kind of trick or illusion manifested by some creative or imaginary source beyond my own mind's eye. Suffice it to say, this spectacle was merely a matter of timing. It was simply the right time of year, with the right weather conditions, on the right day and moment to be on top of that mountain.

People go nuts over a beautiful cloudless day with an uninterrupted sky and unobstructed sun. I used to value and prize those types of days over all others as well, but not any longer. With the right amount of clouds, from the right height and angle, they can give the world a depth and character that a pure blue sky and yellow sun simply could not.

The day wasn't without its drawbacks though, as all of the things that made the landscape more beautiful were once again chipping away at my deteriorating body. The wind, cold, and rocks were exceptionally bad. Darkness fell as we made a mad dash through the twilight in an attempt to reach the stream we aimed for that evening.

As I descended a steep rock face that was mottled with jagged rocks all the way down and even more jagged ones at the bottom, I slipped and lost my footing. As I slipped, I began stepping and leaping from rock to rock faster than my brain could process which ones were safe to step on. I was going down with my own momentum while trying to keep my feet beneath me. Eventually, my feet were unable to keep up with the forward momentum of my body as I began to lean and fall towards the jagged rocks at the bottom. I was falling head over heels towards the rocks, when in a last ditch effort of self-preservation, I pushed off hard on the last rock my feet touched. This movement propelled me off the trail and over the remaining rocks where I landed face and shoulder first in a bunch of pine saplings before barrel rolling several times (with my pack still on) and coming to a final stop on my face. I was thankful I only suffered a mildly deep scratch on my inner thigh. It could have been much worse, and despite our valiant efforts, darkness beat us to Orbeton Stream.

This section of the trail we were on was the location of a very eerie occurrence back in July of 2013. Several miles before Orbeton Stream was a shelter by the name of "Poplar Ridge." We stopped at this shelter for maybe fifteen minutes as we snacked and took a break. Even though this story was high profile at the time, I will leave out the woman's name for the sake of privacy.

Poplar Ridge Shelter was the last place anyone ever saw the northbound female hiker known as "Inchworm" ever again. She had befriended two southbound female hikers at that shelter the night before, and they had taken a photograph of her the next morning before she hiked out. That picture was the last known photograph of her before she disappeared without a trace.

Inchworm was supposed to meet her husband twenty-two miles further north at a road crossing where he was waiting for her. She was expected to arrive at the road two days after staying at Poplar Ridge, but when she didn't show up by early afternoon of the third day, her husband notified authorities.

What ensued was one of the biggest searches in Maine's history. In the end, this search wouldn't turn up a single shred of evidence at that time. There was no backpack, no trekking poles, no nothing. Inchworm had vanished without a trace. They couldn't find a single piece of evidence to even make a guess as to what happened to her. Somewhere between Poplar Ridge Shelter and the road ME 27, she had seemingly vanished off the face of the earth.

Witness accounts from other hikers in the area at the time of her disappearance provided no revelations in attempting to figure out what happened to her. In fact, there was almost no evidence that she had even made it to the next shelter at Spaulding Mountain only eight miles away from Poplar Ridge. She had planned to stay at that shelter before reaching ME 27 the next day. It was widely believed she vanished somewhere along the eight-mile stretch between Poplar Ridge and Spaulding Mountain Shelter.

While camping down at Orbeton Stream, we were essentially smack dab in the area where she had disappeared. When I think back to that stretch of trail, I can remember almost every single step of it; mostly due to the beauty and challenging nature of that particular section, which made it so memorable. If there was a single observation I could make about that stretch between Poplar Ridge and ME 27 during the time I was there in late September, it would be the presence of hunters, moose, and remote logging roads. I remember seeing close to a dozen different hunters that were stealth camped and scouting the trail, as well as the surrounding forests. I knew they were hunters because most of them had their orange vests on, but more importantly, I asked them. All of them confessed to be searching out prime moose locations.

I couldn't help but imagine different scenarios in which Inchworm could have gone missing as I made my way through that section. It's almost certain that she didn't disappear through any fault of her own. Something happened to her by an outside intervention of someone or something else, but what? Mistaken identity by a hunter who covered up his accident? Was she abducted at one of the logging roads? Could an animal have been responsible? All of these could be likely if it wasn't for the fact that there was no trace of any kind of struggle or violence anywhere. As we passed through that area, the mystery still remained unsolved...

My best guess would be that she encountered someone on a logging road that either offered her a ride with bad intentions, or forced her into a vehicle. I believed the reason no trace of her had been found was due to the fact that there wasn't a trace to be found, because she was nowhere near that stretch of forest any longer. She was most likely somewhere far away, where no one would ever think to look. Maybe she wasn't even that far away, but just far enough not to be considered a likely place. It was again my personal belief that she wouldn't be found in the vicinity of the Appalachian Trail due to the scope of effort that had already been placed around it, and a result that turned up nothing.

Regardless of what happened, it was very eerie to be in a remote location where someone with bad intentions possibly visited on a regular basis. It gave me the strange feeling that I was constantly being watched. To add to the eeriness, there were multiple posters, signs, and memorials pertaining to Inchworm and her disappearance throughout that section.

On September 24th, we were gaining on our companions as we estimated we'd catch them after one more big day. The daily climbs had been long, arduous, and plentiful. I felt like the three of us were Aragorn, Legolas, and Gimli tracking down Merry and Pippin (DSOH and Schweppes); this was my internal "Lord of the Rings" analogy.

We had almost zero contact with our other companions, so most of our estimations on how close we were getting were based on how far we thought they'd been going on a daily basis. We looked at the layout of the terrain and the availability of water, as well as the low areas to camp, then made a guess as to how far they moved from day to day. Our plan was simply to guess where they stopped on a certain day, then make sure we pushed ourselves further. My feet were holding up fairly well with the super glue, as the stinging razor blade feeling was gone. With the stinging gone, they were left with only a constant soreness.

I completed a big climb up Lone Mountain, when the trail had pleasantly leveled off for several miles to my intense satisfaction. I felt good and moved along at a fast clip, more or less oblivious to anything besides my immediate surroundings. I was some distance ahead of Laser and Lobster while Katana was keeping about twenty feet ahead of me as we wound our way through the high pines.

We skirted the side of Lone Mountain, not far from the top, with a fairly steep incline to our right and an even steeper decline to our left, when we came to a short straightaway. Not long after hitting the straight away, I heard in two rapid secessions "THUDTHUD...THUDTHUD" before seeing Katana flatten herself to the trail as an enormous Bull Moose leapt clear across the path no more than six feet in front of her! It was moving so fast that it looked like nothing more than a big brown blur. It hit the ground several feet down the slope and kept right on going as it snapped the branches from trees, and trampled the ones that lay strewn all over the ground. The vibrations through the earth were astounding, as I felt them travel up through the soles of my feet and into my bones.

Katana attempted to give chase as I gave myself a head rush while I yelled at her to stop. Thankfully, due to the intensity of my shouts, she obeyed. The moose stopped only fifty yards down the slope and turned right, as it paralleled the trail for several more seconds, weaved through the trees and gave a few snorts before it turned left down the mountain and disappeared. The entire ordeal lasted between ten and fifteen seconds-tops. I couldn't believe my good fortune to have seen a Moose in New Hampshire and then again in Maine.

That second encounter had me thinking... more so than the first one. I hadn't even noticed the behemoth as it stood and then walked just off the side of the path. I'd only heard its hooves hit the ground twice before he leapt across the trail. I assumed that was two bounds from wherever he was standing when he first noticed me or Katana. I couldn't help but wonder what would have happened if he hadn't seen Katana or myself until a few moments later. He could've jumped over Katana, trampled her, or jumped straight through me. I would have been impaled, carried off, or at the very least had my entire skeleton fractured by the momentum of the beast's movement.

Around noon, I stopped on the summit of Spaulding Mountain and had lunch with Lobster and Laser. The top of this mountain lay 1,984.4 miles into my journey and meant that I was almost exactly two hundred miles from the summit of Katahdin. I had reached the "two- hundred-miles-left" mark; it felt bitter sweet and slightly nostalgic. My mind drifted back in an attempt to remember where I'd been at the first two-hundred-mile mark of the trail. The summit of Clingmans Dome in the Smokey Mountains was exactly where I had been.

I found it funny that the first and last two hundred mile marks would fall directly on the summits of mountains. I remembered that day atop Clingmans, laying on the summit with fellow hikers, many of which were no longer on the trail. Tourists passed by, looking at us like vagrants lying around on the ground with our dirty clothes and backpacks. I remembered that Lobster and Viking had been there. Those were the golden days. The days when living outside was still new and the routines weren't quite second nature yet.

Due to the distances we were pushing over the difficult terrain, we often found ourselves hiking into the night as we attempted to meet our daily goal for miles. I missed the days when there was still light in the sky until nine, but now it was pitch black by seven.

We were hell bent on finishing the climbs over North and South Crocker Mountain when darkness had fallen and we still had five miles left. Lobster and I were together, while Laser was somewhere behind us. He knew the game plan and the stopping point, so we had every confidence that he would meet us later that night. As we continued on through the dark, the terrain became increasingly rocky as our pace got slower and slower. At one point there was a loud crash and snapping of branches above us on the right as another Moose made its getaway, heading up the hill. We seemed to have stumbled upon the Moose Mecca of that region, because not ten minutes after that we heard an eerie call that sounded like a cow's "moo," but not as drawn out. It was much shorter with a slightly different pitch, and the call continued randomly for several minutes before it stopped altogether.

For the first time in a long time, we called it a day before reaching our goal. We fell a couple miles short, but the going had been so slow that we figured it would make more sense to make it up in the morning; after we had rested and there was more light.

Laser caught up with us twenty minutes later and recounted his run-in with a moose that stood on the side of the trail about fifteen minutes before finding us. He said it made a loud call, and when he turned towards the noise, the moose had been right there, only yards away. He professed that it scared him shitless and that he was relieved we had stopped early due to the fact that he wasn't too keen on continuing alone.

That night as I lay in my hammock, I heard the sounds of big creatures moving nearby. The creaks, cracks, and snaps of bending and breaking branches filled the forest air around my little bubble. I didn't venture to guess what they were, because deep down I already knew. It didn't bother me so long as none of them came crashing through my hammock.

I crushed the next day, and it felt fantastically good to do more than twenty miles over such difficult terrain. The Bigelow Mountains were the last big mountains of Southern Maine, and as such, I viewed them as the last difficult thing I'd have to overcome before Katahdin.

Before I reached the first Mountain, I hit the two-thousand-mile mark of the trail. I can't even begin to convey how good it felt to see that two thousand mile sign; because I could now officially say that I'd walked "thousand(s)" of miles through forests and over mountains. I'd walked two thousand miles over just about everything you could possibly walk over in order to get to that sign; I could hardly believe it.

A text had come through from DSOH that morning informing us they were planning on stopping at an area called Flag Staff Lake that night. Flag Staff was on the other side of the Bigelow Mountain range and over twenty miles from where I began the day's hike. I made up my mind to complete the entire mountain range that day no matter what. After the two thousand mile-milestone, I set to work on the Bigelows. I only took two breaks throughout the entire day. One break for lunch and one break for water. Katana was a total trooper, despite the difficulty.

First, there was a two-thousand-foot climb. Next, there was a level-off, and then another one-thousand-foot climb. This put me on the top of South Horn Mountain where I had a quick lunch. From the summit of South Horn I could see the next two mountains I'd have to conquer in the distance. I descended South Horn and blew through the next two miles before climbing another one thousand feet to the top of Bigelow Peak. Moving on, I

313

descended another five hundred feet, hiked over some level, yet rocky ground, for a quarter mile and then ascended five hundred more feet to the summit of Avery Peak. I kept going and plummeted two thousand feet down to Stafford Notch before climbing another eight hundred feet to the top of Little Bigelow Mountain. The summit of Little Bigelow was a plateau for nearly two miles before darkness caught me in the middle of another two-thousand-foot descent. I had conquered the Bigelows, but Laser and Lobster were somewhere far behind when I pulled out my headlamp and continued my journey towards Flagstaff.

While on the plateau of Little Bigelow, I made one of the worst and most desperate decisions of my entire hike. It was a warm day and the trail had been devoid of almost any water sources. As fate would have it, I skipped one in anticipation of getting water from the next one, only to find the next one was dry. After that, I'd inadvertently missed the next source in my haste to finish the big day. I was dehydrated and thirstier than I'd ever been on the entire journey. I was desperate for a drink of water in any form that I could get it.

As I was traversing the plateau, I happened upon a very weak spring that wasn't listed on my map. It was hardly a trickle of water that was coming out of some rocks that were level with the muddy ground. The water was really nothing more than a shallow pool of muddy slush that was less than an inch deep. I tried skimming water off the top and managed to get half a water bottle full. As I attempted to filter it, the muddy content of the water was too high for the filter and clogged it. I wouldn't be able to unclog it until I had access to clean water. Still desperate for a drink, I replaced the filter with a bandana that I always carried. I strained the water through the cloth and into my second water bottle feeling thoroughly clever. The water came out yellow with more bits of particulate than I could count. After straining it the first time, I shook out the bandana as well as the first water bottle and strained it a second and third time before risking a drink. The water was still a pale yellow and slightly gritty on the way down, but my thirst was quenched.

With my head finally on straight after quenching my thirst, I immediately regretted drinking the water. Not twelve feet past where I'd collected it; within the same muddy puddle was a pile of moose droppings. My heart sank and my stomach churned as I realized that I was probably going to be punished for that drink of water. I pretty much accepted in that moment that there was going to be repercussions. I didn't know it at the time, but I would be lucky enough for those repercussions to set in much later...

I still had four miles to go when the batteries in my headlamp expired on me. I barely had a flicker of light that I could only see when I pointed my headlamp straight at the ground. It did nothing for me when I looked out into the darkness. I had no batteries left due to the depletion of my spares from all the recent night hiking we'd been doing. If I wanted to make it the rest of the way to Flagstaff, it was going to be in near blindness. Under the thick canopy of the trees, it was almost too dark for one's eyes to adjust. The fine line between what was the path and what was the forest, was a tough one to navigate.

Some people couldn't imagine walking through the wilderness alone at night, let alone doing it without any kind of illumination. I used to be one of those people... and I won't lie to you, it's very eerie. It's incredibly silent, except for the random animal noises, the sounds of your feet, and your own breathing. Despite that eeriness, there is also a surreal feeling of calmness and confidence that's derived from overcoming your paranoid thoughts of "what's out there?" Go for a walk in a strange new forest by yourself without a flashlight. I promise you won't regret it, and you haven't lived until you do.

Without my light, I had to be almost on top of the white blazes in order to see them. The trail suddenly dumped me onto an old dirt road. I guessed it was an old logging road or service road. Regardless of what kind it was, I hated being on back roads at night. To me it was scarier than being in the forest. You never knew who might be out there driving or walking around on them...

To my dismay and frustration, the trail didn't pick up directly across the road. As I took off my pack and strained my eyes against the darkness I tried to see what my map said. I read the words "turn east on road," but couldn't discern any distances. From previous experiences coming across many other roads like this in the wilderness, I knew the trail wouldn't be merged with the road for very long. I walked east down the old road while skimming the tree line on the far side in an attempt to spot any white blazes or openings of a path. I couldn't find any on my first pass, so I doubled back and searched again. I did this several times over the course of half an hour, but couldn't find a single sign of the trail. I was very close to giving up, setting up camp and figuring it out in the morning.

As I made, what I decided was going to be my last pass, I noticed the grass was a little more beaten down in one area than the others. I stopped and strained to look through the trees and vegetation, but couldn't see any blazes or a definitive trail. I took several steps into the tree line before I noticed I was on a rough and narrow path. I decided to follow it a little ways and see if any blazes appeared. As I walked slowly and kept my eyes peeled, to no avail, the path began to quickly steepen and go up hill. I silently told myself I would walk to the top of the climb and if I didn't find a blaze, then I would make camp and try again in the morning. Sure enough, like a lighthouse's beacon to the weary lost sailor, I found a blaze at the very top of the climb. I was back in business and on my way once again.

I continued on through flatlands, marshes, and over several streams before I finally reached the shore of the lake. I was excited at the thought of seeing DSOH and Schweppes again, but as I walked the edge of the water, there was no sign of them or anyone else. Positive that I was in the right spot, I continued to search, but search as I may, I was still alone. I gave up and made camp near the shore.

The sounds around this lake were unbelievable. A pack of coyotes raised hell somewhere nearby while the rhythmic sounds of a barred owl kept up in between the coyote's cries. The most prominent sound however, were the loons. I have no idea how many were on this lake, but they were calling to each other like their lives depended on it. So much so, that it was almost too much of a good thing... almost.

What made the wail of those loons so incredibly overwhelming was how much they were echoing across the lake. One call would echo more than a half dozen times so fast that the echoes overlapped other echoes. A loon would begin its long, mournful wail, and before the original call was even finished, the echoes were already back and overlapping the original call, as well as the previous echoes. It was essentially echoes on top of echoes, on top of original calls, added to more echoes of other loons; it was a continual flow of haunting calls. I can't even begin to explain to you how strange it was to hear. The original sounds and the resulting overlapping echoes would carry on for so long that the noise would develop into a steady siren of the loon variety. It was one hell of a lullaby nature provided to drift off to sleep.

With the completion of the Bigelows, I had vanquished the worst of what Maine had to throw at me. From there on out, it wasn't quite gravy, but nowhere near as rocky, mountainous, or steep as it had been since the early days of Vermont. For the first time in a long time, I was able to peacefully stroll beneath the pines, birches, poplars, and maples, as well as a myriad of other trees and shrubs. The knowledge that the "worst" was behind me put my mind at ease.

Every leaf was a different color, and as the sun shone down through the canopy, the hues of the leaves transformed the rays of light to whatever shades they pleased. I walked through a haze of yellow light, then red, orange, and pink. The light shining through the leaves even turned the ground different colors. It was akin to looking through tinted sunglasses that made you perceive everything in whatever color the lenses were.

I never found DSOH or Schweppes that next morning, but I did find Lobster encamped several hundred feet from my position. He'd also continued into the night and reached the lake quite a bit later than I had. He never even noticed my hammock near the shore when he rolled in. There was no sign of Laser and he couldn't be reached on his phone. We were still over a day's hike from the town of Caratunk, but as small a town as it was, we were confident that we would all meet up there.

Despite being cold and uncomfortable almost every day since early on in New Hampshire, we finally had a stroke of good luck. Since the day before the Bigelows, we'd been in the throes of an Indian summer. An Indian summer is a warm dry period that normally occurs in the autumn months after it's already begun to get cold. They usually happened after a killing frost or a cold rain much like the one we had the night before we found the trees ablaze with their fall colors. One day it had been freezing cold, while the next it felt like the late spring days back in Virginia. I couldn't believe the ongoing good fortune I had experienced throughout the adventure. Not only did I get to experience the changing of the seasons and the gorgeous colors, but now I got to enjoy them in a modest summer climate. I couldn't have asked for better.

Around the middle of that afternoon, Lobster and I stopped at a beautiful area called Carry Pond. I had seen smaller bodies of water referred to as lakes on this journey, and for a pond, Carry was enormous. There was a thick throng of trees and rocks lining the edge of the pond that made it very difficult to reach the water's edge as the trail skirted by. Then quite unexpectedly, the trail passed by a short strip of pure white sandy beach, devoid of any rocks or trees. We sat on that sandy beach, waded in the water and laid on our packs for nearly two hours. The surface of the pond was smooth as glass, clear as the Mediterranean, and so shallow that I could walk out for hundreds of feet with the water never going past my hips. The best had truly been saved for last.

After Carry, we pushed on another six miles and made camp at a shelter on the edge of another gorgeous body of water named Pierce Pond. That particular pond was infamous for having taken the life of a twenty-year-old northbound thru-hiker in 2012. After completing close to the exact same twenty-mile day that Lobster and I had just completed, the young man had gone for a swim in that pond. The water had been barely over forty degrees, causing him to develop cramps and drown about thirty-five yards from shore. Rescuers found his body in fifteen feet of water a short time later.

I stood on the same rocks that the drowned hiker had stood on before entering the water and looked out as I pictured him swimming and relaxing on the calm surface. There must have been other people at the shelter who knew he had disappeared while swimming. I wondered what the circumstances had been that day for no one to come to his aid, or if anyone had even suspected he was in trouble. The sun was still hanging lazily above the trees and there was a warm breeze in the air as I stood on the rocks. There was still plenty of light left for a swim, but on this day, at that pond... I decided against it.

We were drawing closer and closer to the final leg of the trek and would hit Caratunk the next day, then our last town of Monson three days after that. Monson would be our final town before entering the last section of the trail dubbed the hundred-mile wilderness. This one-hundred-mile stretch was the most remote area of the entire trail, as there were no roads and no towns along the entire way, except for one dirt road that serves as some kind of emergency route that doesn't really lead to anywhere. The one-hundred-mile wilderness required special planning that hadn't been needed anywhere else.

I was accustomed to carrying no more than three to four days of food at a time, so unless I planned to kill myself with four-twenty-five mile days in a row, plus another day to climb and descend Katahdin, I was forced to carry a lot of extra food. Many hikers have run out of food and gone hungry a day or even days before emerging from the other side of the hundred-mile wilderness. You had to be careful not to overestimate yourself through this remote stretch, or you could wind up foodless. I was as giddy and nervous about the hundred-mile wilderness as I'd been about the Whites, perhaps even more so.

It was a short day into Caratunk, but before getting there, we first had to cross the Kennebec River, which was perhaps several hundred feet across. At a previous time, you were supposed to ford or swim this river; but, after several accidents and drownings, a local outfitter paid a boatman in a canoe to ferry people across at certain times of the day during hiking season.

We arrived early and were able to catch a ride shortly after 9 am. I would love to say that I attempted to cross that huge river with Katana in tow or atop my shoulders, but the boatman was right there and the service was free. There was even a white blaze painted on the bottom of the canoe to make it an official crossing of the trail. Caratunk was less than half a mile from the other side of the Kennebec, and once there, Lobster and I checked in at a local bed and breakfast to wait on word from our friends.

Later that afternoon, DSOH, Schweppes, Laser, AND Powerhouse dragged themselves into Caratunk. I hadn't had a clue if they were ahead, behind, dead, or what. All I knew was that I'd been busting ass throughout all of Maine and somehow they continued to elude me. I soon found out what happened and why we missed each other. Powerhouse had met them in Andover and bypassed some of the worst of early Maine and met up with Schweppes and DSOH. She had plans to redo that section after Katahdin and hopefully after a full mend. The three of them had been sticking together and plugging along ahead of us for days.

On the day they said they were going to be at Flagstaff Lake, they had all contracted a virus that rendered them unable to make it the whole way. I had zero cell phone service like most people through those parts and didn't get the message that they were encamped down a side trail near a stream about eight miles before Flagstaff. The same side trail to water that I missed in my haste to reach the lake. Laser had gone down to get water and stumbled upon them completely by chance. He then decided to stick with them, and they all had been tagging along a short distance behind Lobster and I, for the rest of the way into Caratunk.

With all of us reunited again, I felt like a huge weight had been lifted off my shoulders, as there was no reason to kill myself every day with big miles anymore. On top of that, the Indian summer was holding out, making the threat of biting cold temperatures no longer a factor. Forecasts predicted the favorable conditions to hold out for at least as long as we planned it would take us to reach Katahdin.

We set out for Monson in high spirits, foreshadowed by the sad knowledge that we'd all be saying goodbye soon. We mostly stuck together as we meandered along the mild terrain between Caratunk and Monson. A good mixture of pine needles and autumn leaves covered the ground with some rocks mixed in here and there, with no shortage of tree roots. Of course, as was custom out on the trail, with the good also came the bad. The beautifully colored leaves that now blanketed the forest floor concealed many a rock and root that I frequently stumbled over. The trail began to look smooth and flat, but that was nothing more than an illusion put on by the leaves. Each day the leaf blanket grew thicker and thicker, as bigger and bigger obstacles were concealed beneath its beauty.

During the climb up Pleasant Pond Mountain, I noticed a big pile of fur and bones on the right side of the trail. Upon closer examination I realized they were the remains of a moose. I looked over and around them, searching for a bone worthy of taking as a souvenir, but it seemed everyone that had passed by since this animal's death had been of the same mindset. There was nothing collectible left, so I gave up and continued my trudge up the mountain.

After a few steps, I turned around to give the remains a final glance. As I turned, I noticed a skull nestled in a pine tree branch about ten feet off the ground on the opposite side of the trail and away from the remains. It was a strange sight to behold because the skull lay there so perfectly, as if it were watching everyone who passed beneath it. I guessed someone had shoved it up there to look like some kind of totem or perhaps to place it out of reach in hopes they could return to claim it later. Either way, I reached up with my staff, put the end through the eye socket and lowered it down.

As far as skulls go, it was in very good shape. All that was missing was the bottom jaw, but the top jaw had all its teeth and they were in good shape as well. The brain cavity was empty and besides a few strips of leathery decomposing skin hanging off, it was more or less clean and odorless. Being such a remarkable find, I did what any self-respecting mountain man would do. I wrapped it in my pack cover, strapped it to the top of my pack and kept on hiking.

The rest of the stretch between Caratunk and Monson was a mixture of pleasant strolls along bubbling rivers, slogs through muddy pits, and short climbs over mossy rocks. For the most part it was easy and enjoyable, but there was one other big climb up Moxie Bald Mountain where I became lost in a dense fog and couldn't find the trail for the better part of twenty minutes.

One thing in great abundance between the two towns were river crossings. In no other state will you ford more rivers than you do in Maine. Sometimes you got lucky and could rock hop across fairly long stretches of river without getting wet or removing your shoes. More often than not, rock hopping wasn't an option as you were forced to wade or swim across if there had been an abundance of rain recently. Luckily it had been a relatively dry several weeks up there and the rivers were, for the most part, calm and shallow. I had to remove my socks and ankle brace in order to save them from being soaked in the freezing waters on only several occasions.

Schweppes took a pretty good fall at one of those shallow crossings one day that almost put a strain on our friendship. There was a shallow brook that had more than enough rocks to hop across without getting our feet wet. The biggest obstacle of this crossing was the last hop to shore. That last hop was a little bit longer than the other hops and required more of a leap, as well as a little bit of faith in the soft, loose earth that you were aiming for on the other side.

I crossed first, and upon landing on the other side after the final leap, I felt my feet slide in the mud very quickly beneath me. It happened so fast that my body didn't have time to react, and the ordeal was over before it was bad enough for me to fall. From an onlooker's perspective, it probably looked like I'd stuck the landing perfectly without any trouble. Normally, I would've turned around and warned Schweppes that there was a bit of a slick spot on the landing and to watch out for it; but for some reason, I thought it would be humorous to watch and see if the same thing happened to him. My reasoning was that I'd made it across without knowing what I was getting into and there was no reason he couldn't either.

I leaned on my staff as I watched Schweppes begin his little trip across the shallow brook. On his final leap, I held my breath. As soon as his feet landed, they shot forward lightning fast as he landed on his ass in the mud. My eyes widened as it happened, but as soon as I was sure he was ok, I couldn't stop myself from laughing hysterically. I felt really bad about the whole thing, but at the same time it was humorous.

Schweppes didn't think it was funny at all, and in a twisted way, his lack of humor for the situation made it even funnier on my end. After about thirty minutes of giving me hell for laughing at him and threatening to finish the rest of the trail by himself, he finally lightened up and we were both able to laugh about it. I apologized to him and explained in all honesty that I wasn't really laughing at him, so much as laughing at the irony of him actually falling, when all I'd expected was a small foot slide, much like the one I had.

When we finally reached the road into Monson, three days after leaving Caratunk, I was filled with a mixture of emotions. Excitement, sadness, anxiousness, and nostalgia swirled around like a storm within me. The first thing I did in Monson was visit the post office and mail the moose skull to my friend Keegan back in Florida. He was the kind of guy that appreciated a good animal skull specimen. I attempted to discreetly wrap the head in bubble wrap before wedging it into a large cardboard box as the woman behind the counter watched curiously. For the return address I simply wrote "Maine Wilderness." I figured he'd be able to guess who it came from, since I was probably his only friend that was known to be in the wilds of Maine at that time.

All of us checked into a local Hostel and did our final resupply at a little mom and pop bakery that catered to hikers with a nice selection of backpacking type foods. That would be the last time any of us did anything together in a town on this hike. We were in no hurry to leave and decided to take one last zero day before the last "BIG ZERO" of being done with the trail and no longer needing to hike. That's what the end of the trail was referred to by us. We called it "The last zero day," "The Big Zero," or "The zero to end all zeros." We had nothing but time on our hands to come up with silly names for things.

There was another saying out there that some people didn't understand or were unable to adhere to. That saying was, "Last one to Katahdin wins." What this simply meant was that it's not a race. If you didn't have any time or money constraints on this hike, then there's no reason in the world to rush through it or make a race out of it. I mean what are you racing to? To go back to work? To sit in traffic? To deal with superficial people living in a made-up, materialistic world every day? That doesn't sound like a very good trade-off to me personally. There were plenty of crappy days out there in the woods, but as I mentioned before, they still beat a good day at work. In fact, there are probably more crappy days out there than good ones, but that made the good ones even better. This brings me to another little secret. Once I was done with the trail and looked back on it all, everyday seemed like it was a good day...even the absolute worst.

With the availability of social media, it was very easy to follow and see what fellow-hikers were doing. This late in the game, there were dozens of hikers I'd met along the way that had either finished or gone home. Talking to them via text and seeing posts online, it was more than apparent that every single one of them was going through some kind of post trail depression and wished they were still out there leading the simple life. I was in no way, shape, or form, looking forward to being done and dealing with my own post trail depression.

CHAPTER 18: 100 MILE WILDERNESS & KATAHDIN

"Better Than I Ever Imagined!"

My first view of Katahdin, 70 miles' distance by trail.

I wasn't even an hour into the hundred-mile wilderness before I realized I was captivated once again. The terrain was rolling hills of varying difficulty and everywhere you looked were ponds, islands, pine groves, waterfalls of various sizes, rivers, and rapids. I was blown away, as every couple hundred yards an epic and picturesque location would reveal itself, offering a once in a lifetime camping spot. I would've made those hundred miles last a month if I could have, but unfortunately you couldn't hike that way through this portion of the trail due to supply constraints.

At one point, I rock hopped my way through a mud pit when I stepped onto a log that looked fairly solid. As I placed my full weight onto the leading leg, the log and my foot sank knee deep into the mud. All I could do was laugh, as I felt like Maine was saying, "Welcome to the home stretch!"

Laser, Schweppes, and I stopped at a large waterfall that plummeted over fifty feet before plunging into what looked like the most perfect swimming hole I'd ever seen. We passed on the swimming, but gave the spot the proper admiration it deserved. We strolled along all afternoon taking in the scenery, and around 5 pm we came to another large river that we crossed using a rope.

While on the other side, I sat on a rock drying out my feet and waiting on Schweppes and Laser to cross. Katana came over and lay right next to me with a large rib bone in her mouth. I looked at her in surprise. "Where did you get that?" I said out loud while looking around. I don't know how I missed it before, but directly behind me was another mangled moose carcass that was still in the fairly early stages of decomposition. The wind must've been just right, because I hadn't smelled a thing. I didn't take any souvenirs from this one, because most of it was gone or still tangled in rotting skin and hair.

Four miles later, we came across the last thing I'd ever expected to find on that stretch. We happened upon a very old and overgrown road bed. There was no gravel or anything, only a "vehicle wide" path that had been cleared through the forest and was becoming overgrown. Tacked to a tree was a sign that read: "If this sign is up, there is trail magic a quarter mile down the road to the east." With our curiosities peaked, we decided to check it out.

We followed the road in the growing darkness to arrive at a small hunting cabin nestled in the trees on the crest of a very small hill. It was quite literally in the middle of nowhere and came as quite the surprise to us. We came to find out, the older gentleman who owned the cabin had a son that thru-hiked the trail years ago, but had passed away in the last year. Now the man stayed at the cabin for months on end providing trail magic for passing hikers in memory of his son. It was an incredibly touching gesture and as far as locations for trail magic go, this was by far the most unexpected. We had been told to expect nothing during this stretch of trail. The man had an enormous cooler full of beer and cooked more hot dogs than you could eat by yourself. I thought this sort of kindness and generosity was over at that point in the journey, but as always, the trail surprised me once again.

Day two in the hundred-mile wilderness was a rough day to say the least. It rained around 3 am that morning and continued steadily for the entire day. The abundance of loose leaves on the ground were soaked, which caused them to cling to everything they touched. Once more, the terrain turned treacherous with rollercoaster climbs and steep descents, while rocks and roots covered in moss were almost constant. All of that, combined with the recent onset of moisture, was an accident waiting to happen.

It could be said that the way rocks covered the trail in northern Pennsylvania was synonymous to the way tree roots covered the trail throughout the hundred-mile wilderness. This was yet another case of "you gotta see it to believe it," because my description simply wouldn't do it justice. There were endless blankets of roots, growing and twisting in every fashion imaginable. They were raised, looped, hooked, crooked, snaked, and slicker than snot when they got wet. They tripped you, snagged you, grabbed you, and caused you to slip at any moment you experienced a lapse in concentration. Even when you concentrated, the roots still managed to get the best of you. Despite the absolute beauty of the surrounding landscape and terrain, the day got old really quick, mostly due to the focus required to monitor every step where you were about to set your feet. When you looked down at your feet, you missed all the good stuff; when you looked up at the good stuff, you tripped. It was a lose-lose situation that became simultaneously grueling and mentally draining.

Around eleven miles into the day as I crossed over "Mount Three and a Half," my foot caught on a root causing me to trip and stumble. I would've recovered from the initial trip, but during the stumble I ran right into a fallen pine log that further continued my downward plunge. I will attempt to paint a picture of that situation for you...

When a fallen pine tree has been sitting for a while, the branches will naturally rot or snap off over time. Unfortunately, the branches never snap off perfectly flush with the trunk of the tree. A fallen pine will usually be covered in thick, hard, sharp protruding spikes of varying lengths that used to be branches. If you land on one of them in an uncontrolled manner, I guarantee you will get impaled.

As I tripped onto this fallen pine and continued to fall, self-preservation kicked in immediately. Realizing I was about to land on a tree full of daggers, I leapt over it, propelling myself off the trail while attempting to barrel roll so that my pack would hit first and provide a cushion. I only managed a half roll before landing in a thicket of more old pine branches. I turned my head and put out my hands and arms to shield myself as I landed with a series of snaps, crushing and breaking branches. Countless sharp sticks and twigs stuck into my body, scraping my hands, arms, and thighs. My bare thighs got the worst of it, as they were covered in shallow scratches and scrapes that were slowly leaking blood. For some reason my hands were burning and throbbing too, although I suffered no cuts on them. Having to plant my hands in the thicket to lift myself out was incredibly uncomfortable, with dozens of sharp twigs and sticks pressed into my face, palms, and forearms as they took on the brunt of my weight. My pack got caught up in some bigger branches, subsequently keeping me pinned down and forcing me to put more weight on my hands as I struggled to push myself up and free of the tangle of branches. In the end, I couldn't even get myself free without Laser's assistance in untangling my pack.

The whole scenario had me really frustrated, as well as in a great deal of physical discomfort. My entire body felt as if it was on fire as the mixture of sweat and rain water flowed across my new cuts and scratches. That was not how I wanted to hike. Not feeling that way, not in that frame of mind, and not on the last leg of my journey. I only wanted happy thoughts and good times through that final stretch, not pain or misery. I decided I needed to take a step back and take it easy. After several more miles I called it a day on the side of "Third Mountain," five miles short of my goal for the day. Schweppes and Laser decided to stay with me, while Powerhouse, Lobster, and DSOH pressed on.

It poured rain all night and all morning. It rained so hard and steadily that I wasn't about to pack up all my gear in those drenching conditions. I reasoned that I'd spent a great deal of time in the pouring rain on this journey and wasn't about to spend my last days letting it make my life difficult. The downpour was so bad that Laser's rainfly malfunctioned, soaking him and most of his gear during the night. He was having a rough time of it, and since he was soaked already, he packed up all of his things and set out. Schweppes and I couldn't bring ourselves to get up and pack our things in the deluge. He lay in his tent and I lay in my hammock as we waited... and waited ...and waited for the rain to abate.

Every now and then one of us would call out to the other, "Do you think we should just make a run for it?" Then the other would say "Eh, let's give it another thirty minutes and see if it lightens up, I'm pretty comfortable." If we were honest with ourselves, I think we were stalling because we didn't want the adventure to end. On any other day, we would've grit it out and packed up.

The stalling went on until after 1 pm when we finally started hiking again. Just like the previous day, the terrain was a rollercoaster of rocks and roots. Taking our sweet time, we made it another five miles to a fairly wide but relatively shallow river crossing with fast moving water. We slowly waded across without any mishaps as I carried Katana. I had one close call when I stumbled into a deep hole that brought the water up to almost my waist, after being barely knee deep. However, I quickly recovered. By the time we had gotten across, dried our feet, and put our socks, shoes, and ankle braces back on, it was after 4 pm - with the sun hanging low in the sky. Since we had a three-thousand-foot rollercoaster climb right in front of us, we decided not to risk it at night, and instead saved it for the next day.

As far as distances went, that day was a complete wash; we might as well have not hiked at all. We squandered almost an entire day in the hundred-mile wilderness, but had eaten our food like we hiked a full day. The hole we were digging ourselves into was getting deeper. Not to mention, we had yet again allowed our companions to pull ahead of us. We now had to play catch up if we were going to reach Katahdin together. It wasn't like they could sit and wait for us, because food was a major factor you couldn't overlook in the hundred-mile wilderness. Everyone would be sprinting to Katahdin in an attempt to outrun their hunger.

Day four in the wilderness was a gorgeous day that will stick with me for the rest of my life. We knew we had to put in some huge miles in order to catch our friends, but the only problem was that we had a range of four big mountains to cross first. Our companions had probably crossed them the day before and were now on easy street, steam rolling over more level sections. We had to knock out the entire mountain range, then cover as much ground after that as we physically could, if we wanted to have a chance at catching them.

We started off at a killer pace on the uphill, as the mountain peaks ascended in rollercoaster fashion towards the highest and final peak of the range called White Cap Mountain. We crushed the first climb called Gulf Hagas Mountain, descended it, then crushed the second mountain named West Peak. While coming down West Peak the elastic lace on my right sandal broke, but after taking five minutes to re-lace it and knot the broken ends together, I was good to go again. We ascended and descended Hay Mountain before stopping to have lunch and then tackled White Cap as the last good climb of that day.

We reached the summit of White Cap around 1 pm as the sky was once again filled with wispy gray clouds that hung over the landscape, casting their Rorschach shadows across the autumn earth. The summit was windy and the view to the south was breathtaking beyond measure. While the view south was fitting of a day's worth of admiration, I wanted nothing more than to look north. I wanted to see if I could finally glimpse my final destination. I pushed through some small pines and shrubs before emerging onto a small rocky clearing on the northern side of the summit. I looked out onto the landscape as my eyes fell upon an enormous mass rising out of the earth, towering high above everything else.

I'd never seen it before, but knew as if by instinct, it was Katahdin. I sat down on a rock and stared across the great expanse at it. So long had I been walking towards this object, that up until that moment, it might as well have been a figment of my imagination... but no longer. It was real now because I had seen it with my own eyes. I didn't know what to expect when I saw it, but I was surprised by the emotions that began to swell up inside me. I can't really explain them to you as I couldn't really explain them to myself, but it was as if my body simultaneously remembered everything it had gone through in order to get me to that point and then decided for itself... "Yes, it was all worth it..."

After more than twenty minutes of staring at the mountain, completely entranced, we pushed on. We were only seventy miles from Katahdin by way of the trail, but it felt like I could reach out and touch it. We descended White Cap and entered one of the most beautiful mossy pine forests that I've ever seen before or since. As darkness fell for the 191st time on this journey, we still had five miles to go in order to reach our mileage goal. Two miles into that five, my headlamp bit the dust again.

I couldn't figure out why the batteries were dying so fast, as they used to last me for weeks in the beginning. Now they were only lasting a few days at best. Either the batteries up north were lacking in quality or something malfunctioned in my headlamp and drained the batteries quicker. After all the punishment and weather that my poor little headlamp had been through, I can't say I was surprised.

I was forced to walk behind Schweppes and build a mental picture of all the rocks and obstacles he passed over before I got to them in the darkness. As I walked behind and slightly to the side of him, I was able use his headlamp to my advantage, but over the last three miles I tripped a dozen times and fell down twice. On one of the falls, I actually ended up doing a half-sideways somersault over a big rock. If one thing was certain, I never fell down more times anywhere else than I did in Maine.

We finally finished our twenty-six-mile day when we arrived at an empty shelter with no familiar faces in sight. No faces period for that matter. I could hear what sounded like a big waterfall nearby, but without my headlamp, I couldn't see anything under the total darkness of the trees. I looked forward to having a good look at the source of the cascading sounds in the morning. I couldn't get visions of Katahdin out of my head as the sounds of rushing water ushered me to sleep.

When daylight dawned, I emerged from my hammock to discover I was hanging next to a breathtaking waterfall. It cascaded down into an even more perfect swimming hole than the one we'd seen on our first day in the hundred-mile wilderness. If not for our haste, I would've jumped in and savored Mother Nature's swimming pool.

The plan for day five was simple. "Go as far as we could in an attempt to catch up to our friends." The entire day was mostly flat besides the roots, rocks, and mud. We made good time, but there were no big climbs and no great views as we trudged in a light rain all day. We had lunch by the side of a gorgeous lake in a peaceful pine grove, but as I took inventory of my food, I realized it was dangerously low. I had enough for one more normal day of eating, but I was going to have to make it stretch for two long days before I could get a small resupply at a camp store on the edge of Baxter State Park; at the end of the hundred-mile wilderness.

Baxter State Park was something that had been troubling me since about halfway through Maine. I'd known it was going to be a problem since the day Katana joined me, but now that I'd finally arrived, I found myself very nervous. Baxter had a very strictly enforced "No dogs or domestic animals" policy and a very heavy ranger presence with checkpoints in and out of the park and even out on the trail. Only registered service dogs were allowed to enter, and even then, had to be checked in first before entering the park. Despite the rules, I was dead set on getting Katana into that park and onto the summit of Katahdin. She hadn't come this far and overcome all the obstacles to NOT summit the final mountain with me. I didn't know what the fines or penalties would be for getting caught, but I heard they could be pretty steep. I decided I was willing to take the risk...

Only fifteen miles of the National Appalachian Trail actually reside in Baxter State Park. Those were the last fifteen miles of the journey that would consist of two days-worth of hiking. Ten miles into Baxter to the base of Katahdin on the first day, then five miles up to the summit and five miles back down on the second day. I made up my mind that Katana was coming with me no matter what. If I got caught before reaching the summit, then I risked getting kicked out of the park without finishing the trail. Even if that happened, I would still night hike in and summit on a different day. I was unwavering in my resolve to reach the finish line with my little dog...

All of this weighed heavily on my mind as I drew closer and closer. I didn't know how I was going to handle it, or what I was going to do until I got there and saw how the situation unfolded with my own eyes. We wrapped up a twenty-two-mile day in the rain with soggy bodies and high hopes. It had poured all day and all that night. It was such a shame, although fitting at the same time, that my last days out there were so wet and filled with rain. Looking back, I wouldn't have changed a thing.

For the second day straight, and the fourth day in the hundred miles' wilderness, the rain came down with a vengeance. It was nearly the fourth full day of rain we had since we entered the hundred miles, and it came down as hard as it ever had for almost the entire day. Despite the obstacles, we knew we had to be closing in on our friends.

At 9 am we caught Laser still asleep in his Hammock in the middle of a pine grove. "One down, three to go!" He didn't know where DSOH, Powerhouse, or Lobster were, only that they were ahead. We waited on him to pack up in the rain before pushing on. We passed more raging rivers and cascading waterfalls as we slogged through the muddy forest.

Of all the mud and roots I'd ever encountered out there, that day took home the prize as having the most. The torrential downpour made it orders of magnitudes worse, as it was quite literally like hiking through a swamp. More than once, the rain got so heavy that I had to tilt my head down so that I could breathe normally. Heavy lightning rolled in sometime in the early afternoon as the bright flashes and deafening crashes of thunder, mixed with the deluge of rain, mud, roots, and rocks made for a surreal, dramatic, and tremendous send-off.

Eight miles after we scooped up Laser, we caught DSOH and Powerhouse. "Three down, one more to go!" I broke away and pushed ahead of everyone else as Katana bounded ahead of me. She kept looking back at me periodically as if to say, "We camp now?" "No little dog, we're almost completely done..."

The up-hills turned into rivers! I'm not exaggerating even a little bit when I say there was so much water coming off those mountains that the trail had literally become shin deep in rushing water. It was difficult to discern if water had always come down the trail, or if it was simply a product of all the rain. It just seemed like there was so much water, it couldn't have only been a result of all the rain that caused it. I concluded there must have been a slow trickle coming down that had swelled and turned violent by all the flooding. I'll never know, because I only climbed those mountains once, and it was during that storm.

My final climb before reaching the edge of Baxter State Park was a five-hundred-foot rise called the Rainbow Ledges. The top was a bald slab of rock with an unobstructed view of Katahdin. The base of that final mountain was only sixteen miles away as the thru-hiker hikes, and twenty-one miles to the summit. Katahdin was massive compared to anything else around it, and the top was shrouded in clouds.

Schweppes and Laser caught up to me while I sat down and ate my last oatmeal cream pie on the Rainbow Ledges. As if by magic, the rain cut off and the sky opened up, showering us with warm sunlight instead of rain. We pushed on another six miles as the rain continued to stay away. We finally emerged from the trees, stepped out onto a crude road, and just like that, the One Hundred Mile Wilderness was over. I was completely out of food and starving!

We walked a short distance down the road and began crossing Abol Bridge. The sun was setting and the light faded quickly as we stopped halfway across to gaze at Katahdin, looming up beyond the water, and behind the silhouettes of conical pine trees.

The next thing I'm about to say will seem unbelievable, but there were eyewitnesses and fuzzy pictures to support what I'm about to share. In the light of dusk, sitting in a tree with Katahdin as the backdrop, was a bald eagle. "Is this even real life?" I thought, "How much more perfect could this get?" Forget about the rain, the mud, and misery, because there was a bald eagle perched in a tree, during sunset, in front of the most famous and daunting mountain of the entire trail. For me, the timing of this national bird's appearance symbolized the dual representation and synchronicity of "freedom" as it related to the culmination of my long journey... it was truly poetic. It felt like a dream where I could wake up at any moment and still be in my bed back in Florida.

We made it to the small camp store and did a modest resupply for two days. Options were severely limited, and I mostly bought Oreos and powdered doughnuts. Along with a half dozen other hikers that we caught up to, we all sat outside the camp store into the late hours and talked about the journey while we enjoyed one of the last nights we'd spend with each other. Surprisingly and sadly, Lobster was nowhere to be found. We hadn't seen him since the first day in the hundred miles and he was nowhere to be seen that night. There was no way he was further along than we were, but nobody there had seen him. None of us had any idea what could've happened to him. We were a little concerned, but figured there was a reasonable explanation for it.

October 9th, day 194 of the trail was a decisive day. The plan was to hike ten miles to a campsite at the base of Katahdin and spend the night there. We were in no hurry as it was some of the last miles we'd spend together; we didn't even start hiking until noon. We knew there was a ranger checkpoint directly on the trail very soon after we got off the road, but we didn't know what to expect or how it would be set up. Laser hiked ahead of us to scout it out.

He came back and informed us that there was a small Kiosk on the side of the trail with a ranger sitting outside it. He also informed us that there was no way around it without being noticed. This was the worst case scenario that I hoped I wouldn't have to confront. Most of my plans had involved circumnavigating any checkpoints, or night hiking Katana in discreetly. I wanted to do these last miles with my friends and not by myself in the dark. It was time to put a plan into action that I had previously never practiced, nor tested to see if it would work.

I took everything out of my pack, except for my hammock that was stuffed on the bottom. I lowered Katana into my backpack with minimal fuss and closed the top so that only her head was peeking out. Then I stretched my rain cover over the top of all of it. "Voila!" The pack cover was big enough to conceal her, yet loose enough that she could still move her head around with plenty of room to breathe. You couldn't even tell there was a dog in there as long as she didn't move or make a sound. Since Katana was usually as silent as the dead, I wasn't worried about her generating a ruckus. I was only concerned that she might get uncomfortable and shift around at some critical point during our stop at the kiosk. To my immense relief, once situated inside the pack, she didn't move or fuss. In fact, she seemed to be very comfortable just sitting in there. My companions each took a few pieces of my gear and stuffed them in their packs to help me out. I could've never done this without their help and support, and I am immensely grateful.

My heart was pounding as we approached the checkpoint. I was nervous beyond words and praying to the trail gods that Katana would continue to sit still. We reached the kiosk and the Ranger, where he proceeded to ask us questions as well as inform us of several park policies. He gave us weather updates and talked about seemingly anything and everything related to Baxter State Park. I felt incredibly guilty and hoped that I didn't look as guilty as I felt. I hoped beyond hope that Katana wouldn't get restless and move her head that now protruded as an awkward bulge on the top side of my pack. If there was any question that could be asked about my ensemble, it would've been... "Why was I using a pack cover on such a beautiful day?"

The Ranger wouldn't take a breath as he went on and on about park safety and recent problems with bears. "Please don't be popping or breaking any champagne bottles up there because the bears will be attracted to the smell," he cautioned. Then he got a little more serious as he began to slowly walk around behind us. My heart was slamming in my chest as I tried not to suspiciously turn with him so that he wouldn't have a clear view of the back of my pack.

"So..." the Ranger began. "Congratulations on making it this far. It's quite an accomplishment, BUT, before you go any further I'm going to have to ask you to sign the thru-hiker roster so that we have an idea of how many of you are in the park." This was TOO MUCH! I couldn't handle any more stress or anxiety! I was chill as a cucumber on the outside, but on the inside, I wanted to drop to my knees and scream to the heavens, "ENOUGH ALREADY!!!" We signed the roster on the clipboard he gave us and were FINALLY on our way. Once out of sight, we couldn't wipe the smiles off our faces. Since we had no way of knowing if we'd run into any other Rangers along the way, I kept Katana in the pack. I did pull the pack cover halfway down so that her head was exposed, but I walked in front of Laser so that he could pull it back over in case we ran into anyone. She didn't squirm or kick, and as far as I could tell, this was a step up from riding on my shoulders.

We strolled along the path that was nearly completely flat and obstacle free before reaching another river about five miles in. This one was actually more than waist deep with a raging current due to the recent torrential rains. There was a side trail that bypassed the river to a bridge; but that wasn't the AT and I wasn't about to skip a section after remaining true to every step the entire way. We decided to risk crossing the river despite the inherent and painfully obvious dangers. Furthermore, we decided to attempt rock hopping it.

The rocks were very spaced out and also quite slick from the frothing rapids that lapped over them. Some of the rocks we planned to cross were actually slightly submerged, and with a pack on, it made the task exponentially difficult. Laser crossed first, using my newest staff to lean on as he took big steps from rock to rock. The sort of falling steps that you wouldn't be able to take without something in your hand to steady yourself and manage your forward momentum. Laser made it across with no close calls and only slightly wet feet. It was mine and Katana's turn to go next. Everything that followed was captured on video.

I began to cross cautiously, as I pushed my staff into the water in an attempt to brace it against the rocks on the bottom, so as to lean on it and steady myself. I proceeded to take long hopping strides from rock to rock as I made my way across the frothing river. Katana was calm inside my pack while peering out to see what was going on as we slowly made our way across. About three quarters of the way over, I brought the staff back out of the water and attempted to adjust my grip on it. As I did so, I lost my grasp and dropped it into the river. To my horror and dismay, I watched helplessly as it was immediately swept away by the current.

The fact that I was now basically stranded on this rock with Katana in my backpack was the least of my worries at that moment (I could've hopped in and dragged myself across if I really needed to). I'd carved that staff from a Magnolia tree back in Florida two weeks prior to embarking on my adventure and it had been with me for every inch of the 2,175 miles that I'd hiked up until that point. Originally, the staff had been over six feet long, but after more than two thousand miles, it had worn down to barely reach my shoulder. My trail name was carved into the handle, and it had tremendous sentimental value to me. The thought of losing it with only ten miles left to go was unbearable!

As it hit the water and swept away, everyone fell silent as I watched it go for several seconds in disbelief. Then I turned back to Schweppes who was filming, looked at him and put my hands on top of my head in further disbelief. Suddenly Schweppes began screaming, "IT'S STUCK! IT'S STUCK! HURRY LASER!" as he pointed down the river. I turned to see it caught on some rocks a couple hundred feet down from my position, near the shore on the far side. Laser sprinted down the bank and was thankfully able to grab it before it washed away again. The original staff was saved once more! He passed it back to me and I was able to finish crossing without further mishap. Everyone else made it across without incident, as we steadily kept on, and took our time.

Not more than a mile later, we came to another swift and deep river crossing. It was an "iffy" decision, but we were able to rock hop it once again. We did this only after we grabbed a small, fallen pine tree and bridged the gap between two rocks that were too far apart. We were able to use the small pine as the base of a single step between the two rocks, so that we didn't have to balance on it.

Schweppes was the last one to cross when another hiker materialized out of the trees behind him. It was Lobster. "Guess who I found!" he yelled excitedly over the rushing water in his Jersey accent. "NO FLIPPING WAY!" I yelled across the river. Just as Lobster finished saying it, Viking, Baguette, Bangarang, Grizelle, and Dancing Feather emerged behind him. They were five of the original members of his group from the beginning of the trail. There were several more that never made it or finished already, but this was the core group. Viking had driven back to Maine to summit Katahdin again with his friends. It was the most unexpected thing that could've happened as a fairy tale ending began to unfold for this adventure. It was hugs all around as no one could contain their excitement.

Lobster had caught up with Baguette, Bangarang, Grizelle, and Dancing Feather in the hundred-mile wilderness and gotten to Abol Bridge the same day, but earlier than we did. It had still been pouring rain, so they'd caught a ride into the nearest town of Millinocket over twenty miles away. They'd gotten back to the bridge a little after we crossed into Baxter and had been a short distance behind us the entire day.

Together we finished the last five easy miles to the campground as darkness set in. Being a State Park, the campground was your typical car camping campground with narrow roads, cleared out spaces with designated fire rings, and plenty of parking. Rangers randomly patrolled the area, as it cost money to reserve a spot. You come to expect nothing less from the State and National Parks that our tax dollars already pay for, but luckily, DSOH's dad had driven up for the occasion and had a spot reserved for us.

We quickly made our way to the designated camp spot where I slipped back into the trees as far as I could and set up. Next, I tucked Katana away inside my hammock. I was in the clear for now. All I had to do was get her to the summit the next day. I didn't care what happened after that, so long as we made it.

October 10th, Day 195 was the big day! It was the culmination of the entire journey and I hadn't slept a wink the night before. I couldn't stop thinking about the significance of the big day and the entire journey in general. One thing that was blatantly apparent was that the Indian summer was gone, while the freezing temperatures were back. This was only fitting for the last day I suppose, but I had no complaints. My excitement was palpable, albeit laden with a heavy dose of melancholy; knowing the adventure and my time with all these amazing people I had grown to call my family, would be coming to an end that day.

We didn't break down camp or put anything away. We left everything where it was in anticipation of our return. I carefully packed Katana back into my bag as we hit the trail before 7 am. Lobster and the rest of his original group weren't up yet, but we couldn't wait. I had to get an early start if I was to get Katana up there relatively unnoticed. Besides, I figured we'd still be at the summit soaking it all in by the time they got up there anyway.

It was five miles and nearly four thousand three hundred feet of climbing to the summit. The first mile was gradual and almost didn't take us anywhere in regards to altitude. After that first mile, things began to get a bit steeper as the rocks got bigger and we were forced to start scrambling. The temperature began to drop and the winds picked up as we climbed higher and higher while the trees grew smaller and smaller. It wasn't long before the trees began to have frost on them and soon became completely frozen in a prison of ice and frost combined.

After more than an hour of ascending, we finally broke through the tree line as pure amazement and no small amount of nervousness greeted me. I'd known Katahdin was going to be tough. I'd heard from many that it was the hardest climb of the entire trail. That information had never fazed me because its difficulty didn't matter. It was the last thing I had to do in order to achieve my goal, and I was going to do it no matter what. Any amount of difficulty, pain, and suffering would be tolerable for that last climb.

When I looked above me, my heart nearly stopped. It was the equivalent of a "Mahoosuc Notch," but literally going straight up. Enormous boulders and stones were tossed together and stacked up. The sheer steepness and intimidating size of the boulders and climb wasn't even the heart stopper. Every inch of it was covered in ice and snow crystals. The entire mountain looked like an enormous pile of giant ice cubes. I would be completely lying if I said I wasn't scared. I'd never seen anything like this before in my life. I hadn't even brought my gloves with me for the final climb. I'd only brought Katana in my pack, while I was wearing everything else that I thought I'd need for the final ascent.

As we stood there staring at what lay before us, I turned to everyone and called out over the howling wind, "They're gonna make us earn it today!" Who is "they" you ask? The Gods? The trail creators? Mother Nature? Put quite simply, it's all of the above. "They" represented every obstacle, challenge, and set back that had ever stood in our way along the entire journey. "They" was an all-encompassing statement today, and "they" were trying very hard to stop us. Even without the addition of the ice, this easily would've been the most challenging climb of the entire trail, no contest.

I brought the CatFox out of the bag for some of it, but the climbing was too technical and slick even for her. Back into the backpack she went, for which I'm sure she was grateful.

Many-a-time we reached areas that made us call out, "They must be joking!" and "Are they trying to kill us!" At one point my hands became numb and I got a little worried. We still had a couple miles to go over all the madness, and it was only getting worse as we got higher. I pulled the sleeves of my goose-down jacket over my hands and continued climbing. The wind was so harsh that it was causing the moisture in our beards to freeze on the side that was facing into the wind. For nearly two hours we climbed over the ice boulders, shrouded in clouds, unable to see above or below for more than a hundred feet or so. As we climbed and climbed, a voice rose up behind us. "Thank god I caught you guys!" it called out. Lobster had made it! He'd left ahead of his group in an attempt to catch up with us, but had the same plan in mind to wait for them at the top.

Finally, we reached the Tablelands, a vast plateau made up of smaller rocks and boulders that were slightly more manageable to traverse. It looked like vast, frozen tundra up there and was by far my favorite part of Katahdin... besides the top of course. You could look all around the immediate plateau and see the sudden dropoff that plummeted back towards earth. Although there was nothing to see through the thick white clouds that engulfed us, it was incredibly surreal. Upon reaching the tablelands, we only had a little over a mile to go to the summit sign, so I let the CatFox out of the bag. She was amazed by the wintery wonderland that surrounded us as she bounced around, rolling in the ice crystals, and knocking them off rocks with her nose.

Over the last half mile or so, the trail that was marked by cairns slowly began to slope back up. It got steeper and steeper, as we knew this would be it… the final ascent. Lobster began to play "Teenage Wasteland" by "The Who" over his portable speakers as we slowly made our way up over the final climb. At that moment I couldn't think of a more perfect approach song for the occasion as the intro rang in my ears over the last couple hundred yards.

Then, slowly materializing out of the fog, as if waking from a dreamy haze… we saw the sign; the sign that marked the summit of Katahdin, as well as the northern terminus of the Appalachian Trail…the sign that marked the completion of an amazing accomplishment as well as the end of an extraordinary journey. I slowly walked up to the sign and placed my right index finger on the front of it for maybe two seconds before dropping my hands back to my side. DONE.

The feeling I felt in that moment was the equivalent of the biggest collective sigh that I've ever had in my entire life. My whole body relaxed as I felt every fiber in my being exhale, as if I'd been holding my breath for the last 195 days. It was a tremendous feeling as I felt tears swell up in my eyes uncontrollably. About half a dozen frozen tears squeezed out before my emotions turned to pure elation as we all began congratulating and hugging one another. "That was one hell of a ride!" I said out loud to no one in particular. My rollercoaster came to a stop… almost.

We all took individual pictures with the sign, as well as some group pictures. Katana even got her own solo picture with the sign that I like more than any other picture I've ever taken of her. There was one more thing I couldn't forget while up there, the final Lion King picture. I climbed back onto the sign and thrust little CatFox out above my head and into the wind. "EPIC" is the only word that comes to mind.

Since it was freezing with thirty-mile-per-hour sustained winds, with gusts much stronger than that, we decided to start heading downward. With the adrenaline subsided, everyone was freezing, but true to his word, Lobster remained behind to wait for Viking and the rest of the group.

It was close to noon as we made our way back down Katahdin with Katana still out of the pack. It was mission accomplished and I didn't care what happened to me now that the journey was over. The clouds were beginning to lift and the view that was uncovered was spectacular. It was as profound as the best view I'd seen prior to Katahdin- but ten times greater! It was so dramatic, colorful, and powerful, I could think of no better vision to be left with at the end of such an amazing and memorable adventure.

I'd fallen quite a distance behind everyone else while trying to keep Katana corralled as she played in the ice crystals. I wasn't going to put her back in the pack until we reached the scrambles again. Continuing down, we reached the Tablelands where I ran into another hiker that was headed to the top. He wasn't wearing a uniform, but all of his matching blue gear gave him an "official" look.

He stopped next to Katana and knelt down to pet her. "This is a fine looking dog, may I ask if it's a service dog?" he asked. "The jig is up!" I thought to myself. I suppose I could've lied to him and said that she was a service dog, but being forthright seemed like the right path at this stage. I'd been caught fair and square in my game of cat and mouse, so I decided to spill the beans. "No she is not," I replied. "Are you aware that it's against park policy to have non-service animals up here?" he continued. "Yes I am," I replied. He seemed a little surprised at my honest answers and a little unsure of what to do. This led me to believe that he was probably not a ranger and probably only someone who worked closely with the park or was friends with those who did.

After the pause, the last thing he said to me was, "You know you're cheating the system by having a dog up here, right?" Now it was my turn to think. I stood in silence for several moments contemplating my response and whether to reply with the first thing that popped into my head. "Do you know why I came out here on this journey for six and a half months?" I asked him. He didn't say anything but made an inquiring expression. "Because fuck the system," I said before turning and continuing on. He didn't say another word to me and I never looked back to see what he did, but I was positive he called down to alert officials.

I didn't say or mean this to be directly nasty or disrespectful to the man, but meant it as a general and emphatic statement as to "why" I did what I did. Maybe that wasn't the best thing to say to someone in that situation and I'm sure it came off as arrogant and entitled; but in my flurry of emotions, it felt right at the time. In a way, this whole journey had felt like "sticking it" to "the man." Kind of like, "Look at me! I can live in the woods, not work, do what I want, and be happy without having to deal with your stupid social norms, rules, and expectations of being a productive drone to society!" This felt like the cherry on top of it all. In that moment I accepted that I was busted, and that rangers would be coming up to intercept me, or at the very least, be waiting down at the bottom. My fear and nervousness was gone, as I prepared to face the consequences of my actions.

I congratulated other thru-hikers as they passed me on their way up to experience the feelings that I had just experienced and was still experiencing. Further and further down I went; still I met no Rangers. It took over four hours to reach the bottom and still I encountered no resistance or authority. I began to get a feeling of "maybe I can get out of here clean." I left Katana in the pack for the last easy mile back to camp.

There were still no Rangers when we got there, and my nerves were all worked up again as the game of cat and mouse was suddenly back on.

Another hiker informed me that a group of Rangers was standing around, a short distance down the road at the only exit. They looked like they were waiting for something, stopping every car that went by. We packed up, but I kept Katana in my pack as I threw all of my individual pieces of gear into the back of DSOH's father's SUV. I got in the back seat and put the pack on my lap with Katana quietly nestled inside.

As we drove down the road, the Rangers waved for us to stop. My heart stopped at the same time as the vehicle. One of the Rangers poked their head almost completely through the driver's window and asked, "There's no dog in this vehicle is there?" "Nope, no, nope, not here," came the small chorus from all of us as we stared back at him stupidly. While the lead Ranger engaged DSOH's father, the other rangers walked around the vehicle and peered through the windows. My body was surging with anxious trepidation and adrenaline, as everything boiled down to this final exchange. The lead ranger was putting a lot of focus on DSOH in the front passenger seat who also had a small backpack sitting on his lap.

The ironic thing was that DSOH's backpack actually had gear in it. The backpack on my lap was the one with the DOG in it, but no one was putting any extra focus on me. The ranger kept his stare on DSOH and repeated, "Are you sure there aren't any LAP dogs in here?" with extra emphasis on the word "lap." DSOH kept his poker face stare that he always wore for every single one of his bone dry jokes and replied, "I'm just a person, not a dog." "Ok, you folks have a good one, congratulations!" the ranger replied as we pulled away. "MADE IT!" I could hardly contain my excitement at getting away almost completely clear. Not long before that final exchange, I'd accepted that this little foray of mine was going to set me back some serious bucks or worse, but now I was home free! This was the real cherry on top! Sticking it to the "system" one last time and getting away with it; a victimless crime...as we took only photographs and left only footprints.

We arrived in the town of Millinocket more than twenty miles later and checked in at a hotel. After checking in, we dropped by a traditional thru-hiker restaurant called the "AT Café." There were a handful of other thru-hikers in there that had finished on that day or were going to finish the next day. Everyone was asking me if I'd been caught, because every thru-hiker that was there that day, or that knew me, had known about Katana and my plans of summiting with her. Apparently the Rangers had checked every vehicle before and after us, even questioning a bunch of individual thru-hikers about it. Every single one of them had covered for me; the feeling of solidarity was amazing.

The Journey was now over, and I was very near to being financially broke. Without enough money to buy a plane ticket or even rent a car, I was presented with a new problem that I'd put very little thought into prior to and during the adventure. "How the hell am I going to get home?"

...Done...

My Favorite Picture

The Final Lion King

CHAPTER 19: Post Trail

"Nostalgia, Nostalgia, Nostalgia…"

From Millinocket we were able to ride with DSOH's father to the city of Bangor. None of us really had a plan as he dropped Powerhouse, Schweppes, and I off at the Bangor Airport. From the airport I was able to split a rental car cost three ways with Powerhouse and Schweppes, but my problems didn't stop there. Powerhouse had signed for the vehicle and she was only going as far south as Maryland. This presented Schweppes and I with a slight problem of where to go from there.

In the end, I called my girlfriend and she was able to take off from work and meet me near Washington D.C. Since she had taken a week off from work, we decided that we'd make a road trip out of the drive back. She had never been that far north, so we decided to stay with my aunt in D.C. and take a tour of downtown. Then we drove up to New York and stayed with my Staten Island family for a couple of days. For the second time that year, I toured the city of Manhattan. We offered to bring Schweppes along, but he didn't want to intrude and was anxious to get back home, so he caught a bus back to southern Virginia.

On our way back down to Florida we stopped and stayed with Schweppes' family for three days before continuing on. We were welcomed as family and were afforded the opportunity to visit some familiar places along the trail while in the area. I was amazed at how clearly I remembered little parts of the trail, despite the immense amount of landmarks and distances that swirled around my memory of the entire trek.

When I began this Journey, I'd begun with certain goals, anticipations, and expectations in mind. I can say with absolute certainty that my expectations and anticipations of the trail were nothing like the actual reality. Everything I had thought and expected from the trail was different, and exceeded, in more ways than I could ever hope to put into words.

I had set goals for myself before embarking on the trail that were designed to be met while I was out there. I wanted to condition myself to live with less, as well as build confidence in myself and my abilities. I'd wanted this journey to set me down a lifelong path of adventure, exploration, and travel. I met those goals with phenomenal results…

Even before the trail, I knew that I never had plans to return to the life I led before. I wasn't sure what I was going to do, but I knew that it was going to be different and that I'd figure it out while I was out there.

Not only did I condition myself to live with less, but I came to find that living with less is neither a chore nor a challenge, but absolutely wonderful. I never dreamed I could be so happy with the level of simplification that I reached. I've detached myself from all of the things I don't need, as I'm no longer in the frame of mind of "what can I acquire and own next?" Now my thoughts wander to "Where can I go?" "What can I see?"

"What can I do and experience?" I've realized that with no more than what I can fit in a backpack, the world is my oyster.

My confidence grew exponentially while out on the trail, not only in myself, but in people and the universe in general. I've discovered a newfound respect and faith in humanity and everything around me. While I'm not religious, I have become a much more spiritual being. My fear of the unknown has all but disappeared and I've learned to be more patient and accepting of the inevitable. If it's going to happen anyway, then why let yourself get worked up over it? I've truly learned to go with the flow and be flexible, while my ability to adapt to a multitude of situations and environments has become immensely stronger.

My goal to kindle a fire for travel and adventure was a goal that I might have met just a little too well. I can't decide if reaching it has been a blessing or a curse... as what this adventure has done to me is quite irreversible I fear. I didn't simply kindle a spirit for adventure, but what I can only describe as a bonfire that now burns inside me. An insatiable bonfire that I'm not sure I will have enough fuel to sustain in the way that it wants to be sustained. I now know that I will never be able to lead what would be deemed a "normal life" by today's standard. I've been bitten by the wanderlust bug and the fever I've contracted only seems to have one antidote... continue wandering.

My days are consumed by thoughts of adventures to go on, as well as places to travel and see. The best part is that they no longer seem like unattainable fantasies or daydreams. I've realized that this lifestyle is actually quite easy to attain and may actually be easier than the lifestyles that most people are leading right now. Once you figure out that adventure is what you want out of life and you refuse to be trapped by our society's worship of material things, credit cards, and the obsession to acquire more and more while living beyond one's own means; making adventures happen will only be a matter of priority. Some people find the time to do all kinds of meaningless things (in my opinion) like shop for things they don't need, watch television, or sit at the bar every day at five o'clock. What I'm trying to say, is make your priority whatever it is you want to do in life, and it can happen. If you truly want to do something, you will find a way; if not, you will find an excuse.

My body has felt some physical changes as well. Many have been negative, but there have been some positives. I lost around fifty-five pounds while out on the trail, most of it fat, but a lot of it muscle. My legs have never looked better, but my upper body atrophied and became soft while my shoulders and chest shrank. Despite the massive weight loss, I gained very little definition in my upper body.

As those who followed my adventure expected, I paid the price for not filtering my water for the last seven hundred miles or so of the trail. Very late in Maine I began to feel the symptoms of Giardia, mostly in the form of mild cramping and mild diarrhea. Thankfully, it didn't hit me full scale until I returned home. I lost my appetite and experienced extreme bloating and diarrhea for the better part of two weeks before making an appointment with a doctor. It was gone in less than a week after beginning some powerful antibiotics.

Funny enough, I never tapped into the thirty boxes of food that I left packaged at my parents' house. Out of the entire 195 days, I only had two sent to me. Upon returning home, I had quite a few hours of sifting through food ahead of me. Luckily, most of it was good for years before going bad, and I planned to use some of it for future endeavors.

Another one of the more major side effects of the trail was that I became mildly lactose intolerant (I feel your pain now Laser!). I can eat cheese and most dairy products just fine, but if I drink any kind of pasteurized milk, I am plagued with terrible gas, bloating, and diarrhea. This is a tragedy because I've been a milk drinker my entire life and I'm also a major fan of cereal. The six months that I went without it on the trail was enough to condition my body to develop sensitivity to it. I do still consume milk sometimes, but I always pay the price later.

Starting three days after the trail, my legs began to ache all the way to the bone. I can only describe the feeling as a "growing pain" from childhood, as the bones in my legs felt as if they were expanding non-stop for about five days. I couldn't tell you what caused it, but I was glad when it was over.

My feet had surprisingly fared better than I anticipated, and despite their horrible corpse like appearance and multiple calluses, they haven't caused me too much discomfort since the trail. Although even months later, my feet were still stiff in the morning and I experience random shooting pains in them, it wore off quickly.

On about the second day off the trail, my lower back became extremely tight as it ached all day every day. It ached for weeks on end before the pain finally subsided. It could have been the lack of wearing a backpack every day, but I personally think it was a result of not sleeping in my hammock anymore. I now firmly believe that the natural cradling shape of a properly hung hammock is more beneficial to you than sleeping flat on a bed. I never woke up once out of my hammock with back pain or stiffness for over six months on the trail and I truly believe there's something to it. I now have my hammock hung firmly between two "i-bolts" that are drilled into the studs behind the walls in my room. While I don't sleep in it every night (girlfriend wasn't a fan), I do take frequent naps in it.

One of the positives since completing the trail is the absence of allergies. For as long as I can remember, every year, twice a year, for about two weeks I would have horrible allergies at the onset of spring and the onset of fall. I never experienced those out on the trail, and I haven't experienced them since coming back home. In fact, almost a year after completing the hike, I haven't had any kind of sickness or allergies at all. As I prepare for more hikes, I can only hope that this trend holds.

More positive impacts from the trail, as they related to my life, have to undoubtedly be the sense of calmness that I've gained in all aspects of my life. I first noticed it when I began driving again. Before the trail, driving had been a point of major contention in my life. I never realized what an angry driver I was until I came back from the trail. I found myself no longer bothered by people speeding or cutting me off. I also found myself perfectly content to drive the exact speed limit, while not tailgating those that didn't. After leading a life where it took me days to reach various locations on foot; now when it took a matter of minutes in a vehicle, any speed faster than walking felt more than sufficient to me. In addition to my calmer driving, I found myself not "sweating the small stuff" any longer. Little things that used to annoy me, no longer did so. I'm more accepting and understanding of people and my predicaments, feeling myself "letting things go" much more easily than I used to.

My ankle was in a bad place after the trail, as it remained swollen, and rolled at the drop of a hat when I wasn't wearing a brace. It rolled during activities as low key as walking down the street. I had an MRI done and it was found that almost all of the tendons surrounding my ankle were torn, partially torn, stretched or inflamed. My orthopedic surgeon that had performed four surgeries on me already, three of which were on that ankle, refused to touch it after going over the MRI results. I was instead referred to an ankle specialist at the local "Andrews Institute" where I underwent Lateral Ligament Reconstruction a couple weeks later. Less than four months after that surgery, I was running painlessly on the roads that surround my neighborhood.

Psychologically, I relish the physical feeling of being capable of meeting almost any natural obstacle with the awareness that I can overcome it. I never want to allow my body to fall into such a state that I would not be able to reach a location under my own physical power. I became addicted to the everyday high of endorphins as I climbed mountain after mountain for all of those months. I realized that I could only sustain those feelings by keeping myself active and in a high state of functionality/mobility.

Katana has experienced some changes as well. Completely opposite of me, she actually lost weight when she got home. All the muscle she gained while climbing mountains slowly disappeared after arriving back in Florida. To my immense satisfaction, her newfound obedience stuck with her. We are now able to go on walks and hikes around the local area without needing a leash.

Another one of the biggest things I've noticed with Katana is her level of calm and affection. She is more laid back and not as easily startled as she was before the trail. She was always wound up tight, hyper, jumpy, and frustratingly independent prior to the adventure (qualities that are common in her breed). She's still independent, but enjoys/wants more loving attention, and is always by my side no matter what. She didn't seem to go through any kind of post trail depression like me, as the trip seemed only to have a positive effect on her during and after its completion. I couldn't be happier, or feel a stronger bond with my little CatFox. I can't imagine going on future adventures without her.

I still stay in contact with my friends from the trail, speaking to DSOH, Schweppes, Laser, Coma, Powerhouse, Stardust, as well as many others on a daily to semi-frequent basis. Many of us have met up at different locations since completing the trail, and the lack of commonality from not being on the trail together, hasn't changed our friendships at all. In fact, Schweppes and I plan to hike the other two major trails of North America – the Pacific Crest Trail (PCT) and the Continental Divide Trail (CDT) together in the very near future.

Since coming home, people have had lots of questions for me about the trail. What did I see? What did I do? How did I do it? WHY did I do it? It's all very difficult to explain and anytime one of these questions comes up, a freight train of answers slams into my brain as I find myself unsure of where to begin or how to even explain. So much happened out there that was so interconnected and personal that I couldn't possibly explain it in a way that would make sense to anybody but me. Many of the things that were a huge deal out there and stuck out most in my mind would be considered insignificant or unworthy of mention to most people who had never done a long distance hike. Some of my fondest memories and stories from the trail would make no sense to the average individual who had never been out there or hadn't shared them with me.

Being back in the everyday hustle and bustle of modern life has been a huge adjustment and a great source of post trail anxiety for me. I miss my trail family and the idealistic days of sitting on mountain tops and around campfires in utopian settings that we might have described in passing, as just another day at the office. I wanted to relive those days out on the trail with my friends so badly that it hurts. I've come to accept that all of it exists only as memories and photographs, and that I'll have to continue making new ones. I take solace in knowing that I now have the courage and insatiable lust to pursue and realize all of the things that I want out of life. This journey taught me that ephemerality is the sum of most human activities in this world, and that the secret is to enjoy the moments when everything is going right.

FINAL WORDS

If I had to describe the entire experience of the trail in just a few words and give you the single most useful piece of advice for thru-hiking and life in general, it would be this:

The trail has its ups and downs and you have to decide how you are going to react and handle each and every one of them. What you take within your backpack is not nearly as important as what you take within yourself. Bring a sense of wonder and a willingness to learn and adapt. Keep a positive attitude and your sense of humor at all times, even when the lows are at their lowest. Find humor in everything and laugh at all the bad things that happen to you. Realize the subtle nuances of your suffering are nothing more than blessings in disguise. Pursue your own definition of happiness in the truest and most honest form that you define it to be; but most importantly, NEVER QUIT! Do this and you cannot fail, because everything is what you perceive it to be and what you make of it. Master this frame of mind and you will master yourself and everything that you do.

Human life is fleeting, and in the grand scheme of the universe, our existence doesn't even register. We have a short time with which to make the most of our lives, and in this day and age many people have trouble finding the joy as well as the positives in their life. In our flurry of activities, schedules, trials, and tribulations, we sometimes forget to stop and smell the roses. We forget to acknowledge the moments and events that have positive or neutral impacts on our lives, maybe even taking them for granted. We often overlook our blessings in disguise and fail to see them for what they are, or could be. Learn to slow down and recognize more of these seemingly insignificant instances that are buried throughout the chaos of our lives, and you might find that extra bit of peace and happiness we are all searching for...